THE ROLE OF CENTRAL BANKS
IN FINANCIAL STABILITY:
HOW HAS IT CHANGED?

World Scientific Studies in International Economics

(ISSN: 1793-3641)

Vol. 22 International Trade Policy Formation: Theory and Politics
by Wolfgang Mayer (University of Cincinnati, USA)

Vol. 23 Priorities and Pathways in Services Reform:
Part I — Quantitative Studies
edited by Philippa Dee (Australian National University, Australia)

Vol. 24 Globalizing Information: The Economics of International Technology Trade
by Keith E Maskus (University of Colorado at Boulder, USA)

Vol. 25 Priorities and Pathways in Services Reform: Part II — Political Economy Studies
edited by Christopher Findlay (University of Adelaide, Australia)

Vol. 26 World Trade Organization and International Trade Law: Antidumping, Subsidies and Trade Agreements
by Gary N Horlick (Law Offices of Gary N Horlick, USA & University of Bern, Switzerland)

Vol. 27 European Economic Integration, WTO Membership, Immigration and Offshoring
by Wilhelm Kohler (University of Tübingen, Germany)

Vol. 28 Services Trade Reform: Making Sense of It
by Philippa Dee (Australian National University, Australia)

Vol. 29 The Social Value of the Financial Sector: Too Big to Fail or Just Too Big?
edited by Viral V Acharya (New York University, USA & Centre for Economic Policy (CEPR), UK), Thorsten Beck (Tilburg University, The Netherlands & Centre for Economic Policy (CEPR), UK), Douglas D Evanoff (Federal Reserve Bank of Chicago, USA), George G Kaufman (Loyola University Chicago, USA), & Richard Portes (London Business School, UK & Centre for Economic Policy (CEPR), UK)

Vol. 30 The Role of Central Banks in Financial Stability: How Has It Changed?
edited by Douglas D Evanoff (Federal Reserve Bank of Chicago, USA), Cornelia Holthausen (European Central Bank, Germany), George G Kaufman (Loyola University Chicago, USA) & Manfred Kremer (European Central Bank, Germany)

The complete list of the published volumes in the series can be found at
http://www.worldscientific.com/series/wssie

30 World Scientific Studies in International Economics

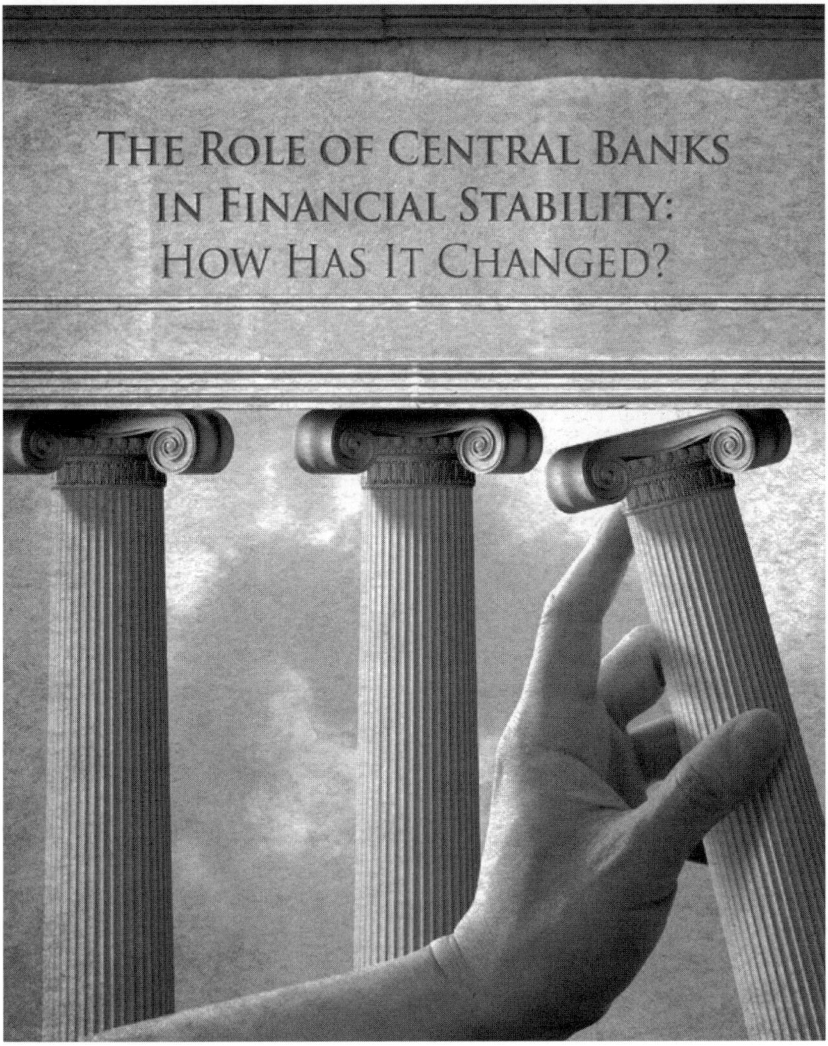

Editors

Douglas D Evanoff (Federal Reserve Bank of Chicago, USA)
Cornelia Holthausen (European Central Bank, Germany)
George G Kaufman (Loyola University Chicago, USA)
Manfred Kremer (European Central Bank, Germany)

World Scientific

NEW JERSEY • LONDON • SINGAPORE • BEIJING • SHANGHAI • HONG KONG • TAIPEI • CHENNAI

Published by

World Scientific Publishing Co. Pte. Ltd.
5 Toh Tuck Link, Singapore 596224
USA office: 27 Warren Street, Suite 401-402, Hackensack, NJ 07601
UK office: 57 Shelton Street, Covent Garden, London WC2H 9HE

British Library Cataloguing-in-Publication Data
A catalogue record for this book is available from the British Library.

World Scientific Studies in International Economics — Vol. 30
THE ROLE OF CENTRAL BANKS IN FINANCIAL STABILITY
How Has It Changed?

ISBN 978-981-4449-91-5

In-house Editor: Yvonne Tan

Typeset by Stallion Press
Email: enquiries@stallionpress.com

Printed in Singapore by World Scientific Printers.

Contents

Preface

The wide-scale financial crisis of recent years has focused attention on the role of central banks in achieving and maintaining financial stability. Indeed, financial stability was the primary reason for the establishment of many of the earliest central banks. But as financial crises diminished in frequency and severity in the post-World War II period, particularly in industrial countries, central banks directed their attention progressively more toward other objectives that were delegated to them by their governments, such as price stability and full employment.

The participants at the Fourteenth Annual Federal Reserve Bank of Chicago International Banking Conference, co-sponsored with the European Central Bank in Chicago on November 10–11, 2011, reevaluated the role of central banks in financial stability. The 160 participants, representing policymakers, financial regulators, financial practitioners, researchers, and academics from nearly 30 countries, focused their discussions on how the role of central banks had changed through time and what it should be.

Specific topics discussed include the history of central banks and financial stability; asset price bubbles and other sources of systemic risk, and how central banks should address them; the sources of past and potential future threats to financial stability; the social productivity of the financial sector; the resolution processes for insolvent large complex financial institutions; too-big-to-fail issues and the associated moral hazard problems; and where appropriate stability policy should go from here.

This volume contains the paper and panel presentations at the conference, including the keynote addresses by major policymakers and practitioners in the United States and abroad. The international nature of the participants expedited the ability to compare experiences across countries and regions, to identify what has and has not worked, and how to move forward most effectively. The publication of the proceedings is intended to disseminate the ideas, analyses, recommendations, and conclusions to a wider audience in the hope that this knowledge may at a minimum mitigate, if not prevent, major widespread financial crises in the future.

Douglas D. Evanoff
Federal Reserve Bank of Chicago

Cornelia Holthausen
European Central Bank

George G. Kaufman
Loyola University Chicago and Federal Reserve Bank of Chicago

Manfred Kremer
European Central Bank

Acknowledgments

Both the conference and this volume represent a joint effort of the Federal Reserve Bank of Chicago and the European Central Bank. Various people at each institution contributed to the effort. The four editors served as the principal organizers of the conference program and they would like to thank all the people who contributed their time and energy to the effort. At the risk of omitting someone, we would like to thank Julia Baker, John Dixon, Ella Dukes, Ping Homeric, Hala Leddy, Rita Molloy, Kathryn Moran, Elizabeth Taylor, Ron Vlasic, Barbara Van Brussel, and Sabine Wiedemann. Special mention should be accorded to Helen O'D. Koshy and Sheila Mangler, who had the primary responsibility for preparing the manuscript for this book, as well as Sandy Schneider and Blanca Sepulveda, who expertly managed the conference administrative duties.

I. SPECIAL ADDRESSES

The (Changing) Role of Central Banks in Financial Stability Policies

Peter Praet*

European Central Bank

More than four years have passed since the onset of the financial crisis. Over these years, central banking functions have been stretched to the limits.

Recent developments demonstrate how fragile our financial system remains, not only because of debt legacy, but more worrisome, because of its mere design.

The public debt crisis in a number of advanced economies is also raising fundamental questions about the role of public debt instruments in our financial system.

Looking backward, one can say that disciplining mechanisms in debt markets have clearly failed, often as a result of mutually reinforcing market and government failures. Too much debt in the public sector is a symptom of both ineffective public governance and ineffective market discipline. Budget rules, such as the no-bail-out provision of the Maastricht Treaty, did not contain the accumulation of debt. In the banking sector, the disciplining role of sight-deposits has proven to be time-inconsistent in the presence of the negative externalities that the failure of a large institution would create. Although the role of monetary policy in the build-up of the crisis is still debated, it does influence in an important way the price of leverage.[1]

---

*Peter Praet is a member of the Executive Board at the European Central Bank. The author thanks Manfred Kremer and Oreste Tristani for their contributions to the preparation of this keynote speech.

[1] See Adrian, T. and H. S. Shin, 2011, "Financial intermediaries and monetary economics," in *Handbook of Monetary Economics*, B. M. Friedman and M. Woodford (eds.), Vol. 3A, Elsevier.

Lack of attention and preparedness to tail-events has been particularly striking. While central banks have always paid attention to the possibility of extreme events in payments and post-trade infrastructures, too little efforts have been devoted to the prevention of the conditions under which emergency liquidity assistance would be provided to the financial sector. Other authorities were concerned, such as supervisors at the micro-level and ministries of finance. The necessity of "constructive ambiguity" was also invoked to keep a low profile.

Preserving financial stability has now become a key policy objective in our societies. Building up a separate macroprudential policy function is considered one of the main elements of the wide-ranging policy reforms in pursuit of this objective. The idea is to entrust the authority in charge of macroprudential policy with the task of monitoring, identifying, and mitigating systemic risks as they emerge. Macroprudential policy, by taking a system-wide perspective, thereby complements microprudential policy, which is mainly oriented toward ensuring the health of individual institutions or markets. But the way to organize this macroprudential function is still work-in-progress, in particular on the role of central banks. There are different views on how to design such a framework and how they should relate to central banks, their governance structures, and their monetary policy strategies.[2] This is essentially related not only to the difficulty to define financial stability in an operational way (contrary to price stability), but also to the number of authorities concerned (central banks, bank supervisors, insurance supervisors, market supervisors, competition authorities, consumer protection authorities, ministries of finance, ministry of justice, resolution authorities) and to the variety of possible tools often assigned to several objectives.

Central banks should undoubtedly assume important roles in macroprudential policies. Central banks bring in essential expertise in analyzing financial systems from an aggregate perspective. They also have proper incentives to mitigate systemic risk *ex ante* since central banks typically have to deal with the fallout from financial crises. Last but not least, involving central banks in macroprudential policy should foster effective coordination between monetary policy and financial stability policies in

[2]See Nier, E., J. Osinkski, L. I. Jacome, and P. Madrid, 2011, "Institutional models for macroprudential policy," IMF, staff discussion note, No. SDN/11/18, November; and also Eichengreen, B., *et al.*, 2011, "Rethinking central banking," Committee on International Economic Policy and Reform, September.

a manner that preserves their autonomy. Policy coordination is likely to become important in light of the strong mutual interdependencies between the financial and the real sectors, and thereby between both policy functions. I will come back to policy coordination later on.

A wide range of different approaches exist to institutionalize central banks' role in the new financial stability frameworks. The different approaches taken largely respond to country-specific circumstances. A "one size fits all" approach simply does not exist. This is also evident in the European Union where individual countries have adopted different approaches.

At the level of the European Union as a whole, a new financial supervisory architecture became operational at the beginning of 2011. It includes three new European supervisory authorities (ESAs) for banking, insurance, and securities markets — which aim to strengthen microprudential supervision — and the European Systemic Risk Board (ESRB) responsible for macroprudential oversight. The ECB ensures the Secretariat function for the ESRB — without prejudice to the principle of central bank independence — and is also in charge of providing analytical, statistical, administrative, and logistical support to this new EU body. Moreover, central bankers hold the majority in the ESRB's decision-making body, the General Board.[3] The main tasks of the ESRB are to monitor and assess systemic risk and to issue warnings and, where necessary, recommendations to the relevant policymakers which are not legally binding but depend on the principle of "comply or explain."

However, the ECB's contribution to financial stability does not rely exclusively on its responsibilities for an effective functioning of the ESRB.

[3]The General Board consists of the following members with voting rights: the president and the vice-president of the European Central Bank (ECB); the governors of the national central banks of the member states; one member of the European Commission; the chairperson of the European Banking Authority (EBA); the chairperson of the European Insurance and Occupational Pensions Authority (EIOPA); the chairperson of the European Securities and Markets Authority (ESMA); the chair and the two vice-chairs of the Advisory Scientific Committee (ASC) of the ESRB; the chair of the Advisory Technical Committee (ATC) of the ESRB; and the following members without voting rights: one high-level representative per member state of the competent national supervisory authorities (the respective high-level representatives shall rotate depending on the item discussed, unless the national supervisory authorities of a particular member State have agreed on a common representative), and the president of the Economic and Financial Committee (EFC) of the Ecofin, which is the only representative of finance ministries.

Obviously, the way the ECB conducts monetary policy also impacts on financial stability. Some people call for vast changes in central banks' institutional set-up and their monetary policy strategies with a view to pursue price stability and financial stability as coequal objectives. In my view, by contrast, major changes in the institutional and strategic framework of monetary policy are not necessary. But business as usual in central banking will not do it, either.

Business as usual would imply adhering to what has become known as the "Jackson Hole consensus." According to this pre-crisis consensus view, central banks should only respond to asset prices and financial imbalances to the extent that they affect the shorter-term inflation forecast.[4] If financial imbalances still emerged, central banks should follow a "mop-up" or "cleaning" strategy after the burst of the bubble. Maintaining price stability is simply the best that central banks could do to contribute to financial stability.

This view implied a strict separation between monetary policy and financial stability policy. Central banks had been well aware of the importance of financial stability for the smooth conduct of monetary policy and of their varied responsibilities in ensuring financial stability on the other hand. Yet, the importance of the possible implications of financial imbalances were underestimated and not systematically integrated in the analytical apparatus supporting monetary policy. This flaw in the intellectual underpinning misled central banks to downplay their financial stability functions and supported the general view that monetary and microprudential policy can be conducted separately, with monetary policy instruments geared toward achieving macroeconomic stability, and financial regulation and supervision aimed at preserving financial stability in the spirit of Tinbergen's policy assignment rule.[5]

However, it has become clear by now that this strictly dichotomous view is flawed since monetary policy and financial stability policy are intrinsically linked to each other, given the powerful interactions between financial and economic conditions. As the recent crisis forcefully

---

[4]See, for example, Bernanke, B. and M. Gertler, 1999, "Monetary policy and asset price volatility," *Economic Review of the Federal Reserve Bank of Kansas City*, 4th Quarter; and the response by Cecchetti, S. G., *et al.*, 2000, "Asset prices and central bank policy," Geneva Reports on the World Economy No. 2, London: Center for Economic Policy Research, July.

[5]See Mishkin, F. S., 2010, "Monetary policy strategy: Lessons from the crisis," paper presented at the ECB Central Banking Conference, Monetary Policy Revisited: Lessons from the Crisis, Frankfurt, November 18–19.

demonstrated, the previous mainly microprudential orientation of financial regulation and supervision proved unable to curb the tendency of the ever more complex and opaque financial system to generate excessive amounts of systemic risk. The unravelling of the associated financial imbalances brought about the biggest financial and economic disaster since WWII which, in turn, severely impacted on the conduct of monetary policy. As the monetary policy transmission mechanisms were affected, central banks had to take "unconventional" measures.

The crisis also taught us that "cleaning" rather than "leaning" against financial imbalances can simply become too costly to be ignored *ex ante*. In addition, we also learned not to underestimate the moral hazard associated with the asymmetry in the previous consensus view of monetary policy.

In the light of the obvious breakdown of the Jackson Hole consensus, the view has become more popular that under certain circumstances, central banks may be well-advised to actively lean against the emergence of financial imbalances in order to mitigate systemic risk and the associated longer-term risks to price stability and economic welfare.[6]

At the ECB, we have always emphasized one tool which helps us maintain a medium to long-run orientation: the "monetary analysis." The monetary analysis is one element of the ECB's two-pillar framework — in addition to the economic analysis — for the regular assessment of risks to price stability. But we have always foreseen that monitoring monetary and credit developments is also part of an overall framework for addressing asset price misalignments. The analysis of trends in money and credit developments allows us to assess risks to price stability well beyond the typical shorter-term forecast horizons.

This notwithstanding, for what concerns the monetary policy strategy, significant efforts are still to be undertaken in building up an appropriate analytical framework linking the various sources of systemic risk to economic outcomes over long policy horizons. This may robustify the ECB's two-pillar monetary policy strategy to better cope with risks of highly uncertain, low probability, but very costly events such as financial crises.

A better understanding of the transmission channels that exist between the financial and the real sectors is therefore of the essence. While some headway has been made in studying non-conventional transmission channels such as the risk-taking channel, other issues still remain

[6]See, for example, Borio, C., 2011, "Central banking post-crisis: What compass for unchartered waters?" BIS, working paper, No. 353, September.

work-in-progress.[7] For example, what is the influence of interest rates on risk tolerance? What is the interrelation between funding and market liquidity? What are the determinants of the leverage cycle, and which role is played by financial innovation? Given the complexity of the issues involved, one has to admit that the development of an operational framework linking monetary policy to the various forms of systemic risk is extremely complicated and poses severe intellectual challenges.

Financial stability risks may also arise from excessive monetary policy activism geared toward buying insurance against adverse macroeconomic and/or financial stability conditions. For instance, central banks might threaten future economic and financial stability if they keep policy rates too low for too long in the aftermath of a crisis.[8] In the context of the present crisis, the risk of missing the right time to exit from unconventional monetary policy measures offers a case in point.

In the light of these insights, it should be clear that monetary policy cannot do it alone. Financial stability should mainly be pursued by microprudential and macroprudential policies.[9]

Also, in order to achieve price and financial stability, a pairing of appropriate policies by all relevant authorities is indispensable. One avenue might be to give an agent the specific mandate to assess the financial stability impact of regulatory and tax changes when relevant.

However, policy coordination is in general not easy. Coordination might be impaired by problems of time inconsistency when the objective functions of the authorities involved may differ. For instance, governments may

---

[7]For a recent overview see Adrian, T. and H. S. Shin, 2011, "Financial intermediaries and monetary economics," in *Handbook of Monetary Economics*, B. M. Friedman and M. Woodford (eds.), Vol. 3A, Elsevier.

[8]See, for instance, Maddaloni, A. and José-Luis Peydró, 2011, "Bank risk-taking, securitisation, supervision, and low interest rates: Evidence from the Euro-area and the U.S. lending standards," *Review of Financial Studies*, Vol. 24, No. 6.

[9]In fact, such a division of labor receives support from the latest research conducted within the Macroprudential Research (MaRS) network of the European System of Central Banks. Under most circumstances, it turns out that financial imbalances are better addressed by macroprudential policy measures (e.g., counter-cyclical loan-to-value ratios) rather than by a monetary policy "leaning against the wind." See Beau, D., L. Clerc, and B. Mojon, 2011, "Macro-prudential policy and the conduct of monetary policy," Banque De France, occasional papers, No. 8; and Lambertini, L., C. Mendicino, and M. T. Punzi, 2011, "Leaning against boom-bust cycles in credit and housing prices," Banco de Portugal, working paper, No. 8/11.

succumb to the temptation to respond to electoral pressures or lobbying activities from the financial industry. A macroprudential authority might also be endowed with too much discretion in its instrument setting. These potential policy failures may therefore favor a more rules-based approach toward the macroprudential policy. This applies to both policy tools addressing the time dimension of financial stability (like counter-cyclical capital requirements or loan-to-value ratios) and tools relating to the cross-section dimension (like capital surcharges for SIFIs, leverage ratios, bank merger and acquisition policy, limits to business organization, etc.). As the financial system is highly adaptive, one has to be aware that controlling only the time dimension of financial stability is not sufficient. For example, similar rates of asset price inflation in the real estate markets may not imply similar risks to financial stability even when occurring at similar points in the financial cycle. A proper assessment of systemic risk always requires a thorough analysis of borrower and lender fragilities as well as of the whole intermediation process.

Policy coordination is also particularly challenging in a currency union when credit cycles (e.g., real estate cycle) are not synchronized. Moreover, monetary integration in the European Monetary Union has advanced at a much higher pace than the integration of financial stability and fiscal policies. An important step forward was allowing the ESRB to make country-specific recommendations, but a further strengthening of its powers might still be needed.

To conclude, challenges are immense both on the technical side as well as on the governance side to safeguard financial stability. In essence, the task consists in reinforcing disciplining mechanisms in private and public debt markets. There is a need to act in a number of areas. Central banks have an important role to play as coordinator/facilitator/initiator. They also have the proper incentives to do so in order not to overburden monetary policy.

The Role of Central Banks in Financial Stability: How Has It Changed?

Willem H. Buiter*
Citigroup

1. The Rediscovery of Financial Stability by the Central Banking Community of the Advanced Economies

A long time ago, in a galaxy far, far away, most academic monetary economists working on advanced economies and quite a few central bankers believed that the sum total of central banking was captured by an operationally independent central bank setting short-term interest rates to pursue a one- or two-dimensional macroeconomic stability objective. The macroeconomic stability objective was (and is) often just price stability, typically defined as the pursuit of some target rate of inflation for some broadly defined index of goods and services. Some countries have dual objectives, involving both price stability and some real activity objective, like employment, unemployment or output. The Fed has a triple macroeconomic stability mandate, involving maximum employment, stable prices and moderate long-term interest rates. An exchange rate objective sometimes substitutes for or complements the price stability objective.

When the North Atlantic financial crisis erupted in August 2007, the economics profession in the advanced economies and some central bankers rediscovered financial stability. Those working in and on emerging markets and developing countries of course never fell victim to the "central bank independence and (flexible) inflation targeting" blind spot. The lesson has been sharp: there can be little doubt that for any central bank faced with

*Willem H. Buiter is the chief economist of Citigroup Inc. The author would like to thank Anne Sibert and Ebrahim Rahbari for many helpful discussions on this subject, and Deimante Kupciuniene and Antonio Montilla for valuable research assistance. The views and opinions expressed are those of the author and cannot be attributed to Citigroup or to any other organization with which he is affiliated.

a potential conflict between price stability (or macroeconomic stability) on the one hand and systemic financial stability on the other, the primacy of financial stability has been rediscovered with a vengeance. Systemic financial stability trumps price stability or macroeconomic stability every time — anywhere. This has been true even for the European Central Bank (ECB). I expect that by the time the European sovereign and banking crises are over, the financial stability role of the ECB will have been enhanced to a scale not seen elsewhere since the crisis started in 2011. If it is not, there will at most be a rump euro area (EA) left, consisting essentially of a "greater Deutschmark zone," when the dust of history settles on the EA crises.

2. Financial Stability: What is It?

I view policies to promote financial stability as having four dimensions.

The first is the prevention and/or mitigation of asset and credit booms, bubbles and busts. There is a long-standing debate, often referred to as lean vs. clean, between the BIS, led by William White (2006a,b), and most of the rest of the economics profession, led by Alan Greenspan (2008) and by Ben Bernanke and Mark Gertler (Bernanke and Gertler, 1999, 2001; Bernanke, 2002, 2005). The BIS favors using interest rates to lean against the wind in asset and credit markets, raising rates when booms or bubbles threaten, even when the general price level and the level of economic activity are on target. The Greenspan–Bernanke school favors letting credit and asset booms and bubbles run their course and using monetary policy aggressively after a bubble bursts to minimize the damage caused by these financial upheavals.

The second dimension of financial stability policy is the prevention and/or mitigation of funding liquidity crises for systemically important financial institutions (SIFIs) and for the sovereign. This is the lender of last resort (LLR) role of central banks. A lender of last resort provides liquidity to solvent but illiquid counterparties. In the classic Bagehot approach, this liquidity is provided against good collateral and at a penalty rate (Bagehot, 1873). The Bagehot approach is, however, too restrictive and I shall use the term "lender of last resort role" just in the sense of lending to solvent but illiquid counterparties. I recognize, of course, that illiquidity is almost always the product of fear of insolvency.

The central bank as LLR is an essential financial stability prop, not only for the private sector but also for the sovereign. Like banks, sovereigns suffer from maturity and liquidity mismatch among their assets and liabilities.

Sovereigns with non-trivial financial deficits and a sizable stock of debt with a range of maturities outstanding have regular funding needs. The main assets of the sovereign are highly illiquid: the net present discounted value (NPV) of future taxes and the NPV of future cuts in public spending. So even if the sovereign is solvent, provided it can get funded at yields that reflect the market's belief that the sovereign *is* solvent, it could be tripped into a fundamentally unwarranted payments default should the market instead adopt the "self-fulfilling fear equilibrium belief" that the government is not solvent. A lender of last resort capable of issuing an unquestionably liquid instrument (base money) in any amount is necessary to trump the "fear equilibrium" or "sovereign debt run equilibrium" that always threatens the sovereign, just as the LLR is necessary to prevent solvent but illiquid banks from succumbing to a bank run. The truth of this proposition has been underlined several times since the start of 2010 in the case of the euro area with its multiple sovereigns. It is equally true, however, in the case of the U.S., where a single sovereign faces the central bank.

The third dimension of financial stability is the prevention and/or mitigation of market liquidity crises involving markets for systemically important financial instruments. This is the market maker of last resort (MMLR) role of central banks, first elaborated in Buiter (2008).

Fourth is the prevention and/or mitigation of solvency crises for systemically important financial institutions. This includes recapitalization of SIFIs through a variety of mechanisms — by raising capital in the markets, by selling assets, by running down maturing loan books or through other forms of deleveraging, through the tax payers or one of their agents (which may result in majority public ownership or full nationalization), by the mandatory conversion of unsecured creditors, including senior unsecured creditors into shareholders and, ultimately, by the mandatory conversion of secured creditors into shareholders.

Solvency gaps can only be filled through an unrequited transfer of resources. This means that either the fiscal authority will have to be involved or that the central bank will act in a quasi-fiscal manner. The fiscal and quasi-fiscal roles of the central bank are a key focus of this essay.

The prevention or mitigation of market illiquidity and funding illiquidity crises is not just intended to address problems caused by and for private actors. Even in the modern, post-World War II era, recurrent sovereign debt crises in emerging markets have reminded us of the potential fragility of sovereign finances. The insolvency crises faced by the Greek, Portuguese, and Irish sovereigns; the liquidity crises rocking Italy, Spain, and lurking behind them, Belgium, France, and Austria; the growing spreads over Bunds now encountered even for the Netherlands and Finland; and finally, the failed German sovereign debt auction of November 23, 2011; and the fact that the CDS spread on five-year German sovereign debt has in recent months exceeded 100 basis points, all suggest that financial stability is a sovereign concern throughout the euro area. I would argue that although the U.S. federal government continues to be the beneficiary of a global safe haven demand for its debt, the protective buffer against the bond market vigilantes provided by the global reserve currency status of the U.S. dollar, the size of the U.S. economy, the independence of its courts, and the depth, breadth, and liquidity of its financial markets — the size of this buffer against normal market discipline is finite, not open-ended. More than that, I suspect that the U.S. federal government buffer against the bond market vigilantes is in the process of being eroded by a steady sequence of unsustainable federal deficits and by a growing suspicion in the U.S. and the global capital markets that the U.S. federal fiscal institutions and policymaking processes may not be up to the job of achieving federal fiscal sustainability.

3. Prevention

Prevention requires foresight. The record of the leading central banks in this regard has been woeful during the decade leading up to the financial crisis that erupted in August 2007.

Both the current and the previous chairs of the Federal Reserve Board were cheerleaders for deregulation and financial innovation, including subprime mortgage securitization — that deadly concoction of social engineering and financial engineering (see Greenspan, 2004, 2005a,b; and Bernanke, 2006, 2007a,b).

In April 2005, Greenspan asserted:

> Innovation has brought about a multitude of new products, such as subprime loans and niche credit programs for immigrants. Such developments are representative of the market responses that have driven the financial services industry throughout the history of our country. With these advances in technology, lenders have taken advantage of credit-scoring models and other techniques for efficiently extending credit to a broader spectrum of consumers.... The mortgage-backed security helped create a national and even an international market for mortgages, and market support for a wider variety of home mortgage loan products became

commonplace. This led to securitization of a variety of other consumer loan products, such as auto and credit card loans (Greenspan, 2005a).[1]

As late as November 1, 2006, Bernanke stated:

> The growth of subprime mortgage lending is one indication of the extent to which access to credit has increased for all households, including those with lower incomes. In 1994, fewer than 5 percent of mortgage originations were in the subprime market, but by 2005 about 20 percent of new mortgage loans were subprime. Indeed, the expansion of subprime lending has contributed importantly to the substantial increase in the overall use of mortgage credit. From 1995 to 2004, the share of households with mortgage debt increased 17 percent, and in the lowest income quintile, the share of households with mortgage debt rose 53 percent (Bernanke, 2006).

In fairness, he went on to warn:

> Although the emergence of risk-based pricing has increased access to credit for all households, it has also raised some concerns and questions, which are magnified in the case of lower-income borrowers. For example, although subprime lending has grown substantially, are prime credit products sufficiently available and do lenders effectively compete in all communities, including historically underserved communities? (Bernanke, 2006).[2]

On June 5, 2007, Bernanke stated that: "The troubles in the subprime sector seem unlikely to seriously spill over to the broader economy or the

---

[1]In the same speech, Greenspan (2005a) also states: "Improved access to credit for consumers, and especially these more-recent developments, has had significant benefits. Unquestionably, innovation and deregulation have vastly expanded credit availability to virtually all income classes. Access to credit has enabled families to purchase homes, deal with emergencies, and obtain goods and services. Home ownership is at a record high, and the number of home mortgage loans to low- and moderate-income and minority families has risen rapidly over the past five years."

[2]Bernanke's speech continues: "How well are lower-income borrowers matched with credit products and loan terms that fit their circumstances? Are borrowers aware of the terms and conditions of their loans, and more generally, are consumers sufficiently well informed to be wary of potentially misleading marketing tactics and to shop effectively among lenders? Some evidence, including recent Federal Reserve research on consumers holding adjustable-rate mortgages, suggests that awareness could be improved, particularly among borrowers with lower incomes and education levels. This research suggests the need for greater financial literacy and increased access to financial counselling...." (Bernanke, 2006).

financial sector" (Bernanke, 2007a). As late as August 2007, Bernanke was singing the only slightly qualified praises of mortgage securitization.[3]

Early in the crisis, especially during the weeks between the first seizure of the wholesale funding markets in August 2007 and the bank run on Northern Rock that followed that bank's request for emergency funding from the Bank of England in September 2008, those in charge of the UK central bank did not recognize that in order to be tough with banks, you need a special resolution regime (SRR) or orderly resolution regime for banks with prompt corrective action, bridge bank creation capacity and all that, and a well-functioning deposit insurance regime. The UK had none of these.

The ECB even today does not know enough about the creditworthiness of its thousands of eligible counterparties to allow it to make informed decisions about their creditworthiness. Some national regulators and supervisors continue to deny the ECB the relevant information, sometimes because of national laws that prohibit passing on such information.

The Fed and the ECB understood, from the first, their lender-of-last-resort responsibilities *vis-à-vis* banks, and in the case of the Fed, *vis-à-vis* non-bank SIFIs like AIG. The Bank of England did not. The ECB understood its market maker of last resort responsibilities well before the Fed and the Bank of England. This is ironic, as intermediation through financial markets is a much larger share of total intermediation in the UK and the U.S. than in the euro area, where intermediation through banks remains the dominant form of intermediation.

The ECB, even today, denies that there is such a thing as the lender-of-last-resort role of the central bank *vis-à-vis* the sovereigns of the euro area.[4]

---

[3]"In some ways, the new mortgage markets came to look more like a textbook financial market, with fewer institutional 'frictions' to impede trading and pricing of event-contingent securities. Securitization and the development of deep and liquid derivatives markets eased the spreading and trading of risk. New types of mortgage products were created. Recent developments notwithstanding, mortgages became more liquid instruments, for both lenders and borrowers" (Bernanke, 2007b).

[4]In response to a question about whether to keep the euro area in one piece, the ECB would consider becoming the lender of last resort to governments, the new ECB President, Mario Draghi, at his first press conference and Q&A session following the November 3, 2011, meeting of the Governing Council of the ECB, answered: "... what makes you think that the ECB becoming the lender of last resort for governments is what is needed to keep the euro area together? No, I do not think that this is really within the remit of the ECB. The remit of the ECB is maintaining price stability over the medium term" (source: www.ecb.int/press/pressconf/2011/html/is111103.en.html).

Its outright purchases of sovereign debt in the secondary markets under the Securities Markets Programme (SMP) are rationalized as part of the job of central bank as MMLR. The argument is that for the interest rate channel of the monetary transmission mechanism to work properly, key financial markets, including the sovereign debt markets, have to function in an orderly, transparent manner. Disorderly, illiquid sovereign debt markets impair the proper functioning of the monetary transmission mechanism and this constitutes a valid ground for central bank intervention in these markets, including through outright purchases of sovereign debt.[5]

Why did our central banks, regulators and supervisors fail to recognize the imbalances as they were building up? Regulatory capture is an important part of the answer. Defective economic analysis, produced by defective economic training for much of the generation of central bankers in charge since the beginning of this century, accounts for much of the rest (see Buiter, 2009a).

Regulatory capture can be direct or cognitive. Whatever the incidence of *direct* capture (inducing regulators and supervisors to act in the interest of the industry they supervise or regulate rather than in the public interest they are committed to serve, by offering financial or positional rewards or by creating the expectation that such rewards may be forthcoming in the future), cognitive capture is the rule rather than the exception. In this crisis, blind faith in the self-regulating properties of financial markets played a major role, with Alan Greenspan as the prophet of socially beneficial self-regulation and Ben Bernanke and many others providing the scholarly underpinnings. It was the triumph of market fundamentalist religion over science.

This suggests the desirability of having multiple, overlapping regulatory and supervisory bodies, properly staffed and funded, with regular turnover of the top personnel and a significant role for "outsiders" and independent

[5] See, e.g., the comment of Draghi, at the same press conference and Q&A session following the November 3, 2011, meeting of the Governing Council of the ECB: "The Securities Markets Programme (SMP) always has had, and was meant to have — as it has been stated since the very beginning — three characteristics. First of all, it is temporary. Second, it is limited in its amount and, third, it is justified on the basis of restoring the functioning of monetary policy transmission channels. So we should keep this in mind because this in a sense answers all the questions that one might have. The relationship with conditionality should be viewed from this perspective. We want our monetary policy to function. And I think that is where the main justification for the SMP lies" (source: www.ecb.int/press/pressconf/2011/html/is111103.en.html).

members in key decision-making committees. These multiple regulators and supervisors should co-operate but also to some degree be in competition with each other. Only in this way can we minimize the risk of regulatory capture and groupthink. Instead we are at risk, in the UK, in the U.S., and in the euro area, of concentrating far too much regulatory power in a single institution, namely the central bank.

Prevention requires early warning systems; indicators of financial stress and strain must be developed, updated and monitored constantly. At the most general level, financial stability is always the result of excessive leverage and excessive mismatch of duration, liquidity, currency denomination, and other relevant characteristics. Despite the enduring role of leverage and mismatch, their manifestations in any particular place and time are forever changing. The combination of rapid financial innovation and lack of transparency promote repeated failures of supervisors and regulators to understand the risks embedded in the financial systems whose stability they are responsible for.

4. Regulate Risky Behavior, Not Institutions

Regulators and supervisors must monitor risky behavior, risky products, practices, and instruments, no matter where they occur. If a certain kind of behavior passes the "duck test" for posing excessive financial instability risk, it must be addressed, regardless of whether the entity or entities engaged in that behavior call themselves banks, non-bank financial institutions, or non-financial enterprises. The range of institutional victims and culprits in the financial crisis is long and very heterogeneous. Northern Rock in the UK was a home-loan bank funded 75 percent in the money markets, 25 percent through deposits. Bear Stearns and Lehman did not take deposits at all and were pure investment banks. AIG was an insurance company — one that operated a rogue investment bank in its UK subsidiary. Fannie and Freddie were government-sponsored entities. IKB Deutsche Industriebank was a German industrial bank. WestLB and the other German Landesbanken were publicly-owned regional banks. Commerzbank was a German universal bank. The Greek government is a sovereign.

I therefore like the feature of the new (post-Dodd–Frank) U.S. financial regulatory regime that makes it possible to attach SIFI designation to non-bank financial intermediaries also. Under the new regime, the Financial Stability Oversight Council (FSOC) is empowered to identify "systemically important" non-bank financial companies, to put such companies under regulation by the Federal Reserve, and to recommend higher prudential standards for the Federal Reserve to impose on these companies. The key features shared by all these institutions, and by many others that failed or had to be rescued by the state, were (as noted in Section 3): excessive leverage, excessive mismatch, and lack of transparency.

Leverage is a measure of the degree to which someone is exposed to the risk of an asset or instrument (price risk, default risk, counterparty risk, etc.) without owning the instrument. Debt — borrowed money — is one of the oldest and still very common ways to increase leverage for an owner or equity investor. The risk can be on balance sheet or off-balance sheet; it can be explicit or embedded in derivatives, including options, futures, margin, and other financial instruments.

Mismatch of maturities, liquidity, currency denomination, etc., is the second key characteristic of risk. Some degree of mismatch is clearly unavoidable, if any worthwhile investment project is to be undertaken. Maturity transformation by banks and other financial institutions is a key activity with considerable economic and social value. So is liquidity transformation, as when illiquid and non-tradable loans are securitized and made marketable and liquid. However, any privately profitable and potentially socially useful activity will, if taken to its logical extreme, result in dysfunctional behavior. Examples include using overnight funding to finance long-term assets traded in markets that could suddenly turn illiquid, or securitization without the retention of a significant first-loss tranche by the originator of the securitized loans. This does not mean, of course, that the socially optimal scale of any activity that can be taken to excess is zero.

Lack of transparency. When entire asset classes and layers of financial intermediaries fail to appear on or disappear off the radar screen of the regulatory and supervisory authorities, the risk of systemic financial instability can rise sharply. Much financial innovation and financial engineering is motivated primarily by regulatory or tax arbitrage, and by the desire to be invisible or incomprehensible to regulators or supervisors.

Solutions to or at least mitigation of some of these financial instability problems are, in principle, not too difficult technically. They are, however, likely to run into strong political resistance. Obvious dos and don'ts are the following:

(1) Require banks and other SIFIs to hold much more capital, in the economic sense of unconditionally loss-absorbing own resources.

Modigliani–Miller teaches us that capital structure does not matter. Incomplete markets, which create the possibility of bankruptcy, and the fact that bankruptcy is costly, put the first nail into the Modigliani–Miller coffin: Costly bankruptcy tells us we need more capital. The fact that all contract enforcement is imperfect and costly creates a further host of complications, which I have no time to address here.

Modigliani–Miller relies crucially on the assumption that households can undo, through homemade increases or reductions in leverage, any change in leverage introduced by companies whose debt or equity they own. This homemade leverage mechanism breaks down because only corporations have limited liability. Households don't. Distortionary taxes are another reason for Modigliani–Miller to fail. In particular, the fact that many countries have corporate tax systems, in which interest on corporate debt is deductible from the corporate tax base but dividends and retained earnings are not, creates a bias toward excessive corporate debt issuance. Asymmetric information and limited liability creates agency problems with corporate managers, who may have an incentive to create excessive leverage if executive earnings are related to profits or share prices. This problem is even more acute if the equity stake of management itself is leveraged by being in the form of stock options.

(2) End interest-deductibility for corporate debt.
(3) Relate executive pay to the value of the firm (equity plus debt) rather than just to equity. Do not pay top bank officials in share options.
(4) Rethink limited liability for some financial institutions.

An example of this class of proposals is Kotlikoff's proposal for "limited purpose banking." Kotlikoff (2010) recommends unlimited liability for all leveraged financial institutions. Limited liability would apply only to pure pass-through mutual funds. Although interesting, this proposal has (at least) two weaknesses. First, how does one differentiate a financial institution from a non-financial enterprise? Every non-financial enterprise has a financial balance sheet. The treasury department of a commodities trader can easily turn into a derivatives trading platform and from there into an investment bank. That is how Enron started off. GE started off as a manufacturer. Second, there is the "too-big-to-fail" problem or the "too-politically-connected-to-fail" problem, which does not go away when there is unlimited liability. An unlimited liability, highly leveraged entity could grow too big or could become too interconnected with other financial entities to be allowed to fail. Limited liability does not solve the too-big-to-fail problem.

(5) Do not confuse liquidity and funding with capital and, specifically, do not turn liquidity into a private good.

Liquidity is not a substance but a property of financial instruments. It is subject to network externalities, and is fundamentally a matter of beliefs and trust. With confidence, optimism, and trust, any security will be liquid. Without these, nothing is liquid. Therefore, for both funding liquidity and market liquidity, the provider of the ultimate, unquestioned source of (domestic currency) liquidity is a necessary participant in any socially efficient arrangement. The central bank must always be ready to act as the ultimate source of funding liquidity (as lender of last resort) and as the ultimate provider of market liquidity (as market maker of last resort) (see Buiter, 2008). It is unwise and inefficient to force private financial institutions to hold emergency or stress-level stocks of liquid assets during normal times. The Liquidity Coverage Ratio and the Net Stable Funding Ratio of the new Basel III arrangements risk forcing unnecessary levels of liquidity on banks and other financial institutions. This would be especially damaging if, as I suspect, domestic sovereign debt will be declared a suitable source of liquidity for all seasons in most countries. This will permit regulators and sovereigns to conspire to use financial repression to stuff large amounts of unwanted public debt into the portfolios of captive, regulated entities at below fair yields, in the name of prudence, liquidity management, and financial stability.

(6) Create a special resolution regime for banks and other SIFIs that can restructure about-to-fail SIFIs at the speed of light, say by applying good bank–bad bank model at the speed of light.

Prompt corrective action and bridge bank constructions should be readily available. All unsecured creditors — subordinated, junior and senior — of banks must know that they are at risk of haircuts or of mandatory conversion of their debt into equity. All unsecured debt is CoCos, either *ex-ante* or *ex-post*. Living wills operate at a different frequency from crisis management, but are an integral part of it. Where possible, the SRR and living wills should be introduced at an international level. Ideally, there would be a global SRR for global SIFIs (GSIFIs). Europe can at least make a start with a European Resolution Authority for EU cross-border SIFIs.

(7) Introduce Islamic finance for all.

There is too much debt in the public sector, the banking sector, and the household sector. Rather than running this down painfully by asset sales and by running financial surpluses, the excessive debt should be either written down or converted into equity. Once the stock problem has been solved, new debt issuance should be subject to much tighter limits than before for financial institutions, households, and sovereigns. Although non-financial corporates were not part of the excessive debt problem this time, limits on indebtedness should also be designed for them.

For households, the main debt problem concerns excessive mortgage debt characterized by negative equity. The existing household mortgage debt that is in negative equity could, at the request of the household, be converted into an Islamic-style mortgage, with the negative equity transferred explicitly to the mortgage lender. The mortgage payment would be changed into a fixed rent component and an equity purchase component, which the household could speed up, slow down, or even reverse (selling equity back to the bank), subject to certain verifiable conditions being satisfied. All new residential mortgages would have the features of an Islamic mortgage.

For banks and other financial institutions, excessive leverage can, for near-insolvent entities, be reduced by converting unsecured subordinated, junior and senior debt into equity. Even for systemically important institutions, the principle should be adhered to, that the last unsecured creditor is fully written down or converted into equity before a cent of public money goes in.

For public debt, equitize the public debt outstanding, if necessary by a "voluntary" restructuring into securities like real GDP growth warrants or floating rate debt, where the nominal interest rate is some constant plus the growth rate of nominal GDP. With declining real GDP and/or deflation, this would allow the sovereign to amortize its debt when the public finances are at their most vulnerable, rather than being faced with a fixed interest burden. Robert Shiller (2003) has proposed a range of useful risk-sharing liabilities for the sovereign.

5. Regulation and Resolution Need to be Global in Scope

Central banks coordinated well in cutting rates and making currency swap lines available. The Fed was generous in allowing U.S. subsidiaries of foreign banks access to many of its special facilities. But this was improvised, messy, and mostly unaccountable to the ultimate beneficial owners of the central bank — taxpayers and other citizens — until the Fed was forced, by lawsuits or by Congressional action, to reveal the information. We need global agreements on host country and home country responsibilities for branches and subsidiaries of SIFIs.

As pointed out in the previous section, in addition to internationally harmonized and preferably uniform and uniformly enforced regulation and supervision, we need cross-border resolution regimes for all GSIFIs. A case can be made that there should be further restrictions on cross-border financial activities by GSIFIs, whether through subsidiaries or branches, unless there is a proper cross-border resolution regime and a cross-border living will.

Of course, resolution of cross-border GSIFIs may require an international fiscal burden-sharing regime if adequate capital resources cannot be found elsewhere. A cross-border TARP — or taxpayer-funded SIFI recapitalization fund or regime — is hard to visualize, except possibly for the European Union, which is likely to achieve banking sector union (with its necessary minimum fiscal backup necessary for bank recapitalization) long before it achieves significant wider and deeper fiscal union in other dimensions.

6. Macroprudential Instruments

6.1 *Leaning against the wind in asset markets and credit markets*

Here, Bernanke *et al.* are right (Bernanke and Gertler, 1999 and 2001). Short-term interest rates, even if you have the world's greatest communication policy to leverage the announcement effects of future short-term interest rates, are not very powerful instruments for influencing asset valuations and credit growth. You need macroprudential instruments. We need these even more to mitigate the procyclical consequences of many aspects of the current and likely future regulatory regimes, including Basel 2, 2.5, and 3.

Among the many macroprudential countercyclical instruments that have been proposed are countercyclical capital requirements for banks (either through countercyclical capital surcharges or through countercyclical risk weights), Spanish-style dynamic provisioning, countercyclical loan-to-value ratios and debt-to-income ratios in residential mortgage markets, countercyclical margin requirements in equity markets, countercyclical variations in margins, or haircuts in repo markets, or a countercyclical land tax. Very little is known about the operating characteristics of these instruments, as most of them have never been implemented.

An important issue concerns the control of these new macroprudential instruments. Some of them are quasi-fiscal or explicitly fiscal in nature. It would be politically difficult to entrust them to an operationally independent central bank. At the same time, it would be necessary to coordinate the usual instruments of monetary policy with the setting of the macroprudential instruments, and a separate macroprudential regulator might make this difficult logistically and politically.

7. The Fiscal Role of the Central Bank

There is an unavoidable fiscal dimension to a central bank's activities. Central banking is an immensely profitable monopoly, especially in a fiat economy. The net present value of its future seigniorage, even if it faithfully executes, say, an inflation target mandate of 2 percent per annum, can be vast. Extremely conservative estimates made by us for the ECB/Eurosystem of the NPV of future non-inflationary currency issuance range from around €2 trillion to multiples of that amount. For the Fed, it is easy to come up with conservative estimates of the NPV of future seigniorage in excess of $7 trillion. That NPV gets distributed to the proximate beneficial owners, the Treasury, after deducting the cost of running the central bank. Through the Treasury, the seigniorage revenues of the central bank end up with the ultimate beneficial owners of the central bank: the citizens and residents of the country, as taxpayers and beneficiaries of public spending.

In addition to the generation of seigniorage revenue, central banks manage significant and often complex portfolios. By taking on credit risk, often at less than *ex-ante* fair rates of remuneration, central banks during this crisis have risked distributing the NPV of its future seigniorage to the parties that succeeded in offloading the credit risk on it, instead of to the Treasury. In a well-functioning political-economic system, with proper accountability for all agents of the state, the taking on of credit risk by the central bank should occur subject to agreement from the taxpayers or their trustee, the Treasury, or the Parliament or Congress to which both the central bank and the Treasury are ultimately accountable. There has been no prior approval by the appropriate Parliament/Congress of the taking on of material credit risk by the central bank either in the case of the ECB or for the Fed. Nor has there been, thus far, proper *ex-post* accountability by these two central banks for the way in which this risk was taken on and managed. Under the Dodd–Frank Act, both the *ex-ante* authorization of risky portfolio management decisions and other quasi-fiscal actions, and the *ex-post* accountability of the Fed will be enhanced. No such enhancement in governance for and accountability of the ECB is in the works.

7.1 *A little seigniorage arithmetic*

As noted, the traditional contribution of the central bank to the sovereign's funding needs are seigniorage, the stream of profits earned by the central bank through its ability to issue base money. In a modern fiat money economy, base money, M, is the sum of the stock of currency, C, and commercial bank reserves held with the central bank, R, which in turn is the sum of required reserves, R^r, and excess reserves, R^e. It pays an interest rate that is typically below the risk-free market rate of interest. Currency typically pays a zero interest rate, $i^c = 0$. The interest rate on required reserves, i^r, and on excess reserves, i^e, is set by the central bank. In addition, currency is irredeemable — the holder of a given amount of currency has no other claim on the issuer than for the same amount of currency. For all practical purposes, the stock of bank reserves can also be viewed as irredeemable — at most, the holder can insist on redemption in the form of currency.

So:

$$M = C + R, \tag{1}$$

$$R = R^r + R^e. \tag{2}$$

I will define seigniorage in period t, S_t, as the flow of period t profits derived from base money issuance. Let M_t be the stock of base money at the end of period t, with similar notation for all other asset stocks; Δ is the backward difference operator.

$$\begin{aligned} S_t &= M_t - (1 + i_t^c)C_{t-1} - (1 + i_t^r)R_{t-1}^r - (1 + i_t^e)R_{t-1}^e \\ &= \Delta M_t - i_t^c C_{t-1} - i_t^r R_{t-1}^r - i_t^e R_{t-1}^e. \end{aligned} \tag{3}$$

We can rewrite Equation (3) more compactly in terms of the (weighted) average interest rate on the monetary base, i^m, as follows:

$$S_t = \Delta M_t - i_t^m M_{t-1}, \tag{4}$$

where

$$i_t^m = i_t^c \left(\frac{C_{t-1}}{M_{t-1}}\right) + i_t^r \left(\frac{R_{t-1}^r}{M_{t-1}}\right) + i_t^e \left(\frac{R_{t-1}^e}{M_{t-1}}\right). \tag{5}$$

Let Y denote real GDP and P the GDP deflator. The proportional growth rate of real GDP in period t is denoted $\gamma_t = \frac{Y_t - Y_{t-1}}{Y_{t-1}}$ and the rate of inflation of the GDP deflator is denoted $\pi_t = \frac{P_t - P_{t-1}}{P_{t-1}}$. Seigniorage as a share of GDP, $s_t = \frac{S_t}{P_t Y_t}$, is therefore given by:

$$s_t = \frac{\Delta M_t}{P_t Y_t} - \frac{i_t^M}{(1+\gamma_t)(1+\pi_t)} m_{t-1}, \tag{6}$$

where $m_t = \frac{M_t}{P_t Y_t}$ is the monetary base as a share of GDP, the reciprocal of the income velocity of circulation of base money.

The net present discounted value of current and future seigniorage at the beginning of period t,denoted $NPV_t(S)$, is defined as:

$$NPV_t(S) = E_t \sum_{j=t}^{\infty} I_{j,t}(M_j - (1 + i_j^m)M_{j-1}), \tag{7}$$

where E_t is the expectation operator conditional on information at time t, and $I_{j,t-1}$ is the (stochastic) nominal discount factor between periods j and t, defined by

$$\begin{aligned} I_{j,t} &= \prod_{k=t+1}^{j} I_{k,k-1} \quad \text{for } j > t \\ &= 1 \quad\quad\quad\quad\quad \text{for } j = t. \end{aligned} \tag{8}$$

The one-period risk-free nominal interest rate in period t, i_t, is defined by:

$$\frac{1}{1+i_t} = E_t I_{t+1,t}. \tag{9}$$

An empirical implementation of Equation (7) is a heroic task, which we tackle by making the heroic simplification of stationarity. Specifically, we assume that the proportional growth rate of the monetary base is a constant μ and that the short nominal interest rate is a constant i. I also restrict the consideration of the monetary base to the currency component, omitting required and excess reserves issuance as a source of seigniorage. This means that we set $M = C$ and $i_j^m = 0$ in Equation (7). I therefore err on the side of underestimating the size of the NPV of future seigniorage.

It follows that in this stationary environment, the NPV of current and future currency issuance is given by:

$$NPV_t(S) = \left(\frac{1+i}{i-\mu}\right)\mu C_0, \tag{10}$$

where C_0 is the initial value of the stock of currency.

A standard Cagan-style demand function for currency takes the form

$$\frac{C}{P} = kY^{\alpha}e^{-\beta(i-i^c)} \\ k, \alpha, \beta > 0 \tag{11}$$

where P is the general price level and Y some scale variable like real GDP. With i^c, the interest rate on currency zero (because of historical accident and the lack of imagination of our central bankers), it follows that at a constant nominal interest rate, the growth rate of the stock of currency, μ, the rate of inflation, π, and the growth rate of real GDP, γ, are related as follows:

$$1 + \mu = (1+\pi)(1+\gamma)^{\alpha}. \tag{12}$$

The NPV of current and future currency issuance can therefore be written as:

$$NPV(S) = \left(\frac{1+i}{1+i-(1+\pi)(1+\gamma)^{\alpha}}\right)((1+\pi)(1+\gamma)^{\alpha}-1)C_0. \tag{13}$$

The Global Economics team at Citi have recently produced estimates of long-run currency demand functions for the euro, the U.S. dollar, the pound sterling, and the Japanese yen, based on Equation (11), allowing for non-stationarity, common trends, and structural breaks in the relevant series.

The estimation yields a very robust estimate for the output elasticity of currency demand for the euro (and for the three other currencies) of around 0.8, implying that every one percent increase in real output calls forth a 0.8 percent increase in real money balances held. The interest rate semi-elasticity of currency demand is somewhat less precisely estimated. The average coefficient value estimated is around 3 for the euro area (but considerably higher for the U.S. and for Japan), implying that a 1 percent increase in a short-term nominal market interest rate (our opportunity cost measure) implies a 3 percent decrease in currency balances.[6] To arrive at estimates

[6]Full details of the data used, the estimation methodology, and the result will be made available in a forthcoming publication.

Table 1. Present Discounted Value of Future Seigniorage in the Euro Area ($\alpha = 0.8$; $\beta = 2.9$).

EUR (bn)	Interest/Discount Rate (i)				
Real Growth Rate (γ)	3.5%	4.0%	4.5%	5.0%	5.5%
0.5%	€1,886	€1,273	€956	€763	€632
1.0%	€3,717	€2,065	€1,421	€1,078	€865
1.5%	€13,090	€3,817	€2,216	€1,553	€1,189
2.0%	Infinite	€10,966	€3,888	€2,345	€1,670

Note: α represents the long-run income elasticity of the money demand function, and β the corresponding interest rate semi-elasticity.
Source: Citi Investment Research and Analysis.

of the present discounted value of seigniorage, we need to combine our estimated coefficients with assumptions about future real growth rates for the euro area and discount rates for the stream of seigniorage revenue. Reasonable conservative estimates for the former would be around 1 percent on average for the euro area, while a 4 percent nominal discount rate may be appropriate for the latter.

Table 1 presents the estimates for the value of Eurosystem seigniorage based on these benchmark assumptions as well as a number of alternative assumptions for growth rates and interest rates. As the table indicates, the resulting value would be just over €2 trillion at a 1 percent average real growth rate and with a discount rate of 4 percent. Raising the average growth rate of real GDP to 1.5 percent almost doubles the estimate of the value of seigniorage. Note that the relevant growth rate here is the average growth rate in the future, with the horizon being very long (infinite, actually).

Above, we noted that the output elasticity of currency demand is estimated extremely precisely and robustly, including across different samples, different statistical methodologies, and different countries. There is therefore little need to dwell on the impact of different assumptions about this elasticity. The interest rate semi-elasticity is less precisely estimated. However, the quantitative impact of different values for this elasticity is rather limited, reducing the estimated value of seigniorage in our benchmark case (for a real growth rate of 1 percent and a nominal interest rate of 4 percent) by 3 percent if the elasticity is 4 rather than 3 and raising it by 3 percent if the elasticity is 2.

Table 2. Present Discounted Value of Future Seigniorage in the United States ($\alpha = 0.8$; $\beta = 7.2$).

USD (bn)	Interest/Discount Rate (i)				
Real Growth Rate (g)	3.5%	4.0%	4.5%	5.0%	5.5%
0.5%	\$1,727	\$1,150	\$849	\$664	\$540
1.0%	\$3,186	\$1,795	\$1,226	\$918	\$724
1.5%	\$8,669	\$3,096	\$1,839	\$1,285	\$974
2.0%	Infinite	\$7,077	\$3,005	\$1,864	\$1,329

Note: α represents the long-run income elasticity of the money demand function, and β the corresponding interest rate semi-elasticity.
Source: Citi Investment Research and Analysis.

Table 3. Present Discounted Value of Future Seigniorage in the United Kingdom ($\alpha = 0.8$; $\beta = 1.7$).

GBP (bn)	Interest/Discount Rate (i)				
Real Growth Rate (g)	3.5%	4.0%	4.5%	5.0%	5.5%
0.5%	£98	£67	£51	£41	£34
1.0%	£182	£105	£74	£56	£46
1.5%	£514	£183	£111	£79	£62
2.0%	Infinite	£432	£183	£116	£85

Note: α represents the long-run income elasticity of the money demand function, and β the corresponding interest rate semi-elasticity.
Source: Citi Investment Research and Analysis.

The corresponding estimates and calculation for U.S. dollar, sterling, and yen currency demand are given in Tables 2, 3, and 4, respectively.

By any standards, these estimates of the NPV of non-inflationary seigniorage are large numbers. For the euro area, at 2 percent inflation, 1 percent real GDP growth and a 4 percent nominal interest rate, it comes to more than €2 trillion (see Table 1). For the U.S., with 2 percent inflation, real GDP growth at 2 percent and a 4 percent nominal discount rate, the NPV of future non-inflationary seigniorage is more than \$7 trillion.

These numbers underestimate the non-inflationary loss-absorbing capacity or *NILAC* of the central bank for a number of reasons. First, it

Table 4. Present Discounted Value of Future Seigniorage in Japan ($\alpha = 0.7$; $\beta = 12.1$).

Yen (trn)	Interest/Discount Rate (i)				
Real Growth Rate (γ)	3.5%	4.0%	4.5%	5.0%	5.5%
0.5%	¥136	¥90	¥65	¥50	¥40
1.0%	¥225	¥131	¥89	¥66	¥51
1.5%	¥457	¥203	¥125	¥88	¥66
2.0%	¥2,438	¥360	¥185	¥120	¥86

Note: α represents the long-run income elasticity of the money demand function, and β the corresponding interest rate semi-elasticity.
Source: Citi Investment Research and Analysis.

ignores required reserves or assumes they are paid the market opportunity cost and therefore do not represent a source of profit to the central bank. Even if this were correct currently, it is at the discretion of the central bank, which sets both the reserve requirement and the rate of remuneration on required reserves. The required reserve ratio for the euro area was recently (on December 8, 2011) lowered to 1 percent of eligible deposits from 2 percent. Second, it ignores excess reserves or assumes they, too, are paid their market opportunity cost. Again, their remuneration rate, just like the remuneration rate on all the central bank's non-monetary liabilities, are instruments of the central bank, although the availability of private and other sovereign substitutes limits the ability of the central bank to extract rents from these liabilities.

Third, it ignores the conventional loss-absorption capacity of central banks — in the case of the Eurosystem, about €81 billion of capital plus reserves plus probably around €320 billion of gold and foreign exchange revaluation gains.

Finally, as shown in Buiter (2007b), the intangible asset that has to be added to the conventional balance sheet of the central bank to obtain its non-inflationary loss absorption capacity due to the monopoly of currency issuance is not just the NPV of future currency issuance, but the sum of the NPV of future currency issuance and the initial stock of base money, about €875 billion for the euro area. This means that the non-inflationary loss-absorption capacity of the Eurosystem with $\gamma = 1$ percent, $\pi = 2$ percent, and $i = 4$ percent, is at least €3.2 trillion — enough to get excited about. These resources are, of course, taxpayers' resources and should be accounted for properly.

8. How Different is the Fiscal Role of the Central Bank in the U.S. from that in the Euro Area?

8.1 *The ability and willingness to use the anticipated and unanticipated inflation taxes*

As regards the *ability*, that is, the technical or instrumental capacity of the central bank to fund government budget deficits or inflate away the real net present value of servicing the outstanding stock of public debt, there is no significant difference between the Fed and the ECB/Eurosystem. The ECB can, from a purely technical, instrumental perspective, use seigniorage or the anticipated inflation tax to fund the deficits of any, some, or all of the 17 sovereigns that are part of the euro area, just as the Fed can for the U.S. federal government (and indeed for any of the 50 state governments and any of the countless local government entities). The ECB cannot purchase sovereign debt in the primary issue markets or lend to sovereigns directly, but it can purchase any amount of sovereign debt in the secondary markets — although it has thus far restricted its outright purchases of sovereign debt (mainly periphery sovereign debt through the Securities Market Programme (€211 billion outstanding on December 30, 2011)) to levels much below that of the other leading central banks.

The ECB also has the same technical capacity as the Fed (or the Bank of England) to use unanticipated inflation to reduce the real NPV of servicing the euro-denominated sovereign (and private) debt in the euro area. The U.S. certainly holds an advantage over the UK as regards its ability to impose a capital levy on government bond holders through unanticipated inflation. The average maturity of the outstanding stock of U.S. Treasury debt is only around five years, while in the UK it is just over 13 years.[7] The euro area average maturity is around 6.3 years. This means that the inflation surprise would have to be larger in the U.S. if it is to achieve the same absolute or percentage reduction in the real cost of sovereign debt service on the outstanding debt. Both in the euro area and in the U.S., the share of index-linked or foreign-currency-denominated sovereign debt in total sovereign debt is small. Of the $15.5 trillion federal debt outstanding

[7] For the euro area, the source is Eurostat; for the U.S. and the UK, the source is the IMF.

at the end of fiscal year 2011, of which $9.9 trillion was held by the public, only 3.5 percent (5.6 percent) was index-linked.[8] Less than one percent of euro area sovereign debt is denominated in non-Euro currencies.

In comparing the Fed and the ECB, the real issues are, first, the *legal or constitutional ability* of these two central banks to use seigniorage or the unanticipated inflation tax to improve the solvency of their sovereigns, and, second, their *political ability* or *willingness* to act as lender of last resort for their sovereigns, and/or to impose an unanticipated capital levy on the holders of their sovereign's debt.

It is clear that as far as the EU Treaty is concerned, there are only minor, insignificant legal constraints on the ability of the ECB/Eurosystem to act as lender of last resort for the 17 sovereigns of the euro area. The primary objective of the ECB is price stability. However, the ECB/Eurosystem is also mandated to support financial stability.[9] If excessive sovereign debt and/or excessive sovereign deficits threaten financial stability, acting as lender of last resort for one or more of the sovereigns and/or inflating away the burden of the sovereign debt may be the lesser evil if deflation and financial collapse are the alternative.

As noted, the Treaty also forbids the ECB from lending directly to any sovereign or from purchasing its debt in the primary issuance markets. However, there is no Treaty impediment to outright purchases of sovereign debt in the secondary markets. Since the Securities Market Programme was activated in May 2010, the Eurosystem has purchased outright around €211 billion of euro area sovereign debt. Every euro area member state's central bank held sovereign debt outright on its balance sheet even before the EMU was created. And of course, the individual member states' central banks prior to 1999, as well as the Eurosystem since 1999, have accepted hundreds of billions of euros worth of euro area sovereign debt as collateral in repos and other collateralized transactions with eligible counterparties. As the counterparties in these transactions included (and include) banks that were either insolvent (kept alive by regulatory forbearance and by the willingness of the ECB/Eurosystem to fund insolvent banks that offered as collateral securities issued by or guaranteed by insolvent sovereigns) or at risk of insolvency should the sovereigns whose debt they offered as collateral turn out to be insolvent, these collateralized loans were at times economically equivalent to outright purchases of sovereign debt.

[8] Source: U.S. Treasury.

[9] See Article 127.5 FTEU.

The ECB rejects a role as lender of last resort to sovereigns. It has, however, already gone far beyond that role. A lender of last resort lends to entities that are illiquid but most likely solvent. As noted earlier, in the pure Bagehot (1873) model of the lender of last resort, the LLR lends only against good collateral and at a penalty rate. Instead, in its first interventions in support of illiquid sovereigns, the ECB purchased debt issued by sovereigns (Greece, Ireland, and Portugal) that were not just illiquid but almost certainly insolvent as well. Funding into insolvency means going well beyond a lender of last resort role *vis-à-vis* sovereigns.

Such restrictions as those which the Treaty imposes on the balance sheet of the central bank apply only to the asset side of the balance sheet — the ban on direct lending to the sovereigns by the ECB and the NCBs and the prohibition of sovereign debt purchases in the primary markets by the ECB and the NCBs. There are no Treaty restrictions on the liability side of the central bank. Specifically, there is no restriction on "monetary financing" by the Eurosystem of euro area sovereign debt nor is there a requirement that purchases of sovereign debt in the secondary markets by the Eurosystem be sterilized. There is a lot of popular mythmaking to the contrary, and there are non-specific references to the "spirit of the Treaty," but the truth of the matter is that there was no agreement on these issues among the authors of the Treaty, and this lack of agreement is reflected accurately in the open-ended and ultimately permissive approach of the Treaty to sovereign debt purchases by the central bank and to the monetization of sovereign debt. It is a classic EU fudge that does not rule out any course of action.

The notion that the U.S. sovereign is not at risk of default because it can always force the Fed to monetize its debt and deficits is politically naive and technically incorrect. It is true that the Fed is "a creature of Congress." The Fed is governed by the Federal Reserve Act, which can be repealed or amended by the Congress. But for the members of the Board of Governors and of the FOMC to vote by majority in favor of a deliberately inflationary resolution of the U.S. sovereign debt problem, an "inflationist" majority would have to be found among the seven Board members and the five voting regional Fed governors. The Congress would therefore have to be able to pack the Board with inflationist members. The current members certainly would not oblige. In addition, amendments to the Federal Reserve Act and to the Full Employment and Balanced Growth Act (better known as the Humphrey–Hawkins Full Employment Act) would likely be required, as both include stable prices or stable purchasing power of money among the objectives of the Fed.

Such packing of the Board of Governors and the FOMC with inflationists and/or the passing of inflationist amendments to the Federal Reserve Act and the Full Employment and Balanced Growth Act are possible but politically highly unlikely. The legal changes would require either an inflationist majority in both Houses of Congress and an inflationist President, or an inflationist super-majority in the Congress capable of overcoming a presidential veto. The personnel changes on the Board would require that the President nominate and the Senate confirm inflationist appointments.[10]

So, while it is true that the Fed is "a creature of Congress," and that the institution is constrained by, and indeed at times appears to live in fear of, anticipated congressional reactions to its actions, the political conditions that would have to be satisfied for the U.S. sovereign to be able to compel or induce the Fed to monetize its debt and deficits are unlikely to be satisfied any time soon. It is difficult to envisage circumstances under which either both the Congress and the executive/White House would be dominated by parties that consider sovereign default to be more harmful than monetization and inflation, or under which there is a super-majority in the Congress that holds the view that sovereign default is worse than inflation and that can override a presidential veto of congressional legislation to instruct the Fed to monetize the federal debt and deficit.

In fact, the most vocal elements in Congress on issues of monetization, QE, and debauching the currency are as rabidly anti-monetization of sovereign debt and deficits as those of any parliament in the euro area. One candidate for the Republication nomination for the U.S. presidency, Governor Rick Perry of Texas, has come very close to accusing Chairman Ben Bernanke of treason because of Bernanke's support for QE.[11] Another candidate for the Republican nomination, Congressman Ron Paul, wants to abolish the Fed (which he considers to be an immoral institution) and replace it with a gold standard. Rather than being inflationist, the U.S. body politic appears to have a surprisingly large quota of anti-inflation nutters. I therefore conjecture that the likelihood of an attempt at an inflationary

[10]The seven members of the Board of Governors are appointed by the President and confirmed by the Senate for a 14-year term.

[11]"If this guy prints more money between now and the election, I dunno what y'all would do to him in Iowa but we would treat him pretty ugly down in Texas. Printing more money to play politics at this particular time in history is almost treasonous in my opinion." — Governor Rick Perry on Monday, August 15, 2011, Burns and Haberman, Politico.com. See www.politico.com/news/stories/0811/61448.html.

resolution of the U.S. federal fiscal problems is not significantly greater than an inflationary resolution of the sovereign debt problems of the euro area member states.

8.2 *Technical/economic obstacles to an inflationary solution of the U.S. and euro area sovereign debt problems: The seigniorage Laffer curve*

Unanticipated inflation can be used to reduce or even wipe out the real net present value of servicing the outstanding public debt, as long as this debt is not price index linked or exchange rate indexed. The rates of inflation may be high, but it can be done.

However, even if the entire stock of sovereign debt were wiped out, there would remain sizable non-interest sovereign deficits or primary deficits in the U.S. For the U.S., the IMF estimate of the general government structural or cyclically corrected deficit as a share of GDP in 2010 is 5.1 percent. The corresponding euro area figure for 2010 is 1.6 percent.

Although it is complicated to do a real-time analysis of the maximum amount of seigniorage revenue that can be extracted once inflation is fully anticipated, it is rather easy to provide a steady-state or long-run benchmark. The currency demand function in Equation (11) can be written as $c = kY^{\alpha-1}e^{-\beta i}$, where $c = C/(PY)$ is the ratio of currency to GDP — the reciprocal of the income velocity of circulation of currency. There can be a steady state or balanced growth path only if currency demand is proportional to GDP, that is, $\alpha = 1$. For the U.S., the point estimate for α is 0.8 and is statistically insignificantly different from 1 at conventional significance levels. Assuming α to be too high biases the results toward overestimating the amount of seigniorage that can be extracted.

With $\alpha = 1$, the long-run base money demand function becomes:

$$c = ke^{-\beta i}. \tag{14}$$

In the long run, if $\alpha = 1$, the growth rate of the nominal stock of base money equals the growth rate of the nominal GDP (see Equation (12)). Also, when the actual and anticipated rates of inflation are the same, the nominal interest rate, the real interest, r, and the inflation rate are related as follows: $1 + i = (1 + r)(1 + \pi)$. It follows that seigniorage as a share of GDP can be written as:

$$s = ((1 + \pi)(1 + \gamma) - 1)ke^{-((1+r)(1+\pi)-1)}. \tag{15}$$

Assume that the long-run growth rate of GDP and the long-run real interest rate are independent of the fully anticipated rate of inflation. It follows that the inflation rate that maximizes long-run seigniorage as a share of GDP, $\hat{\pi}$, is given by:

$$\hat{\pi} = \left(\frac{1}{\beta} - \gamma\right)\left(\frac{1}{1+\gamma}\right). \tag{16}$$

The maximum long-run share of seigniorage in GDP, $\hat{s}$, is therefore given by:

$$\hat{s} = \frac{1}{\beta} k e^{-\left[\frac{r-\gamma}{1+\gamma} + \frac{1}{\beta}\left(\frac{1+r}{1+\gamma}\right)\right]}. \tag{17}$$

The long-run real interest rate for the U.S. is probably not all that different from the long-run growth rate of real GDP. Assuming $r = \gamma$, we have:

$$\hat{s} = \frac{1}{\beta} k e^{-\frac{1}{\beta}}. \tag{18}$$

The U.S. estimates for β, (minus) the semi-elasticity of real base money demand with respect to the financial opportunity cost of holding base money (some nominal interest rate minus the own return on base money — zero for currency), tend to be high — the point estimate reported earlier was $\beta = 7.2$, although it is statistically poorly determined. I will further flatter the conclusion in favor of a high-revenue yielding inflation tax also considering the case where the interest semi-elasticity is as low as -2.0.

Note that k is the long-run ratio of the monetary base to GDP when the nominal interest rate is zero. The opportunity cost of base money, or at least the opportunity cost of holding currency, has been just about zero in the U.S. since the beginning of 2009. As of November 2, 2011, there was just over \$1.0 trillion worth of Federal Reserve notes outstanding; \$1.5 trillion worth of commercial bank overnight deposits (reserves) were also held with the Federal Reserve System. U.S. nominal GDP for 2011 is likely to be around \$15.0 trillion. This gives us an estimate of k based on currency alone of 0.067, that is, the long-run stock of U.S. currency at a zero nominal interest rate is 6.7 percent of GDP. If we were to consider instead an estimate of k for the entire stock of base money, our estimate of k would be 0.167 or 16.7 percent of GDP.

When $\beta = 7.2$, maximum long-run seigniorage as a share of GDP considering only currency issuance is therefore only 0.8 percent of GDP. Considering both currency issuance and commercial bank reserves held with the Fed, and assuming (1) that base money demand tracks currency demand, and (2) that the Fed pays a zero interest rate on both required and excess reserves, the estimate of maximum long-run seigniorage as a share of GDP is just 2.0 percent of GDP. The cyclically adjusted primary deficit of the U.S. general government for 2010 is, as we noted earlier, estimated to be 5.1 percent of GDP. Seigniorage cannot fill that gap. Assuming a 2.5 percent per annum real GDP growth rate in the long run, this insufficient maximal seigniorage would be extracted at an inflation rate of 11.1 percent per annum.

If we assume instead (and counterfactually) that $\beta = 2.0$, maximum long-run seigniorage as a share of GDP considering only currency issuance is just over 2.0 percent of GDP. Considering both currency issuance and commercial bank reserves held with the Fed (and making the same assumptions about reserve demand and remuneration as before), the estimate of maximum long-run seigniorage as a share of GDP is 5.1 percent of GDP. Because the cyclically adjusted primary deficit of the U.S. general government for 2010 is estimated to be 5.1 percent of GDP, seigniorage can just fill that gap if the broad seigniorage definition is used. Assuming a 2.5 percent per annum real GDP growth rate in the long run, this seigniorage would be extracted at an inflation rate of 46.3 percent per annum.

No doubt, at nearly 50 percent inflation, either the Fed would have to compensate excess reserves, or excess reserves would vanish rapidly, reducing the maximum amount of seigniorage that could be extracted to something much closer to the 2 percent of GDP that we estimate as the inflation tax yield from currency issuance alone. Noting that these calculations are based on estimates of the income elasticity of base money demand and of the interest semi-elasticity of base money demand that are deliberately slanted to exaggerate the likely revenues yielded by the anticipated inflation tax, it is clear that the U.S. sovereign could not fund anything like its existing cyclically corrected primary deficit through money issuance alone. Any attempt to do so would lead to accelerating inflation and, ultimately, hyperinflation.

For the euro area, 2011 GDP is likely to come out at around €9.8 trillion (IMF estimate). On October 11, euro currency outstanding was around €863 billion and bank reserves held with the Eurosystem was €775 billion. The currency-based estimate of k for the euro area is therefore around 8.8 percent of GDP and the base money estimate is 16.7 percent of GDP. Assume that for the euro area, the real interest rate is 2.0 percent and the growth rate of real GDP 1.0 percent. With $\beta = 2.9$ (the estimate used in Table 1), the maximum long-run currency-based estimate of seigniorage as a share of GDP for the euro area is therefore 2.1 percent, higher than the 0.8 percent obtained for the U.S. with $\beta = 7.2$. The base money-based estimate for the euro area is 4.0 percent of GDP, also higher than its U.S. counterpart when $\beta = 7.2$. If we redo the calculations for the euro area with $\beta = 2.0$, the currency-based estimate is 2.6 percent of GDP. The broad base money-based estimate is close to that for the U.S., at 5.0 percent of GDP. If the IMF's estimate of the cyclically corrected primary general government balance for the euro area in 2010 of 1.6 percent is correct, seigniorage alone could fill the primary gap in the euro area. Assuming a trend growth rate of real GDP of 1.0 percent per annum, and a real interest rate of 2.0 percent, it would do so at an annual inflation rate of around 22 percent based on the currency-only calculation, or just under 10 percent based on the broad-base money definition.

9. Quasi-Fiscal Activities of the Central Bank

In addition to the overtly and unavoidable fiscal activities of the central bank associated with the distribution of seigniorage revenues, central banks are involved in a wide range of transactions and other activities that are *ex-ante* or *ex-post* equivalent from an economic perspective to subsidies or taxes, even if they are not formally or legally labelled as such and even though they generally are not subject to the same parliamentary/congressional scrutiny and oversight as explicit taxes, transfers and subsidies. These quasi-fiscal activities of the central bank can involve private, public, domestic or foreign entities.

Among the quasi-fiscal instruments used by central banks during the financial crisis are the following:

- The level of required reserves for eligible deposits;
- The remuneration of both required and excess reserves;
- The terms and conditions on which central banks purchased illiquid assets from private, public, domestic, and foreign counterparties; and
- The terms and conditions on which central banks have accepted illiquid and other hard-to-value collateral from eligible counterparties, including the valuation of the collateral and the haircuts imposed on these valuations.

Central banks have taken on significant credit risk during the crisis. If this was not priced properly *ex-ante*, that is, if the risk-adjusted expected return to the assumption of private and public sector credit risk by the central bank did not at least cover the appropriate opportunity cost of funds to the central bank, such actions involve an *ex-ante* quasi-fiscal subsidy. Even if the central bank took on credit risk on the correct terms *ex-ante*, the *ex-post* realization of risk could still result in *ex-post* quasi-fiscal transfers or taxes. It is a key question whether even taking on properly priced credit risk is a legitimate task of the central bank. I believe it is not. Unfortunately, when the political arena within which a central bank operates is crooked and badly distorted, such quasi-fiscal activities by the central bank may constitute the lesser evil.

The Bank of England followed a clear policy under which purchases or acceptance as collateral of anything but high-grade financial instruments could only be done with a full guarantee or indemnity from the UK Treasury. As long as the UK Treasury is most likely solvent, that is indeed the proper division of labor.

Both the Fed and the ECB have taken on massive credit risk during the crisis. The Fed has taken on only private credit risk (as long as the U.S. sovereign is most likely solvent); the ECB has taken on both private credit risk and the credit risk of potentially insolvent sovereigns from the euro area periphery. The Fed parked much of its risky private exposures in off-balance-sheet SPVs like Maiden Lane and Maiden Lane 2. The TALF could potentially have exposed the Fed to up to $1 trillion of risky private assets with a U.S. Treasury indemnity of at most $100 billion. The ECB/Eurosystem now holds €211 billion worth of risky EA periphery sovereign debt outright on its balance sheet. By lending to (near-) insolvent banks that offer as collateral instruments issued by or guaranteed by (near-) insolvent sovereigns, the ECB/Eurosystem is exposed to many hundreds of billions of euros worth of convoluted private and public credit risk. The ELAs (Emergency Liquidity Assistance facilities) are notionally an exposure of national central banks (guaranteed by the national sovereign), not of the Eurosystem or the ECB, but if the national sovereign involved is itself insolvent, ELA exposure becomes ECB/Eurosystem exposure nevertheless.

Secrecy is one of the traditional hallmarks of central banking. In this crisis, the opaqueness of central banks' actions has set new records. Some of it may be necessary, at least temporarily so as to ensure that market-sensitive and other confidential information does not become public prematurely or in a distorting or unfair manner. Most of it appears to be motivated by the all-too-human desire to maximize power and minimize accountability and the risk of being asked difficult or embarrassing questions about the form and substance of central bank interventions during the crisis. Central banks, most notably the ECB and the Fed, have been stonewalling all attempts to produce greater openness, transparency, and accountability. In the case of the Fed, it was only the threat of lawsuits,[12] the continuing threat of legislative initiatives like Representative Ron Paul's "audit the Fed" proposals, and the heavy hand of the Dodd–Frank Act that have forced the U.S. monetary authorities to begin to come clean on their interventions on behalf of domestic and foreign financial institutions since late 2007.

The ECB thus far has refused to disclose, even after the passing of an appropriate time interval, exactly what securities it has bought outright under the SMP and at what prices. It has also refused to make public either the valuation methods it uses to price illiquid financial instruments it is offered as collateral, or the actual valuations assigned to the illiquid instruments it has accepted as collateral. The haircuts applied to these valuations are supposed to be in the public domain, but many market observers believe that the actual haircuts imposed on Greek banks offering Greek sovereign debt as collateral at the Greek central bank are higher than the posted official haircuts.

The identities of the counterparties in the Eurosystem's and ELAs' transactions are also not revealed, even after the passing of a suitable period of time. This complete lack of openness, transparency, and accountability for the ECB's and NCB's use of public resources — ultimately resources belonging to the taxpayers and other citizens of the euro area — is extraordinary. With a Eurosystem balance sheet of around €2.1 trillion and a non-inflationary loss absorption capacity (NILAC) of at least €3.2 trillion, one would have hoped that the European Parliament, to which the ECB is formally accountable (mainly through the quarterly hearings with its Committee on Economic and Monetary Affairs (ECON)), would have insisted on a full accounting for the quasi-fiscal activities of the ECB/Eurosystem. Thus far, however, the ECON has been something of a toothless paper tiger.

[12]When the Fed refused to identify the recipients of almost $2 trillion of emergency loans or the nature and provenance of the troubled assets it had accepted as collateral, Bloomberg News requested details of the Fed lending under the U.S. Freedom of Information Act and filed a federal lawsuit on November 7, 2008, seeking to force disclosure. The Bloomberg lawsuit was Bloomberg LP vs. the Board of Governors of the Federal Reserve System, 08-CV-9595, U.S. District Court, Southern District of New York (Manhattan). On August 25, 2009, the Court ruled in favor of Bloomberg News.

10. Instruments of the Modern Central Bank

The financial crisis has provided a timely reminder that the policy instruments of the central bank extend beyond the setting of some short-term nominal interest rate. Even before the crisis struck, it was common knowledge that the announcement effects of monetary policy decisions were likely to be more significant drivers of economic activity than the monthly setting of some overnight rate. Providing projections of future policy interest rate paths or publishing contingent rules for setting future interest rates is now part of the "acquis central bancaire."

The size and composition of both sides of the balance sheet of the central bank (and the proliferation of off-balance-sheet assets and liabilities like swaps and many other contingent claims and derivatives) have greatly expanded the central bank's instrumentarium. The Fed and the Bank of England conduct (or have conducted) many of their rescue operations through off-balance-sheet special purpose vehicles (SPVs) like the Maiden Lane SPVs of the Fed mentioned before, or the Special Liquidity Scheme (now closed for new business) and Asset Purchase Facility of the Bank of England.

Quantitative easing (or Large-Scale Asset Purchases), credit easing (aka qualitative easing), enhanced credit support, and operation twist have entered the central bank dictionary since the official policy rate has reached levels so low that it could not be cut further, either because of the availability of a zero nominal interest rate store of value (currency) or because of the extreme psychological discomfort this would cause for central bankers unable to contemplate (indirectly) imposing negative nominal interest rates on commercial bank depositors.

All the unconventional measures mentioned in the previous paragraph are "poor man's monetary policy." QE at the zero lower bound (ZLB) or the effective lower bound (ELB), when the assets the central bank purchases are traded in orderly markets, has very little effect on anything. The Fed's and Bank of England's assertion that there is evidence of significant impacts (at least in asset markets) (see D'Amico and King, 2010; Joyce *et al.*, 2010; Hamilton and Wu, 2011; and Swanson, 2011) is quite unconvincing, and has recently been refuted quite convincingly in a BIS study (Meaning and Zhu, 2011). Inevitably, all these studies rely on high-frequency event studies, which are inherently incapable of demonstrating the presence or absence of *lasting* effects, even of the identification of the impact effect were to be convincing.

Nothing happens when the economy is at the ELB on the liability side when the central bank engages in QE. Excess reserves held by commercial banks just sit there idly. QE, credit easing, or enhanced credit support have significant effects at the ELB, if you intervene on the asset side in disorderly markets. Examples are purchases of securitized mortgages during the subprime mortgage-backed securities crisis or purchases of securities issued by most likely solvent, but most certainly illiquid sovereigns like Spain and Italy during 2011 and 2012. In the future, central bank purchases (or acceptance as collateral) of securitized commercial loans, including SME loans, the Wilshire stock index, REITs, etc., could play a similar role.

This brings me to the inevitable conclusion that it is time to get serious about abolishing the zero lower bound or effective lower bound on risk-free short nominal interest rates. It is only the hidebound conservatism of our central bankers that prevents them from undertaking the minor institutional and practical innovations that would make it as easy, operationally, to set the central bank's official policy rate at minus 5 percent as at plus 5 percent.

I have written extensively on this subject (see Buiter and Panigirtzoglou, 2001, 2003; Buiter, 2005, 2007a, 2008, 2009b, 2010a; Hall, 1997; Goodfriend, 2000; Fukao, 2005; Eisler, 1932; Gesell, 1916; and Gaitskell, 1969). The socially most efficient way of getting rid of the ELB would be by doing away with currency completely. An alternative due to Gesell (1916) would tax currency holdings. A third approach, due to Eisler (1932), decouples the numéraire or unit of account role of money from its medium of exchange or means of payment role. The central bank would introduce a potentially variable exchange rate between bank reserves with the central bank (the dollar) and a new currency (the rollad). There would be no physical dollar currency issued by the state. By setting the rollad at a forward discount relative to the dollar, the central bank can implement an arbitrarily large negative interest rate for the dollar.

11. The Institutional Division of Labor for Financial Stability: Who Does What?

Different countries organize the management of financial stability in different ways and there is a wide range of proposals for alternative arrangements. When it comes to deciding which institution does what, two key points have to be kept in mind. First, the Treasury (the sovereign) has to be the central player on the financial stability team whenever taxpayers' money is put at risk. Second, do not fall into the common trap of thinking that centralization is the solution to every coordination problem — avoid the "central planning fallacy."

The Bank of England is a prime example of this central planning fallacy. Under the new regime proposed by the UK government, the Bank of England would have control over interest rates through the MPC, which has a majority of internal or executive Bank of England members; it would have control of macroprudential oversight through the Financial Policy Committee (FPC), which would also have a majority of executive Bank of England members; it would have control over microprudential oversight, through the Prudential Regulation Authority (PRA); and it would run the Resolution Authority. Every aspect of financial regulation and supervision, except market conduct — aka the protection of widows and orphans — will be under the control of the Bank of England. The governor of the Bank of England chairs the MPC, the FPC, and the PRA. He will also be in charge of the UK Resolution Authority. To top it off, he is also a vice-chair of the European Systemic Risk Board — the EU proto-macroprudential body. This adds up to an impossibly heavy workload. Even if it were feasible, it would not be desirable to concentrate so much power in one person.

I have no firm views on the relative merits of the twin peaks model (prudential and conduct of business), the three pillars model (banking, insurance, and securities) or the integrated model, in which all supervision is concentrated in one organization. I would just want to note that "markets," that is, maintaining orderly, liquid, and well-functioning markets, is also a macroprudential issue, not just a conduct or widows-and-orphans issue, although of course some conduct issues arise in markets as well as in institutions.

The setting of the official policy rate (the Federal Funds target rate in the U.S., the Refi rate in the euro area, and the Bank Rate in the UK) could be delegated to an operationally independent body, the Monetary Policy Committee or MPC, say, outside the central bank. Presumably, the MPC would set the usual trio of rates: a central rate, a (lower) deposit facility rate, and a (higher) loan facility rate. Conventionally, this rate-setting function is performed by a body that is part of the central bank, often with a majority of its members drawn from among the central bank's executives. It is not clear why this is the best location for the MPC.

The exchange rate *regime* (fixed, floating, multiple exchange rates) is a political decision that has to be made by the Treasury. Exchange rate management within a regime (e.g., foreign exchange market interventions in spot or forward markets) should be the responsibility of the monetary authority — the central bank, or if the MPC is outside the central bank, the

MPC and the central bank jointly. The stock of official gold and foreign exchange reserves should be transferred to the central bank as legal owner, not just as manager. The common practice of having the Treasury in charge of/responsible for exchange rate management, even within a given exchange rate regime — as is the case, for instance in the U.S. and Japan — is as incomprehensible as it is unhelpful to effective monetary and exchange rate management. Anyone who has tried to explain this arrangement in a world with a floating exchange rate and perfect international capital mobility to a class full of undergraduates will know what I am talking about.

The lender of last resort and market maker of last resort roles — the provision of funding liquidity and market liquidity — can only be the responsibility of the central bank. The size and composition of the balance sheet of the central bank, including its collateral policy, are matters for the central bank, constrained of course by the interest rates set by the MPC, and subject to the constraint that if the central bank takes on credit risk greater than that of its sovereign, it should only be able to do so with a full guarantee or indemnity of the sovereign, and therefore only subject to the consent of the sovereign.

Macroprudential policy (countercyclical capital requirements, loan-to-value ratios, margin requirements, even a countercyclical land tax or property tax) should be conducted by a macroprudential regulator, which need not be the central bank. If it is the central bank, the central bank should not be in charge of microprudential regulation, to avoid obvious conflicts of interest. If the central bank is not in charge, the macroprudential regulator has to work closely with the central bank and the MPC, and with the Treasury whenever taxpayers' money is at risk.

Microprudential policy should really not be led by the central bank, even if the central bank is not the lead macroprudential agency. The central bank's unavoidable LLR and MMLR roles are too likely to create conflicts of interest should the central bank also act as lead microprudential regulator. Although the central bank should not be in the lead, it should work closely with the microprudential regulator.

There is no reason for the central bank to be the bank or SIFI resolution authority. In the U.S., this task is performed by the FDIC. It will always require the approval of the Treasury for any decision that puts public money at risk.

More generally, solvency support for systemically important financial institutions needs to be decided by a body that includes representatives from the resolution authority, the macroprudential authority, the microprudential authority, the LLR and MMLR, and the Treasury. The Treasury should have veto power in any decision to put public resources at risk in support of the solvency of individual private institutions.

The U.S., through FSOC (the Financial Stability Oversight Committee), brings all agencies involved in systemic financial stability together under the chairmanship of the Secretary of the Treasury. That seems a rather sensible arrangement. In the UK's new proposed arrangement, the central bank is all-powerful, although the Treasury, through its monopoly of the power to tax, will no doubt play an important, but not explicitly spelled out, role. In the euro area, there is no EA-wide fiscal authority, only an EA-wide quasi-fiscal authority, namely the ECB/Eurosystem. This is reflected in the composition of the European Systemic Risk Board, which draws a majority of its voting members, including its chair, from the ECB's Governing Council, and has no voting member that represents any Treasury, national or supranational.

12. Competence and Independence

The providers of macroprudential and microprudential oversight will require a whole new set of skills. If central banks are going to play a significant role in these areas, they will need these skills. So far, central banks are dominated by monetary economists and macroeconomists, with a bit of finance (the asset-pricing variety, not corporate finance) thrown in. Where they have a regulatory or supervisory function, the ranks of the supervisors are made up of accountants and lawyers — box tickers. These skills and professions all have their uses but need to be complemented by finance experts, including corporate finance experts, experts on micro market functioning and on dysfunctional markets, experts on game theory and mechanism design, including auctions, and on industrial organization.

More independent experts will have to be brought in and for shorter terms. Groupthink, cognitive capture, and direct capture are ever-present threats. An eight-year, non-renewable term should be the maximum anyone can serve in any capacity as a regulator, supervisor, or member of the MPC.

13. Legitimacy, Accountability, Transparency

Central banks have great powers, derived from their monopoly over the creation of unquestioned domestic-currency liquidity. From this they derive their roles as lender of last resort and market maker of last resort. As Tables 1–4 demonstrate, they command vast resources — taxpayers' or citizens' money. With growing macroprudential and microprudential powers, the influence of central banks will only grow further.

The people in charge of central banks are political appointees, unelected and without any real "input legitimacy," except for the small amount conferred by their nomination and confirmation processes. It is therefore important that an institution led by unelected technocrats be properly accountable, formally and substantively.

Formal accountability is a key aspect of the mechanism through which the agent (or trustee) is held responsible for his actions. It involves the agent/trustee giving, *ex-post*, a statistical or judicial explanation for events, actions, and outcomes. Such formal accountability requires that those to whom account is given (the principal) can properly monitor the actions of the agent. The principal must have enough information to be able to make an informed judgment as to how well the agent has performed.

Clear objectives for the agent and the most complete possible information about the choice set and the actions of the agent are necessary for formal accountability to be possible. Formal accountability requires openness and transparency, at least *ex-post.* Whether, in the case of the ECB, it is enough to know the objectives of the ECB and to observe the narrowly defined actions of the monetary authority (typically the interest rate decisions), or whether more detailed and comprehensive information about the actions of the ECB (such as individual voting records, if voting takes place) and greater procedural transparency (minutes) are also required, continues to be a subject of disagreement (see, e.g., Buiter, 1999; and Issing, 1999).

Substantive accountability means that following such reporting, explanation, and justification, *judgment* (or other pleasant or unpleasant consequences for the agent) may follow.

There is substantive accountability if the reporting, explanation, and justification is "payoff-relevant" for the party doing the reporting, that is, if there can be punishments, sanctions, or rewards for those deemed responsible for actions or outcomes. It is clear from its own website that the ECB has a minimalist interpretation of formal accountability and considers substantive accountability inconsistent with independence. If one searches the ECB's website for "Accountability," one can find a reasonable definition of formal accountability ("accountability" to the ECB) under the heading "Accountability and Transparency":

> Accountability: To help the ECB carry out its mandate to guarantee price stability, it has been granted political independence. But this independence

> needs to be balanced with accountability. Accountability is the legal and political obligation of the ECB to explain and justify its decisions to the citizens of Europe and their elected representatives. Accountability is enhanced by a high degree of transparency.[13]

A second statement on accountability can be found also.[14] From this statement it is clear that what I call formal accountability is identified with reporting obligations imposed by the Treaty (the Statute of the ESCB and of the ECB) and by appearances before the Committee on Economic and Monetary Affairs (ECON) of the European Parliament to give evidence.

The reporting obligations are minimal and the ECB does not go beyond them in any meaningful way. Quoting again from the ECB's website:

> According to the Statute, the ECB is required to publish quarterly reports on the activities of the Eurosystem as well as a consolidated Weekly Financial Statement. In addition, it has to produce an Annual Report on its activities and on the monetary policy of the previous and the current year. The Annual Report has to be addressed to the European Parliament, the EU Council, the European Commission and the European Council.
>
> To fulfil the requirements of the Statute, the ECB publishes:
>
> - a Monthly Bulletin
> - a consolidated Weekly Financial Statement
> - Annual Reports
>
> Besides that, the ECB produces a range of other task-related publications.[15]

Note that, as discussed in Section 9, this interpretation of reporting obligations appears to be quite consistent in the eyes of the ECB, with a refusal to provide any information that would allow outside parties to evaluate the quasi-fiscal activities of the ECB/Eurosystem.

The fact that the ECB does not reveal the individual voting records of the members of its Governing Council, the freely admitted failure to have formal votes for interest rate decisions at all (these decisions apparently emerge "by consensus"), and the absence of minutes or other records of the decision-taking meetings, continue to be an anomaly standing in the way of judging the competency of the individual members and the degree

[13] See www.ecb.int/mopo/strategy/comm/html/accountability.en.html.

[14] See www.ecb.int/ecb/orga/accountability/html/index.en.html.

[15] See www.ecb.int/ecb/orga/accountability/html/index.en.html.

to which they adhere to their commitment to serve the EMU-wide interest rather than their national interests.

The Treaty makes the European Parliament the institution to which the ECB is formally accountable. The ECB describes its relations with the European Parliament in a way that suggests that there is a material degree of (formal) accountability through these interactions.[16]

In fact, the ECON and the European Parliament in general are woefully ineffective as regards holding the ECB to account. Past presidents of the ECB have stonewalled awkward questions, refused to answer them point-blank, and generally run circles around the MEPs. It is therefore quite appropriate that the ECB tends to refer to the quarterly sessions with the ECON not as "evidence sessions," "hearings," or "testimony," but as "dialogues." Dialogues occur between equals, not between principal (the Parliament) and agent or trustee (the ECB). The party that is held to account is not the equal of the party to whom it is accountable.

The Fed and the Bank of England also have oral and written reporting obligations to, respectively, the U.S. Congress and the UK Parliament. In the case of the Fed, there has been a significant increase in formal accountability since it engaged in multi-trillion dollar quasi-fiscal balance sheet operations in the first two years of the crisis. All other operationally independent central banks in representative democracies also have both oral and written reporting obligations that are rather more onerous than those of the ECB. For the Fed and the Bank of England, the oral reporting sessions/hearings/evidence sessions are rather more taxing affairs than those for the ECB. There can be little doubt that the ECB has the

[16]"The European Parliament, as the institution which derives its legitimacy directly from the citizens of the EU, plays a key institutional role in holding the ECB to account. Since its establishment, the ECB has maintained a close and fruitful dialogue with the European Parliament. The President of the ECB regularly reports on the ECB's monetary policy and its other tasks at his hearings before the European Parliament's Committee on Economic and Monetary Affairs (ECON), which take place quarterly. Moreover, the President appears before the plenary session of the Parliament to present the ECB's Annual Report, on which Parliament, as a rule, adopts a resolution. Other members of the ECB's Executive Board also appear before the European Parliament. In addition, informal discussions take place between ECB representatives and members of the European Parliament on the policies of the ECB and other issues where the ECB has specific expertise. Beyond that, the ECB replies to written questions by MEPs, which are published together with the ECB's answers in the Official Journal of the EU and on the ECB's website." (See www.ecb.int/ecb/orga/accountability/html/index.en.html.)

lowest degree of formal accountability of any central bank in an advanced economy.

As regards substantive accountability, it is not surprising that truly operationally independent central banks have effectively no substantive accountability at all. Independence probably *has* to mean that those in charge of monetary policy cannot be fired except for incapacity or serious misconduct, and that financial remuneration and working conditions likewise cannot be used to reward or punish them for mere incompetence. It ought to mean also that monetary policymakers cannot be sued in civil courts or be dragged into criminal courts for actions taken in their capacity as monetary policymakers. In the advanced industrial countries, we have not (yet) witnessed recourse to the law by those disgruntled with the conduct of monetary policy. The legal immunities and liabilities of central bankers in the performance of their monetary policymaking tasks are, however, an uncharted area in the advanced economies, although not in emerging markets and developing countries.

In the case of the ECB, substantive accountability (such as the right to fire ECB Executive Board members and NCB Governors for incompetence, or to dock their pay for incompetence or a failure to faithfully implement their mandate) is non-existent. The protections enshrined in the Treaty are backed up by the fact that the European Court of Justice is the only body that can dismiss ECB Executive Board members. De facto the same absence of substantive accountability exists, as regards the risk of being fired, for the members of the Federal Reserve Board of Governors and for the members of the UK's MPC. It is perhaps not quite as clear that an enraged U.S. Congress or House of Commons could not try to dock the pay of the national monetary policymakers.

The Fed and the Bank of England both have limited but material formal accountability and very limited substantive accountability. The ECB has very limited formal accountability and no substantive accountability. I fear that this will undermine the legitimacy and longer-term political viability of the institution, especially now that it has gained these comprehensive financial stability responsibilities and is engaging in such vast quasi-fiscal operations.

The ECB asserts that it has all the legitimacy it needs. It has input legitimacy because it is a creature of the European Treaties. It has process legitimacy because it is accountable. After all, it regularly publishes the documents it is required to produce by the Treaty; its president and other Executive Board members have periodic dialogues with the Committee on

Economic and Monetary Affairs of the European Parliament; its president presents the annual report to the whole European Parliament; and its entire Executive Board talks to the media. It has output legitimacy because it does a good job pursuing its price stability mandate and does so in a verifiable way, with an operational, quantitative inflation measure.

This kind of independence, limited formal accountability, and absence of substantive accountability may be tolerable if all a central bank does is set interest rates. It is not adequate and will not remain politically tolerable if that central bank acts as lender of last resort, market maker of last resort, and quasi-fiscal actor on a huge scale. It would seem unavoidable that sooner rather than later, the fact that the central bank is an agency of the state and that its resources are taxpayers' money will become politically relevant. Such central banks should be accountable substantively and formally to a much higher degree than has been the norm thus far, even in the U.S. and the UK. The ECB will not be able to retain its independence if it continues as the least accountable central bank in the world whilst accumulating steadily greater regulatory powers and playing an ever-expanding quasi-fiscal role.

Subject to the requirement of temporary confidentiality for commercially sensitive and market-sensitive transactions, the public and Parliament or Congress should know every aspect of what the central bank has done, particularly:

- What securities it has bought outright, from whom and on what terms;
- What collateral it has accepted, from whom and on what terms; and
- Which counterparties it has agreed to deal with or turned down.

The crisis of central bank accountability is in large part not of the central banks' making. Instead, it reflects a failure of political institutions, processes, and leadership. In the EA, the ECB is forced into a lender of last resort role *vis-à-vis* sovereigns and even beyond that, into a position of having to fund likely or manifestly insolvent sovereigns, banks, and other systemically important financial institutions because the alternative would be a financial catastrophe. The fundamental problem is that the EA and EU political leadership could not agree on the creation of a €3 or €4 trillion EFSF/ESM liquidity facility, and on the matching quid-pro-quo for such liquidity support: orderly restructuring of insolvent sovereigns and banks (with PSI); fiscal austerity and deep structural reform enforced through a (possibly temporary) loss of national sovereignty over fiscal policy and wider economic policy for financial beneficiary countries; and the creation of a European banking union, with a common regulator/supervisor, a common resolution agency, a common bank recapitalization facility, and common deposit insurance arrangements.

In a more sensibly arranged future universe, the problem of reconciling central bank independence in the conduct of conventional monetary policy — interest rates and QE — which is probably desirable, with central bank accountability, will be resolved by reducing the regulatory and supervisory roles of the central bank and by taking the central bank out of the quasi-fiscal game completely.

Eliminating the quasi-fiscal role of the central bank will require that each central bank obtain a full guarantee/indemnity from its sovereign (in the case of the ECB, this should be a joint and several guarantee from all 17 EA sovereigns) for any credit risk the central bank takes on that is higher than that of its sovereign (in the case of the ECB, for any credit risk it takes on that is higher than that of a joint and several guarantee from all 17 EA sovereigns). This means that the central bank will have an envelope or limit, beyond which it cannot go as regards credit risk exposure, without permission from the Treasury and without a full guarantee from its Treasury. The central bank may have to argue in public for an increase in its credit risk-bearing capacity, but it cannot engage in any unilateral, non-sovereign-guaranteed increase in its credit risk exposure.

The terms and conditions associated with all the central bank's on-balance-sheet and off-balance-sheet activities will have to be in the public domain, subject to a suitable time lag to allow for confidentiality concerns and market sensitivity.

This would put an end to most of the quasi-fiscal activities of the central bank, this opaque form of taxation and subsidization without representation. While it is highly desirable to put an end a.s.a.p. to this making of budgetary policy by the central bank without the approval of Parliament or Congress, it will not happen while the current financial crisis continues. I hope that when the next financial crisis comes around, a comprehensive, legal, regulatory, and institutional division of labor between the central bank, the Treasury, and the regulatory/supervisory authorities will have been put in place in the euro area, the U.S., the UK, and elsewhere to minimize — preferably eliminate — the need for an operationally independent and therefore substantively unaccountable central bank to engage in fundamentally inappropriate and illegitimate quasi-fiscal actions.

The quasi-fiscal activities of the Bank of England have been limited to the acceptance of illiquid collateral from eligible counterparties on terms not revealed to the public. The scale of this (relative to the size of the banking sector or GDP) has probably been much smaller than in the U.S. or the euro area. Both the Fed and the ECB continue to engage in quasi-fiscal activities on a large scale. They did not seek this quasi-fiscal role or want it. They were forced into it by a desire to prevent a financial disaster with potentially catastrophic consequences for the real economy. In the U.S., the real culprit is the fiscal gridlock and paralysis at the heart of the U.S. federal government. In the euro area, the defining problems are the institutional fiscal vacuum at the heart of the euro area and the lack of political leadership in the EU. There is no supranational, federal fiscal authority of any kind in the euro area. In the U.S., the combination of constitutional checks and balances and political polarization produces a federal fiscal decision-making process that is so dysfunctional that it resembles the euro area fiscal vacuum.

The quasi-fiscal actions of the ECB and the Fed are contributing to a democratic deficit and accountability crisis. We need to reform this perverse division of labor between unaccountable central banks lacking legitimacy and fiscal authorities that, although accountable and legitimate, lack the capacity to act. Central banks, because of a failure of institutional design, deep political pathologies, and lack of foresight and political leadership, have been and continue to be forced to perform tasks for which they are not suited and for which they lack the political legitimacy. It is time to restrict them again to the important but limited roles they were designed for.

14. Conclusion

The roles of central banks in the advanced economies have expanded and multiplied since the beginning of the crisis. The conventional monetary policy roles — setting interest rates in the pursuit of macroeconomic stability and acting as lender of last resort (LLR) and market maker of last resort (MMLR) to provide funding liquidity and market liquidity to illiquid but solvent counterparties — have both been transformed. With official policy rates near or at the effective lower bound, the size of the central bank's balance sheet and the composition of its assets and liabilities have become the new, "poor man's," monetary policy instruments. The lender of last resort and market maker of last resort roles have expanded to include solvency support for systemically important private financial institutions and, in the euro area, the provision of liquidity support and solvency support for sovereigns also.

Concentrating too many financial stability responsibilities, including macroprudential and microprudential regulation, in the central bank risks undermining the independence of the central bank, where it is likely to be useful — setting interest rates and the LLR and MMLR functions.

The non-inflationary loss-absorption capacity (NILAC) of the leading central banks is vast. For the ECB/Eurosystem, we estimate it at no less than €3.2 trillion; for the Fed, at over $7 trillion. This is taxpayers' money that is not under the effective control of the fiscal authorities. The central banks have used their balance sheets and their NILACs to engage in quasi-fiscal actions that have been essential to prevent even greater financial turmoil and possible disaster, but that also have important distributional impacts between sectors, financial institutions, individuals and nations. The ECB was forced into this illegitimate role by the fiscal vacuum at the heart of the euro area; the Fed by the fiscal paralysis of the U.S. federal government institutions.

References

Bagehot, Walter, 1873, *Lombard Street: A Description of the Money Market*, London, UK: Henry S. King and Co.

Bernanke, Ben S., 2002, "Deflation: making sure 'it' doesn't happen here," remarks before the National Economists Club, Washington, DC, November 21.

Bernanke, Ben S., 2005, "The global saving glut and the U.S. current account deficit," remarks at the Sandridge lecture, Virginia Association of Economics, Richmond, VA, April 14.

Bernanke, Ben S., 2006, "Community development financial institutions: Promoting economic growth and opportunity," speech given at the Opportunity Finance Network's Annual Conference, Washington, DC, November 1.

Bernanke, Ben S., 2007a, "The housing market and subprime lending," speech given via satellite to the 2007 International Monetary Conference, Cape Town, South Africa, June 5.

Bernanke, Ben S., 2007b, "Opening remarks, housing, housing finance, and monetary policy," speech at the Federal Reserve Bank of Kansas City Economic Symposium.

Bernanke, Ben S. and Mark Gertler, 1999, "Monetary policy and asset price volatility," *Quarterly Review*, Federal Reserve Bank of Kansas City, December.

Bernanke, Ben S. and Mark Gertler, 2001, "How should central bankers respond to asset prices?," *American Economic Review Papers and Proceedings*, Vol. 91, pp. 253–257.

Buiter, Willem H., 1999, "Alice in Euroland," *Journal of Common Market Studies*, Vol. 37, No. 2, pp. 181–209.

Buiter, Willem H., 2005, "Overcoming the zero bound: Gesell vs. Eisler: Discussion of Mitsuhiro Fukao's 'The effects of 'Gesell' (currency) taxes in promoting Japan's economic recovery,'" *International Economics and Economic Policy*, Vol. 2, Nos. 2–3, pp. 189–200.

Buiter, Willem H., 2007a, "Is numérairology the future of monetary economics? Unbundling numéraire and medium of exchange through a virtual currency with a shadow exchange rate," *Open Economies Review*, Vol. 18, No. 2, pp. 127–156.

Buiter, Willem H., 2007b, "Seigniorage," *Economics, the Open-Access, Open-Assessment E-Journal*, Vol. 1, No. 10, pp. 1–49.

Buiter, Willem H., 2008, "Central banks and financial crises," paper presented at the Federal Reserve Bank of Kansas City's symposium, Maintaining Stability in a Changing Financial System, Jackson Hole, WY, August 21–23.

Buiter, Willem H., 2009a, "The unfortunate uselessness of most 'state of the art' academic monetary economics," Maverecon blog, *Financial Times*, March 3, reproduced by VoxEU, available at www.voxeu.org/index.php?q=node/3210.

Buiter, Willem H., 2009b, "Negative nominal interest rates: Three ways to overcome the zero lower bound," *The North American Journal of Economics and Finance*, available online, October 20, hardcopy publication, 2009–2010.

Buiter, Willem H., 2010a, "Don't raise the inflation target, remove the zero bound on nominal interest rates instead," *Citi Economics, Global Macro View*, March 5.

Buiter, Willem H., 2010b, "Games of chicken between the monetary and fiscal authority: Who will control the deep pockets of the central bank?," (long version), *Citi Economics, Global Economics View*, July 21.

Buiter, Willem H., 2011, "Accountability of the Bank of England," *Citi Economics, Global Economics View*, June 1.

Buiter, Willem H. and Nikolaos Panigirtzoglou, 2001, "Liquidity traps: How to avoid them and how to escape them," in *Reflections on Economics and Econometrics: Essays in Honour of Martin Fase*, Wim F.V. Vanthoor and Joke Mooij (eds.), Amsterdam, Netherlands: De Nederlandsche Bank NV, pp. 13–58.

Buiter, Willem H. and Nikolaos Panigirtzoglou, 2003, "Overcoming the zero bound on nominal interest rates with negative interest on currency: Gesell's solution," *Economic Journal*, Vol. 113, No. 490, pp. 723–746.

D'Amico, S. and T. King, 2010, "Flow and stock effects of large-scale treasury purchases," Finance and Economics Discussion Series, Board of Governors of the Federal Reserve System, working paper, No. 2010-52.

Eisler, Robert, 1932, *Stable Money: The Remedy for the Economic World Crisis: A Programme of Financial Reconstruction for the International Conference 1933*; with a preface by Vincent C. Vickers, London, UK: The Search Publishing Co.

European Central Bank, 2002, "The accountability of the ECB," *Monthly Bulletin*, November, available at www.ecb.int/pub/pdf/other/pp45_57_mb200211en.pdf.

Fukao, Mitsuhiro, 2005, "The effects of 'Gesell' (currency) taxes in promoting Japan's economic recovery," Discussion Paper Series, Institute of Economic Research, Hitotsubashi University, Tokyo, Japan, No. 94, June, available at http://hi-stat.ier.hit-u.ac.jp/.

Gaitskell, H., 1969, *Four Monetary Heretics: Douglas — Social Credit, Soddy — Bank Credit, Gesell — Free Money, Eisler — Stable Money*; with an introduction by M.F. Lloyd Pritchard, Christchurch: Lyn. Christie and Son, Ltd.

Gesell, Silvio, 1916, *Die Natürliche Wirtschaftsordnung*, Rudolf Zitzman Verlag; available in English as *The Natural Economic Order*, 1958, London, UK: Peter Owen Ltd.

Goodfriend, Marvin, 2000, "Overcoming the zero bound on interest rate policy," *Journal of Money, Credit and Banking*, Vol. 32, No. 4, pp. 1007–1035.

Greenspan, Alan, 2004, "Economic flexibility," speech via satellite to the HM Treasury Enterprise Conference, London, England, January 26.

Greenspan, Alan, 2005a, "Consumer finance," remarks at the Federal Reserve System's Fourth Annual Community Affairs Research Conference, Washington, DC, April 8.

Greenspan, Alan, 2005b, "Risk transfer and financial stability," remarks via satellite to the Federal Reserve Bank of Chicago's Forty-first Annual Conference on Bank Structure, Chicago, Illinois, May 5.

Greenspan, Alan, 2008, "We will never have a perfect model of risk," *Financial Times*, March 16.

Hall, Robert E., 1997, "Irving Fisher's self-stabilizing money," *American Economic Review, Papers and Proceedings*, Vol. 87, No. 2, pp. 436–438.

Hamilton, J. and J.C. Wu, 2011, "The effectiveness of alternative monetary policy tools in a zero lower bound environment," National Bureau of Economic Research, working paper, No. 16956.

Issing, Otmar, 1999, "The Eurosystem: Transparent and accountable or 'Willem in Euroland,'" *Journal of Common Market Studies*, Vol. 37, No. 3, pp. 503–519.

Joyce, M., A. Lasaosa, I. Stevens, and M. Tong, 2010, "The financial market impact of quantitative easing," Bank of England, working paper, No. 393.

Kotlikoff, Laurence J., 2010, *Jimmy Stewart Is Dead: Ending the World's Ongoing Financial Plague with Limited Purpose Banking*, Hoboken, NJ: John Wiley and Sons.

Meaning, Jack and Feng Zhu, 2011, "The impact of recent central bank asset purchase programmes," *BIS Quarterly Review*, December, pp. 73–83.

Shiller, Robert J., 2003, *The New Financial Order: Risk in the 21st Century*, Princeton, NJ: Princeton University Press.

Swanson, E., 2011, "Let's twist again: A high-frequency event-study analysis of Operation Twist and its implications for QE2," *Brookings Papers on Economic Activity*, Spring, pp. 151–188.
White, William, 2006a, "Procyclicality in the financial system: Do we need a new macrofinancial stabilisation framework?," Bank for International Settlements, working paper, No. 193, January, available at www.bis.org/publ/work193.pdf.
White, William, 2006b, "Is price stability enough?," Bank for International Settlements, working paper, No. 205.

Pursuing Financial Stability at the Federal Reserve

Janet L. Yellen*
Board of Governors of the Federal Reserve System

Let me begin by thanking the Federal Reserve Bank of Chicago for inviting me to participate in this important conference on the role of central banks in financial stability. As you know, the Dodd–Frank Wall Street Reform and Consumer Protection Act of 2010 (Dodd–Frank Act) assigned the Federal Reserve a central role in the new framework for achieving and maintaining financial stability. I am grateful for this opportunity to explain how we, together with other regulators, have been moving forward to fulfill our new responsibilities.[1]

The Dodd–Frank Act instituted substantial changes to financial-sector supervision and regulation in the United States in direct response to the serious deficiencies in the regulatory framework that were revealed, all too painfully, by the financial crisis and the associated deep recession. One key change was the requirement that U.S. financial regulators take a "macroprudential approach" to supervision and regulation. In my remarks today, I want to describe how this approach is being put into practice at the Federal Reserve. I will touch on both our own regulatory and supervisory responsibilities and our responsibilities as a member of the multi-agency Financial Stability Oversight Council (FSOC), which the Dodd–Frank Act established to promote a more comprehensive approach to monitoring and mitigating systemic risk.

---

*The author is Vice Chair of the Board of Governors of the Federal Reserve System. The comments were delivered on November 11, 2011, at the Federal Reserve Bank of Chicago's Fourteenth Annual International Banking Conference, Chicago, Illinois. The views are those of the author and not necessarily those of others in the Federal Reserve System.

[1] I am indebted to Federal Reserve Board staff members Rochelle Edge, Andrea Kusko, Andrew Levin, and Nellie Liang for their assistance in preparing these remarks.

I should note that an important part of putting the macroprudential approach into practice is establishing a new regulatory infrastructure, including the FSOC and its working-committee structure. In addition, individual regulatory agencies have made organizational changes needed to fulfill their new responsibilities. At the Federal Reserve, we have re-oriented our supervision of large bank holding companies, and we have created a new office called the Office of Financial Stability Policy and Research, which plays a key role in monitoring financial risks, analyzing the implications for financial stability, and identifying approaches for mitigating identified risks.

1. Overview of the Macroprudential Approach

The explicit incorporation of macroprudential considerations into our structure for financial regulation and oversight represents a major innovation in our thinking about how financial stability is most effectively achieved. In contrast to the traditional, or "microprudential," approach to regulation and supervision, which focuses on the safety and soundness of *individual* financial institutions, markets, and infrastructures, the macroprudential approach also calls for attention to the financial system *as a whole*.

In particular, financial institutions are typically linked together in a complex web of relationships, and hence the sudden failure of a single institution can generate spillover effects on other firms and potentially place the entire financial system at risk. Such externalities are most evident for very large institutions and financial market utilities but may also arise within a set of small or medium-sized firms that are engaged in activities with highly correlated returns. Therefore, the macroprudential approach focuses on achieving financial stability by reducing systemic risk — that is, the risk of a financial disruption that is severe enough to inflict significant damage on the broader economy. Ideally, this approach is done through preemptive policies that restrain risks to the financial system before they develop into crises.

Macroprudential policies address several forms of systemic risk. One form of risk can be described as structural — such as the presence of systemically important financial institutions (SIFIs) or systemically important payment, clearing, or settlement infrastructures or activities, whose failure or financial distress could have outsized destabilizing effects on the rest of the financial system. Another form of risk can be described as cyclical and includes, for example, elevated asset prices and excessive credit growth that arise in robust economic times but can leave the balance sheets of both large and small financial firms vulnerable to downturns in the credit cycle. Attentiveness to these various channels is critical in the monitoring of systemic risk and the formulation of appropriate macroprudential policy responses. In particular, some risks are best allayed by policies that are structural in nature and thus do not change as economic conditions evolve, whereas others are best addressed by policies that are sensitive to economic developments. Indeed, selecting the right policies to address specific forms of systemic risk is important for ensuring that reasonable risk-taking and innovation continue to take place in financial markets so as to foster broader productivity gains, economic growth, and job creation.

A key question for central banks is how macroprudential policies fit together with monetary policy. The evolving — though by no means settled — consensus is that monetary policy is too blunt a tool to be routinely used to address cyclical risks to financial stability, and that more targeted micro- and macroprudential tools should be used to address these risks. I agree that targeted prudential policies should be the first line of defense against threats to financial stability. However, because their effectiveness in practice is not yet proven, I would not rule out the possibility that monetary policy could be used directly to support financial stability goals, at least on the margin.

2. Identifying and Addressing Structural Forms of Systemic Risk

I want to turn now to structural sources of systemic risk and discuss how macroprudential policy can be used to mitigate them. Structural vulnerabilities may go largely unnoticed until they are exposed in financial crises — and at considerable cost. Indeed, many of the regulations now being implemented under the Dodd–Frank Act, as well as the international agreements relating to bank capital and liquidity standards, are a reaction to the events of 2007 through 2009. Such responses include regulations and reforms that address risks resulting from the existence of SIFIs and systemically important financial market utilities (FMUs) as well as other efforts to improve the resilience of important financial markets and infrastructure.

Because the material distress or failure of a SIFI can have outsized effects on the financial sector and the real economy, the Dodd–Frank Act empowers the Federal Reserve to reduce the probability of such events through tougher prudential standards, including enhanced risk-based capital and leverage requirements, liquidity requirements, an early remediation regime, and restrictions on activities. The Act also requires the Federal Reserve to consider systemic risk effects when reviewing and ruling on applications for mergers among financial firms. In addition, to ensure that the failure of a SIFI can occur without serious damage to the financial system, the Act gives the Federal Reserve and the Federal Deposit Insurance Corporation new tools, such as improved resolution planning by firms and an orderly liquidation authority. The Act also requires centralized clearing of standardized over-the-counter (OTC) derivatives and introduces margin requirements for non-cleared derivatives and other measures to strengthen the integrity and functioning of financial markets.

Efforts to develop these rules have been progressing well. The Federal Reserve will soon release for comment its proposed rule on enhanced prudential standards that would apply to large bank holding companies and systemically important non-bank financial firms. It also recently approved a final rule implementing the resolution plan requirement. Let me note that in these instances, as in all its rule-making responsibilities, the Federal Reserve is attentive to aligning the rules required by the Dodd–Frank Act with international agreements, such as higher capital standards and new liquidity standards for large banks and capital surcharges for the largest global SIFIs.

The Federal Reserve, working with other financial regulators, has issued a number of proposed and final rules relating to such areas as the centralized clearing of derivatives, swap margin requirements, and the designation of systemically important FMUs and non-bank financial firms. The proposed rule for designating non-bank financial firms was put out for comment in October.[2] This rule specifies a process for designating such institutions, starting by analyzing firms that exceed a size threshold and exhibit characteristics, including excessive leverage and reliance on short-term funding, that could contribute to systemic risk if the firm were to become distressed.

Less discernible progress has been made to date, however, in addressing other key vulnerabilities that came to the fore during the financial crisis. Indeed, short-term funding markets remain an important source of structural risk. Despite some significant reforms that enhance liquidity and impose additional restrictions on portfolios, money market funds are still susceptible to liquidity constraints largely because of attributes like their rounded net asset value (NAV) feature and the low risk tolerance of their investors. Options for further reforms being considered by the Securities

---

[2]See Financial Stability Oversight Council, 2011, "Authority to require supervision and regulation of certain non-bank financial companies" (PDF), second notice of proposed rule-making and proposed interpretive guidance, FR Doc. 2011-26783, *Federal Register*, Vol. 76, October 18, pp. 64264–83.

and Exchange Commission (SEC) include a mandatory floating NAV to mute the incentive for investors to be the first to redeem, capital buffers to allow funds to deal better with actual and potential losses while sustaining a stable NAV, and limits on redemptions both to provide more time for fund managers to address problems and to emphasize to investors that money market funds do not guarantee bank-like liquidity.[3]

The tri-party repurchase agreement (repo) market also continues to exhibit important vulnerabilities. In particular, the settlement process for tri-party repo trades continues to rely on massive amounts of intraday credit and, as a result, remains vulnerable to a decision by a clearing bank to withhold funding from a market participant in default or perceived as facing distress. The FSOC has recommended reforms to deal with these problems, and an industry task force has taken some key initial steps in that direction — for example, by coordinating the implementation of a robust confirmation process for tri-party trades. But more needs to be done. Indeed, given the centrality of this market to the financial system, taking further steps to reduce its vulnerabilities should be given a high priority.

In addition to addressing the unfinished business from the financial crisis, financial stability authorities and market participants need to be alert to new structures and products, not just those that caused problems in the past. New financial products — for example, exchange-traded funds and collateralized commercial paper — may foster more efficient intermediation, but they may also raise systemic risk if they increase the complexity and interconnectedness of the financial system.

Authorities need to collect data and monitor risks associated with new products before the risks become salient. To improve the quality of financial-sector data and facilitate the analysis of data for the FSOC and its member agencies, the Dodd–Frank Act created the Office of Financial Research within the Treasury Department. The office has initiated a project to design a global classification system based on unique legal entity identifiers to identify parties to financial contracts. This system would allow market participants to better measure on a consolidated basis their counterparty risk across products and other dimensions. In addition, the SEC and the Commodity Futures Trading Commission recently issued a new reporting

---

[3]Box D of the FSOC 2011 annual report provides a fuller discussion of the financial-sector vulnerabilities implied by money market funds. See Financial Stability Oversight Council, 2011, *Financial Stability Oversight Council 2011 Annual Report* (22 MB PDF), Washington: FSOC, "Box D: Money market funds," pp. 50–51.

form for hedge funds and certain other private investment funds, which will provide more information on their size, concentration, funding, and investments; this additional information should shed some valuable light on an important segment of the financial sector for which we have not had consistent data.

3. Identifying and Addressing Cyclical Forms of Systemic Risk

Turning next to cyclical forms of systemic risk, we are working to develop good measures of such risks, to monitor them on an ongoing basis, and to be aware of how they could unwind in a destabilizing way. On that score, at the Federal Reserve, we regularly monitor measures of leverage and maturity mismatch at financial intermediaries, and we look at asset valuations, underwriting standards for loans, and credit growth for signs of a credit-induced build-up of systemic risk. We also monitor various systemic risk measures for the largest banking firms. These measures capture financial market perceptions of the risk such a firm could impose on the broader financial system were it to become stressed. Such measures are based on firms' stock prices, credit default swap premiums, and stock price volatility, as well as the correlation in asset prices across firms.

In addition, we use regular stress tests of the nation's largest banking organizations to evaluate the ability of these firms to withstand worse-than-expected outcomes for the economy. These tests are based on detailed confidential data about the balance sheets of the large banks and provide a comprehensive and rigorous assessment of how their financial conditions would evolve over a multi-year period if economic and financial conditions were to deteriorate. The stress tests started in 2009 with the Supervisory Capital Assessment Program (SCAP), and they continued with the Comprehensive Capital Analysis and Review (CCAR) in late 2010 and early 2011, in which we evaluated the capital planning processes of the firms and responded to requests to resume or increase shareholder payouts.

In a couple of weeks, we will begin CCAR 2012, building on the previous CCAR, and roughly a year from now, we will conduct the annual supervisory stress tests mandated by the Dodd–Frank Act. The Dodd–Frank tests will involve a larger group of banking organizations than the 19 firms covered in the SCAP, and will be extended to include any financial institution the FSOC designates as systemically important. As additional data are collected on significant credit exposures, stress tests may evolve into an effective way to identify linkages across systemically important institutions that could lead them to fall into financial distress at the same time.

Another important element in identifying financial-sector vulnerabilities is the continued vigilance to the financial risks that might emerge in parts of the financial sector for which data are very scarce or that have developed more recently and are thus less well-understood. The regulatory community has been working hard to fill these knowledge gaps. For example, in response to the need to improve the monitoring of leverage, particularly outside of the traditional banking system, the Federal Reserve instituted in 2010 a quarterly survey on dealer financing terms (the Senior Credit Officer Opinion Survey on Dealer Financing Terms).[4] This survey collects qualitative information on the leverage that dealers provide to financial market participants in the repo and OTC derivatives markets. This information complements the data on counterparty credit exposures that supervisors collect on a confidential basis from large, complex financial institutions and higher-frequency data on liquidity profiles. In addition, the Board staff is working in the context of the flow of funds accounts to develop measures of reliance by non-financial businesses on non-bank, volatile sources of funds — that is, the shadow banking sector. Such measures would permit us to track this source of risk through the business cycle.

Cyclical vulnerabilities seem relatively quiescent at present. Still, such vulnerabilities could easily emerge, especially once the economy starts to expand more robustly. Regulators need to look ahead and be ready to respond. A number of macroprudential policy tools could, in principle, be used to address heightened cyclical vulnerabilities — some of which have been used in other countries and others that have been proposed but not yet tried. Examples of tools that have been used in other countries include time-varying caps on mortgage loan-to-value ratios and household debt-to-income ratios, which have been used in Korea and Hong Kong, and dynamic provisioning for losses by banks, which has been employed in Spain. The Basel III package of reforms that was agreed to last year includes a countercyclical capital buffer that can be imposed when excessive growth of risk-taking in credit markets results in an unacceptable level of systemic risk. Another policy that has been put forward but not yet tried is countercyclical margins and haircuts for funding contracts, as proposed by the Committee on the Global Financial System.[5]

---

[4]The Senior Credit Officer Opinion Survey is available on the Board's website at www.federalreserve.gov/econresdata/releases/scoos.htm.

[5]See Committee on the Global Financial System, 2010, "The role of margin requirements and haircuts in procyclicality" (PDF), CGFS Papers No. 36, Basel, Switzerland: Bank for International Settlements, March.

Of course, U.S. policymakers will need to examine such policy tools in depth before implementing them here. As a first step, policymakers need to establish that countercyclical policy tools address cyclical vulnerabilities more effectively than simpler tools that are constant over the course of the cycle do.[6] In addition, in taking lessons from abroad, policymakers need to be aware of institutional differences that may prevent tools from having the same effects in the United States as they do elsewhere. A further issue is that the literature on the efficacy of macroprudential tools in limiting the build-up of cyclical systemic risks is still at an early stage. Even for policies that have been used in other countries, the number of papers that evaluate their effectiveness is relatively small, and isolating the effect of a specific policy amid an array of economic and financial developments is a persistent challenge. Nonetheless, these papers are encouraging — at least to the further consideration of the use of cyclical policy tools — and this literature, which also includes more theoretical analyses of such policies, is a vibrant and growing one that should yield useful insights in coming years.[7]

---

[6]Examples of constant, through-the-cycle policy tools are *time-invariant* caps on loan-to-value (LTV) and debt-to-income (DTI) ratios and *time-invariant* floors on margins and haircuts, which can likely play some role in limiting the build-up of cyclical vulnerabilities (even if they do not go as far as countercyclical policies).

[7]Current empirical work on this topic includes a number of interesting country case studies on LTV and DTI policies. For example, see Bank of Korea and International Monetary Fund, 2011, "Managing real estate booms and busts" (PDF), summary from the BOK-IMF workshop, Seoul, Korea, April 11–12. For a difference-in-difference econometric analysis of dynamic provisioning in Spain (with implications for countercyclical capital buffers), also see Gabriel Jiménez, Steven Ongena, José-Luis Peydro, and Jesús Saurina, 2011, "Macro-prudential policy, countercyclical bank capital buffers and credit supply: Evidence from the Spanish dynamic provisioning experiments" (PDF), unpublished paper, Banco de España, March. An example of model-based analysis is a study of LTV ratios in the context of calibrated general-equilibrium macro models by Luisa Lambertini, Caterina Medicino, and Maria Teresa Punzi, 2011, "Leaning against boom-bust cycles in credit and housing prices" (PDF), Banco de Portugal Working Papers 8/11, Lisbon, Portugal: Banco de Portugal, March; another example of model-based analysis is a study of countercyclical capital buffers in the context of calibrated general-equilibrium macro models by Ian Christensen, Césaire Meh, and Kevin Moran, 2011, "Bank leverage regulation and macroeconomic dynamics" (PDF), paper presented at the Regulation of Systemic Risk conference sponsored by the Board of Governors of the Federal Reserve System and the *Journal of Money, Credit and Banking*, Washington, September 15–16.

4. Current Challenges

Let me finish with a few words about current challenges to financial stability. In particular, concerns about European fiscal and banking issues have contributed to strains in global financial markets that pose significant downside risks to the U.S. economic outlook. U.S. banking institutions have manageable levels of direct exposure to the peripheral European countries but more substantial links to financial institutions in the larger European economies. In addition, some major European banks that obtain appreciable short-term wholesale U.S. dollar funding from U.S. money market funds appear to be facing significant funding pressures. In light of such international linkages, further intensification of financial disruptions in Europe could lead to a deterioration of financial conditions in the United States.

The European rescue package announced in late October indicates a strong commitment by European leaders to address the issues stemming from sovereign debt. The package was a step in the right direction, but many details of the plan were unclear, and the measures would require rigorous implementation. The continued rise in sovereign debt spreads for some countries, more generalized market volatility, and political turmoil that we have seen in recent days speak to the need for forceful action to stabilize the situation.

We, along with other supervisors, are actively engaged in ensuring that U.S. financial institutions are appropriately managing their credit and liquidity risks. To limit the spread of funding stresses, we have in place dollar liquidity swap lines with a number of foreign central banks. We are monitoring European developments very closely, and we will continue to do all that we can to mitigate the consequence of any adverse developments abroad on the U.S. financial system.

5. Conclusion

The Federal Reserve and other U.S. financial regulators have accomplished a great deal since the Dodd–Frank Act was enacted a little more than a year ago. We have put into practice an institutional framework for undertaking a macroprudential approach to supervision and regulation, and we have implemented processes for identifying and responding to sources of systemic risk. However, much remains to be done, including further work to close the gaps in the data coverage of the financial sector and to deepen our understanding of the effectiveness of different policy tools. The bottom line is that developing an effective macroprudential policy is critical to preserving financial stability and supporting overall U.S. economic activity. Accomplishing this objective will be a considerable challenge, but it is one of great importance.

II. THE ROLE OF CENTRAL BANKS IN FINANCIAL STABILITY: HISTORICAL REVIEW AND CRITIQUE

Financial Stability: Lessons Learned from the Recent Crisis and Implications for the Federal Reserve

Nellie Liang*

Board of Governors of the Federal Reserve System

This paper addresses some lessons learned about financial stability during the recent financial crisis, with a particular focus on the implications for changes at the Federal Reserve. Changes also are driven by the passage of the Dodd–Frank Wall Street Reform and Consumer Protection Act of 2010 (DFA).[1] DFA addresses significant shortcomings and gaps in the regulatory structure of large complex financial institutions, and relies heavily on preemptive policies to reduce the likelihood that the firms fail. However, it also limits the tools available to regulatory agencies to address a crisis once it is underway. This emphasis on preemptive actions may reflect an apparent belief among many in the Congress that the actions taken by regulators in 2008 and 2009 to address the financial crisis as it unfolded, while effectively preventing a financial collapse, may have increased moral hazard problems going forward. DFA is silent on reforming short-term funding markets — a central propagation channel in the crisis — and leaves the task of reform to the regulatory agencies. The lessons learned and DFA have altered the ways that the Federal Reserve, other regulators, and firms conduct their business and assess systemic risks to foster financial stability.

*Nellie Liang is the director of the Office of Financial Stability Policy and Research, Board of Governors of the Federal Reserve System. The views presented here are the author's and do not necessarily reflect those of the Board of Governors or its staff. The author thanks Tobias Adrian, Jim Clouse, Dan Covitz, Bill English, Mike Gibson, Andrea Kusko, Andreas Lehnert, and Mark Vanderweide for helpful comments, and Valentin Bolotnyy and Steven Hopper for excellent research assistance.

[1]This paper is based on remarks delivered at the Fourteenth Annual International Banking Conference at the Federal Reserve Bank of Chicago on November 10, 2011.

This paper contains two major sections. Section 1 presents four important lessons for the Federal Reserve that came out of the crisis; it includes a brief review of the actions taken by the Fed during the crisis, as well as some insights from the literature on the causes and consequences of financial crises. Section 2 addresses how the Fed is reshaping its organization, policies, and governance in the aftermath of the crisis to meet its expanded mandate for financial stability under DFA.

1. Lessons Learned

The financial crisis exposed serious deficiencies in the existing financial regulatory framework and cast doubt on some widely held perceptions about the relationship between financial stability and other economic policy objectives. It also challenged the Federal Reserve to find new ways to fulfill its traditional central banking functions for financial and monetary stability and offered important lessons that should be heeded as the Fed implements DFA and works to improve the resilience and performance of the financial sector.

To set the stage for lessons and implications, the Federal Reserve has several functions relating to financial stability, including: (1) maintaining the stability of the financial system, if necessary by serving as lender of last resort; (2) conducting monetary policy — currently according to the dual mandate, which treats maximum employment and price stability as co-equal policy objectives; and (3) serving as primary supervisor for bank holding companies and state member banks.

Lesson 1. Pre-crisis regulatory policies were not sufficient to ensure financial stability. Perhaps the most important lesson is that there were notable gaps in the pre-crisis regulatory and supervisory structure. In part, the gaps reflect more rapid development of financial practices than in the regulatory structure. In particular, the regulatory system was built largely around ensuring the safety and soundness of *individual* depository institutions, often evaluated by capital-to-risk-weighted assets ratios, which tend to be lagging indicators of performance. Regulators and regulated firms alike paid insufficient attention to systemic risk externalities that the firms could impose on other parts of the financial system and real economic activity. Risk externalities, such as fire sales driven by de-leveraging, contagion from common exposures or lack of information, and complexity, have the potential to transmit and amplify distress of an individual firm to other parts of the financial system and disrupt real economic activity (see Bernanke and Gertler, 1989; Allen and Gale, 2005; Brunnermeier and Pedersen, 2009; and Caballero and Krishnamurthy, 2008). Overall, risk management practices were not sufficiently forward- or outward-looking.

In addition, insufficient attention was paid to the rapidly growing shadow banking sector, which had its roots in regulatory capital arbitrage and greater demand for private alternatives to insured deposits from, for example, money market mutual funds and institutional cash pools. Securitizations, asset-backed commercial paper (including SIVs), and broker-dealers often use short-term debt from liquid markets to purchase long-term illiquid assets (see Pozsar *et al.*, 2010; Gorton and Metrick, 2012; and Covitz, Liang, and Suarez, 2013). But shadow banks are susceptible to runs on their short-term debt, which is not covered by deposit insurance, leaving the financial system highly vulnerable.

Although shadow banks are vulnerable to runs, the existing resolution regime for commercial banks did not apply to these institutions. Bankruptcy was the only formal process available for resolving financial institutions other than insured depositories. Because the bankruptcy courts focus not on systemic risk, but on maximizing proceeds to creditors, the idea of addressing financial claims through the bankruptcy process raised concerns about further destabilizing the financial system during the crisis.

Lesson 2. The pursuit of price and economic stability is not sufficient for financial stability. The extended period of price and economic stability that preceded the financial crisis lulled many into believing that stable macroeconomic conditions were sufficient to foster financial stability. Monetary policy during this period was geared largely toward sustaining the so-called "Great Moderation," and based on the argument that bubbles are hard to identify and crises hard to predict, it responded to financial factors only to the extent that they affected the outlook for inflation or real activity. Because identifying bubbles *ex ante* with certainty is virtually impossible, having to clean up after a bubble burst was viewed as preferable to acting too frequently and unduly restricting credit.

However, financial institutions responded to the period of stability by increasing leverage (Adrian and Shin, 2008). And because the financial regulatory structure is procyclical, in part because capital requirements are often based on recent historical experience, it too facilitated the build-up of risks (Kashyap and Stein, 2004). In any event, we learned that highly leveraged institutions or asset values driven up by leverage and maturity mismatches in assets and liabilities can pose substantial risks to financial stability.[2] Furthermore, cleaning up after the crisis has been costlier and has taken longer than had been expected.

Lesson 3. The traditional tools of the Fed are not sufficient for the worst crises. The first traditional tool in the Fed's central banking toolkit is monetary policy. As financial strains increased in short-term funding markets in the fall of 2007, the Fed started to lower short-term interest rates. However, the federal funds rate is subject to a zero lower bound, which was encountered relatively early in the financial crisis. Of course, additional stimulus could be — and was — provided through large-scale asset purchases (LSAPs); the LSAPs seem to have eased pressures in short-term funding markets somewhat, but they likely entailed costs as well. While research suggests that there are benefits to reducing the federal funds rate sooner to combat a crisis (Reifschneider and Williams, 2000), some recent research suggests that conventional monetary policy may be less effective during periods of stress than in more normal times. Hubrich and Tetlow (2011) use a Markov-switching VAR model to identify "stress events," which the model associates with periods of elevated financial stress, highly accommodative monetary policy, and a weak outlook for economic activity. They found that although monetary policy was eased during each "stress event" since the 1970s, the policy actions seem to have had only small effects on real economic activity.

The second traditional tool is the discount window, which serves as a backstop source of short-term funds to insured depository institutions (DIs). However, insured depositories are typically reluctant to borrow from the discount window, apparently because a liquidity constraint might be taken as a sign of a solvency problem, and indeed the stigma appeared to intensify in the crisis. The Fed's initial efforts to spur the use of the discount window (through a lowering of the spread between the primary rate and the federal funds rate and an extension of the terms of the lending) apparently did little to ease the stigma. Accordingly, in December 2007, the Fed introduced the Term Auction Facility (TAF), under which predetermined amounts of discount window credit were auctioned against a broad range of collateral. TAF apparently helped to overcome the stigma somewhat, presumably because of both the competitive auction format and the availability of large fixed amounts of credit.

[2]See Woodford (2011).

Shadow banks, however, did not have access to the discount window, and these institutions were subject to investor runs. To address the problems of broker-dealers and the dysfunction in the tri-party repo market, the Fed provided discount-window-like lending to non-DIs under the determined "unusual and exigent" circumstances. This was done through the Term Securities Lending Facility, which allowed primary dealers to exchange less-liquid securities for terms of 28 days at an auction-determined fee, and the Primary Dealer Credit Facility, which allowed primary dealers to borrow at the same rate at which DIs could access the discount window. The Fed also provided backstops for money market mutual funds through the Asset-Backed Commercial Paper Money Market Mutual Fund Liquidity Facility, and for issuers of commercial paper through the Commercial Paper Funding Facility.

The Fed's performance as lender of last resort under "unusual and exigent" circumstances during the crisis was consistent with Bagehot's dictum to "lend freely at a high rate, on good collateral." Lending freely on good collateral during a financial crisis can be useful because it can help prevent solvent financial institutions from selling assets at fire-sale prices in order to meet the demands of depositors and other sources of funding; the creation of several new lending facilities under Section 13(3) of the Federal Reserve Act largely followed this dictum. Moreover, the new facilities were priced to be unattractive in normal times, and thus to unwind automatically as market conditions improved. Of course, whether collateral will turn out to be good or bad depends in part on the success of the actions; for example, the collateral is likely to be good if fire sales are prevented, but may not be if they are not. Also, fire-sale effects can last a long time should financial risks spill over to economic activity more broadly.

An interesting consequence of these activities was the emergence of timely, sophisticated valuation of collateral as an important new area of central banking. Indeed, for the Supervisory Capital Assessment Program — the original stress tests — more than 150 Federal Reserve staff worked for many months to value the legacy assets on the banking and trading books of the 19 largest bank holding companies, based on unprecedented detail about the specific assets collected from the firms. And when the Term Asset-Backed Securities Loan Facility (TALF) was established, an army of "central bankers" turned "investment bankers" was required to evaluate the consumer and small business loans that were used as collateral in new securitizations.

In the event, however, the liquidity provided by the Federal Reserve programs alone was not sufficient to solve the fundamental credit problems, and fiscal and other authorities were also needed to stem the crisis. In particular, the Troubled Asset Relief Program (TARP) provided by Congress was used to purchase equity from financial institutions and thus served as a source of backstop capital for banks; the TARP also was used in a subordinated position to the Fed in the TALF program to restart securitization. In addition, the Housing and Economic Reform Act provided taxpayer funds to the GSEs; the Treasury authorized funds from the Exchange Stabilization Fund to guarantee money market mutual funds after the collapse of Lehman Brothers; and under the Temporary Liquidity Guarantee Program, the FDIC provided a guarantee for bank holding company and bank debt under the systemic risk exception.

The new programs in which the Federal Reserve participated, from expansion of discount window terms to loans to help restart securitization of consumer and small business loans, generated a good deal of controversy. These new creative programs brought the central bank squarely into the spotlight because its balance sheet was being used in unconventional ways.

Lesson 4. An escalation of the tension between financial stability and moral hazard frequently accompanies a crisis and creates hard decisions for policymakers. Although some tension between financial stability and moral hazard is likely always present, that tension escalated significantly during the crisis. One reason may be the asymmetry in timing in that the consequences of financial instability are immediate and apparent, while the effects of moral hazard may take some time to become evident. The difficult choices facing the authorities during the crisis were also likely compounded by the lack of consensus on the relative importance of financial stabilization *vis-à-vis* moral hazard: Some argue that a crisis is not the time to teach the lessons of moral hazard, while others believe that moral hazard, and its perpetuation, is in fact the principal reason for why crises occur.[3] On that score, I believe that the strong focus on preemptive policies in DFA largely reflects the view of many in Congress — reinforced by widespread perceptions that the policies adopted to counter potential market-wide stresses were essentially bailouts of firms — that authorities leaned too heavily on

[3] See Caballero (2010) and Cochrane (2010) for differing views.

fostering financial stability during the crisis at the expense of exacerbating moral hazard.[4]

2. Implications for the Federal Reserve

Dodd–Frank Act. As often occurs after a major crisis, the events prompted the enactment of legislation designed to prevent a repeat of that episode. Indeed, DFA, which was signed into law in July 2010, is an expansive piece of legislation (16 titles, 880 pages) that is significantly reshaping the financial regulatory and supervisory environment. A key feature of the Act is the explicit incorporation of macroprudential considerations into the U.S. regulatory structure. This means that regulators now have to pay attention to the state of the financial system *as a whole* as well as to the safety and soundness of *individual* financial institutions, markets, and infrastructures. Another key feature is the strong emphasis on preemptive policies, designed to reduce moral hazard and systemic risk associated with the expectation of bailouts. These policies include, for example, enhanced prudential standards for banking firms and systemically important non-bank firms, living wills, and a new resolution mechanism for financial institutions that could pose systemic risk if they were to be resolved through bankruptcy. The Act also set up stronger supervision requirements, including a program of regular stress-testing by both banking supervisors and the firms themselves, and more stringent data and disclosure requirements. At the same time, DFA puts more restrictions on the use of tools to address a crisis once it is underway. The explicit incorporation of macroprudential considerations, along with the emphasis on preemptive policies, represents a major innovation in the approach to achieving financial stability.

In the end, however, the Dodd–Frank Act basically maintains the current structure of the financial system. In particular, it leaves the basic bank holding company model essentially intact and does not radically alter the activities or organizational structures of insured depositories. It also does little to reform the wholesale funding markets, leaving to financial regulators the crucial task of devising plans to address the risks in these fragile markets.

---

[4]Regardless of one's view on the appropriate weight to attach to moral hazard, some recent research suggests that the lender of last resort cannot commit to withhold liquidity *ex post*, even if it would reduce incentives for excessive risk-taking, primarily because leverage building is a strategic complement among firms. See Farhi and Tirole (2009).

To put the new macroprudential approach into practice, DFA assigned expanded financial stability responsibilities to many existing regulators, and created new organizations. One is the Financial Stability Oversight Council (FSOC), tasked with identifying and mitigating threats to the financial stability of the United States, promoting market discipline by eliminating expectations that the government will shield private parties from losses in the event of financial firms' failures, and responding to emerging threats to U.S. financial stability. The FSOC is chaired by the Secretary of the Treasury and has ten voting members, including the Chairman of the Federal Reserve, and five non-voting members. Two of its important responsibilities are the designation of systemically important non-bank financial institutions and financial market utilities. The FSOC also is required to make recommendations to promote financial stability, but it does not replace the primary regulator for writing guidance or rules, or for supervision. The Act also created the Office of Financial Research within the Treasury Department, which is tasked with improving the quality of financial-sector data and facilitating the analysis of data for the FSOC and its member agencies.

Organization at the Fed. To meet its new expanded mandate for financial stability responsibilities, the Fed is incorporating lessons learned from the financial crisis for supervision and regulation, and setting up a new organizational structure to assess risks to financial stability. The intent is to take a more deliberate and coordinated approach, utilizing its expertise across different areas and skills, to monitor and promulgate policies in pursuit of financial stability.

Even before the enactment of DFA, the Fed was strengthening the supervision of the largest, most complex financial firms. It created a committee with supervisors and other experts, including economists and financial market analysts from across the Reserve Banks, to oversee the supervision of these firms and incorporate macroprudential considerations into the supervisory process. This committee is using more sophisticated quantitative methods and incorporating interconnections between firms to evaluate their expected performance and risk, and the risk the firms might pose to the broader financial system. The Fed is using a similar body to help supervise systemically important financial market utilities.

In addition, the Fed created the Office of Financial Stability Policy and Research (OFS) at the Board to coordinate monitoring and analysis of potential financial systemic risks to the financial system and the economy, including developing quantitative measures of systemic risks, to work with supervision of the largest complex firms, and to help design and analyze macroprudential policies to promote financial stability. The OFS is expected to play a major role in breaking down silos among economists, financial market experts, and supervisors, and thereby facilitate better internal communication and coordination of information and policy formulation. It will also support the Fed's role as a member of the FSOC, including working with other member agencies to identify potential risks and evaluate potential mitigating actions.

Financial stability framework. Promoting financial stability involves monitoring risks to identify threats to financial stability. This activity primarily entails identifying vulnerabilities in the financial system, through which a variety of shocks could be transmitted and amplified and harm other parts of the financial system and real economy. It also entails developing and implementing policies to address these identified vulnerabilities.

Sources of systemic risk can be described as structural — those that are present under all macroeconomic conditions. Such risks are present because large complex banking firms, or payment, clearing, and settlement firms that provide a critical service can fail, and could have outsized destabilizing effects on the rest of the financial system. Another structural risk is that shadow banks are vulnerable to runs. Sources of systemic risk can also be cyclical — those that build up in a buoyant expanding economy. Asset bubbles built from excessive credit or a high degree of maturity mismatch in the financial system are examples of cyclical systemic risks.

The main goal of macroprudential policies is to increase the resiliency of both institutions and markets and build a financial system that holds risk in less fragile ways so that systemic risks do not build. To address structural risks, new proposed regulations under DFA emphasize higher standards, better supervision, and a resolution mechanism for large financial institutions. In particular, these firms will be required to hold more capital and better quality capital, reduce liquidity risk, and limit single counterparty exposures. In addition, requirements include supervisory and firm stress tests, early remediation rules, and viable recovery and resolution plans — so-called "living wills." Such regulations should provide incentives to firms to become simpler.

In addition, regulators are working to reform the shadow banking sector and strengthen resilience in short-term funding and other critical markets. In particular, as noted in the FSOC 2011 Annual Report, money market funds and the tri-party repo market continue to exhibit critical vulnerabilities. Improving the standardization of over-the-counter derivatives markets with centralized clearing is another high-priority item.

The challenge of understanding and mitigating cyclical risks — for example, elevated asset prices and excessive credit growth that arise in robust economic times but can leave the balance sheets of financial firms vulnerable to downturns in the credit cycle — may be even more daunting. In part, this involves the monitoring of measures of leverage and maturity mismatch at financial intermediaries. Asset valuations, underwriting standards for loans, and credit growth should also be scrutinized for signs of a build-up of systemic risk. In addition, some promising work is under way — both in the United States and abroad — to design and evaluate policy tools to mitigate cyclical risk. Examples of such tools include variable capital requirements, countercyclical margin requirements, restrictions on loan-to-value ratios, interest on reserves, and taxes on liabilities. That said, the experience with such tools is limited, especially in the more developed economies, and the literature on their efficacy is still at an early stage.

A related issue is how macroprudential policies fit together with monetary policy. In the past, the goals of monetary and macroprudential policies were generally well-aligned, and the Tinbergen separation principle — that is, separate tools for separate goals — was largely taken for granted. On the whole, this principle retains considerable support, given monetary policy may be too blunt a tool to address some risks to financial stability that arise from narrow sources, though some researchers have started to question whether it should still apply. For example, with recent research suggesting that accommodative monetary policy could impair financial stability by contributing to the build-up of leverage or excessive reliance on short-term funding, it seems reasonable to think about whether such considerations might warrant some weight in monetary policy decisions — and, if so, under what circumstances (Woodford, 2011). In any event, this debate will surely remain a lively and important one for years to come.

Similarly, the goals of micro- and macroprudential policies are generally well-aligned, but conflicts can arise, such as when economic activity is weak. For example, allowing banks to "release a capital buffer" to promote lending could help support economic activity in the early phase of a recovery, while having banks hold on to their capital could leave them in a better position in case economic conditions were instead to worsen. Macroprudential regulators will need to determine how to balance competing objectives.

This framework follows DFA and emphasizes preemptive policies which are designed to increase the resilience of the financial sector so that it can absorb rather than amplify shocks. The intent is to reduce the likelihood of future crises and the costs when they occur. DFA also has restricted the tools available to regulators to respond to crisis. In particular, DFA puts additional restrictions on the Fed's use of emergency lending facilities to prevent expectations of a bailout, requires that the names of borrowers and amounts from these facilities be disclosed to Congress within seven days, prohibits the use of the Exchange Stabilization Fund to guarantee money market mutual funds, and eliminates the systemic risk exception to the least cost resolution. Because of these changes, it is all the more critical that an effective program of preemptive actions be put into place.[5] These changes also increase the uncertainty about how authorities would respond to a future crisis.

Governance. Finally, from the perspective of governance, DFA requires the Fed to engage more closely with other agencies, including fiscal authorities, in its pursuit of financial stability. This closer engagement is likely to be especially evident during times of crisis, given the new restrictions on the Fed's authority to use 13(3) emergency lending powers, which stipulate that any new facility should not be expected to impose losses on taxpayers, must be broad-based, and must be approved by the Secretary of the Treasury. To some observers, such ties with the Treasury may raise concerns about compromising the independence of the Fed and undermining its power to promote price stability and maximum employment.

However, because these changes help to clarify the responsibilities of the Fed *vis-à-vis* those of the Treasury, they may in fact be useful in resolving *ex post* conflicts, real and perceived, about the emergency use of public funds. Still, some have called for a formal agreement that sets forth the specific roles of the two entities.[6] Such an agreement could build on the joint statement issued during the crisis on appropriate roles for the Federal Reserve and the Treasury, and could help reduce misperceptions.[7]

3. Conclusion

In summary, the experience of 2007–2009 offers some important lessons for the Federal Reserve. These lessons, along with the new responsibilities

---

[5]See Kohn (2011).

[6]For example, Goodfriend (2011) has proposed an agreement similar to the 1951 Treasury-Fed accord.

[7]The Role of the Federal Reserve in Preserving Financial and Monetary Stability; see www.federalreserve.gov/newsevents/press/monetary/20090323b.htm.

assigned under DFA, have significant implications for internal processes, policies, and governance at the Fed. Considerable progress has been made to identify and monitor sources of systemic risks and to evaluate alternative macroprudential regulatory policies. Implementing higher capital standards for systemically important firms, supervisory stress tests and requiring firms to conduct their own stress tests, and requiring living wills also may encourage regulated firms to become simpler. However, much remains to be done, including collecting and disseminating data in a way that promotes better risk management by the private sector and supports quantitative supervisory practices. These data would also foster research by outside analysts and academics, which could be an important input to the risk analysis and the design of effective policy tools by the regulators.

References

Adrian, T. and H.S. Shin, 2008, "Liquidity and leverage," Federal Reserve Bank of New York, staff report, No. 328.

Allen, F. and D. Gale, 2005, "From cash-in-the-market pricing to financial fragility," *Journal of the European Economic Association*, Vol. 3, No. 2–3, pp. 535–546.

Bernanke, B. and M. Gertler, 1989, "Agency costs, net worth, and business fluctuations," *American Economic Review*, Vol. 79, No. 1, pp. 14–31.

Brunnermeier, M.K. and L.H. Pedersen, 2009, "Market liquidity and funding liquidity," *Review of Financial Studies*, Vol. 22, pp. 2201–2238.

Caballero, R., 2010, "Crisis and reform: Managing systemic risk," prepared for the Angelo Costa lecture delivered in Rome, March 23. Forthcoming in *Rivista di Politica Economica*.

Caballero, R. and A. Krishnamurthy, 2008, "Musical chairs: A comment on the credit crisis," *Financial Stability Review*, Banque de France, Vol. 11, pp. 1–3.

Cochrane, J., 2010, "Lessons from the financial crisis," *Regulation*, Vol. 32, No. 4, pp. 34–37.

Covitz, D., N. Liang, and G. Suarez, 2013, "The evolution of a financial crisis: Collapse of the asset-backed commercial paper market," *Journal of Finance*, forthcoming.

Farhi, E. and J. Tirole, 2009, "Leverage and the central banker's put," *American Economic Review*, Vol. 99, No. 2.

Financial Stability Oversight Council, 2011, *Annual Report*.

Goodfriend, M., 2011, "Central banking in the credit turmoil: An assessment of Federal Reserve practice," *Journal of Monetary Economics*, Vol. 58, No. 1, pp. 1–12.

Gorton, G.B. and A. Metrick, 2012, "Securitized banking and the run on repo," *Journal of Financial Economics*, forthcoming.

Hubrich, K. and R. Tetlow, 2011, "Financial stress and economic dynamics: The transmission of crises," European Central Bank, working paper.

Kashyap, A.K. and J.C. Stein, 2004, "Cyclical implications of the Basel II capital standards," *Economic Perspectives*, Federal Reserve Bank of Chicago, First Quarter, pp. 18–31.

Kohn, D., 2011, "Will the Federal Reserve be able to serve as lender of last resort in the next financial crisis?," prepared remarks for the Long-Term Effects of the Great Recession conference, Federal Reserve Bank of Boston, October 18–19.

Pozsar, Z., A. Tobias, A. Ashcraft, and H. Boesky, 2010, "Shadow banking," Federal Reserve Bank of New York, staff report, No. 458.

Reifschneider, D. and J.C. Williams, 2000, "Three lessons for monetary policy in a low-inflation era," *Journal of Money, Credit and Banking*, Vol. 32, No. 4, pp. 936–966.

Woodford, M., 2011, "Inflation targeting and financial stability," prepared for The Future of Central Banking conference, Einaudi Institute for Economics and Finance, Rome, Italy, September 30, 2010.

Role of Central Banks in Financial Stability: Lessons from the Experience of the Bank of Japan

Takeo Hoshi*
Stanford University, NBER, and TCER

1. Introduction

Rosengren (2011) defines financial stability as the "ability of the financial system to consistently supply the credit intermediation and payment services that are needed in the real economy if it is to continue on its growth path." Thus, financial stability is lost when the financial system fails to provide the services and harms the real economy. It is important to note that turmoil in the financial system that accompanies failures of financial institutions does not necessarily jeopardize the financial stability. For example, a large number of savings and loan institutions failed in the 1980s U.S., but other financial institutions were able to step up and increase financial intermediation without serious impact on the real economy, as Rosengren points out.

Conversely, continuation of financial institutions does not guarantee consistent provision of intermediation service and could compromise the financial stability. Even when there are no failures of financial intermediaries, if they fail to allocate credit to worthy borrowers, this can harm the real economy. A clear example here is the problem caused by zombie banks and zombie firms studied by Kane (2000), among others. Zombie banks are those banks that are economically insolvent but are kept alive by bank regulators. They have a tendency to gamble by making too-risky investments, because their downside is limited. Zombie firms are non-financial counterparts of zombie banks. Their profitability is too low to stay in the market in

*Takeo Hoshi is the Henri H. and Tomoye Takahashi Senior Fellow in Japanese Studies at Shorenstein Asia Pacific Research Center at Stanford University and Professor of Finance, by courtesy, at Stanford Graduate School of Business.

a normally competitive market, but they are kept alive by their banks. They continue to produce, demand funds, and hire human capital that could be deployed elsewhere in more productive ways. By competing for precious resources, they hinder the expansion of healthy firms and new entrants, and hurt the process of creative destruction.

Financial stability often emerged as an important policy objective in many countries, but it was sometimes confused with stability/continuation of individual financial institutions. The experience in Japan, which this paper studies, provides a clear example of such a case. The Japanese government and its central bank, the Bank of Japan, have intervened frequently to maintain financial stability, but the interventions often aimed at protection of individual financial institutions rather than the functions of the entire financial system. When the Bank of Japan intervened to maintain financial stability, it also encountered a potential trade-off between the policy to protect healthy functioning of the financial system and the policy to deal with economic recession that accompanied financial instability.

This paper examines the Japanese government's policies to maintain financial stability in both pre-war and post-war years, and derives some general lessons. The paper especially focuses on the role of the Bank of Japan in the last 20 years, when the Japanese economy experienced a long period of stagnation, often called the lost decade (or two). The paper is organized as follows. We start by reviewing the Japanese government's policy responses to a series of financial instability in the 1920s in the next section. We observe that the role for the Bank of Japan in dealing with financial instability gradually increased over time. Starting from the events in the 1920s is important because the basic stance of the banking regulations that try to maintain financial stability by not allowing any bank to fail was established then and continued to the post-war era. Section 3 reviews the policy stance toward financial stability that lasted until the financial crisis in the 1990s. Section 4 examines the policy responses to the financial crisis and economic stagnation during the 1990s and the 2000s. This was the period right after the Bank of Japan obtained legal independence. Special attention is paid to the Bank of Japan's interactions with other regulators such as the Financial Services Agency (FSA). Section 5 builds a simple model that shows the trade-off between policy toward financial stability and monetary policy, and uses it to understand the Bank of Japan's policy in the late 1990s and the 2000s. Finally, in Section 6, the paper concludes by deriving general lessons from the experience in Japan on the role of central banks in maintaining financial stability.

2. Financial Instability in the 1920s

The Bank of Japan (BOJ) was established as the central bank in 1882. The bank was organized as a joint stock company, but it was tightly controlled by the government. The shareholders were limited to Japanese citizens, and they had to be approved by the Ministry of Finance before they could buy shares of the BOJ. The government was to monitor the business of the BOJ and had the power to prohibit not only the actions that violated the Bank of Japan Act or the charter, but also anything that was considered to be detrimental to the government's interest. Under this heavy influence of the government, the BOJ often provided funds to private sector banks and industrial firms directly in the name of maintaining financial stability.

The first systematic rescue loans by the BOJ happened in the post-war recession of 1920. Japanese industries expanded very rapidly during World War I, and suffered from over-extension when the war ended. In the spring of 1920, crashes in stock and commodity markets led to a financial crisis. Many banks were rumored to be in trouble and the depositors ran to their branches. From April to July 1920, there were 169 bank runs in total (BOJ, 1958, pp. 547–548). To respond to the crisis, the BOJ took several measures. First, the BOJ provided liquidity to the banking sector. For those banks that already had accounts at the BOJ, the BOJ increased the lending by relaxing the collateral requirements. In some cases, the BOJ extended loans without any collateral. The BOJ also extended credits to those banks that did not have prior transactions with the BOJ through purchase of government bonds that the banks held with repurchase agreements.

In addition to the banking sector, the BOJ provided liquidity to stock exchanges (Tokyo, Osaka, and Nagoya) and major corporations in the industries that were hard hit by the recession, such as sugar refinery, mining, and textile industries. Figure 1 shows the amount of the BOJ loans (advances and discounts) that include these emergency loans to banks and industries from 1917 to 1930. The amount almost doubled from around 400 million yen in late 1919 to 800 million yen in April 1920.

The liquidity provision by the BOJ was apparently effective in calming down the financial markets toward the end of 1920. The banking sector continued to be fragile, however. The boom during WWI encouraged many

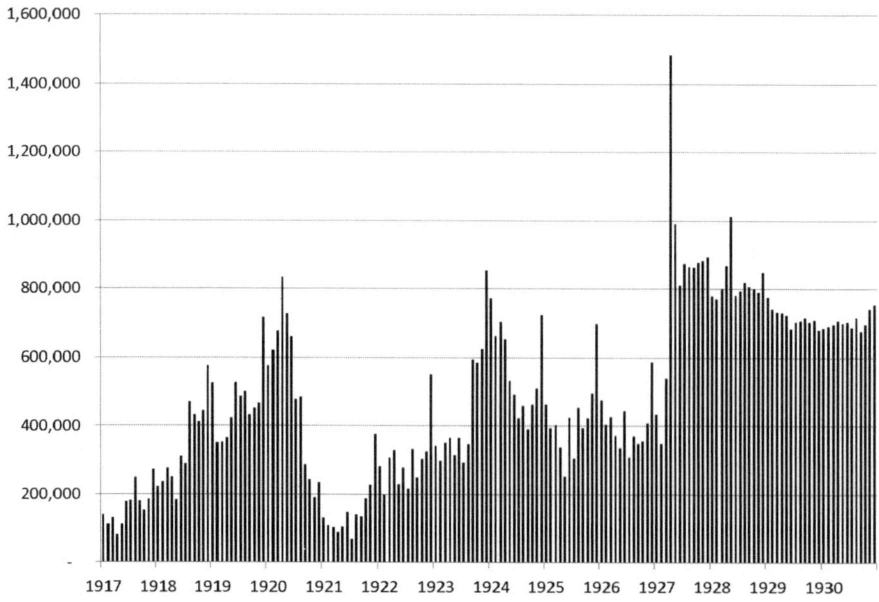

Figure 1. BOJ Advances and Discounts (Thousand Yen).

Sources: Bank of Japan (1928), pp. 12–13; Bank of Japan (1964), Statistical Appendix, pp. 2–3.

businesses to over-extend, only to get into trouble when the economy cooled down after the war. Many banks were saddled with non-performing loans to those customers. The problem was especially serious for so-called "organ banks," which are financing arms of corporations run by the insiders of banks. The loans of these banks were concentrated on those to the related companies, and the health of the banks deteriorated quickly when the related companies' performance deteriorated.

Bank runs again spread nationally in late 1922 and 16 banks suspended the deposit withdrawals. The BOJ intervened again to lend directly to the troubled banks. The financial instability, however, did not stop. The BOJ provided rescue loans again in 1923 when a series of bank runs happened in central Japan. Figure 1 shows that the BOJ loans that once dipped below 100 million yen in 1921 started to increase again in 1922 and 1923.

On September 1, 1923, Tokyo and the surrounding areas were hit by a massive earthquake with a magnitude of 7.9. The number of casualties was estimated to exceed 140,000, and the total amount of property damage was as high as 30% of GNP. The financial system stopped functioning as most of the banks in Tokyo were physically destroyed. The government responded by quickly passing a moratorium on financial payments until the end of September. This was followed by the Earthquake Bill Discounting Loss Guarantee Act (passed on September 27), which made the BOJ provide a large amount of rescue loans. Under this scheme, private sector banks were allowed to bring the bills that were issued by the companies in the affected areas and that had been discounted by the banks to the BOJ for rediscounting. The BOJ offered a two-year window for the bills to be repaid. When the earthquake bills were supposed to be repaid at the end of those two years, however, it was deemed too soon, so the banks were given two more years. In the event that the BOJ were to incur losses from the earthquake bills, the government was supposed to cover the BOJ's losses up to a certain amount. Figure 1 shows that the BOJ loans jumped by more than 200 million yen in September 1923 and stayed high for a while.

A major problem of this policy of helping the banking sector to recover from the shock of the earthquake was that the "earthquake bills" included the bills that were already non-performing even before the earthquake. Even if the economy recovered from the earthquake shock, those bills were not likely to be repaid. Worse, continuing to provide credit to those firms slowed down the necessary economic restructuring that Japan needed after the credit boom during WWI was over.

In 1927, as the expiration of the Earthquake Bills Act drew near, banks that were rumored to have a large amount of (probably non-performing) earthquake bills started facing difficulty in raising funds. In March, the government submitted a bill that allowed the government to grant government bonds equivalent in amount with the earthquake bills to private banks so that they could use government bonds as collateral for loans from the BOJ, but the Diet refused to pass this bill. In the meantime, the finance minister's statement that the failure to pass the bill was already forcing a bank in Tokyo to close (although the bank was actually not closed, yet) precipitated a full financial panic. The bank faced a run and was indeed closed the next day. By the end of April, 31 more banks closed. On April 22, the Bank of Japan, all banks, and all trust companies closed for two days.

The BOJ was again forced to step up in liquidity provision during the financial crisis of 1927. Figure 1 shows that the BOJ loans almost tripled from around 540 million yen at the end of March 1927 to 1,480 million yen at the end of April 1927. The amount came down to around 800 million yen before the end of 1927, but the high amount of BOJ loans around 700 million yen persisted throughout the 1930s. As Kato (1957) argued, the series of financial instability in the 1920s solidified the BOJ's role as a large "rescue fund" that the government can use.

As Patrick (1971) points out, an important lesson that the Ministry of Finance learned from the financial instability in 1927 was that bank failure should be avoided. The government tried to prevent any more bank failures by making the banks bigger. The government raised the minimum level of capital required for a bank in the Banking Act of 1927 and encouraged mergers to advance concentration of the banking industry. By the end of 1928, the number of banks dropped by 20% from 1,283 to 1,031. In the next five years to 1933, the number of banks almost halved to 538. During wartime, the government encouraged further consolidation of the banking industry by advancing the "one prefecture, one bank" principle. By the end of the war in 1945, the number of banks in Japan had dropped to 61.

The BOJ seem to have learned a different lesson. The BOJ rescue loans may have helped to contain financial instability, but they also allowed many banks and companies that should have been restructured to survive without serious restructuring. This may have slowed down the economic restructuring that the Japanese economy needed following the over-extension during the war years. By keeping part of the BOJ assets in those rescue loans, the flexibility of monetary policy in adjusting the money supply and the interest rates was also harmed. As early as 1928, Eigo Fukai, who later became the BOJ governor in the 1930s, lamented the situation that the BOJ had been pulled into:

> Ever since the Bank of Japan's emergency rescue loans to Masuda Bank and Seventy-Fourth Bank in 1920 during the so-called post-war reactionary recession, the emergency measures were not reserved for emergency anymore. The Bank of Japan is now viewed as having responsibility of rescuing the industries, especially the financial industry. There were some precedents of rescue operations by the BOJ before 1920, but they consisted of slightly relaxing the collateral requirement or making loans on personal guarantees and were very rare. Since 1920, however, the industries have taken the BOJ rescue for granted and do not feel ashamed of asking for help. The tools for the rescues have become more involved, and the attempts to solve problems of the industries are conducted with the sacrifice of the Bank of Japan (Eigo Fukai, lecture in 1928, quoted by Kato, 1957, p. 325; author's translation).

3. Convoy System to Prevent Bank Failures

The basic stance of avoiding financial instability by not allowing any bank to fail continued and was solidified in the post-war period.[1] Indeed, no banks failed during the 50 years from 1948 to 1995. Whenever a bank got into trouble, the Ministry of Finance, which was responsible for bank regulation, approached a bigger and healthier bank to absorb the troubled bank. As Hoshi (2002) pointed out, the Ministry of Finance was able to provide regulatory rewards to the acquiring bank under the heavily regulated banking regime of Japan.

The government also continued to be able to influence the Bank of Japan to come to the rescue of troubled financial institutions. The Bank of Japan Act had been revised in 1942 to further increase the power of the government. The law specified the BOJ's mandate to be "properly enhancing the national economic power," and allowed the government to heavily influence the BOJ's actions. The rescue loans that the BOJ was already making to banks and non-financial firms were institutionalized as "special loans" under Section 25 of the Act. The Bank of Japan Act was largely unchanged after the war.

The BOJ used the Section 25 "special loans" for the first time after the war during the recession of 1965. During the recession, Yamaichi Securities, one of the four biggest securities houses, faced financial difficulty, which was feared would spread to other financial institutions. To prevent a financial crisis, Finance Minister Kakuei Tanaka (who later became prime minister in the early 1970s) asked the BOJ to provide a special loan to Yamaichi Securities, to which the BOJ complied. The BOJ also made a special loan to a smaller securities house, Oi Securities. These measures were effective in avoiding a financial crisis.

The BOJ's rescue during the 1965 recession was exceptional in the post-war period. During the rapid economic growth period, only a few financial institutions experienced financial troubles and when they did, larger financial institutions were usually willing to absorb them. The Ministry of

[1] Immediately following the end of the war, Japan experienced an economy-wide insolvency problem caused by government repudiation of war debts. Although there are some interesting lessons to be learned from this experience and the policy responses, which are discussed in Hoshi (1995), they are not concerned with the role of the central bank in maintaining financial stability.

Finance (MOF) was able to provide regulatory rewards to those institutions that absorbed the failing banks. As Hoshi (2002) showed, the number of branches for each bank was restricted by regulation, and acquiring the branch network of a failing bank was profitable. Thus, the MOF did not have to pressure the BOJ to bail out failing banks.

This situation started to change in the late 1980s as the financial industry was gradually deregulated. Having more branches did not necessarily mean more profits anymore. The MOF started to have a harder time convincing large banks to absorb the failing financial institutions. The government, however, did not abandon its policy of not failing any banks to protect financial stability. When some banks began to get into trouble after the bubble burst in the early 1990s, the government first responded by expanding the role of the Deposit Insurance Corporation (DIC).

The government started to use an explicit financial subsidy from the DIC to encourage banks to rescue failing banks. The first case of DIC-assisted rescue was that of Tōhō Sōgo Bank. The MOF asked Iyo Bank, a healthier regional bank in the same region, to absorb Tōhō Sōgo. Iyo agreed and received subsidized loans of 8 billion yen for five years from the DIC with the interest rate 500 basis points lower than the government bond yield of the same maturity. The role of the DIC in assisting rescue mergers was later expanded. The size of DIC assistance was initially limited to be no more than the cost of paying off the insured deposits of the bank that was rescued. The reform of the Deposit Insurance Act in 1995, however, allowed the DIC to provide financial assistance that exceeded the cost of paying off the insured depositors "temporarily." This temporary exception was to be phased out on March 31, 2001, but was later extended by one more year. In 1997, the Deposit Insurance Act was revised again and the DIC was allowed to provide financial assistance (again "temporarily") to mergers that did not involve any failing institutions or mergers between failing institutions.

The BOJ was called upon to help indirectly by providing funds to the DIC first, and directly by making special loans to failing or failed banks later. For example, when the Deposit Insurance Act was revised in 1995, the DIC's credit line with the BOJ was expanded to 1 trillion yen. The BOJ also revived the special loans and started providing assistance to many failed financial institutions. The institutions that the BOJ assisted through special loans included Hyogo Bank (August 1995), Kizu Credit Union (August 1995), Hanwa Bank (November 1996), Kyoto Kyoei Bank (October 1997), Hokkaido Takushoku Bank (November 1997), Yamaichi

Securities (November 1997), Tokuyō City Bank (November 1997), and Midori Bank (which was created out of Hyogo Bank that failed in 1995; May 1998).

4. Bank of Japan After the New Bank of Japan Act of 1998

The banking crisis in Japan reached its peak in late 1997. November began with the failure of Sanyo Securities, a mid-sized securities house. Sanyo defaulted on the overnight interbank loan market (call market) and filed for bankruptcy. This was the first post-war default in the call market. Other financial institutions that were considered to have solvency problems also faced difficulty securing funds. In the same month, Hokkaido Takushoku Bank, a major bank, Yamaichi Securities, one of the big four securities houses, and Tokuyō City Bank, a regional bank in Sendai, all failed. Interbank markets froze up, and the situation was similar to the global financial crisis in 2008, as Hoshi and Kashyap (2010) point out.

The government responded by arranging with the BOJ and the DIC to be ready to provide as much as 30 trillion yen (17 trillion to protect depositors at failed banks and 13 trillion to inject capital into undercapitalized banks). In March 1998, 1.8 trillion yen was distributed to 21 banks for recapitalization, but it was not sufficient to calm down the market. Very much like after a similar capital injection in the U.S. 10 years later under the Troubled Asset Relief Program, the crisis continued. It was only after nationalization of two major banks (Long-Term Credit Bank of Japan and Nippon Credit Bank) and the second round of capital injection in the spring of 1999, based on serious inspection of individual banks (very much like the stress tests in 2009 in the U.S.), that the financial market calmed down.

During the crisis, two important institutional changes took place. First, the Bank of Japan Act was revised substantially for the first time since 1942. The new law became effective as of April 1, 1998. Second, the financial supervisory functions that primarily resided in the MOF were separated out, and the Financial Supervisory Agency was established in June 1998 as the regulator of essentially all the financial institutions that operate in Japan. Both of these changes were already planned before the peak of the crisis.

As Cargill *et al.* (2000) explain, one of the most important changes in the new BOJ Act was granting the BOJ with legal independence from the government. The goal of the monetary policy is specified as "contributing to healthy development of the national economy through achieving price stability." The clause on BOJ special loans (Section 25 in the old law) survived in the new law as Section 38, but now the law specifies that the BOJ gets to decide whether such loans are necessary, without being influenced by the government.

The monetary policy was already accommodative when the new Bank of Japan Act commenced in April 1998. After the collapse of the bubble, the BOJ quickly cut the target overnight interest rate, and the rate had been at 0.5% since September 1995. In the middle of the banking crisis, the new BOJ continued the accommodative monetary policy. In February 1999, the Bank of Japan cut the target rate to zero. The BOJ later (4/9/1999) added that the policy will continue "until the threat of deflation subsides." The zero interest rate policy (ZIRP) is usually interpreted as the limit of traditional expansionary monetary policy that tries to stimulate aggregate demand by lowering the interest rate. During the global financial crisis of 2007–2009, many central banks, including the Federal Reserve Banks, adopted the ZIRP. The Bank of Japan's interpretation, however, was slightly different.

In the "Change of the Guideline for Money Market Operations" that the BOJ published at the start of the ZIRP (February 12, 1999), it stated:

> In order to bring the Japanese economy back to a solid recovery path, it is important not only to provide support from monetary and fiscal sides but also to steadily promote financial system revitalization and structural reforms.

The BOJ did not consider that expansionary macroeconomic policy alone would be able to fix the Japanese economy. The Japanese economy suffered from the over-extension during the bubble period. Without restructuring and "revitalization," the economy would continue to stagnate. In other words, the shortage of aggregate demand, which expansionary macroeconomic policy may have been able to help, was not considered to be the main cause of the recession. The ZIRP only buys time for necessary restructuring. With this message, the BOJ seems to have tried to clarify its view that the government must work hard to promote "financial system revitalization and structural reforms" to put the Japanese economy on a recovery path.

The Financial Supervisory Agency initially moved rather aggressively to clean up the banking sector. It started out by examining all the major banks and then moved on to regional banks. By the summer of 1999, the agency had finished all the examinations. Five regional banks were found to be undercapitalized and they subsequently closed.

As the financial markets calmed down after the second round of recapitalization in 1999, the government's commitment to structural reforms seems to have waned. The Financial Reconstruction Commission (FRC), which led the nationalization process of failed banks and the recapitalization of others, had a series of chairs who seemed to be more eager to protect the incumbent political party's interests. The Financial Supervisory Agency was subsumed into the newly created Financial Services Agency (FSA) in July 2000. The new FSA also took over the functions of the FRC and the MOF's Financial System Planning Bureau.[2]

In August 2000, the BOJ surprised many by terminating the ZIRP although the inflation rate was still negative. This appeared to violate the earlier commitment to continue the ZIRP until the threat of deflation was gone. Two policy members objected and the government observers to the policy meeting asked for the postponement of the decision, but the majority approved the termination of the ZIRP.

Umeda (2011, Chapter 4) studies how the BOJ reached the decision to terminate the ZIRP based on the minutes of the policy board meetings, especially the one on August 11, 2000, that decided the termination. The discussion in that meeting (and in several of the previous ones) was centered on the interpretation of the commitment to continue the ZIRP until the threat of deflation subsided. Given that they did not have a precise measure of the threat of deflation, it was natural to see disagreements arise among the policy board members. In the end, the majority agreed that the economy had recovered sufficiently to make the possibility of accelerating deflation remote.

The majority of policy board members also stressed the "side effect" of the ZIRP that suppressed the role of interest rates in allocating financial resources effectively. With the interest rate stuck at zero, the short-term financial markets stop functioning, they argued. Although it was not stated explicitly, the policy board members may have also been concerned with the slow pace of economic restructuring and structural reforms. The BOJ considered that the ZIRP alone would not be effective. The ZIRP was just buying time for structural reforms that were essential for the economic recovery, but the FSA did not seem to be committed to complete the reforms.

The termination of the ZIRP turned out to be premature. Japan went back into recession. The BOJ eventually decided to cut the policy rate back to zero in March 2001. At this point, the BOJ announced that it would start targeting the outstanding balance of current accounts (CAB; bank deposits

[2]See Hoshi and Ito (2004) for more on this reorganization of the FSA and its performance.

at the BOJ) instead of the call rate. This was the start of the quantitative easing (QE). The BOJ stated that the policy would be in place until the CPI inflation rate is 0% or higher. The initial target level of the CAB was set at 5 trillion yen, but was subsequently raised to 6 trillion yen (8/14/2001), 10–15 trillion yen (12/19/2001), over 15 trillion yen (2/28/2002), and 15–20 trillion yen (10/30/2002). The BOJ also started to announce the monthly amount of purchase of the Japanese government bonds (JGB) in August 2001. The outright purchase of JGBs increased gradually from 600 billion yen per month (8/14/2001) to 800 billion yen (12/19/2001), 1 trillion yen (2/28/2002), and 1.2 trillion yen (10/30/2002).

A notable feature of the QE announcements during this period was that the BOJ's statement sometimes confirmed the understanding that the QE was to be supplemented by the government efforts on structural reforms, which the BOJ continued to see as essential for the recovery. For example, the BOJ stated the following after the policy board meeting on February 28, 2002:

> To realize the full permeation of the effects of strong monetary easing, it is essential to strengthen a financial system and ensure its stability by making a swift move to resolve the non-performing loan problem. It is also vital to make progress in structural reform on the economic and industrial fronts through tax reform, streamlining of public financial institutions, and deregulation. The Bank strongly hopes that both the government and the private sector, in particular financial institutions, will take more determined and effective steps in this regard ("On Today's Decision at the Monetary Policy Meeting," February 28, 2002).

The following remark was made after the policy meeting on October 30, 2002:

> In order to ensure the abundant liquidity provision by the Bank leading to the revitalization of the economy, improvement in credit allocation function of capital markets is important in addition to the strengthening of the financial intermediary function of banks. In this regard, the Bank will closely monitor the impact of expected government measures to accelerate the resolution of the NPL problem on corporate financing and explore possible measures to secure the smooth working of corporate financing ("Change in the Guideline for Money Market Operations," October 30, 2002).

These statements show that the BOJ believed that the QE had to be accompanied by the government's earnest efforts in forcing the banks to remove the non-performing loans from their balance sheets and encouraging economic restructuring. Without such coordination, the BOJ believed the side effects of the QE would dominate any benefits it might have.

The quantitative easing continued for almost five years. The governor of the BOJ changed from Masaru Hayami to Toshihiko Fukui in March 2003, but Governor Fukui continued the QE, raising the CAB target further. The target level was increased to 17–22 trillion yen (3/25/2003), 22–27 trillion yen (4/30/2003), 27–30 trillion yen (5/20/2003), and 27–32 trillion yen (10/10/2003).

On the government side, Junichiro Koizumi became prime minister in April 2001. He was exceptionally reform-minded and tried to push structural reforms on several fronts under the slogan "no growth without reform." He especially stressed the need to clean up the non-performing loans in the banking sector. He asked the Minister of Financial Affairs, Hakuo Yanagisawa (who was the first and effective chair of the FRC) first and then Heizo Takenaka after the fall of 2002, to force the banks to remove the non-performing loans from their books. The government set the goal of reducing the non-performing loans at the major banks by half by March 2005, and succeeded.

Thus, the BOJ and the government seem to have coordinated their policies successfully between 2001 and 2005. The government and the FSA were finally serious about resolving the non-performing loans problem. The BOJ supported the efforts through accommodative monetary policy. Figure 2 shows the size of the BOJ's balance sheet from 2001 to 2011. The BOJ balance sheet expanded about 50% during the quantitative easing.

5. Monetary Policy and Prudential Policy

The BOJ's policy responses during the banking crisis in the 1990s and the early 2000s suggest interesting interactions between policy to avoid financial instability and monetary policy. Central bank provision of credit can ease the liquidity problem in financial markets and at individual financial institutions. It does not solve the solvency problem of financial institutions, however, which is often at the core of financial instability. Ideally, one would want to combine the ample liquidity provision by the central bank with strict bank supervision to encourage necessary restructuring. In reality, however, the bank regulators may be reluctant to force the restructuring. Kane (1993) makes a similar point in discussing the problems of

Figure 2. BOJ Total Assets (Trillion Yen).

Source: Bank of Japan (http://www.boj.or.jp).

bank regulation with a deposit insurance scheme:

> Bankers want deposit insurance as a competitive advantage. Politicians want deposit insurance as a way to avoid being embarrassed by bank failures. Because they are more directly answerable to politicians and bankers than to taxpayers, in practice government regulators are pulled more toward avoiding failures and subsidizing deposit-institution operations than they are toward minimizing taxpayer loss exposures (Kane, 1993, p. 336).

The fact that financial instability almost always leads to recession adds to the tension. The central bank would want to loosen the monetary policy to stimulate aggregate demand, but such expansionary monetary policy can also bail out poorly performing banks and firms and slow down their restructuring. The problem is especially serious when the policy interest rate hits the zero bound, which happened in Japan in the late 1990s (and in other major countries in late 2008). When a central bank runs out of room for rate cutting, the only monetary policy tools left for the central bank are non-traditional varieties such as quantitative easing and credit easing, which end up providing direct supports for banks regardless of their financial health.

The Bank of Japan understood the potential problem of expansionary monetary policy in slowing down the necessary restructuring of the industries. It repeatedly mentioned the potential side effects of the ZIRP or the QE, and considered the problem very important. This attention to the side effects, however, seems to have made the BOJ's monetary policy not expansionary enough.

This section presents a simple game theoretic model of the interaction between monetary policy and prudential policy. The model helps us understand the Japanese experience better by showing that if monetary policy and prudential policy are determined by different authorities, the equilibrium may show lower inflation (or more deflation) and slower economic restructuring than either policy authority desires.

The model presented here is similar to Nordhaus (1994) and Dixit and Lambertini (2003), both of which model a lack of coordination between the monetary authority and the fiscal authority. In the model of Nordhaus (1994), both the equilibrium interest rate and the budget deficit end up higher than the levels either authority considers optimal. The monetary authority does not want to cut the interest rate, because it does not expect the fiscal authority to cut the budget deficit. Dixit and Lambertini (2003) explore the implications for aggregate output and price level in a similar setup. They show that the equilibrium output is lower and the equilibrium price level is higher than the levels that either policy authority considers optimal.

The closest to the model in this paper is the one by Cargill and Guerrero (2007). They also model a game between the monetary authority and the fiscal authority in the context of the Japanese economic policy making. They show that the interaction between the BOJ and the MOF (as fiscal authority) may have led to deflationary biased monetary policy.

The model here is concerned with the interaction between the BOJ (monetary authority) and the FSA (bank regulator). The central bank is assumed to have the following preference function:

$$V_M = -\frac{1}{2}(x - x_M^*)^2 - \frac{b}{2}(u - u^*)^2, \tag{1}$$

where u is the unemployment rate and x is the extent of economic restructuring. The asterisk denotes the optimal level of the variable for the policy authority, and the subscript is the identifier of the policy authority. The subscript M stands for the monetary authority.

The bank regulator is assumed to have the following preference function:

$$V_R = -\frac{1}{2}(x - x_R^*)^2 - \frac{b}{2}(u - u^*)^2 - \frac{a}{2}s^2. \tag{2}$$

Here, s is the supervisory effort for the bank regulator, which is costly. The subscript R stands for bank regulator. Both the central bank and the bank regulator are assumed to have the same optimal level of unemployment, but the levels of the economic restructuring that they consider optimal are different.

It is assumed that $x_R^* < x_M^*$. The optimal level of economic restructuring is lower for the bank regulator. This may reflect the political pressure that the regulator feels as the quote from Kane (1993) above suggests. A legally independent central bank would not feel such political pressure very much.

The extent of economic restructuring is assumed to be influenced by two factors: the supervisory effort of the bank regulator (s) and the inflation rate denoted by π. Economic restructuring advances with more effort of the bank regulator but is slowed down by high inflation (as a result of quantity easing, for example):

$$x = s - \pi. \tag{3}$$

The model assumes a (short run) Phillips curve that takes the following form:

$$u = u^* + \gamma x - \alpha\pi. \tag{4}$$

The usual term on the inflation expectation is suppressed because we consider only one shot game here. The Phillips curve here assumes that the economic restructuring increases the unemployment (at least in the short run).

The central bank is assumed to maximize its objective function (1) with respect to the inflation rate taking the bank regulator's action as given. The bank regulator is assumed to maximize its objective function (2) with respect to the supervisory efforts taking the central bank's action as given. It is straightforward to calculate the reaction function of each policy authority. The central bank's reaction function is:

$$\pi = \frac{x_M^* + (1 + b\gamma)s}{1 + b(\gamma + \alpha)^2}. \tag{5}$$

The bank regulator's reaction function is given by:

$$s = \frac{x_s^* + [1 + b\gamma(\gamma + \alpha)]\pi}{1 + b\gamma + a}. \tag{6}$$

The equilibrium is given by a pair (π, s) that satisfies both Equations (5) and (6).

It is also straightforward to calculate the bliss point for each policy authority, which is the pair (π, s) that maximizes the objective function of one policy authority. The bliss point for the central bank is given by:

$$\pi_M = \frac{\gamma}{\alpha} x_M^*,$$
$$s_M = \frac{\gamma + \alpha}{\alpha} x_M^*. \tag{7}$$

The bliss point for the bank regulator is:

$$\pi_R = \frac{b\gamma\alpha - a}{b\alpha^2 + a[1 + b(\gamma + \alpha)^2]} x_R^*,$$
$$s_R = \frac{b\alpha(\gamma + \alpha)}{b\alpha^2 + a[1 + b(\gamma + \alpha)^2]} x_R^*. \tag{8}$$

Given our assumption $x_R^* < x_M^*$, we can show:

$$\pi_R < \pi_M$$
$$s_R < s_M. \tag{9}$$

Thus, if one policy authority can determine both inflation and supervisory efforts, the bank regulator will choose lower inflation and lower level of supervisory efforts than the central bank.

Figure 3 depicts the Nash equilibrium of the game. The central bank's reaction function is steeper than the bank regulator's reaction function. We see the equilibrium level of supervisory effort is lower than what either policy authority considers optimal. The equilibrium inflation rate is also lower than the ideal rate for either policy authority. Given the low level of supervisory effort, the central bank is reluctant to generate higher inflation because that would undermine the economic restructuring. Given the low inflation rate, the bank regulator is reluctant to exert supervisory effort because that would push the unemployment rate too high.

If the policymakers coordinated their actions, both parties could be better off. The bank regulator could promise to step up efforts to advance

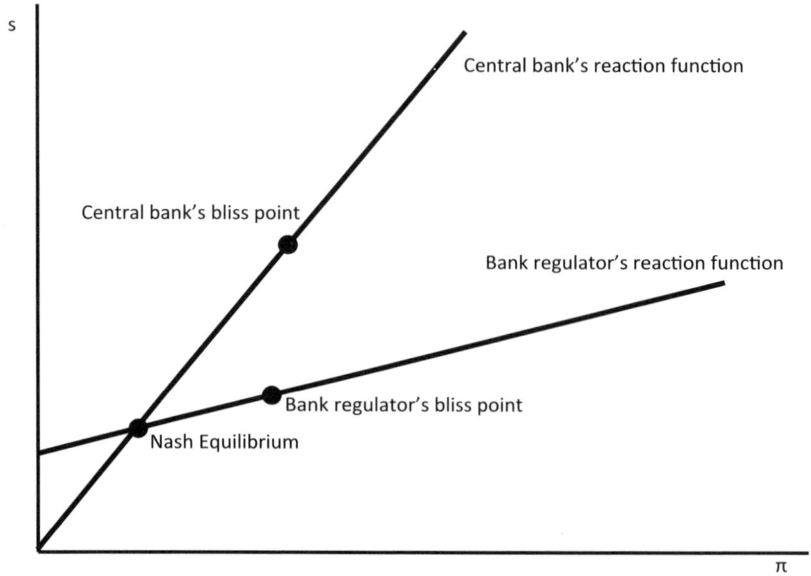

Figure 3. Non-Cooperative Equilibrium of the Game.

economic restructuring, so that the central bank could generate higher inflation without worrying about its negative impact on economic restructuring. The central bank could promise to increase the inflation rate, so that the bank regulator could encourage economic restructuring without worrying about the negative impact on unemployment.

One may question the assumption of this model that the central bank cares about the level of economic restructuring. This seems to be a reasonable assumption, at least in the financial crisis. Okina and Shiratsuka (2003) point out that the effectiveness of monetary policy depends on the health of the financial system. Thus, they argue:

> Once a financial system tumbles into a critical situation, the boundary between monetary and prudential policies becomes extremely ambiguous (Okina and Shiratsuka, 2003, p. 92).

During a financial crisis, the central bank would have to care about the health of the financial system even if it is only concerned with using monetary policy to influence just traditional aggregate variables.

Angelini, Neri, and Panetta (2011) study a dynamic general equilibrium model with a banking sector that allows them to formally analyze how the transmission of monetary policy is affected by macroprudential policy. They also explore the implications of interactions between the monetary authority and the macroprudential authority when different organizations are in charge of two policies.

The simple model in this paper seems to capture an important aspect of interactions between monetary policy and prudential policy in Japan. Before 2001 or so, the bank regulator seemed to be not very serious in resolving the non-performing loans problem. The Bank of Japan looked reluctant to commit to aggressively expansionary monetary policy. In August 2000, the Bank of Japan terminated the ZIRP when the economy still suffered from deflation. Starting around 2002, however, the BOJ and the government appeared to have established better coordination. Under the leadership of Prime Minister Koizumi, the government finally forced the major banks to deal with the non-performing loans. The BOJ continued and expanded the quantitative easing.

Such coordination seems to be absent during the more recent period. As Harada *et al.* (2011) report, the bank supervision by the FSA has been relaxed after the global financial crisis. The FSA encouraged banks to help small and medium-sized enterprises (SMEs) that were facing financial trouble in the global recession by rescheduling their loans. In return, the FSA allowed the banks to classify those restructured loans as normal as long as some loose conditions are being satisfied (such as a plan for future restructuring). As a result, the disclosed amount of non-performing loans for Japanese banks did not increase after the global financial crisis, although the Japanese economy suffered substantially from the crisis. For regional banks, the amount of non-performing loans actually fell between 2008 and 2011.

The Bank of Japan worked with other central banks to provide liquidity (especially U.S. dollar liquidity) into the markets at the peak of the global financial crisis in 2008, but was somewhat slow in going back to non-traditional monetary policy such as quantitative easing. The expansion of the BOJ balance sheet was much slower than that of the Federal Reserve. Figure 2 shows that the BOJ's effort in this aspect was more timid than its own QE during the 2001–2006 period.

6. Lessons from the Experiences of the Bank of Japan

The experiences of Japan in dealing with financial instabilities imply some general lessons on the role of the central bank in maintaining financial stability. First, the Japanese experiences confirm that stability of the financial system is different from the stability of individual financial institutions. Failures of individual financial institutions do not necessarily lead to financial instability. Conversely, absence of failure does not necessarily imply financial stability. Protecting failing financial institutions can inhibit healthy economic restructuring and may impair the functions of the financial system. Both in the 1920s and during the banking crisis in the 1990s, the Japanese government tried to avoid failures of financial institutions and forced the Bank of Japan to rescue many failing banks and industrial firms. The policy to avoid failures as much as possible slowed down the economic restructuring and prolonged the stagnation.

Second, consideration for financial stability can influence the monetary policy. An argument often made in this context is that the central bank may pursue too-loose monetary policy to avoid financial instability. In the case of Japan, the problem was in the opposite direction. The BOJ seemed to have understood the problems of protecting failing financial institutions. In the 1990s and the early 2000s, when the Japanese government did not seem to be seriously pushing for disposal of non-performing loans from bank balance sheets, the BOJ often pursued too-tight monetary policy.

Thus, the third lesson is the importance of coordination between prudential policy and monetary policy. The central bank and the bank regulator can make both parties better off by coordinating their policies. The BOJ and the Japanese government seemed to have achieved such successful coordination in the mid-2000s.

One obvious way to make the policy coordination easier is to make the central bank a bank supervisor as well. If the BOJ had been responsible for both bank supervision and monetary policy, it would have implemented more stringent prudential policy and more expansionary monetary policy. The Japanese experience may provide another support for the argument that the central bank should be closely involved in prudential policy.

References

Angelini, Paolo, Stefano Neri, and Fabio Panetta, 2011, "Monetary and macroprudential policies," working paper, Banca d'Italia.

Bank of Japan, 1923, *Sekai Sensō Shūryō-go ni okeru Honpō Zaikai Dōyōshi* (*History of Financial Instability in Japan after the World War*). Reprinted in

1958 in Bank of Japan, *Nihon Kin'yū-shi Shiryō: Meiji-Taishō Hen* (*Data for Japanese Financial History: Meiji-Taisho Volumes*), Vol. 22, pp. 385–735.

Bank of Japan, 1928, *Shōwa 2 nen Honpō Keizai Tōkei* (*Economics Statistics of Japan: 1927*). Reprinted in 1958 in Bank of Japan, *Nihon Kin'yū-shi Shiryō: Meiji-Taishō Hen* (*Data for Japanese Financial History: Meiji-Taisho Volumes*), Vol. 22.

Bank of Japan, 1964, *Nihon Kin'yū-shi Shiryō: Shōwa Hen* (*Data for Japanese Financial History: Showa Volumes*), Vol. 9.

Cargill, Thomas F. and Federico Guerrero, 2007, "Japan's deflation: A time-inconsistent policy in need of an inflation target," *International Finance*, Vol. 10, pp. 115–130.

Cargill, Thomas F., Michael M. Hutchison, and Takatoshi Ito, 2000, *Financial Policy and Central Banking in Japan*, Cambridge, MA: MIT Press.

Dixit, Avinash and Luisa Lambertini, 2003, "Interactions of commitment and discretion in monetary and fiscal policies," *American Economic Review*, Vol. 93, pp. 1522–1542.

Harada, Kimie, Takeo Hoshi, Kaoru Hosono, Satoshi Koibuchi, and Masaya Sakuragawa, 2011, "Japan in the global financial crisis," in *The World in Crisis: Insights from Six Financial Regulatory Committees*, pp. 245–295, available at www.aei.org/paper/economics/financial-services/the-world-in-crisis/.

Hoshi, Takeo, 1995, "Cleaning up the balance sheets: Japanese experience in the postwar reconstruction and recapitalization," in *Corporate Governance in Transitional Economies: Insider Control and the Role of Banks*, Masahiko Aoki and Hyung-Ki Kim (eds.), Washington, DC: The World Bank, pp. 303–359.

Hoshi, Takeo, 2002, "The convoy system for insolvent banks: How it originally worked and why it failed in the 1990s," *Japan and the World Economy*, Vol. 14, pp. 155–180.

Hoshi, Takeo and Takatoshi Ito, 2004, "Financial regulation in Japan: A sixth year review of the financial services agency," *Journal of Financial Stability*, Vol. 1, No. 2, pp. 229–243.

Hoshi, Takeo and Anil K. Kashyap, 2010, "Will the U.S. bank recapitalization succeed? Eight lessons from Japan," *Journal of Financial Economics*, Vol. 97, pp. 398–417.

Kane, Edward J., 1993, "What lessons should Japan learn from the U.S. deposit-insurance mess?" *Journal of the Japanese and International Economies*, Vol. 7, pp. 329–355.

Kane, Edward J., 2000, "The dialectical role of information and disinformation in regulation-induced banking crises," *Pacific-Basin Finance Journal*, Vol. 8, pp. 285–308.

Kato, Toshihiko, 1957, *Honpō Ginkō-shi Ron* (*Treatise on Banking History in Japan*), Tokyo, Japan: University of Tokyo Press.

Nordhaus, William D., 1994, "Policy games: Coordination and independence in monetary and fiscal policies," *Brookings Papers on Economic Activity*, Vol. 2, pp. 139–216.

Okina, Kunio and Shigenori Shiratsuka, 2003, "Japan's experience with asset price bubbles: Is it a case for inflation targeting?" in *Asset Price Bubbles: The Implications for Monetary, Regulatory, and International Policies*, William C. Hunter, George G. Kaufman, and Michael Pomerleano (eds.), Cambridge, MA: MIT Press, pp. 81–99.

Patrick, Hugh T., 1971, "The economic muddle of the 1920s," in *Dilemmas of Growth in Prewar Japan*, James W. Morley (ed.), Princeton, NJ: Princeton University Press, pp. 211–266.

Rosengren, Eric S., 2011, "Defining financial stability, and some policy implications of applying the definition," keynote remarks at the Stanford Finance Forum, June 3, available at www.bos.frb.org/news/speeches/rosengren/2011/060311/index.htm.

Umeda, Masanobu, 2011, *Nichigin no Seisaku Keisei* (*Monetary Policy Making at the BOJ*), Tokyo, Japan: Toyo Keizai Shimposha.

Overcoming the Fear of Free Falling: Monetary Policy Graduation in Emerging Markets

Carlos A. Vegh*
University of Maryland and NBER

Guillermo Vuletin
Colby College

1. Introduction

As is well-documented by now, developing countries have traditionally pursued procyclical fiscal policy.[1] In other words, governments have tended to follow expansionary fiscal policy during booms and contractionary fiscal policy in recessions, thus exacerbating the underlying business cycle (the so-called "when it rains, it pours" phenomenon).

Figure 1 illustrates procyclical fiscal policy on the spending side, by plotting the cyclical components of government spending and real GDP for 94 countries during the period 1960–2009.[2] Black bars denote industrial countries, while light bars indicate developing countries. The visual impression is quite striking: While an overwhelming majority of light bars lie on the right side of the picture, indicating a positive correlation or procyclical government spending in developing countries, a majority of black bars lie on

*Carlos A. Vegh is a professor of economics at the University of Maryland; Guillermo Vuletin is an assistant professor of economics at Colby College. This paper was prepared for a conference on "The role of central banks in financial stability: How has it changed?," organized by the Federal Reserve Bank of Chicago on November 10–11, 2011. The authors are grateful to Pablo Federico, Agustin Roitman, and conference participants for helpful comments and suggestions.

[1]See Kaminsky, Reinhart, and Vegh (2004) and the references therein.

[2]Real government expenditure is defined as central government expenditure and net lending deflated by the GDP deflator.

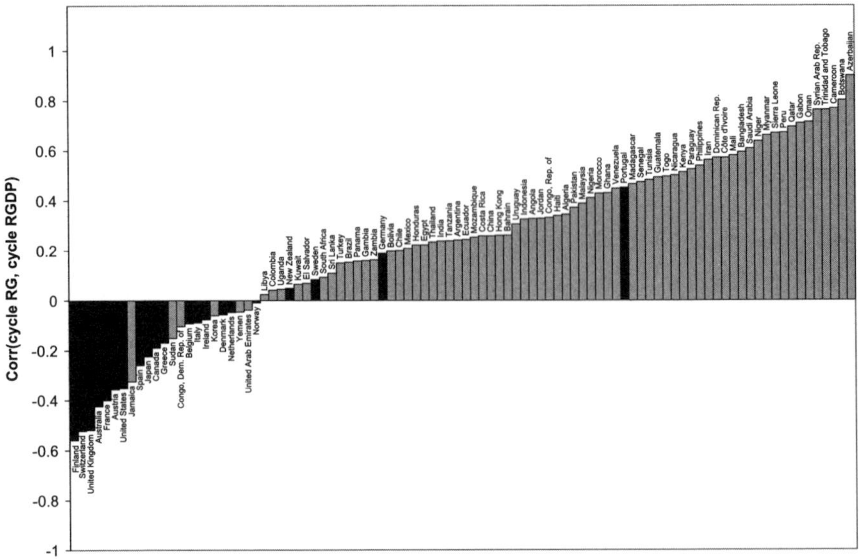

Figure 1. Country Correlations between the Cyclical Components of Real Government Spending and Real GDP, 1960–2009.

Notes: Dark bars are industrial countries and light bars are developing countries. The cyclical components have been estimated using the Hodrick–Prescott filter. A positive (negative) correlation indicates procyclical (countercyclical) fiscal policy.

Source: Frankel, Vegh, and Vuletin (2011).

the left side, indicating a negative correlation or countercyclical government spending in industrial countries.[3] Explanations for this puzzling behavior of fiscal policy in developing countries range from imperfect access to international capital markets (Gavin and Perotti, 1997; Riascos and Vegh, 2003) to political pressures for additional spending in good times (Talvi and Vegh, 2005; Alesina and Tabellini, 1990; Ilzetzki, 2011).

Over the last decade, however, many emerging countries have managed to escape the fiscal procyclicality trap and actually become countercyclical (see Frankel, Vegh, and Vuletin, 2011). To illustrate this "graduation" phenomenon, Figure 2 repeats Figure 1 for the period 1960–1999, while Figure 3 focuses on the decade 2000–2009. While Figure 2 essentially

[3]The same is true on the taxation side. As shown in Vegh and Vuletin (2011), tax rate policy tends to be procyclical in developing countries and acyclical in industrial countries.

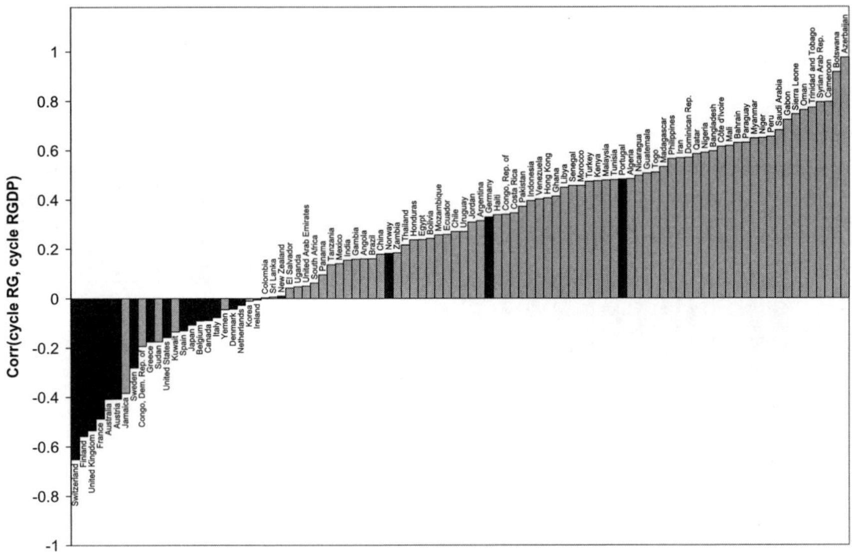

Figure 2. Country Correlations between the Cyclical Components of Real Government Spending and Real GDP, 1960–1999.

Notes: Dark bars are industrial countries and light bars are developing countries. The cyclical components have been estimated using the Hodrick–Prescott filter. A positive (negative) correlation indicates procyclical (countercyclical) fiscal policy.

Source: Frankel, Vegh, and Vuletin (2011).

conveys the same message as Figure 1, Figure 3 shows an obvious shift of light bars from the right side of the picture to the left. In fact, about a third of developing countries have graduated. Frankel, Vegh, and Vuletin (2011) trace this dramatic shift in policy to improvements in institutional quality, which are reflected in better fiscal institutions and policy rules that require the fiscal authority to meet a certain target for the cyclically adjusted primary balance (Frankel, 2011). This ensures that countries will save in good times and hence be able to dissave in bad times.

While a great deal of attention has been paid to the cyclical properties of fiscal policy, relatively little attention has been devoted to monetary policy. In particular, there has been no attempt, as far as we know, to examine whether the graduation phenomenon alluded to above is also present for monetary policy. Our aim in this paper is thus to: (i) document the extent of monetary policy procyclicality in developing countries relative to industrial countries; and (ii) assess how many countries have graduated, if any, over the

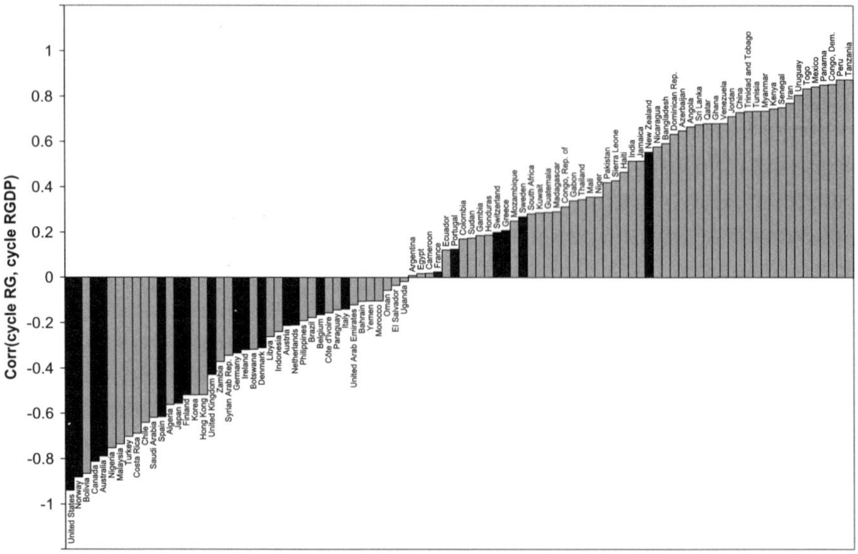

Figure 3. Country Correlations between the Cyclical Components of Real Government Spending and Real GDP, 2000–2009.

Notes: Dark bars are industrial countries and light bars are developing countries. The cyclical components have been estimated using the Hodrick–Prescott filter. A positive (negative) correlation indicates procyclical (countercyclical) fiscal policy.

Source: Frankel, Vegh, and Vuletin (2011).

last decade. In fact, we will show that 40 percent of developing countries in our sample have, on average, pursued procyclical monetary policy over the last 50 years. In sharp contrast, every single industrial country has followed countercyclical monetary policy over the same period. Over the last decade, however, around 35 percent of developing countries have graduated.

We trace this graduation from monetary policy procyclicality to the fact that many emerging markets have overcome what we call the "fear of free falling." In the past — and this is still true, of course, of many developing countries — the depreciation of the domestic currency during bad times (typically characterized by large capital outflows) would force policymakers to raise interest rates to defend the currency. The fear was (is) that a rapidly depreciating currency would plunge the economy into a deeper crisis by encouraging further capital outflows and leading to widespread bankruptcy of firms indebted in dollar terms. The need to raise interest rates to defend the currency would preclude the possibility of using monetary policy to spur the economy, as in industrial countries. As many emerging markets have matured — by undertaking market-friendly reforms and pursuing sounder macroeconomic management — this fear of free falling has subsided, or disappeared altogether, thus allowing policymakers to free policy rates for countercyclical purposes.

The paper proceeds as follows. We first document the shift in the cyclical behavior of monetary policy over the last decade in the developing world. We then show empirically how this graduation process is tightly linked to developing countries overcoming the fear of free falling. Final thoughts close the paper.

2. Graduating Class

This section documents the shift in the cyclical behavior of monetary policy over the last decade in the developing world. To set the stage, Figure 4 plots the cyclical components of short-term interest rates and real GDP for 68 countries for the period 1960–2009.[4] As can be seen, every single dark bar lies on the left side of the figure, indicating that all industrial countries have pursued, on average, countercyclical monetary policy (i.e., higher interest rates in good times). In contrast, 40 percent of light bars (developing countries) lie on the right side, indicating procyclical monetary policy (i.e., lower interest rates in good times). In fact, the average correlation for developing countries is 0.05, compared to 0.41 for industrial countries.

How is monetary policy cyclicality related to fiscal policy cyclicality? Not surprisingly, Figure 5 shows that fiscal and monetary policy cyclicality are strongly related. All countries pursuing procyclical monetary policy (i.e., Corr(cycle i, cycle RGDP) < 0) have also followed procyclical fiscal policy (i.e., Corr(cycle RG, cycle RGDP) > 0). Moreover, countries that tend to be more countercyclical in monetary policy are also less procyclical when it comes to fiscal policy. Given the close relation between the cyclicality of monetary and fiscal policy — and based on the findings in Frankel, Vegh, and Vuletin (2011) regarding fiscal policy graduation — we would expect many developing countries to have also graduated from monetary policy procyclicality.

[4]We take short-term interest rates as a proxy for the stance of monetary policy. In some cases, we have data for overnight interbank interest rates, such as the federal funds rate in the United States. In most cases, however, we rely on discount rates due to their longer availability. Conceptually, any standard open economy model with imperfect asset substitution would allow monetary authorities to use the interest rate as a policy instrument (see, for instance, Calvo and Vegh, 1995; and Flood and Jeanne, 2005).

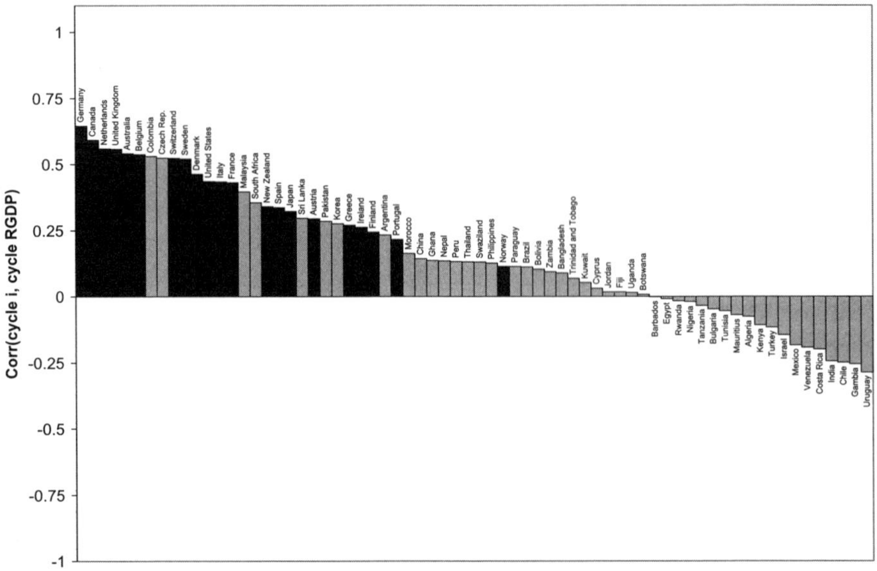

Figure 4. Country Correlations between the Cyclical Components of Short-Term Interest Rate and Real GDP, 1960–2009.

Notes: Dark bars are industrial countries and light bars are developing countries. The cyclical components have been estimated using the Hodrick–Prescott filter. A positive (negative) correlation indicates countercyclical (procyclical) monetary policy. Sample of 68 industrial and developing countries.

Source: World Economic Outlook (IMF), International Financial Statistics (IMF), and Global Financial Data.

To address the issue of monetary policy graduation, we divide the 1960–2009 sample used in Figure 4 into two subsamples: 1960–1999 and 2000–2009. Figure 6 replicates Figure 4 for the period 1960–1999 and conveys essentially the same message. Figure 7, on the other hand, focuses on the period 2000–2009. Once again, the visual image conveyed by Figure 7 is striking when compared to Figure 6. Specifically, the number of light bars on the left side of the picture (i.e., positive correlations) has greatly increased. Around 77 percent of developing countries (36 out of 47) now show countercyclical monetary policy, up from 49 percent (23 out of 47) in Figure 6. Moreover, the average correlation between the cyclical components of short-term interest rates and real GDP in developing countries has increased from −0.02 for the period 1960–1999 (indicating acyclical monetary policy

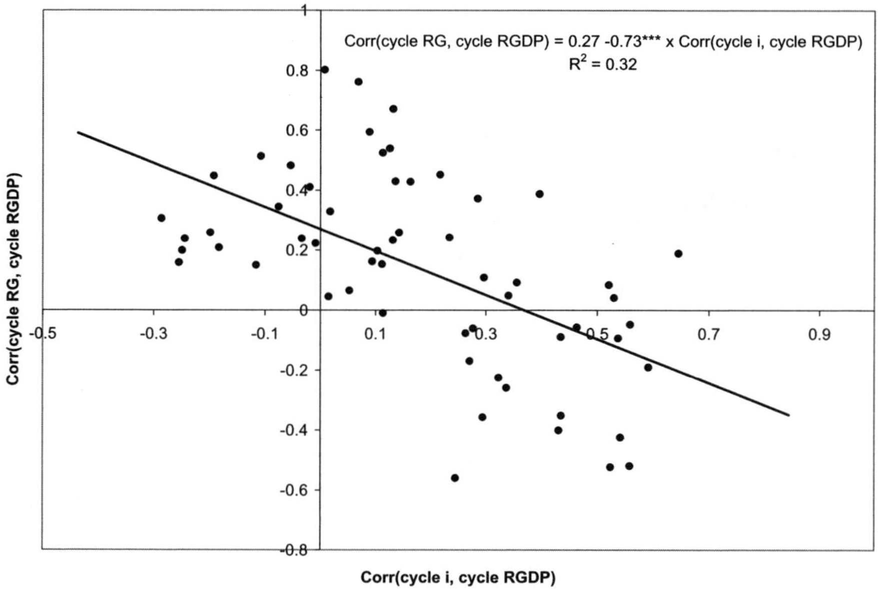

Figure 5. Cyclicality of Fiscal Policy vs. Cyclicality of Monetary Policy, 1960–2009.

Notes: Corr(cycle RG, cycle RGDP) measures country correlations between the cyclical components of real government spending and real GDP. Corr(cycle i, cycle RGDP) measures country correlations between the cyclical components of a short-term interest rate and real GDP. A positive (negative) Corr(cycle RG, cycle RGDP) indicates procyclical (countercyclical) fiscal policy. A positive (negative) Corr(cycle i, cycle RGDP) indicates countercyclical (procyclical) monetary policy.

Sources: Frankel, Vegh, and Vuletin (2011); World Economic Outlook (IMF), International Financial Statistics (IMF), and Global Financial Data.

on average) to 0.28 since the year 2000 (indicating countercyclical monetary policy).

To illustrate the issue of monetary graduation more broadly, Figure 8 presents a scatter plot with the 1960–1999 correlation on the horizontal axis and the 2000–2009 correlation on the vertical axis. By dividing the scatter plot into four quadrants along the zero axes, we can classify countries into four categories:

(1) **Established graduates** (top right): These are countries that have always been countercyclical. Not surprisingly, all industrial countries

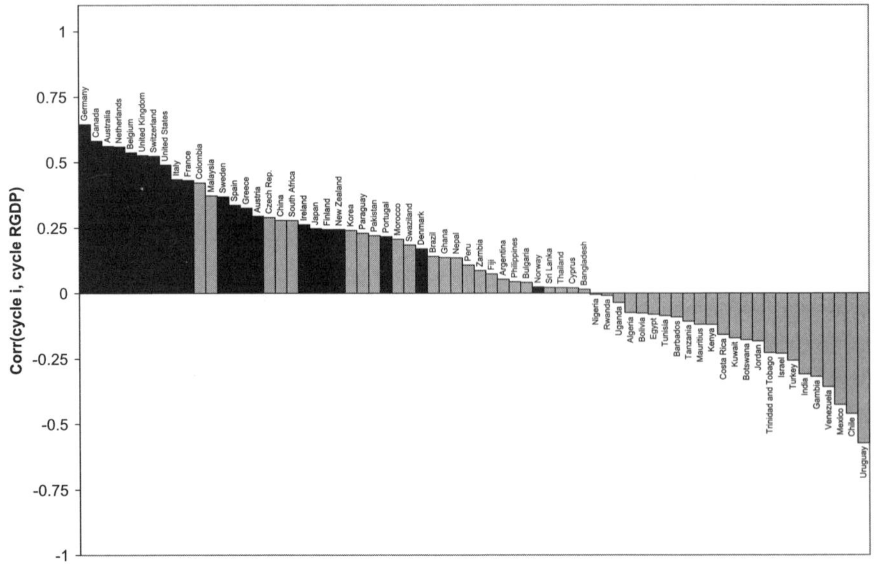

Figure 6. Country Correlations between the Cyclical Components of Short-Term Interest Rate and Real GDP, 1960–1999.

Notes: Dark bars are industrial countries and light bars are developing countries. The cyclical components have been estimated using the Hodrick–Prescott filter. A positive (negative) correlation indicates countercyclical (procyclical) monetary policy. Sample of 68 industrial and developing countries.

Source: World Economic Outlook (IMF), International Financial Statistics (IMF), and Global Financial Data.

belong to this category. About 38 percent of developing countries (18 out of 47) also fall into this category, including Colombia and Korea.

(2) **Still in school** (bottom left): These are countries that have continued to behave procyclically over the last decade. These are all, of course, developing countries, including Costa Rica, Gambia, and Uruguay. Interestingly, this category represents a fairly small set of all developing countries (about 13 percent, or 6 out of 47).

(3) **Back to school** (bottom right): These are countries that were countercyclical during the 1960–1999 period and turned procyclical over the last decade. This small group of countries includes Brazil, China, and Morocco. It is worth noting that taken together, the "back to school" and "still in school" categories represent less than 25 percent of all developing countries (11 out of 47).

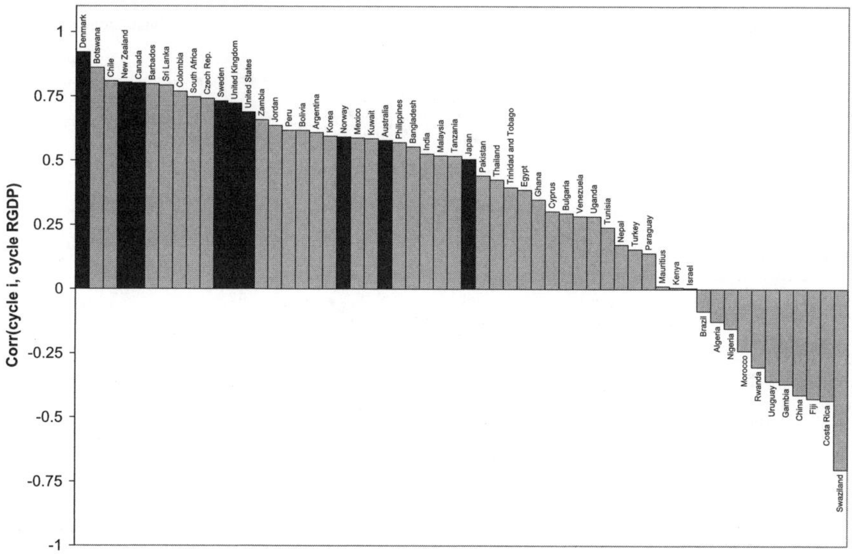

Figure 7. Country Correlations between the Cyclical Components of Short-Term Interest Rate and Real GDP, 2000–2009.

Notes: Dark bars are industrial countries and light bars are developing countries. The cyclical components have been estimated using the Hodrick–Prescott filter. A positive (negative) correlation indicates countercyclical (procyclical) monetary policy. Sample of 56 industrial and developing countries.

Source: World Economic Outlook (IMF), International Financial Statistics (IMF), and Global Financial Data.

(4) **Recent graduates** (top left): These are countries that used to be procyclical and became countercyclical over the last decade. They are all developing countries (18 out of 47) and include Chile and Mexico.

In sum, the evidence suggests that more than a third of the developing world (18 out of 47 countries) has recently "graduated" from monetary policy procyclicality. As a result, about 77 percent (36 out of 47) of developing countries have followed countercyclical monetary policy over the last decade.

3. Graduation and "Fear of Free Falling"

What explains the ability of some developing countries to escape the procyclical monetary policy trap? While there is no doubt that many factors

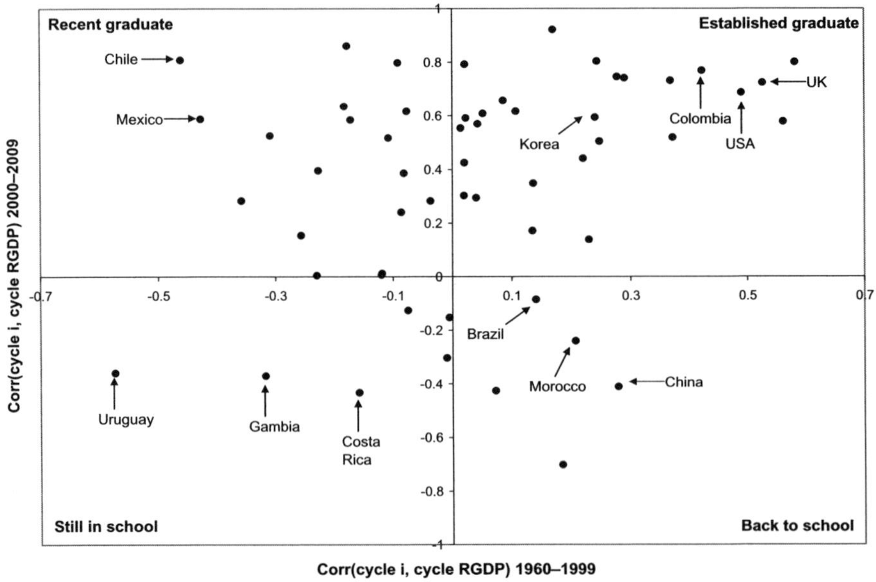

Figure 8. Country Correlations between the Cyclical Components of Short-Term Interest Rate and Real GDP, 1960–1999 vs. 2000–2009.

Notes: The cyclical components have been estimated using the Hodrick–Prescott filter. A positive (negative) correlation indicates countercyclical (procyclical) monetary policy. See Appendix 3 for correlation values for each country. Sample of 56 industrial and developing countries. Established graduates: Argentina, Australia, Bangladesh, Bulgaria, Canada, Colombia, Cyprus, Czech Rep., Denmark, Ghana, Japan, Korea, Malaysia, Nepal, New Zealand, Norway, Pakistan, Paraguay, Peru, Philippines, South Africa, Sri Lanka, Sweden, Thailand, United Kingdom, United States, and Zambia. Still in school: Algeria, Costa Rica, Gambia, Nigeria, Rwanda, and Uruguay. Back to school: Brazil, China, Fiji, Morocco, and Swaziland. Recent graduates: Barbados, Bolivia, Botswana, Chile, Egypt, India, Israel, Jordan, Kenya, Kuwait, Mauritius, Mexico, Tanzania, Trinidad and Tobago, Tunisia, Turkey, Uganda, and Venezuela.

Source: World Economic Outlook (IMF), International Financial Statistics (IMF), and Global Financial Data.

come into play, we believe that a critical channel is the following. In emerging economies, recessions are often associated with capital outflows (and, in fact, are sometimes caused by sudden reversals of capital inflows, the so-called "sudden stops" phenomenon; see Calvo, 1998). This capital outflow triggers a steep depreciation of the domestic currency, which forces the central bank to raise interest rates to defend the currency.[5] We refer to this monetary policy reaction as "fear of free falling" (FFF) and we measure it by computing the correlation between the percentage change of a short-term interest rate and the percentage change of the rate of depreciation.[6] Specifically, a positive correlation indicates that the short-term policy rate increases when the domestic currency is depreciating, indicating the presence of FFF.[7] On the contrary, a zero correlation (or no FFF) suggests that the monetary authority does not systematically respond to exchange rate movements. While a standard Taylor rule would call for a lower interest rate during recessions, the presence of FFF forces policymakers to raise interest rates to defend the currency.[8] Indeed, Figure 9 shows that monetary policy is procyclical for high levels of FFF and becomes more countercyclical as FFF diminishes.

As we might expect, FFF is closely related to other common criteria used to ascertain the soundness of government policy, such as institutional quality. We construct an index of institutional quality (IQ) by calculating

---

[5]The need to defend the domestic currency in bad times is best exemplified by IMF advice during the 1997 Asian crisis. To quote Stanley Fischer (at the time, the First Deputy Managing Director), "[i]n weighing [the question of whether programs were too tough], it is important to recall that when they approached the IMF, the reserves of Thailand and Korea were perilously low, and the Indonesian rupiah was excessively depreciated. Thus, the first order of business was, and still is, to restore confidence in the currency. To achieve this, countries have to make it more attractive to hold domestic currency, which, in turn, requires increasing interest rates temporarily, even if higher interest costs complicate the situation of weak banks and corporations. This is a key lesson of the tequila crisis in Latin America in 1994–1995, as well as from the more recent experiences of Brazil, the Czech Republic, Hong Kong, and Russia, all of which have fended off attacks on their currencies in recent months with a timely and forceful tightening of interest rates along with other supporting policy measures. Once confidence is restored, interest rates can return to more normal levels" (Fischer, 1998).

[6]We borrow the expression "free falling," of course, from Reinhart and Rogoff's (2004) well-known exchange rate regime classification.

[7]Of course, if interest parity held in practice, our measure of FFF would be meaningless because it would always be positive by construction (assuming variations in international interest rates are not significant). But, empirically, it is well-known that interest parity does not hold, particularly in the short run (see, among others, Mishkin, 1984; Frankel, 1991; Chinn and Meredith, 2004; Akram, Rime, and Sarno, 2008; and Burnside, Eichenbaum, Kleshchelski, and Rebelo, 2010). In addition, for more than 90 percent of the countries, we use the discount rate, rather than a short-term or market interest rate.

[8]See Hnatkovska, Lahiri, and Vegh (2008) for a formal model of interest rate defense of the domestic currency in small open economies.

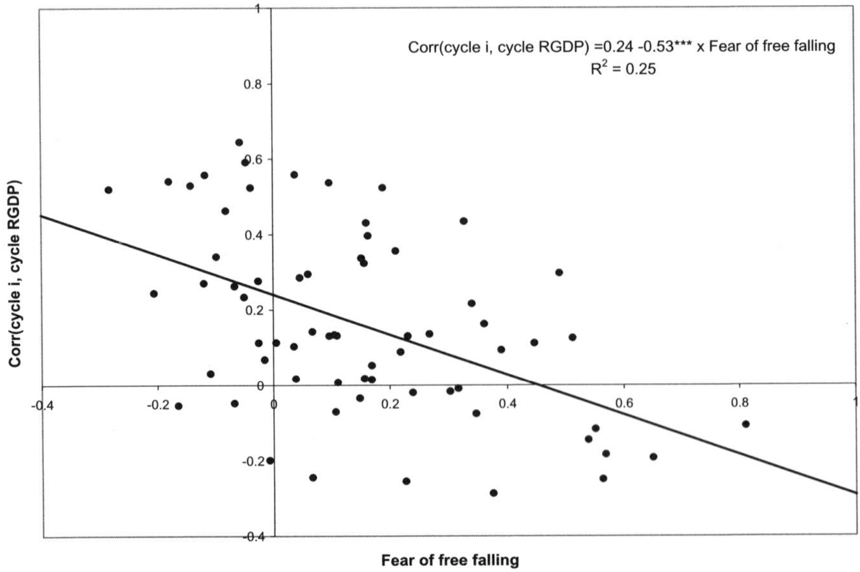

Figure 9. Country Correlations between the Cyclical Components of Short-Term Interest Rate and Real GDP vs. Fear of Free Falling, 1960–2009.

Note: Sample of 66 industrial and developing countries.

Source: World Economic Outlook (IMF), International Financial Statistics (IMF), and Global Financial Data.

the average of four normalized variables from the International Country Risk Guide dataset:

- Investment profile: Factors affecting investment risk that are not covered by other political, economic, and financial risk components. The risk rating assigned is the sum of three subcomponents: contract viability/expropriation, profits repatriation, and payment delays.
- Corruption: Measures corruption within the political system.
- Law and order: Assesses the strength and impartiality of the legal system and the popular observance of the law.
- Bureaucratic quality: Assesses the ability and expertise to govern without drastic changes in policy or interruptions in government services.

The IQ index ranges from 0 (lowest institutional quality) to 1 (highest institutional quality). Figure 10 shows that higher (lower) IQ is associated with lower (higher) FFF. Moreover, Figure 11 shows that in developing

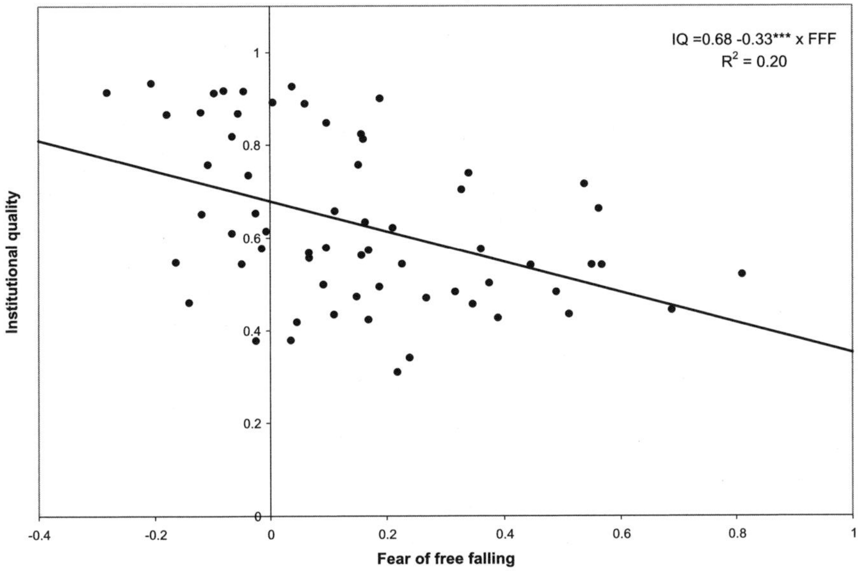

Figure 10. Fear of Free Falling (1960–2009) vs. Institutional Quality (1984–2008).

Note: Sample of 64 industrial and developing countries.

Source: World Economic Outlook (IMF) and International Country Risk Guide (ICRG).

countries, FFF diminishes over time as countercyclicality of monetary policies increases.

Although it is tempting to think of capital flight and FFF as chronic scourges in developing countries, they can change over time. Figure 12 provides some examples of the within-country relation between FFF and cyclicality of monetary policy by plotting, for three different countries, the 20- or 15-year rolling window associated correlations. Panel A shows the case of the United Kingdom, an "established graduate." FFF levels have been consistently around zero and monetary policy has always been countercyclical. At the other extreme, Panel B shows the case of Uruguay, a "still in school" country. FFF levels have ranged between 0.4 and 0.9 and monetary policy has been consistently procyclical. Panel C shows the case of Chile, a "recent graduate." Remarkably, the FFF decreased from values close to 0.9 in the early 1980s to about zero in the late 2000s. In line with our arguments, monetary policy shifted from being strongly procyclical — with values close to Uruguay's — to countercyclical.

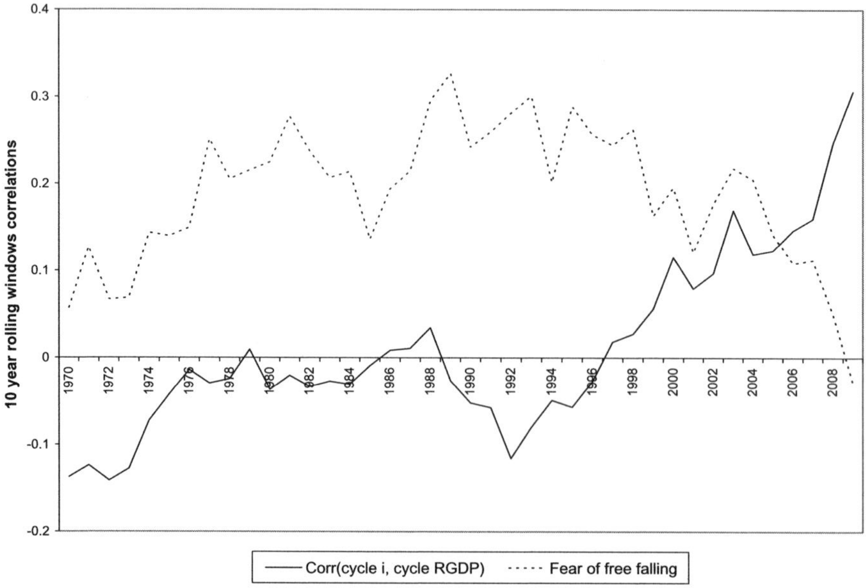

Figure 11. Average Country Correlations between the Cyclical Components of Short-Term Interest Rate and Real GDP vs. Fear of Free Falling (Developing Countries).

Note: Sample of 47 developing countries.

Source: World Economic Outlook (IMF), International Financial Statistics (IMF), and Global Financial Data.

4. Graduation and "Fear of Free Falling" — Regression Analysis

This section uses panel data regressions to exploit the within-country variability as opposed to the cross-section analysis underlying Figure 9. First, we estimate expanded Taylor rules for developing countries (Corbo, 2000; Moron and Winkelried, 2005):

$$i_{it}^c = \alpha + \beta \cdot y_{it}^c + \delta \cdot \pi_{it}^c + \lambda \cdot e_{it}^c + \eta_i + \mu_{it}, \tag{1}$$

where i_{it}^c, y_{it}^c, π_{it}^c, and e_{it}^c are the cyclical components of the short-term interest rate, real GDP, inflation, and exchange rate depreciation, respectively, and η_i is a country fixed-effect. In addition, we will interact FFF with the output cycle to evaluate whether the FFF alters the way in which monetary

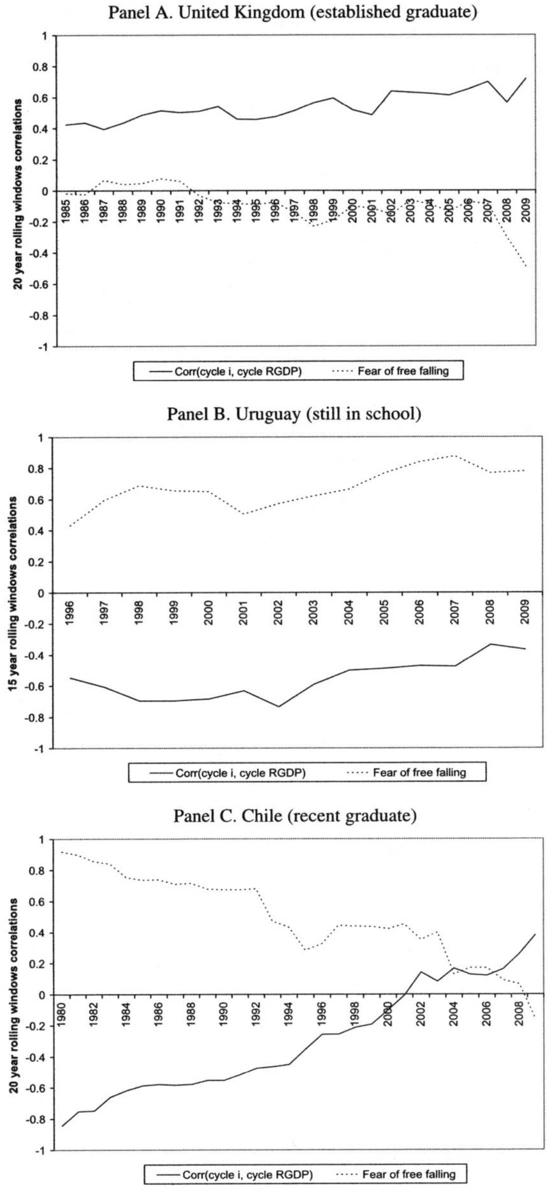

Figure 12. Graduation Examples: Country Correlations between the Cyclical Components of Short-Term Interest Rate and Real GDP vs. Fear of Free Falling.

Source: World Economic Outlook (IMF), International Financial Statistics (IMF), and Global Financial Data.

policy responds to business cycle fluctuations.[9] Specifically, we estimate:

$$i_{it}^{c} = \alpha + \beta \cdot y_{it}^{c} + \delta \cdot \pi_{it}^{c} + \lambda \cdot e_{it}^{c} + \gamma \cdot (FFF_{it} \times y_{it}^{c}) + \phi \cdot FFF_{it} + \eta_i + \mu_{it}. \tag{2}$$

In line with our findings from Figure 9, we expect γ to be negative. This would confirm that interest rates respond more countercyclically as FFF diminishes.

Table 1 shows all panel country-fixed-effects regressions. Columns 1, 2, and 3 estimate the effect of each regressor in regression (1) one at a time. Panel A shows the results for all countries in the sample, which support Taylor rules implications. In particular, column 1 shows that during good (bad) times, the interest rate increases (decreases), indicating that monetary policy is countercyclical. Columns 2 and 3 support the notion that the interest rate is positively related to inflation and depreciation shocks.

In line with our earlier correlation-based analysis, monetary policy is countercyclical in industrial economies (Panel B, column 1) and seems to be acyclical in developing countries (Panel C, column 1). These results continue to hold when we include macroeconomic determinants of interest rate policy two at a time or all together (columns 4–7).

Columns 8–10 estimate different versions of regression (2); column 8 excludes e_{it}^{c}, column 9 leaves π_{it}^{c} off, and column 10 includes all regressors. In all cases, the interaction term γ has a negative sign, as expected. However, it is not statistically significant for industrial countries, supporting the idea that FFF is not an important issue in those cases. In sharp contrast, FFF appears to be critical for developing countries. First, the interaction term between FFF and real GDP cycle is negative, which gives empirical support to the arguments laid out in the previous section. Second, including FFF makes it possible to recover the Taylor rule prediction between monetary policy and business cycle. Indeed, as shown in Panel C, columns 8, 9, and 10, once FFF is included, the coefficient on RGDP cycle becomes positive.

We thus conclude from the empirical analysis that, when FFF is not an issue, monetary policy is countercyclical because the traditional monetary policy reaction dominates. However, as FFF increases, policymakers' concerns regarding sharp depreciations during recessions become more relevant. Eventually, for high levels of FFF, this new suggested channel dominates the traditional one and monetary policy becomes procyclical.

---

[9]FFF is constructed using the 10-year rolling window correlation between the cyclical components of the short-term interest rate and the rate of depreciation of the exchange rate.

Table 1. Panel Regressions. Dependent Variable is the Cyclical Component of Short-Term Interest Rate.

Panel A. All countries	(1)	(2)	(3)	(4)	(5)	(6)	(7)	(8)	(9)	(10)
RGDP cycle	0.48***			0.47***	0.49***		0.47***	1.63***	1.63***	1.66***
	[2.8]			[2.7]	[2.8]		[2.7]	[5.6]	[5.5]	[5.6]
Inflation cycle		0.04***		0.04***		0.04***	0.04***	0.04***		0.04***
		[6.4]		[6.3]		[6.2]	[6.1]	[5.2]		[5.0]
Exchange rate depreciation cycle			0.41**		0.42**	0.29*	0.30*		0.42**	0.33*
			[2.3]		[2.4]	[1.7]	[1.7]		[2.2]	[1.8]
RGDP cycle * Fear of free falling								−3.01***	−3.02***	−3.05***
								[−4.0]	[−4.0]	[−4.1]
Number of observations	2732	2718	2769	2681	2705	2702	2669	2037	2037	2037
Number of countries	68	68	68	68	68	68	68	67	67	67

(Continued)

Table 1. (*Continued*)

Panel B. Industrial countries	(1)	(2)	(3)	(4)	(5)	(6)	(7)	(8)	(9)	(10)
RGDP cycle	5.38***			5.37***	5.67***		5.59***	5.73***	6.01***	5.92***
	[12.3]			[12.0]	[12.8]		[12.4]	[11.1]	[11.7]	[11.4]
Inflation cycle		0.03***		0.01		0.03***	0.01	0.01		0.01
		[2.9]		[1.6]		[2.9]	[1.5]	[1.2]		[1.2]
Exchange rate depreciation cycle			12.20		25.51***	12.55	25.80***		26.60***	26.37***
			[1.5]		[3.3]	[1.5]	[3.3]		[3.1]	[3.1]
RGDP cycle ∗ Fear of free falling								−1.76	−2.06	−2.12
								[−1.3]	[−1.5]	[−1.5]
Number of observations	874	878	893	858	856	871	851	705	705	705
Number of countries	21	21	21	21	21	21	21	21	21	21

(*Continued*)

Table 1. ***(Continued)***

Panel C. Developing countries	(1)	(2)	(3)	(4)	(5)	(6)	(7)	(8)	(9)	(10)
RGDP cycle	0.13			0.13	0.14		0.14	0.95***	0.89**	0.98***
	[0.6]			[0.7]	[0.7]		[0.7]	[2.6]	[2.4]	[2.7]
Inflation cycle		0.05***		0.05***		0.04***	0.04***	0.04***		0.04***
		[5.6]		[5.5]		[5.4]	[5.3]	[4.4]		[4.2]
Exchange rate depreciation cycle			0.40**		0.41**	0.28	0.28		0.39*	0.29
			[2.1]		[2.1]	[1.4]	[1.4]		[1.9]	[1.4]
RGDP cycle ∗ Fear of free falling								−2.26**	−2.22**	−2.30**
								[−2.4]	[−2.4]	[−2.5]
Number of observations	1858	1840	1876	1823	1849	1831	1818	1332	1332	1332
Number of countries	47	47	47	47	47	47	47	46	46	46

Notes: Estimations are performed using country fixed-effects. t-statistics are in square brackets. Constant and fear of free falling terms are not reported. *, ** and *** indicate statistically significant at the 10%, 5% and 1% levels, respectively. Fear of free falling is constructed using the 10-year rolling window correlation between the percentage change of a short-term interest rate and the percentage change of the rate of depreciation.

5. Conclusions

We have documented the fact that over the last decade, more than a third of developing countries have graduated from monetary policy procyclicality and become countercyclical. We have argued that a critical factor in achieving this important policy shift has been overcoming the fear of free falling; that is, the need to defend a rapidly depreciating currency in bad times. This frees the policy rate for countercyclical purposes.

References

Akram, Q. Farooq, Dagfinn Rime, and Lucio Sarno, 2008, "Arbitrage in the foreign exchange market: Turning on the microscope," *Journal of International Economics*, Vol. 76, pp. 237–253.

Alesina, Alberto and Guido Tabellini, 1990, "A positive theory of fiscal deficits and government debt," *Review of Economic Studies*, Vol. 57, pp. 403–414.

Burnside, Craig, Martin Eichenbaum, Isaac Kleshchelski, and Sergio Rebelo, 2010, "Carry trade and momentum in currency markets," Duke University and Northwestern University, mimeo.

Calvo, Guillermo A., 1998, "Capital flows and capital-market crises: The simple economics of sudden stops," *Journal of Applied Economics*, Vol. 1, November, pp. 35–54.

Calvo, Guillermo A. and Carlos A. Vegh, 1995, "Fighting inflation with high interest rates: The small open economy case under flexible prices," *Journal of Money, Credit and Banking*, Vol. 27, pp. 49–66.

Chinn, Menzie and Guy Meredith, 2004, "Monetary policy and long-horizon uncovered interest parity," *IMF Staff Papers*, Vol. 51, No. 3, pp. 409–430.

Corbo, Vittorio, 2000, "Monetary policy in Latin America," Central Bank of Chile, working paper, No. 78.

Fischer, Stanley, 1998, "The IMF and the Asian crisis," available at www.imf.org/external/np/speeches/1998/032098.HTM.

Flood, Robert and Olivier Jeanne, 2005, "An interest rate defense of a fixed exchange rate?," *Journal of International Economics*, Vol. 66, pp. 471–484.

Frankel, Jeffrey, 1991, "Quantifying international capital mobility in the 1980s," in *National Saving and Economic Performance*, Chicago: University of Chicago Press.

Frankel, Jeffrey, 2011, "A solution to fiscal procyclicality: The structural budget institutions pioneered by Chile," in *Fiscal Policy and Macroeconomic Performance*, Luis Felipe Céspedes and Jordi Galí (eds.), forthcoming. Also available as NBER, working paper, No. 16945.

Frankel, Jeffrey A., Carlos A. Vegh, and Guillermo Vuletin, 2011, "On graduation from fiscal procyclicality," NBER, working paper, No. 17619.

Gavin, Michael and Roberto Perotti, 1997, "Fiscal policy in Latin America," *NBER Macroeconomics Annual*, Vol. 12, pp. 11–61.

Hnatkovska, Viktoria, Amartya Lahiri, and Carlos Vegh, 2008, "Interest rates and the exchange rate: A non-monotonic tale," NBER, working paper, No. 13925.

Ilzetzki, Ethan, 2011, "Rent-seeking distortions and fiscal procyclicality," *Journal of Development Economics*, Vol. 96, pp. 30–46.

Kaminsky, Graciela, Carmen M. Reinhart, and Carlos A. Vegh, 2004, "When it rains, it pours: Procyclical capital flows and macroeconomic policies," *NBER Macroeconomics Annual*, Vol. 19, pp. 11–82.

Mishkin, Frederic, 1984, "Are real interest rates equal across countries? An empirical investigation of international parity conditions," *Journal of Finance*, Vol. 39, pp. 1345–1357.

Moron, Eduardo and Diego Winkelried, 2005, "Monetary policy rules for financially vulnerable economies," *Journal of Development Economics*, Vol. 76, pp. 23–51.

Reinhart, Carmen M. and Kenneth Rogoff, 2004, "The modern history of exchange rate arrangements: A reinterpretation," *Quarterly Journal of Economics*, Vol. 119, pp. 1–48.

Riascos, Alvaro and Carlos A. Vegh, 2003, "Procyclical government spending in developing countries: The role of capital market imperfections," UCLA and Banco Republica, Colombia, mimeo.

Talvi, Ernesto and Carlos A. Vegh, 2005, "Tax base variability and procyclicality of fiscal policy," *Journal of Development Economics*, Vol. 78, No. 1, pp. 156–190.

Vegh, Carlos A. and Guillermo Vuletin, 2011, "How is tax policy conducted over the business cycle?," University of Maryland and Colby College, mimeo.

Appendix 1. Definition of Variables and Sources

Gross Domestic Product

World Economic Outlook (WEO-IMF) and International Financial Statistics (IFS-IMF) were the main data sources. Series NGDP (gross domestic product, current prices) for WEO and 99B for IFS-IMF. For Azerbaijan, Bahrain, Kuwait, Libya, Qatar, and United Arab Emirates, data were provided by Middle East Department at the IMF. Data period covers 1960–2009.

GDP deflator

World Economic Outlook (WEO-IMF) and International Financial Statistics (IFS-IMF) were the main data sources. Series NGDP_D (gross domestic product deflator) for WEO-IMF and 99BIP for IFS-IMF. For Azerbaijan, Bahrain, Kuwait, Libya, Qatar, and United Arab Emirates, data were provided by Middle East Department at the IMF. Data period covers 1960–2009.

Consumer price index

World Economic Outlook (WEO-IMF) and International Financial Statistics (IFS-IMF) were the main data sources. Series PCPI (consumer price index) for WEO-IMF and 64 for IFS-IMF. For Azerbaijan and Kuwait, data were taken from Global Financial Data (GFD). Data period covers 1960–2009.

Short-term interest rate

Global Financial Data was the main data source. For the following countries, the short-term interest rate used is the discount window interest rate: Algeria, Argentina, Austria, Bangladesh, Barbados, Belgium, Bolivia, Botswana, Brazil, Bulgaria, Canada, Chile, China, Colombia, Costa Rica, Cyprus, Czech Rep., Denmark, Egypt, Fiji, Finland, France, Gambia, Germany, Ghana, Greece, India, Ireland, Israel, Italy, Japan, Jordan, Kenya, Korea, Kuwait, Malaysia, Mauritius, Mexico, Morocco, Nepal, Netherlands, Nigeria, Norway, Pakistan, Paraguay, Peru, Philippines, Portugal, Rwanda, South Africa, Spain, Sri Lanka, Swaziland, Switzerland, Tanzania, Trinidad and Tobago, Tunisia, Turkey, Uganda, United States, Uruguay, Venezuela, and Zambia. For Australia we used the Australia Reserve Bank overnight cash rate. For New Zealand we used the New Zealand Reserve Bank official cash rate. For Sweden we used the Sweden Riksbank repo rate. For Thailand we used the discount window as well as the repo rate. For the United Kingdom we used the Bank of England base lending rate. Data period covers 1960–2009.

Official exchange rate

World Economic Outlook (WEO-IMF) was the main data source. Series ENDA (exchange rate, national currency per U.S. Dollar). For the United States we used the Dollar per Euro exchange rate. Data period covers 1960–2009.

Institutional quality

International Country Risk Guide (ICRG) was the source of data. Institutional quality is a normalized index that ranges between 0 (lowest institutional quality) and 1 (highest institutional quality). The index was calculated by the authors as the average of four components: investment profile, corruption, law and order, and bureaucracy quality. Data period covers 1984–2008.

Appendix 2. Countries in the Sample

Industrial countries (21)	Developing countries (47)	
Australia	Algeria	Kuwait
Austria	Argentina	Malaysia
Belgium	Bangladesh	Mauritius
Canada	Barbados	Mexico
Denmark	Bolivia	Morocco
Finland	Botswana	Nepal
France	Brazil	Nigeria
Germany	Bulgaria	Pakistan
Greece	Chile	Paraguay
Ireland	China	Peru
Italy	Colombia	Philippines
Japan	Costa Rica	Rwanda
Netherlands	Cyprus	South Africa
New Zealand	Czech Rep.	Sri Lanka
Norway	Egypt	Swaziland
Portugal	Fiji	Tanzania
Spain	Gambia	Thailand
Sweden	Ghana	Trinidad and Tobago
Switzerland	India	Tunisia
United Kingdom	Israel	Turkey
United States	Jordan	Uganda
	Kenya	Uruguay
	Korea	Venezuela
		Zambia

Note: Total number of countries is 68.

Appendix 3. Data on Cyclicality of Monetary Policy, Fear of Free Falling, and Institutional Quality

		Country correlation between the cyclical components of the central bank interest rate and real GDP			Fear of free falling	Institutional quality
Country	Graduating class	Average 1960–2009	Average 1960–1999	Average 2000–2009	Average 1960–2009	Average 1984–2008
Algeria	SS	−0.08	−0.07	−0.13	0.35	0.46
Argentina	EG	0.23	0.05	0.61	−0.05	0.54
Bangladesh	EG	0.09	0.01	0.55	0.22	0.31
Bolivia	RG	0.10	−0.08	0.62	0.04	0.38
Botswana	RG	0.01	−0.18	0.86	0.11	0.66
Brazil	BS	0.11	0.14	−0.09	0.45	0.54
Bulgaria	EG	−0.05	0.04	0.29	−0.07	0.61
Chile	RG	−0.25	−0.46	0.81	0.56	0.66
China	BS	0.14	0.28	−0.41	0.07	0.56
Colombia	EG	0.53	0.42	0.77	−0.14	0.46
Costa Rica	SS	−0.20	−0.16	−0.43	−0.01	0.61
Cyprus	EG	0.03	0.02	0.30	−0.11	0.76
Czech Rep.	EG	0.52	0.29	0.74	−0.04	0.74
Egypt	RG	−0.01	−0.08	0.39	0.32	0.48
Fiji	BS	0.02	0.07	−0.43	0.04	
Gambia	SS	−0.25	−0.32	−0.37	0.23	0.54
Ghana	EG	0.14	0.14	0.35	0.27	0.47
India	RG	−0.24	−0.31	0.53	0.07	0.57
Israel	RG	−0.14	−0.23	0.00	0.54	0.72
Jordan	RG	0.02	−0.18	0.64	0.16	0.56
Kenya	RG	−0.11	−0.12	0.01	0.81	0.52
Korea	EG	0.28	0.24	0.59	−0.03	0.65
Kuwait	RG	0.05	−0.17	0.58	0.17	0.57
Malaysia	EG	0.40	0.37	0.52	0.16	0.63
Mauritius	RG	−0.07	−0.12	0.01	0.11	
Mexico	RG	−0.18	−0.43	0.59	0.56	0.54
Morocco	BS	0.16	0.21	−0.24	0.36	0.58
Nepal	EG	0.13	0.13	0.17	0.11	
Nigeria	SS	−0.02	−0.01	−0.15	0.24	0.34
Pakistan	EG	0.29	0.22	0.44	0.05	0.42
Paraguay	EG	0.11	0.23	0.14	−0.03	0.38
Peru	EG	0.13	0.11	0.62	0.11	0.43
Philippines	EG	0.13	0.04	0.57	0.51	0.44
Rwanda	SS	−0.02	−0.01	−0.30	0.30	
South Africa	EG	0.36	0.28	0.75	0.21	0.62

(*Continued*)

(*Continued*)

		Country correlation between the cyclical components of the central bank interest rate and real GDP			Fear of free falling	Institutional quality
Country	Graduating class	Average 1960–2009	Average 1960–1999	Average 2000–2009	Average 1960–2009	Average 1984–2008
Sri Lanka	EG	0.30	0.02	0.79	0.49	0.48
Swaziland	BS	0.13	0.18	−0.70	0.23	
Tanzania	RG	−0.03	−0.11	0.52	0.15	0.47
Thailand	EG	0.13	0.02	0.43	0.10	0.58
Trinidad and Tobago	RG	0.07	−0.23	0.40	−0.01	0.58
Tunisia	RG	−0.05	−0.09	0.24	−0.16	0.55
Turkey	RG	−0.12	−0.26	0.15	0.55	0.54
Uganda	RG	0.01	−0.04	0.28	0.17	0.42
Uruguay	SS	−0.29	−0.57	−0.36	0.37	0.50
Venezuela	RG	−0.19	−0.36	0.28	0.65	0.44
Zambia	EG	0.09	0.09	0.66	0.39	0.43

Notes: The abbreviations EG, SS, RG, and BS stand for established graduate, still in school, recent graduate, and back to school graduating classes, respectively.

Can We Identify the Financial Cycle?

Mathias Drehmann, Claudio Borio, and Kostas Tsatsaronis*
Bank for International Settlements

1. Introduction

The financial crisis exposed important gaps in macroeconomics. The dominant pre-crisis paradigms viewed finance largely as a side-show for macroeconomic fluctuations. Models rarely included financial variables beyond interest rates. And even strands of the literature that captured richer elements of the interactions between finance and the real economy, such as the role of collateral, fell way short of replicating the strength and occasional virulence of the processes at work. After all, they could not account for financial crises. Since then, a rapidly growing literature has been seeking to incorporate financial sectors into dynamic equilibrium models. But regardless of specifics, any future work requires a better understanding of the stylized empirical regularities of the "financial cycle," with its booms and busts possibly leading to serious financial and macroeconomic strains. This renewed interest notwithstanding, the meaning and characterization of the financial cycle remains elusive.

This paper is a contribution to the budding literature that seeks to characterize the financial cycle. Some of this work has shed only indirect light on the question. It has done so in various ways: by documenting empirically the behavior of the relationship between credit, asset prices, and real economic activity, e.g., Borio *et al.* (1994), Detken and Smets (2004), Schularick and Taylor (2009); in the process of developing leading indicators of financial distress, e.g., Borio and Lowe (2002), Alessi and Detken (2009); and by

* Mathias Drehmann is a senior economist at the Bank for International Settlements (BIS), and Claudio Borio and Kostas Tsatsaronis are also affiliated with BIS. The authors would like to thank Michela Scatigna for her excellent research assistance. The views expressed in this paper are their own and do not necessarily reflect those of the Bank for International Settlements or the Basel Committee on Banking Supervision.

examining the forecasting properties for economic activity of various financial indicators beyond interest rates, e.g., English *et al.* (2005),[1] Borio and Lowe (2004).

More recently, other work has addressed the issue head-on. In particular, Claessens *et al.* (2011a,b) employ classical cycle dating methods ("turning-point analysis") for a large number of countries to identify peaks and troughs in credit, property prices, and equity prices — the three series that they classify as financial-cycle series. They find that cycles in these series considered individually tend to be long and severe, that the cyclical behavior of credit and house prices is highly synchronized, and that there is a strong relationship between the financial and the business cycle. For their part, Aikman *et al.* (2010) rely on frequency-based filters to document the relationship between the credit cycle and the business cycle. They find that there is a distinct credit cycle, whose length and amplitude exceed those of the business cycle, and that credit booms are strongly related to banking crises.

Our study complements and extends this line of enquiry in several ways. We combine the two analytical approaches — turning-point and frequency-based filter analysis — to draw sharper and more robust conclusions; we look not only at individual series but also at combinations of variables, so as to identify a proxy that captures more fully the "financial cycle." We compare short-term with medium-term cycles. Finally, we begin to explore the relationship between the financial cycle, on the one hand, and financial and monetary regimes, on the other. Our analysis covers six countries and the period 1960–2011. We highlight the following findings.

First, the turning-point and frequency-based filter analysis provide a remarkably consistent message, allowing us to identify a distinct "financial cycle." The variables that *jointly* best characterize the financial cycle are credit and property prices. By contrast, equity prices have shorter cycles and exhibit less concordance with the other variables. More importantly, typical business cycle frequencies (up to eight years) are *too short* to characterize financial cycles associated with serious economic disruptions: The average length of the medium-term financial cycle is 15 years.

Second, the financial cycle, so defined, is very closely related to financial crises. *All* the financial crises with domestic origins (i.e., those not

[1]There is a large literature following Bernanke and Boivin (2003) that takes account of financial variables to develop forecasts for variables of interest to monetary policymakers. English *et al.* (2005) use the same techniques.

arising from losses on cross-border exposures) occur at, or close to, the *peak* of the financial cycle. Conversely, most peaks of the financial cycle coincide with financial crises. In fact, there are only three instances post-1985 where the peak is not close to a crisis date, and these correspond to periods when the financial system came under considerable stress (Germany in the early 2000s, Australia and Norway in 2008–2009).

Third, our evidence is consistent with the view that the amplitude, length, and disruptive force of the financial cycle is closely related to the financial, and possibly also monetary, regimes in place (e.g., Borio and Lowe, 2002). Since 1985 — a rough proxy for financial liberalization and, to a lesser extent, for the establishment of credible anti-inflation regimes — the length and amplitude of the financial cycle has increased. The length has doubled (approximately from ten to 20 years). Similarly, the relationship with financial crises has become tighter following financial liberalization.

Finally, we draw attention to what we call the "unfinished recession" phenomenon. This refers to episodes in which policy responses that fail to take medium-term financial cycles into account can contain recessions in the short-run but at the cost of larger recessions down the road. In these cases, authorities may focus too much on equity prices and standard business cycle measures and lose sight of the continued build-up of the medium-term financial cycle, characterized by further increases in the ratio of credit to GDP and in property prices. The bust that follows an unchecked financial boom brings about large economic disruptions.

The rest of the paper is organized as follows. Section 2 describes the data and methodologies. Section 3 presents the results for individual series. Section 4 develops the multivariate analysis, thereby identifying the financial cycle, and considers its relationship with financial crises. Section 5 explores the link of the financial cycle with policy regimes and illustrates the "unfinished recession" phenomenon. Section 6 concludes.

2. Data and Methodology

We analyze the behavior of six variables for seven countries (Australia, Germany, Japan, Norway, Sweden, the United Kingdom, and the United States) over the period 1960–2011 with quarterly data. We select the variables and countries based on relevance and availability. Following common practice, we take GDP as the representative variable for the business cycle.

The financial cycle has been far less researched and is less well-defined than the business cycle. Therefore, in the style of Burns and Mitchell (1946), we look at a number of series to characterize it. This choice of variables is not obvious, but it is hard to imagine that one could do without credit and asset prices (e.g., Kindleberger, 2000; Minsky, 1982). We thus consider five financial variables: (i) credit to the private, non-financial sector; (ii) the ratio of credit to GDP; (iii) equity prices; (iv) residential property prices; and (v) an index of aggregate asset prices, which combines residential property, commercial property, and equity prices (Borio *et al.*, 1994).[2]

Given our focus on longer cycles, we require that variables be available for at least 40 years. This rules out a number of other financial variables that are obvious candidates for inclusion: measures of credit risk assessments, such as spreads between high- and low-risk debt, measures of performance of financial firms (e.g., profits, write-offs, non-performing loans), default rates, and measures of leverage.

All series are in real terms (deflated by CPI) and in logs. The only exception is the credit-to-GDP ratio that is expressed in percentage points. All series are normalized by their respective value in 1985Q1 to ensure comparability of the units.

Our sample includes 11 banking crises (henceforth referred to also as "financial crises"). We follow the dating of crises in Laeven and Valencia (2008 and 2010) and Reinhart and Rogoff (2009). In addition, we use judgment and draw on correspondence with central banks to determine some of the dates.

2.1 *Frequency-based filter analysis*

Historically, the study of the business cycle has focused on the behavior of macroeconomic data with cycles lasting between one and eight years. In our study, we want to focus on two types of cyclical patterns, namely those that have the same periodicity as the business cycle and those that have considerably longer ones.

Our first approach to identify cycles is in the spirit of Comin and Gertler (2006), who study the behavior of medium-term macroeconomic cycles for the U.S. economy. Similarly to their work, we employ a band-pass filter

[2]Ideally, the credit to the private, non-financial sector should cover credit from all sources, but a reliable long-run series is only available for the United States. For all other countries, therefore, we use bank credit. This is not a significant shortcut, however, as other countries have much more bank-centric financial systems.

to isolate short-term cycles, with frequencies between five and 32 quarters (the typical business-cycle frequency-band), and medium-term cycles, with frequencies between eight and 30 years (or 32 and 120 quarters).[3]

We use the band-pass filter suggested by Christiano and Fitzgerald (2003) to isolate the component of each series that corresponds to a particular frequency of fluctuation. We filter the data in annual growth rates (i.e., fourth-order differences of log-levels). To facilitate comparison with the turning-point analysis, we then convert the resulting series into log-levels, by cumulating growth rates from zero, starting at the beginning of the observation period.[4]

2.2 *Turning-point analysis*

The second approach we use seeks to identify cyclical peaks and troughs in the series and was originally proposed by Burns and Mitchell (1946) to date the business cycle. Bry and Boschan (1971) provided a computerized algorithm for monthly series, which was extended to quarterly series by Harding and Pagan (2002). The algorithm involves two key steps: (1) identifying local maxima and minima over a specific window; and (2) imposing censoring rules, so as to guarantee a minimum length of the cycle (i.e., the distance between two consecutive peaks or troughs) as well as a minimum length of each phase (i.e., from peak to trough or trough to peak). In addition, the algorithm requires peaks and troughs to alternate and a trough (peak) to be lower (higher) than the preceding peak (trough).

We employ two different calibrations of the algorithm. For the shorter (business-cycle) horizon, we follow the suggestions of Harding and Pagan (2002). We define local maxima (minima) at time t if the value of the series is the highest (lowest) within the five-quarter window centered at t. We require that cycles have a minimum length of five quarters and that each phase (expansion or contraction) is at least two quarters long. We label this the short-term (ST) algorithm.

---

[3]The choice of 30 years as an upper bound is partly dictated by data availability. It is technically impossible to estimate cycles that have a frequency longer than the span of the available data. Given that some series start after 1960 and a few as late as 1970, we choose to examine cycles that are up to 30 years long. This also insures that the medium-term cyclical components do not include long-term secular trends.

[4]Given that we focus on the cyclical patterns — rather than the exact level — of the filtered series, the starting level is of minor importance, as this amounts to a shift parameter.

To capture cycles that are longer than those typically considered in business cycle analysis, we also implement what we call the medium-term (MT) algorithm. This requires that local maxima and minima occur within a nine-quarter window, and that the minimum cycle length is 40 quarters. Arguably, five years are still at the low-end for a medium-term cycle, but, if anything, the choice biases the methodology toward identifying shorter rather than longer cycles.[5]

We implement both methods as mechanical computer algorithms. This approach identifies the vast majority of peaks and troughs. That said, some manual cross-checking is also necessary.

3. Characterizing Cycles in Individual Series

In this section we compare the behavior of the short- and medium-term cycles in individual variables. We discuss sequentially the results of the frequency-based filter and turning-point methods. We also explore the relationship between the resulting medium-term cycles and financial crises. The messages from this analysis will inform our choices in building a measure of the financial cycle in Section 4.

3.1 *Frequency-based filter analysis: Short-term and medium-term cycles*

Table 1 reports the ratio of the volatility (standard deviation) of the medium-term cyclical component to the short-term cyclical component for the six series across countries. A ratio higher than unity means that the medium-term component is more volatile (i.e., has greater amplitude) than the short-term one. As the two components are independent of each other, the ratio can also be interpreted as their relative weight in accounting for the dynamics of each variable.

We observe that in all cases, the volatility of the medium-term cyclical component exceeds that of the shorter-term one. The cycles of frequencies between eight and 30 years are more important in shaping the behavior of these series than those with shorter duration. This confirms and extends the finding of Comin and Gertler (2006) for U.S. real variables.

---

[5]Extending the minimum length to eight years for the medium-term cycle would only *strengthen* our results while still identifying all the main peaks and troughs associated with crises.

Table 1. Relative Volatility of Short- and Medium-Term Cycles.[1]

	AU	DE	GB	JP	NO	SE	U.S.
Credit	**4.52**	**1.80**	**3.73**	**4.34**	**6.28**	**6.78**	**3.87**
Credit/GDP	**7.36**	**2.83**	**5.28**	**3.39**	**4.99**	**5.98**	**4.92**
EQ	1.72	1.40	1.77	2.14	1.30	1.42	1.41
AAP	1.95	**3.94**	**2.56**	**3.36**	1.60	1.48	**1.75**
HP	1.75	**2.19**	**2.42**	3.05	2.21	**4.91**	**3.91**
GDP	3.25	1.73	1.93	3.06	2.55	1.84	1.51

[1]The figures refer to the ratio of the standard deviation of the medium-term cyclical component to that of the short-term component over the entire sample period. A number greater (smaller) than 1.0 means that the medium-term cyclical component is more (less) volatile than the short-term component. Cells shown in bold denote cases where the ratio of medium- to short-term component volatility for the corresponding series is higher than the corresponding ratio for GDP. Acronyms used here and in subsequent tables and graphs: AU = Australia; DE = Germany; GB = United Kingdom; JP = Japan; NO = Norway; SE = Sweden; U.S. = United States. EQ = Equity prices index; AAP = Aggregate asset price index; HP = House price index.

This pattern is more pronounced for most financial variables. Their medium-term volatility is in many cases much higher than that of the short-term component, often by a factor of two or greater. Moreover, for some financial-cycle variables, the ratio exceeds that for GDP (entries shown in bold). This is the case for all countries for the two credit variables (credit and the credit-to-GDP ratio). The pattern is not as strong for asset prices. Importantly, the ratio for equity prices is never larger than that for GDP. But in four out of seven countries, the ratio for house prices and aggregate asset prices exceeds that for GDP.

Was the amplitude of the medium-term cycle affected by structural changes in the regulatory financial framework over the period 1960–2011? In a rough attempt to capture the financial liberalization wave, we split the period into two halves (pre-1985 and post-1985). Table 2 presents the ratio of the volatility of the medium-term component during the post-1985 period to its volatility during the first half of the period.

For many financial variables, volatility has increased following financial liberalization. For all countries except Japan, the medium-term cyclical component of the credit and the residential price series increased in the

Table 2. Relative Volatility of Medium-Term Financial Cycles Pre- and Post-1985.[1]

	AU	DE	GB	JP	NO	SE	U.S.
Credit	**2.75**	**1.53**	**1.49**	0.85	**2.09**	**1.12**	**2.66**
Credit/GDP	**5.86**	**2.27**	**3.88**	0.99	**2.05**	**1.26**	**4.91**
EQ	0.43	**1.14**	0.51	**1.45**	0.65	**1.36**	**1.78**
AAP	**2.97**	0.68	0.48	0.56	**1.88**	**2.25**	**1.86**
HP	**2.27**	**1.16**	**1.94**	0.49	**1.90**	**1.04**	**3.96**
GDP	0.34	**1.14**	**1.26**	0.84	**1.25**	**2.16**	0.93

[1]For each variable, the figures refer to the ratio of the volatility of the medium-term cyclical component post-1985 to that of pre-1985. A number greater than 1.0 (shown in bold) means that the medium-term cyclical component of the corresponding series was more volatile in the post-1985 period than in the pre-1985 period.

post-1985 period. This is consistent with the fact that Japan never quite recovered from the financial bust in the early 1990s. The increased volatility post-1985 is weaker in the case of equity prices and the aggregate price index, for which this is evident only in four out of the seven countries.

The analysis of the changes in the ratio of the volatility of the medium- to short-term component over the two sub-periods paints a similar picture (Drehmann *et al.*, 2012). The relative weight of the medium-term cyclical component of credit and house prices increased by comparison to that of the shorter-term component in the post-1985 period.

3.2 *Turning-point analysis: Short-term and medium-term cycles*

By applying the turning-point dating algorithm, we obtain a set of peaks and troughs for each series. A subset of those turning points refers to the medium-term cycle of the series. Figure 1 illustrates the results of the algorithm for the case of the United States (the graphs for the other countries are shown in Drehmann *et al.*, 2012). Crosses denote the peaks and troughs of the short-term cycle, and diamonds denote those that are also turning points of the medium-term cycle. Shaded areas indicate NBER recessions, and vertical black lines the beginning of financial crises.

Looking at GDP (upper left-hand panel), our short-term dating algorithm captures NBER recessions well. In many cases, the dating of a peak

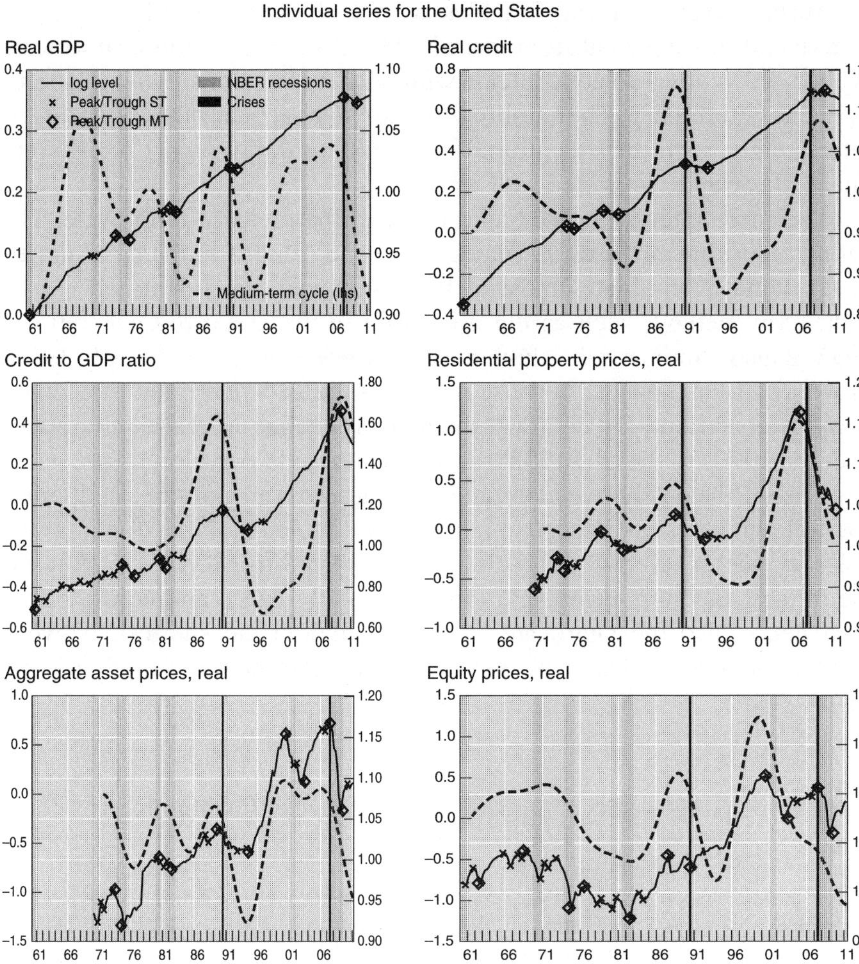

Figure 1. Peaks and Troughs of Short-Term and Medium-Term Cycles.

Note: Series are in log levels and normalized by their respective value in 1985Q1.

Sources: National data; OECD; IMF; BIS estimates; author's estimates.

and subsequent trough coincide exactly with the onset of a recession and the beginning of the recovery. A significant exception is the mild recession in the early 2000s: GDP just stagnated while the NBER recorded a recession because broader measures of macroeconomic activity pointed to a contraction.

Turning to the financial variables, we note that their short-term cyclical patterns differ somewhat from that of GDP. There are far more short-term cycles, which often do not coincide with NBER recessions. This is particularly true before 1985. The amplitude of the cycles appears also much larger. Interestingly, with the exception of real credit, turning points of different financial variables are often well-aligned.

The more interesting messages relate to the medium-term cycle. The dating algorithm captures *all* major peaks and troughs in the data (dotted lines) while it eliminates most of the short-lived ones identified by the short-term method, such as the mini drop in the credit-to-GDP ratio in 1996. It also eliminates the short-run equity price cycles in the early 1970s (lower right-hand panel), because it violates the five-year minimum length of cycle constraint. By contrast, the general decline in real equity prices over the 1970s to the early 1980s is still split into two cycles.

Casting the net more widely, and looking across all countries and series, the following results deserve highlighting (Table 3). First, for all variables, typical medium-term cycles last between 8 to 18 years. Credit has the longest medium-term cycle (around 15–18 years), and equity prices (and hence also the aggregate asset price index) the shortest, between eight and ten years. The cycle in GDP has an intermediate length, around 11–14 years.

Table 3. Characteristics of the Medium-Term Cycle: Turning-Point Method.

	Growth rate[1]		Amplitude[2]		Duration[3]		
Variable	Exp.	Contr.	Exp.	Contr.	Exp.	Contr.	Cycle
Credit	1.7	−1.1	156.5	−10.5	52	13	68
Credit/GDP	1.2	−1.0	42.9	−11.4	32	14	45
EQ	4.5	−5.4	160.1	−46.6	23	15	36
AAP	2.0	−1.5	59.3	−19.4	25	19	45
HP	2.3	−2.9	68.6	−26.3	24	14	38
GDP	0.9	−0.9	79.6	−3.8	53	5	56

Notes:
[1]Quarterly rate, in percent.
[2]Percentage change from trough to peak (expansion) or peak to trough (contraction).
[3]For expansions: trough to peak; for contractions: peak to trough; in quarters.

Second, in general, the contraction phase in the medium-term cycle is significantly shorter than the expansion. This is particularly pronounced for GDP. The typical contraction in GDP lasts only five quarters, whereas financial variables tend to contract for 2–3 years. Contractions in residential property prices are especially drawn out and typically last for around five years.

Third, the data also suggest that medium-term expansions in financial variables include periods of particularly strong growth. For variables that exhibit a relatively steady growth pattern, one can expect the product of the average quarterly growth rate times the average duration of each phase to roughly match the average amplitude. This is the case for GDP. By contrast, for all financial variables, this calculation underestimates the observed amplitudes during expansions.

Finally, post-1985 the length and amplitude of medium-term cycles have increased (tables are shown in Drehmann *et al.*, 2012). This pattern is particularly pronounced for residential property prices, for which cycles are on average twice as long (14 instead of seven years) and the trough-to-peak amplitude rises from 44 percent to 85 percent. The length of credit cycles effectively doubles, from around ten to nearly 20 years.[6] And some of the short-term cycles appear to be short-term reversals rather than full-blown cycles. In particular, short-term cycles that occur *between* turning points of the medium-term cycle are from 20 percent to 60 percent shorter than those for which peaks (or troughs) coincide with medium-term peaks (or troughs).

3.3 *What happens around financial crises?*

It is common to associate financial crises with the bust phase of financial cycles. In Tables 4a and 4b we examine the relationship between these crises and the peaks in the medium-term cycles identified by the two statistical methods. Table 4a refers to the peaks identified by the band-pass filter and Table 4b to those generated by the turning-point algorithm. All numbers are reported in quarters, with a negative (positive) number indicating that the peak in the series occurs prior to (after) the quarter in which the crisis begins.

[6] In the majority of countries, there are no short- or medium-term cycles in the first 10–15 years in credit or GDP as both variables expand continuously. Therefore, there are very few data points to measure the length of the cycle — in particular, from peak to peak — prior to 1985.

Table 4a. Financial Crises and Peaks in the Medium-Term Cycle: Frequency-Based Filters Individual Series.

	Crisis date	GDP	HP	Credit/GDP	Credit	EQ	AAP
AU	1989 Q4	−2	5	−1	−2	−4	−2
DE	2007 Q3	−29	—	12	−38	6	−38
GB	1973 Q4	3	4	−1	−1	−13	−9
	1990 Q2	−6	−3	3	−1	−9	−3
	2007 Q3	−7	0	11	9	−37	−3
JP	1992 Q4	−9	−6	−6	−7	−16	−10
NO	1990 Q4	−18	−10	−6	−9	−8	−31
SE	1991 Q3	−11	−5	−2	−3	−16	−8
	2008 Q3	−11	2	9	8	2	−34
U.S.	1990 Q4	−4	−7	−5	−5	−5	−6
	2007 Q3	−12	−2	6	5	−1	−7
Mean	*(excl DE)*	*−8*	*−2*	*1*	*−1*	*−11*	*−11*

Notes: The figures refer to the distance (in quarters) between a financial crisis date and the nearest peak in the medium-term cyclical component of the corresponding variable. Negative (positive) numbers indicate that the nearest peak precedes (follows) the crisis date.

Table 4b. Financial Crises and Peaks in the Medium-Term Cycle: Turning-Point Method Individual Series.

	Crisis date	GDP	HP	Credit/GDP	Credit	EQ	AAP
AU	1989 Q4	2	−3	5	3	−9	−3
DE	2007 Q3	2	−47	6	7	1	−1
GB	1973 Q4	−2	−1	1	0	−21	−1
	1990 Q2	0	−3	5	3	−11	−3
	2007 Q3	2	0	10	10	−1	−1
JP	1992 Q4	17	−8	0	0	−12	−12
NO	1990 Q4	−14	−11	−2	−3	−2	−13
SE	1991 Q3	−5	−6	−5	−5	−8	−8
	2008 Q3	−3	−4	3	2	−5	−5
U.S.	1990 Q1	1	−2	3	1	−10	−2
	2007 Q3	1	−6	6	6	−1	−1
Mean	*(excl DE)*	*−0.1*	*−4.4*	*2.6*	*1.7*	*−8.0*	*−4.9*

Note: See footnote to Table 4a.

Crises tend to occur close to the peaks of the medium-term cycles in credit, credit-to-GDP, and residential property prices. The only exception is the recent crisis in Germany, which was driven by exposures to financial cycles abroad, notably to the United States and Ireland. Leaving this case aside, on average, fewer than three quarters separate the peaks identified by frequency-based filters and the crisis date, with credit and house price peaking prior to the crisis and the credit-to-GDP ratio immediately after it (Table 4a). The peaks in the other series occur further away. Equity prices and the aggregate asset price index peak, on average, three to four years prior to the crisis. Those for GDP are somewhat closer.

The results of the turning-point approach are broadly similar (Table 4b). While the exact dates of peaks differ slightly from those in the filtered series, the general pattern still holds. In particular, the two credit variables and house prices register peaks near crisis dates, with house prices peaking prior to it and often before the filtered series. On average, GDP peaks now almost coincide with systemic crises while the aggregate asset price index, reflecting the faster adjustment of equity prices, continues to lead crises, by slightly over one year.

Table 5 elaborates further on the relationship between cyclical peaks and crises. Rather than considering only medium-term peaks, it examines also all short-term ones. It classifies a peak as "close" to a financial crisis if it occurs within a 12-quarter window. Three points stand out.

First, all the crises with domestic origin are associated with peaks in medium-term cycles in credit and property prices. Conversely, around 40–50 percent of these peaks are close to crises. And this link tightens after 1985, as in this sub-period around 65–70 percent of peaks are close to crises. Note that there is actually only one crisis in the pre-1985 period, which is the secondary banking crisis in the United Kingdom in the early 1970s, following a period of liberalization. In contrast to credit and property prices, the link between crises and peaks in other series is much weaker, especially for equity prices, where only 20 percent of the peaks are close to crises.

Second, the cycles that coincide with crises tend to be longer and to have greater amplitude. For example, the credit cycle associated with crises is on average four years longer (15 instead of 11 years) and its amplitude from trough to peak is close to 200 percent rather than 120 percent. The findings for the property price cycle are qualitatively similar.

Finally, the table underscores that trying to characterize the financial cycle by looking at short-term frequencies is inappropriate if the aim is to

Table 5. All Cycle Peaks and Financial Crises: Turning-Point Method.

	Amplitude[2]		Duration[3]		#peaks all/post 85[4]		%crises peaks[5] all/post 85[4]
Close to crisis[1]	No	Yes	No	Yes	No	Yes	
Medium-term cycle							
Credit	120	197	45	59	11/5	10/9	48/64
Credit/GDP	26	74	26	43	21/9	10/9	32/80
EQ	145	210	22	26	29/12	8/8	22/40
HP	44	81	20	33	15/4	10/9	40/69
AAP	68	70	24	23	20/10	9/8	31/44
GDP	96	48	54	49	16/8	8/7	33/47
Short-term cycle							
Credit	42	82	19	28	36/14	14/12	28/46
Credit/GDP	10	50	9	24	60/24	14/12	19/33
EQ	45	40	6	5	109/51	24/22	18/30
HP	17	46	9	18	43/22	15/14	26/39
AAP	26	34	9	11	50/30	20/18	29/38
GDP	21	38	20	39	33/13	11/9	25/41

Notes:
[1]Close to crisis is “yes” if the peak in the series occurs within a three-year window around a crisis; it is “no” otherwise.
[2]Percentage change from trough to peak.
[3]In quarters.
[4]All/post 85 indicates whether the whole sample or only data after 1985 are used.
[5]Number of peaks close to crises relative to the number of total peaks.

identify boom and bust phases that could lead to severe macroeconomic disturbances. When using the short-term turning-point method, only between 20–30 percent of identified peaks are close to a crisis, even for the credit series and house prices.

4. Toward a Measure of the Financial Cycle

In this section we combine the messages from the analysis of cyclical patterns in individual variables in order to establish stylized facts about the properties of the financial cycle more broadly. Given the analysis so far, we focus on the medium-term financial cycle.

4.1 *Methodology for the combination of series*

The aggregation procedures to identify a common cycle depend on the method to measure cycles in individual series. For the frequency-based filter method, we simply take the average of the filtered series.[7] For the turning-point method, aggregating peaks and troughs is slightly more involved. Here we follow Harding and Pagan (2005). In essence, the procedure identifies, say, a peak in the common cycle if two conditions are satisfied. The first condition is that the peak corresponds to a local minimum for the median distance of all component series from their closest own peak. The second condition requires that all individual series have an individual peak within a pre-specified window around that date.[8] Troughs are identified equivalently. In addition, the procedure imposes the same constraints on the common cycle as those imposed on individual series to date their own cycles: Peaks and troughs need to alternate, and the length of the cycle and each phase need to satisfy certain censoring rules.[9]

We depart from Harding and Pagan (2005) in one respect. We judge that requiring a two-year window for all series to register peaks is too restrictive for the medium-term financial cycle. We adopt two different values for the width of this window. We identify a turning point in the common cycle if peaks/troughs of the individual series are within six quarters from the turning points in the common cycle (i.e., the maximum cluster width is three years). We also identify "weak" turning points if peaks/troughs of the individual series are further away than six, but no more than 12, quarters from turning points in the common cycle.

4.2 *Selection of series*

To construct the financial cycle, we consider the medium-term cyclical components of credit, the credit-to-GDP ratio and property prices. We therefore omit aggregate asset prices and equity prices. As the analysis has already highlighted, equity prices — and thus also aggregate asset prices — behave

[7]To ensure comparability of different series at this point, it is important that the log level of all individual series is normalized, for which we use the respective (log) level in 1985 Q1.

[8]More precisely, a peak in the common cycle is a local minimum of median distance to the nearest peak across all individual series subject to peaks of the individual series not being further away than x quarters from the peak in the common cycle.

[9]As it turns out, it is immaterial whether we use the censoring rules for the short-term or medium-term cycle: the length of the combined cycle always exceeds five years.

differently from residential property prices and the credit variables. They exhibit far greater short-term volatility and their medium-term cycle peaks are less often associated with crises.

The different behavior in equity prices is also confirmed by the concordance index, proposed by Harding and Pagan (2005). This simple statistic measures the fraction of time in which two series are in the same phase (expansion or contraction). If two series expand and contract at the same time, the concordance between them is 100 percent. If they are always in different phases, their concordance is zero. If two series have fully independent cycles, their concordance measure is 50 percent.

Table 6 confirms the pattern one would expect. The phases in the credit and property price cycles are better aligned (concordance around 70 percent). The medium-term equity price cycle is not very closely synchronized with those of the other financial-cycle variables: The concordance measures range from 53 percent to 59 percent. Given that the aggregate asset price index is a weighted average of both series (as well as of commercial property prices), its synchronicity with the credit cycle is somewhere in between those for equity and property prices.

The frequency-based filters provide a similar picture (Drehmann *et al.*, 2012). The correlation between the filtered series for house prices and the credit series is quite strong and positive: It is close to 60 percent (house

Table 6. Concordance between Financial Variables for the Medium-Term Cycle.[1]

	Credit				Credit/GDP			EQ		HP
	Cr/GDP	EQ	HP	AAP	EQ	HP	AAP	HP	AAP	AAP
AU	91	57	56	84	60	54	76	42	75	66
DE	89	49	59	62	42	63	54	29	67	58
GB	93	53	80	75	48	85	68	55	71	75
JP	77	80	86	81	59	77	76	78	82	96
NO	72	56	72	69	59	52	53	72	81	75
SE	73	62	76	51	58	72	46	57	78	66
U.S.	93	54	79	73	47	71	73	66	68	80
Mean	*84*	*59*	*73*	*71*	*53*	*68*	*64*	*57*	*74*	*73*

Notes: [1]Fraction of time in which two series are in the same phase, in percent. EQ: equity prices, HP: house price, AAP: aggregate asset prices.

prices and credit) and 42 percent (house prices and credit-to-GDP). By contrast, the average contemporaneous correlation between the medium-term cycle cyclical component of equity prices and credit is 37 percent and drops to 15 percent for equity prices and the credit-to-GDP ratio.

On the basis of these findings and the messages from the analysis in the previous section, we base the calculation of the financial cycle on three variables: residential property prices, real credit, and the credit-to-GDP ratio.

4.3 *Results*

Figure 2 summarizes the results for the financial cycle. It shows that both methods provide a very consistent picture. In particular, the identified peaks align well. Moreover, they tend to occur around major financial crises. This is not surprising, given the discussion in the previous section. Nevertheless, the alignment is striking.

Table 7 formalizes this result. It summarizes the information of all the 24 peaks in the financial cycle identified by either method. The table is structured to show, in sequence: (a) the peaks that both methods identify and that coincide with a crisis; (b) the peaks that both methods identify but that do not coincide with a crisis; (c) the peaks identified by the turning-point method but not by the frequency-based filtered one; and (d) the peaks in the filtered series that are not identified by the turning-point method. The date shown is the date that corresponds to the turning-point method, except for the last category, for which it inevitably corresponds to the peak in the filtered series. Taking these dates as a benchmark, the table provides information about the number of quarters to the nearest crisis, to the nearest peak identified by the turning-point method, or to the nearest peak identified in the filtered series. Negative (positive) numbers in these columns indicate that the peak or crisis occurs before (after) the specified date. For the turning-point method, we also show the cluster width and whether the peak could only be identified weakly, i.e., whether the cluster width is in the range of three or six years.

The table underlines that both methods provide a very consistent picture about the peaks in the financial cycle. No fewer than 17 out of 24 peaks are identified by both methods. And in these cases, both methods identify a peak within five quarters — with the exception of Germany in the late 1990s. Even more surprising given the difference in the methodological approaches, the coincidence is so tight that for more than half of these

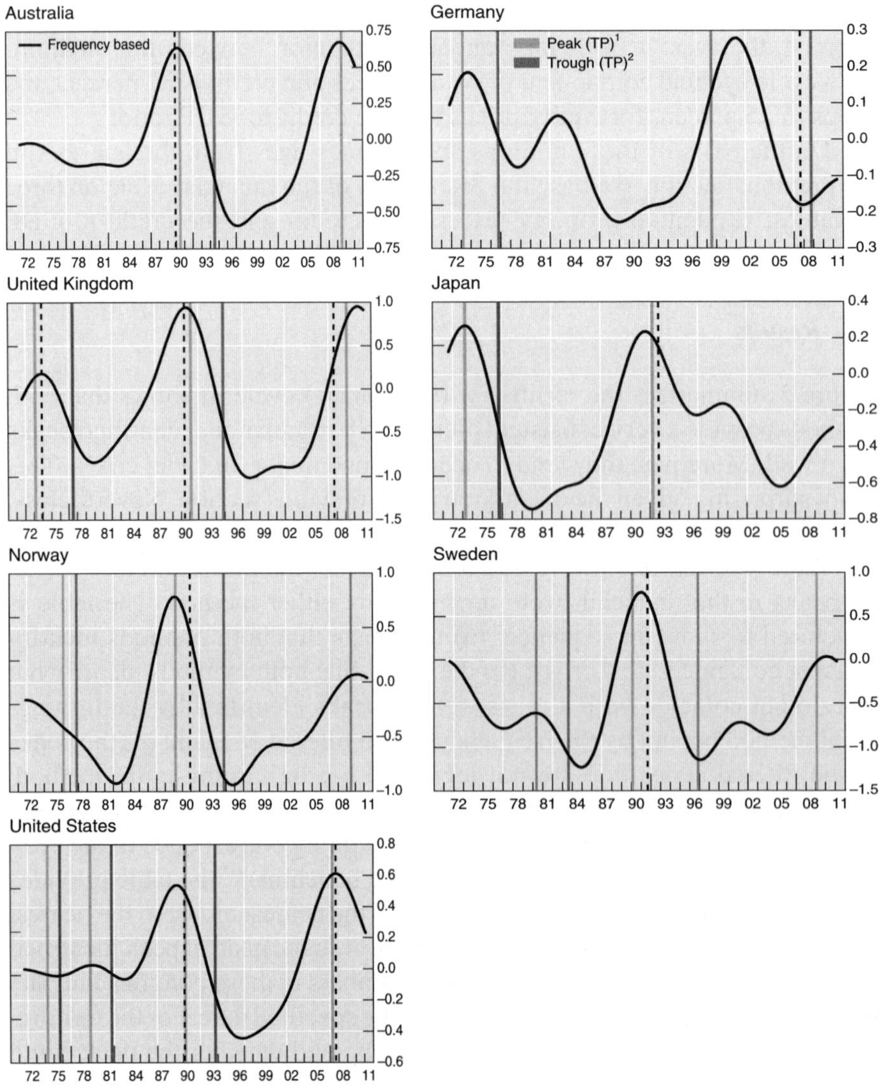

Figure 2. The Financial Cycle: Frequency and Turning-Point Based Methods.

Notes: Gray and black bars indicate peaks and troughs of the combined cycle using the turning-point (TP) method. The frequency-based cycle (solid line) is the average of the medium-term cycle in credit, the credit to GDP ratio and house prices (frequency-based filters). Black vertical lines (dashed) indicate the starting point for banking crises.

Figure 2. (***Continued***)

[1]Peaks are weakly identified in DE 1998q4, NO 2009q2, and SE 1980q4 as the peaks for credit, the credit to GDP ratio and house prices are further than six quarters but no more than 12 quarters apart from the peak in the common cycle.
[2]Troughs are weakly identified in AU 1994q1, GB 1994q2, NO 1977q1, NO 1994q4, and SE 1983q4 as the troughs for credit, the credit to GDP ratio, and house prices are further than six quarters but no more than 12 quarters apart from the trough in the common cycle.

Source: Authors' estimates.

cases both methods identify a peak within half a year.[10] In what follows, we consider only those peaks that are identified by both methods. This seems to be a reasonable choice, given that nearly all the peaks detected only by the filtered series appear to be minor reversals: They can be detected statistically but do not seem to be very meaningful economically. And many of these peaks, including the two identified by the turning-point approach only, occur before financial liberalization.

The last column of the table provides a rough measure of the duration of the financial cycle. It underlies the point that the medium-term financial cycle is quite long and that its length has increased over time. Over the whole sample, the duration of the financial cycle is, on average, around 16 years. For the most recent peaks, it is nearly 20 years, compared with eleven for previous ones.

The most striking result of Table 7 is the high coincidence of financial cycle peaks with crises. This coincidence is so strong that it is worth asking why some peaks in the financial cycle are *not* associated with crises. Post-financial liberalization occurs only three times: in Germany in 1998 and in Australia and Norway in 2009. And even in these cases, the dating seems to capture financial disruptions: All three countries experienced severe strains around those dates, even though our crisis-identification methods do not record full-blown crises (see Section 1). It is well-known that the German banking system was under strong pressure in the early 2000s,

[10]Interestingly, peaks in the filtered series tend to occur more often than not before peaks identified by the turning-point method. In particular around crises, this may be partly driven by the draw-down of credit lines, which results in a measured increase in credit even though stress has materialized already. The medium-term filters seem to filter this out more appropriately.

Table 7a. Financial Crises and Peaks in the Financial Cycles: Peaks for Both Dating Methods Coincide.

		Time to closest[1]				
	Date	Crises	Peak (filters)	Peak (TP)	Cluster width[3]	Duration[4]
Peaks close to a crisis						
GB	2009 Q1	−6	5	0	10	72
SE	2009 Q1	−2	4	0	7	75
U.S.	2007 Q3	0	0	0	12	68
JP	1992 Q2	2	−3	0	8	74
GB	1991 Q1	−3	−2	0	8	69
AU	1990 Q3	−3	−2	0	8	
U.S.	1990 Q3	−2	−5	0	5	44
SE	1990 Q2	5	3	0	1	38
NO	1989 Q3	5	−2	0	9	53
GB	1973 Q4	0	0	0	2	
Mean		*−0.4*	*−0.2*			
Peaks not close to crisis						
NO[2]	2009 Q2	−74	3	0	16	79
AU	2009 Q1	−77	1	0	6	74
DE[2]	1998 Q4	35	9	0	21	100
SE[2]	1980 Q4	43	−2	0	13	
U.S.	1979 Q3	42	−1	0	5	21
DE	1973 Q4	135	−1	0	0	
JP	1973 Q4	76	−2	0	4	
Mean		*25.7*	*1*			

Notes:

[1]Distance (in quarters) between a peak and closest crisis or closest peak using either frequency-based filters or the turning-point method. Negative (positive) numbers indicate that the nearest peak/crisis precedes (follows) the peak date.

[2]The combined cycle is weakly identified as the turning points for credit, the credit to GDP ratio and house prices are further than six quarters but no more than 12 quarters apart from the turning point in the common cycle.

[3]Maximum distance (in quarters) between two peaks of the individual series within one cluster.

[4]Number of quarters from previous peak.

Table 7b. Financial Crises and Peaks in the Financial Cycles: Peaks for Both Dating Methods Do Not Coincide.

		Time to closest[1]				
	Date	Crises	Peak (filters)	Peak (TP)	Cluster width[3]	Duration[4]
Only peaks in the combined cycle using turning-points						
NO	1976 Q2	58	51	0	7	
U.S.	1974 Q2	63	20	0	4	
Only peaks in the combined cycle using filtered series						
SE	2001 Q1	30	0	32		
JP	1999 Q3	−27	0	−29		
DE	1982 Q2	99	0	−36		
AU	1972 Q4	68	0	71		

Note: [1,3,4]See notes to Table 7a.

following the post-unification boom, and that one big bank (Commerzbank) nearly needed official assistance. Similarly, in the wake of the recent crisis, the Australian authorities enhanced deposit insurance schemes and introduced debt guarantees to stabilize the banking system. They also intervened in capital markets to buy residential mortgage-backed securities. And the Norwegian authorities injected NOK 4.1 billion of capital into 28 Norwegian banks.

5. Policy Context: Regime-Dependence and "Unfinished Recessions"

We next go beyond the stylized empirical regularities and consider in more depth the broader policy context that may lie behind them. We explore, sequentially, how the nature of the financial cycle and its interaction with the business cycle may depend on the policy regimes in place ("regime-dependence"), and how policy responses that fail to take medium-term financial cycles into account may contain recessions in the short-run but at the cost of larger recessions down the road (we label this the "unfinished recession" phenomenon).

Our results indicate that the length and amplitude of the medium-term financial cycle (and the associated medium-term business cycle) have increased since the early 1980s. To our mind, as suggested in our analysis, a key factor behind this development is the conjunction of changes in the financial and monetary regimes (Borio and Lowe, 2002). The wave of financial liberalization that took place in the early to mid-1980s allowed financial forces to have full play, reinforcing the procyclicality of the financial system. At the same time, more subdued inflation progressively removed the need for tightening monetary policy as the economy expanded. The stop-go policies of the 1960s to early 1970s naturally prevented financial cycles from gaining strength; the change in regimes in effect loosened the anchors of the financial system, increasing its "elasticity."

The role of changes in the financial and monetary regimes is complementary. In and of itself, financial liberalization is capable of amplifying the financial cycle, as highlighted by the experience of the United Kingdom with Competition and Credit Control in the early 1970s, a period of high inflation. But in those days the rise in inflation, and/or the deterioration of the balance of payments that accompanied economic expansions, would inevitably quickly call for a policy tightening. More recently, the amplitude of recent financial and business cycles has been boosted by positive supply-side developments, not least the globalization of the real economy (Borio, 2007). The combination of higher growth potential and downward pressure on prices turbo-charged the cycle.

Against this backdrop, if the policymakers "overreact" to short-term developments and lose sight of the medium-term financial cycle that may lie behind them, they can store bigger trouble down the road. Arguably, this is what happened both in the mid-1980s/early 1990s and in the period 2001–2007. In both cases, policymakers reacted strongly to collapses in equity prices — the global stock market crashes of 1987 and 2001, which ushered in slowdowns in economic growth and/or actual recessions. As we have seen, however, equity prices are not a reliable indicator of the medium-term financial cycle. In fact, in both episodes, credit and property prices continued to increase, benefiting from a second breath of life. A few years later, the credit and property price booms in turn collapsed, causing serious financial disruptions and dragging down the economy with them.[11] From the perspective of the medium-term financial and business cycle,

[11]The main difference between the two episodes is that the interval between the peaks in equity and property prices was considerably longer in the more recent one, as already conjectured in Borio and McGuire (2004). This, in turn, largely reflects the more delayed emergence of incipient, if any, inflationary pressures in the past decade.

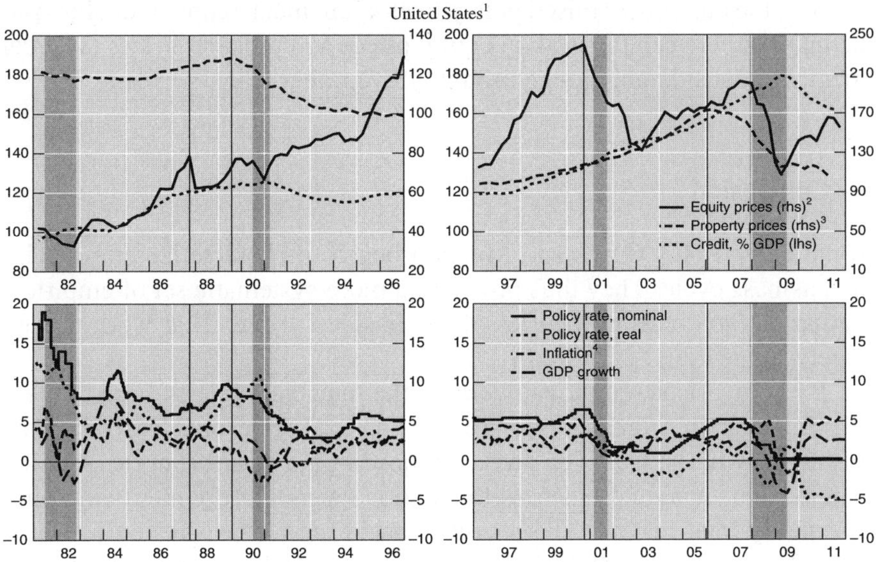

Figure 3. Unfinished Recessions.

Note: The vertical lines denote stock and real estate market peaks in each subperiod.

[1]The shaded areas represent the NBER business cycle reference dates.

[2]1995 = 100; in real terms.

[3]Weighted average of residential and commercial property prices; 1995 = 100; in real terms.

[4]Consumer price index.

Sources: Datastream; national data; BIS estimates.

the slowdowns or contractions in 1987 and 2001 can thus be regarded as "unfinished recessions."

These stylized patterns are evident in Figure 3, which shows the experience of the United States for illustrative purposes.[12] Monetary policy eased strongly in the wake of the stock market crashes and the weakening in economic activity. At the same time, the credit-to-GDP ratio and property prices continued their ascent, soon followed by GDP, only to collapse a few years later. Partly because inflation remained rather subdued in the second

[12]The UK experience is similar as shown by Drehmann *et al.* (2012). For more cases in the earlier episode, see Borio and Lowe (2004).

episode, the authorities raised policy rates again much more gradually. And the interval between the peak in equity prices and property prices (vertical lines) was considerably longer, roughly five rather than two years.

6. Conclusion

In the early 1940s Burns and Mitchell began to characterize empirically the business cycle. They thus provided a more systematic set of empirical regularities to confront theories of the business cycle. That work proved hugely influential.

By comparison, empirical work on the financial cycle is more limited. This is puzzling. After all, notions of the financial cycle, or at least of booms followed by busts, had even predated those of the business cycle. And the idea that financial and business fluctuations were closely intertwined has an equally long history. The recent financial crisis has showed just how untenable this state of affairs is. Our paper is intended as a small contribution to what we hope will become a growing literature that seeks to characterize empirically the financial cycle.

With this in mind we highlight four key conclusions. First, when seeking to identify financial cycles most relevant for macroeconomic disruptions, it is critical to focus on the *medium-term*, not on traditional business-cycle frequencies, i.e., on cycle lengths of at least 15 years. Second, it is possible to identify well-defined medium-term cycles, whose peaks tend to coincide very closely with financial crises and, hence, with serious damage to economic activity. Third, those cycles are best captured by combinations of credit and property prices; equity prices do not fit the picture so well. Fourth, the length, amplitude, and virulence of these cycles have increased since the mid-1980s.

These findings have significant policy implications. We argue that they are consistent with the view that the greater prominence of these cycles is regime-dependent, i.e., that it reflects the conjunction of financial liberalization with monetary policy frameworks that have, over time, become focused on, and quite successful at, delivering near-term price stability. And we note that the authorities should watch out for what we call the "unfinished recession" phenomenon. Policy responses that fail to take medium-term financial cycles into account can help contain recessions in the short-run but at the expense of larger recessions down the road. Arguably, the recent great recession is a case in point.

References

Aikman, D., A. Haldane, and B. Nelson, 2010, "Curbing the credit cycle," paper presented at the Columbia University Center on Capitalism and Society Annual Conference, New York.

Alessi, L. and C. Detken, 2009, "Real-time early warning indicators for costly asset price boom/bust cycles: A role for global liquidity," European Central Bank, working paper, No. 1039.

Bernanke, B.S. and J. Boivin, 2003, "Monetary policy in a data-rich environment," *Journal of Monetary Economics*, Vol. 50, pp. 525–546.

Borio, C., 2007, "Monetary and prudential policies at a crossroads? New challenges in the new century," *Moneda y Crédito*, Vol. 224, pp. 63–101. Also available as Bank for International Settlements working paper, No. 216.

Borio, C., N. Kennedy, and S. Prowse, 1994, "Exploring aggregate asset price fluctuations across countries: Measurement, determinants and monetary policy implications," Bank for International Settlements, economic paper, No. 40, April.

Borio, C. and P. Lowe, 2002, "Assessing the risk of banking crises," *BIS Quarterly Review*, December, pp. 43–54.

_______, 2004, "Securing sustainable price stability: Should credit come back from the wilderness?," Bank for International Settlements, working paper, No. 157.

Borio, C. and P. McGuire, 2004, "Twin peaks in equity and housing prices?," *BIS Quarterly Review*, March, pp. 79–93.

Bry, G. and C. Boschan, 1971, "Cyclical analysis of time series: Selected procedure and computer programs," National Bureau of Economic Research, technical paper, No. 20.

Burns, A.F. and W.C. Mitchell, 1946, *Measuring Business Cycles*, National Bureau of Economic Research, Studies in Business Cycles, No. 2, New York.

Christiano, L. and T. Fitzgerald, 2003, "The band pass filter," *International Economic Review*, Vol. 44, No. 2, pp. 435–465.

Claessens, S., M.A. Kose, and M.E. Terrones, 2011a, "Financial cycles: What? How? When?," International Monetary Fund, working paper, No. WP/11/76.

Claessens, S., M.A. Kose, and M.E. Terrones, 2011b, "How do business and financial cycles interact?," International Monetary Fund, working paper, No. WP/11/88.

Comin, D. and M. Gertler, 2006, "Medium-term business cycles," *American Economic Review*, Vol. 96, No. 3, pp. 523–551.

Detken, C. and F. Smets, 2004, "Asset price booms and monetary policy," European Central Bank, working paper, No. 364.

Drehmann, M., C. Borio, and K. Tsatsaronis, 2012, "Characterising the financial cycle: don't lose sight of the medium-term!," Bank for International Settlements, working paper, No. 380.

English, W., K. Tsatsaronis, and E. Zoli, 2005, "Assessing the predictive power of measures of financial conditions for macroeconomic variables," in "Investigating the relationship between the financial and real economy," Bank for International Settlements Papers, No. 22.

Hamilton, J., 1994, *Time Series Analysis*, Princeton University Press.

Harding, D. and A. Pagan, 2002, "Dissecting the Cycle: A Methodological Investigation," *Journal of Monetary Economics*, Vol. 49, pp. 365–381.

Harding, D. and A. Pagan, 2005, "A suggested framework for classifying the modes of cycle research," *Journal of Applied Econometrics*, Vol. 20, pp. 151–159.

Kindleberger, C., 2000, *Manias, Panics, and Crashes: A History of Financial Crises*, 4th ed., Cambridge, UK: Cambridge University Press.

Laeven, L. and F. Valencia, 2008, "Systemic banking crises: A new database," International Monetary Fund, working paper, No. WP/08/224.

______, 2010, "Resolution of banking crises: The good, the bad, and the ugly," International Monetary Fund, working paper, No. WP/10/146.

Minsky, H., 1982, *Can "It" Happen Again? Essays on Instability and Finance*, Armonk, NY: M.E. Sharpe.

Reinhart, C. and K. Rogoff, 2009, *This Time Is Different: Eight Centuries of Financial Folly*, Princeton, NJ: Princeton University Press.

Schularick, M. and A. Taylor, 2009, "Credit booms gone bust: Monetary policy, leverage cycles, and financial crises, 1870–2008," *American Economic Review*, forthcoming.

III. CENTRAL BANKS AND ASSET PRICE BUBBLES

Low Interest Rates and Housing Bubbles: Still No Smoking Gun

Kenneth N. Kuttner*
Williams College

1. Introduction

The relationship between interest rates and property prices has come under intense scrutiny since the housing boom of the mid-2000s, and the ensuing financial crisis of 2007–2009. Two views have emerged from this experience. One is that monetary policy should respond more proactively to asset price rises, and especially to excesses in the property markets. According to this view, by "leaning against the wind" central banks can prevent or attenuate asset price bubbles, and thus promote financial stability. This would represent a retreat from the Bernanke–Gertler (1999) dictum that monetary policy should respond only to the macroeconomic consequences of asset price fluctuations, rather than to asset prices themselves.[1]

A second, stronger view is that overly expansionary monetary policy is itself the cause of asset price bubbles, and in particular that the Federal Reserve deserves blame for the recent house price bubble. Taylor (2007, 2009) has forcefully articulated this view, which often surfaces in the financial press as well. If so, then monetary policymakers need to be extremely cautious about pursuing expansionary monetary policy, lest it eventually precipitate a financial crisis.

Both of these views rest on the hypothesis that interest rates have an economically significant effect on real estate prices. The validity of that hypothesis may appear self-evident at first glance. Historically, interest rate

*Kenneth N. Kuttner is the Robert F. White Class of 1952 Professor of Economics at Williams College. The author is indebted to Joshua Gallin, Jimmy Shek, and Ilhyock Shim for their assistance with the data; to the Bank for International Settlements for its support of this research; and to Andy Filardo for his comments.

[1] See Kuttner (2011a) for a survey of the arguments for and against this view.

declines do tend to precede periods of house price appreciation, and that was certainly true over the last decade. A more careful examination of the data yields little support for this hypothesis, however. Surveying a number of recent studies and bringing to bear some new evidence on the question, this paper argues that in the data, the impact of interest rates on house prices appears to be quite modest. In fact, the estimated effects are uniformly smaller than those implied by the conventional user cost theory of house prices, and insufficient to account for the rapid house price appreciation experienced in the U.S. and elsewhere.

A link between low interest rates and house price bubbles is especially tenuous. Standard theory says that low interest rates *should* increase house values (or the value of any long-lived asset, for that matter). Consequently, the observation that house prices rise when interest rates fall is not by itself evidence that low interest rates cause bubbles. To make this case, one would have to argue that house prices tend to *overreact* to interest rate reductions, i.e., that appreciations are larger than warranted by fundamentals. The generally muted response observed in the data suggests this is not the case.

The paper begins with a review of the ways in which interest rates can affect house prices, focusing primarily on the conventional user cost model. It goes on to survey some of the existing evidence on the relationship between interest rates and house prices. It then presents two new sets of empirical findings. One is an error correction model involving U.S. data on house prices, rents, and the long-term interest rate. The second is a cross-country exploration of the relationships between interest rates, the monetary base, house prices, and housing credit. Both confirm that the effect of interest rates on property prices is small. However, in some countries, there does appear to be a link between monetary factors — the monetary base in particular — and the property market.

2. Why Interest Rates Affect House Prices

This section reviews the channels through which interest rates affect house prices. While it breaks no new ground theoretically, such a review is useful for two reasons. One is that it gives some structure to discussions as to what constitutes a bubble, as opposed to the normal inverse relationship between interest rates and property prices. A second is that it provides a metric for assessing the economic and quantitative significance of empirical estimates of interest rates' impact on property prices.

2.1 *The user cost framework*

A natural starting point for analyzing the connection between interest rates and property prices is the venerable user cost model which, as argued by Himmelberg *et al.* (2005), provides a useful benchmark for gauging the importance of economic fundamentals. The model is based on the simple proposition that market forces should equate the cost of renting with the all-in risk-adjusted cost of home ownership. The equality is expressed as:

$$\frac{R_t}{P_t} = (i_t + \tau_t^p)(1 - \tau_t^y) + \sigma_t + \delta - \frac{\dot{P}_t^e}{P_t}, \tag{1}$$

where R/P is the rent-to-price ratio, i is the relevant nominal long-term interest rate, δ is the rate of physical depreciation, σ is the risk premium associated with owning a home, and $\dot{P}^e/P$ is expected nominal house price appreciation. The property and income tax rates, τ^p and τ^y, also figure into the calculation, as in Poterba (1984). Equivalently, subtracting the expected rate of inflation π^e yields an expression in terms of the real interest rate and the rate of real house price appreciation,

$$\frac{R_t}{P_t} = [(i_t + \tau_t^p)(1 - \tau_t^y) + \sigma_t + \delta - \pi_t^e] - \left(\frac{\dot{P}_t^e}{P_t} - \pi_t^e\right), \tag{2}$$

where the term in square brackets represents the real user cost, excluding expected real house price appreciation. While obvious at some level, an important and often overlooked point is that the interest rate is one of the economic fundamentals underlying property prices. There is no need to appeal to bubbles to explain why interest rate cuts lead to higher property prices.

The quantitative effects of interest rate changes are easily calculated by differentiating Equations (1) or (2):

$$\frac{1}{P}\frac{\partial P}{\partial i} = -\frac{1 - \tau^y}{UC}, \tag{3}$$

where UC is the right-hand side of Equation (1). Historical values of real user cost (UC) and τ^y can be used to obtain a rough estimate of this sensitivity. With the mortgage rate in the 7 percent range (where it was in the late 1990s), $\delta = 1.3$ percent, $\tau^p = 1.2$ percent, $\tau^y = 21$ percent and expected 10-year consumer price inflation of 2 percent, real UC would have been roughly 6 percent, ignoring the risk premium and assuming zero expected real appreciation. As mortgage rates (and other long-term interest rates) fell in the early 2000s, real UC declined to approximately 5 percent. With real

UC equal to 6 percent, Equation (3) implies that a 10 basis point reduction in the mortgage rate would lead to a 1.3 percent increase in house prices; with real UC equal to 5 percent, the implied increase is 1.6 percent.

Naturally, this calculation is sensitive to assumptions about the unobserved risk premium and user cost terms. Reductions in σ and increases in π^e both increase P (i.e., reduce R/P) *and* increase the sensitivity of house prices to the interest rate. For example, with $\sigma = 0$ and $i = 6$ percent, an increase in the expected rate of real appreciation from zero to 3 percent would double the impact of a change in the interest rate.

2.2 *A dynamic user cost model*

Given that expected house price appreciation increases house prices through its effect on UC, it is tempting to think of any increase in expected appreciation as a bubble. This conclusion is unwarranted, however, as non-zero rates of expected appreciation can arise naturally in the context of a dynamic user cost model. A simple version of such a model, similar to that presented in Poterba (1984), consists of three equations:

$$\frac{\dot{H}}{H} = g(P/C(H)) - \delta, \tag{4}$$

$$R = f(H) + \varepsilon, \quad \text{and} \tag{5}$$

$$\frac{R}{P} = i + \delta - \frac{\dot{P}}{P}, \tag{6}$$

where H is the housing stock, P is the price of housing, R is rent, C is the marginal cost of new houses, i is the nominal interest rate, and δ is the rate of depreciation. Equation (4) represents the flow supply of new houses, and the function g satisfies $g'(\cdot) > 0$ and $g''(\cdot) < 0$. The marginal cost of new housing, $C(H)$, increases with H, so $C'(\cdot) > 0$. Equation (5) represents the demand for housing, and the f satisfies $f'(H) < 0$; ε is a housing demand shock. Equation (6) is the user cost relationship, Equation (1), simplified by the omission of the income and property tax rates. Assuming perfect foresight, the model is readily analyzed using a phase diagram involving P and H, as shown in Figure 1. Equation (4) determines $\dot{H}$, and setting this to zero yields the $\dot{H} = 0$ locus. Combining Equations (5) and (6) gives an expression for $\dot{P}$, and setting this to zero results in the $\dot{P} = 0$ locus. The model exhibits familiar saddle path dynamics. An essential property is that when P is "too high" — meaning above the $\dot{P} = 0$ locus — P is *rising*.

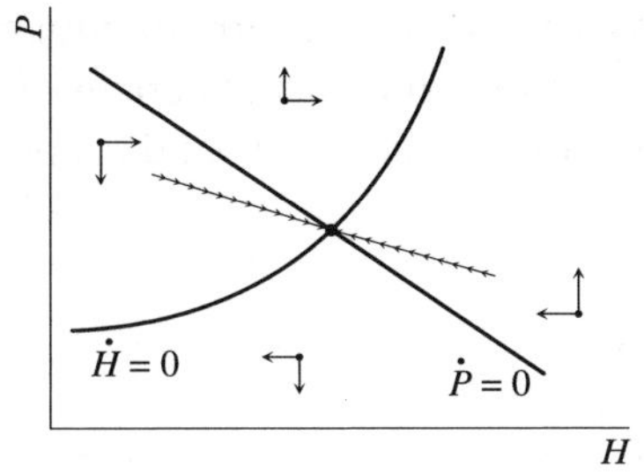

Figure 1. Phase Diagram for the Dynamic User Cost Model.

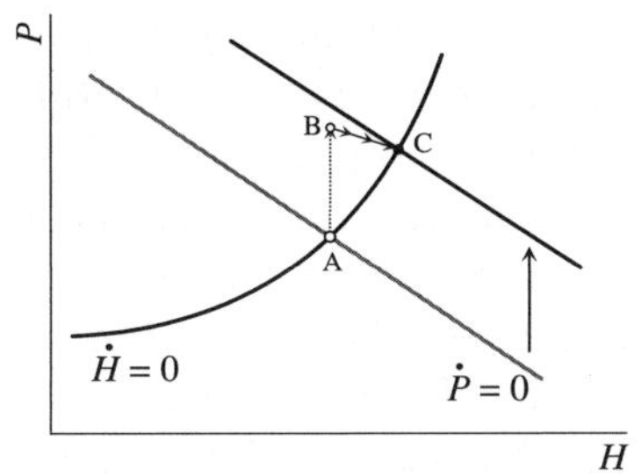

Figure 2. The Effects of an Interest Rate Reduction.

This may be counterintuitive, but it follows directly from Equation (6): Starting from a P that satisfies $\dot{P} = 0$, increasing P reduces the rent-to-price ratio, R/P. The user cost must fall so that households are indifferent between renting and owning. Given i and δ, this can only happen through an increase in expected appreciation.

The model delivers two insights relevant for understanding the link between interest rates and house prices. One is that with zero expected appreciation, the static user cost relationship, represented by Equations (1) and (6), applies only to the steady state. An increase in housing demand or a decrease in the interest rate will shift the $\dot{P} = 0$ locus upward, as shown in Figure 2, and house prices will adjust as the economy moves to its new steady state. Expected appreciations and depreciations are therefore part of the normal adjustment process, and do not necessarily imply the existence of bubbles.

A second insight is that interest rate changes cause house prices to overshoot the steady state. The unanticipated rate reduction depicted in Figure 2, for example, leads to an immediate jump in house prices (from point A to point B in the diagram), followed by a subsequent *decline* (from point B to point C). The initial impact of interest rate changes therefore may exceed what is implied by the simple user cost model presented in the previous section.

2.3 *The credit channel*

The stylized user cost framework clearly leaves out a number of other factors that could potentially affect house prices, and alter prices' interest rate sensitivity. An obvious omission is the supply of credit. Purchasing a house typically requires a loan, and many households are to some extent constrained in terms of the amount they can borrow. While not an explicit part of the framework, the user cost model is useful for thinking about how this might work. Because borrowing-constrained households face a higher shadow cost of credit, the interest rate that appears in these households' version of Equation (6) exceeds the market interest rate, i. An increase in the availability of credit, and the relaxation of borrowing constraints, would reduce this shadow cost. The effects would therefore be similar to those of an interest rate reduction. This is a natural interpretation of the development of the subprime mortgage market in the U.S., and a plausible story for why that market's development was associated with a house price boom. In this interpretation, the price rise would have been the result of a change in fundamentals, rather than a bubble.

To the extent that expansionary monetary policy relaxes credit constraints, an operative credit channel would tend to amplify the effects of monetary policy on house prices. According to this view, a monetary expansion has two effects. The first is to lower the mortgage rate. And second, by easing the availability of credit, the expansion would also increase the demand for owner-occupied housing by more than would be implied by the interest rate reduction alone. The $\dot{P} = 0$ locus would shift up by a larger amount, amplifying the appreciation.

2.4 *The risk-taking channel*

The risk-taking channel is a third mechanism through which monetary policy could affect house prices. According to this view, which has been articulated by Rajan (2005), Borio and Zhu (2008), and Gambacorta (2009), lower interest rates induce intermediaries to take on additional risk in an effort to achieve a certain target rate of return. Dell'Ariccia *et al.* (2010)

worked out a partial equilibrium model in which low interest rates can encourage risk-shifting, and Ioannidou *et al.* (2009) presented evidence suggesting that this mechanism was operative for Bolivian banks over the 1999–2003 period. A general theory of interest rates, risk-taking, and asset pricing has yet to be developed, but presumably the increased demand for risky assets caused by low interest rates would boost the price of risky assets by a larger amount than they would otherwise have risen.

The risk-taking channel maps only loosely into the user cost framework. One interpretation parallels the credit channel. The increased appetite for risk brought forth by low interest rates would make intermediaries more willing to lend, increasing credit supply. The increased availability of credit would allow some credit-constrained households to purchase homes, thus increasing the demand for owner-occupied houses and, assuming imperfect substitutability between the two types of dwellings, decreasing the rent-to-price ratio. An alternative interpretation is that low interest rates somehow reduce σ, the risk premium associated with home ownership. The positive impact of such a reduction on house prices would be the same as an increase in expected home price appreciation. Neither interpretation implies a bubble.

3. Evidence on the Response of House Prices to Interest Rates

This section summarizes the existing literature on the impact of interest rates on house prices, and presents some new evidence on the relationship between user cost and house prices in the U.S. from a simple error correction model. Collectively, the results are consistent with an inverse relationship between house prices and interest rates, but in quantitative terms the effect is modest. It is considerably weaker than implied by the user cost framework, and insufficient to explain the magnitude of most countries' real estate booms.

3.1 *Existing literature*

The cyclical properties of house prices and interest rates are well-documented. Claessens *et al.* (2011), for example, showed that house prices are strongly procyclical in most countries. Ahearne *et al.* (2005) found that low interest rates tend to precede housing price peaks, with a lead of approximately one to three years. While these patterns are suggestive, discerning the impact of interest rates *per se* is complicated by the fact that other macroeconomic factors affecting the demand for housing are varying along with the interest rate. Moreover, it is impossible to tell from purely descriptive analysis whether the magnitude of the house price variations are consistent with the effects implied by user cost theory.

Some indirect evidence on the contribution of interest rates to house price fluctuations was furnished by Campbell *et al.* (2009). Using the methodology developed in Campbell (1991), the authors decomposed house price fluctuations in 23 metropolitan areas in the U.S. into components attributable to real interest rates, rent, and risk premia. They found that risk premia were the principal source of variance in U.S. house prices, and that interest rate fluctuations accounted for a relatively small share.

Another piece of evidence on interest rates' contribution to house prices, and in particular the mid-2000 boom, comes from Dokko *et al.* (2009), who looked at house price forecasts under alternative interest rate paths, directly addressing Taylor's (2007, 2009) assertion that overly expansionary monetary policy caused the boom. They found that deviations from the Taylor rule explained only a small portion of the pre-crisis rise in property prices. Examining nearly 100 years' worth of data for the U.S., Reinhart and Reinhart (2011) reached a similar conclusion.

A number of recent studies have used vector autoregression (VAR) analysis to estimate the impact of interest rates on house prices, four of which are summarized in Table 1. All four documented statistically significant effects of monetary policy on house values, with estimates of the

Table 1. VAR Estimates of Monetary Policy Shocks' Impact on House Prices.

	Effects of 25 bp policy shock		
	Immediate	10 quarters	Long run
Del Negro and Otrok (2007), Fig. 5: U.S., 1986–2005	0.9%	0.2%	≈0
Goodhart and Hofmann (2008), Fig. 3: 17 OECD countries, 1985–2006	0	0.4%	0.8%
Jarociński and Smets (2008), Fig. 4: U.S., 1995–2007	0	0.5%	≈0
Sá *et al.* (2011), Fig. 4: 18 OECD countries, 1984–2006	−0.1%	0.3%	0.1%

impact of a 25 basis point monetary policy shock ranging from 0.3 percent to 0.8 percent.

Del Negro and Otrok (2007) estimated a six-variable VAR on U.S. data spanning 1986 through 2005. The variables included in the system were the house price, total reserves, CPI inflation, GDP growth, the 30-year mortgage rate, and the federal funds rate. Monetary shocks were identified using sign restrictions, and a novel feature of the analysis is its incorporation of latent house price factor derived from a dynamic factor model. Their main finding was that a 25 basis point expansionary monetary policy shock led to a statistically significant 0.9 percent appreciation immediately on impact, decaying to only 0.2 percent after ten quarters.

Goodhart and Hofmann (2008) used a panel VAR to examine the relationship between house prices, macroeconomic variables, and other financial indicators in 17 industrialized countries. The six variables in their model were real GDP growth, CPI inflation, the short-term nominal interest rate, house price growth, broad money growth, and nominal private credit growth. The results revealed Granger-causal relationships between many of the variables, and in particular a causal relationship from interest rates to house prices and credit growth. While resisting the temptation to attach structural interpretations to the shocks, they found that a 25 basis point orthogonalized expansionary interest rate innovation leads to a statistically significant 0.8 percent increase in house prices. In terms of magnitude, this is very similar to the 0.9 percent response reported by Del Negro and Otrok (2007), but the dynamics are very different. In Goodhart and Hofmann (2008), there is no immediate impact; the effect builds slowly, reaching 0.4 percent after 10 quarters and gradually achieving its maximum after 40 quarters. In Del Negro and Otrok (2007), on the other hand, the 0.9 percent peak occurs immediately and dissipates rapidly.

Jarociński and Smets (2008) presented two sets of estimates from Bayesian VARs for the U.S.: one in levels, and an alternative first-difference specification. Their nine-variable models included output, consumption, the GDP deflator, housing investment, the house price, the short-term interest rate, the term spread, a commodity price index, and the money supply. Like Del Negro and Otrok (2007), they identified structural shocks via sign restrictions on the impulse response functions. In the levels VAR, an expansionary 25 basis point monetary policy shock leads to a gradual rise in house prices, peaking at a statistically significant 0.5 percent after ten quarters. This is accompanied by a decline in the long-term interest rate of roughly 10 basis points. The effects subsequently diminish, and 20 quarters after the shock the house price has returned to its mean. The differenced VAR yielded somewhat larger and more persistent estimates, but the confidence intervals are much wider, especially at longer horizons.

Finally, a recent paper by Sá *et al.* (2011) reported panel VAR results for 18 OECD countries from a 12-variable model, using data from 1984 through 2006. In addition to the standard macro variables (output, the price level, consumption, non-residential and residential investment, short- and long-term interest rates, and a measure of credit), the specification also included four variables reflecting global factors: world GDP, world prices, the trade-weighted exchange rate, and the current account balance. Like Del Negro and Otrok (2007) and Jarociński and Smets (2008), the shocks were identified using sign restrictions. The results are remarkably similar to those of Jarociński and Smets (2008). The response to a 25 basis point expansionary shock is initially slightly negative, subsequently rising to a statistically significant but modest 0.3 percent effect after 10 quarters. Over a similar horizon, the long-term interest rate declines by approximately 10 basis points. Interestingly, the response is somewhat larger for countries with more sophisticated financial systems (including the U.S.), where the response at ten quarters is closer to 0.5 percent. For all countries, the effect subsequently diminishes, falling to 0.1 percent after 30 quarters.

These VAR-based estimates are remarkably similar to those reported by Glaeser *et al.* (2010), who used a completely different econometric method. Running a simple regression of the log house price on the real 10-year interest rate, they concluded that a 10 basis point reduction in the interest rate would result in a 0.7 percent rise in house prices.

Because it is specified in terms of the long-term interest rate rather than the short-term policy rate, mapping the Glaeser *et al.* (2010) figure into the VAR literature requires making an assumption about the effect of policy shocks on longer-term interest rates. An estimate of this effect can be gleaned from the VAR results summarized above: In both Jarociński and Smets (2008) and Sá *et al.* (2011), a 25 basis point expansionary monetary policy shock is associated with a reduction in the long-term interest rate of roughly 10 basis points. This is similar to the results in Kuttner (2001), which imply a response of approximately 8 basis points. Using the 10 basis point figure as a rough rule of thumb, the 10 basis point effect implied by the Glaeser *et al.* (2010) regression is comparable to the implications of a 25 basis point monetary policy shock.

All of these effects are quite modest in economic terms, and considerably smaller than the effects implied by standard theory. As previously discussed in Section 2.1, the user cost model suggests that a 10 basis point reduction in the long-term interest rate — the magnitude typically associated with a 25 basis point expansionary monetary policy shock — should cause house prices to rise by 1.3 percent to 1.6 percent, depending on the initial level of interest rates. By contrast, the VAR estimates, which range from 0.3 percent to 0.8 percent, are one-fourth to one-half the magnitude implied by the user cost model.

3.2 *Results from an error-correction model*

While the structural VAR exercises summarized above paid careful attention to the identification of monetary policy shocks, they failed to incorporate the main features of the user cost model sketched in Section 2.1. If real UC and the rate of expected real appreciation are stationary, Equation (2) says that the rent-to-price ratio should also be stationary. Including rent in the model could therefore be useful for understanding why macro variables affect the property market, and for determining whether the observed house price response is excessive relative to the user cost benchmark. This section presents the results from a simple error-correction model of house prices that represents a first step in this direction.

But before developing such an error-correction model, one first has to verify that rents and house prices are indeed cointegrated. As reported in Kuttner (2011b), standard augmented Dicky–Fuller tests consistently reject the null of non-stationarity for the log of the rent-to-price ratio calculated using the Freddie Mac FMHPI index for the 1975Q1 to 2011Q1 sample.[2] This suggests that an error-correction specification would be an appropriate way to model the joint behavior of rents and house prices. The null hypothesis of non-stationarity is also rejected for the real UC variable calculated as described in Section 2.1, using the 30-year conventional mortgage rate.[3]

Following Gallin (2008), these considerations led to the specification of a three-variable vector error correction model involving the log of the house price (the FMHPI index), the log of the rent component of the CPI, and UC.

[2]Non-stationarity is also rejected for the discontinued Freddie Mac CMHPI used in Gallin (2008), the FHFA, and the Census property price indexes. Interestingly, the evidence is weaker for samples ending in the middle of the boom period, since at that time property prices had yet to revert to their mean.

[3]I am indebted to Joshua Gallin for sharing the tax rate and inflation expectations data used in the calculation of real UC.

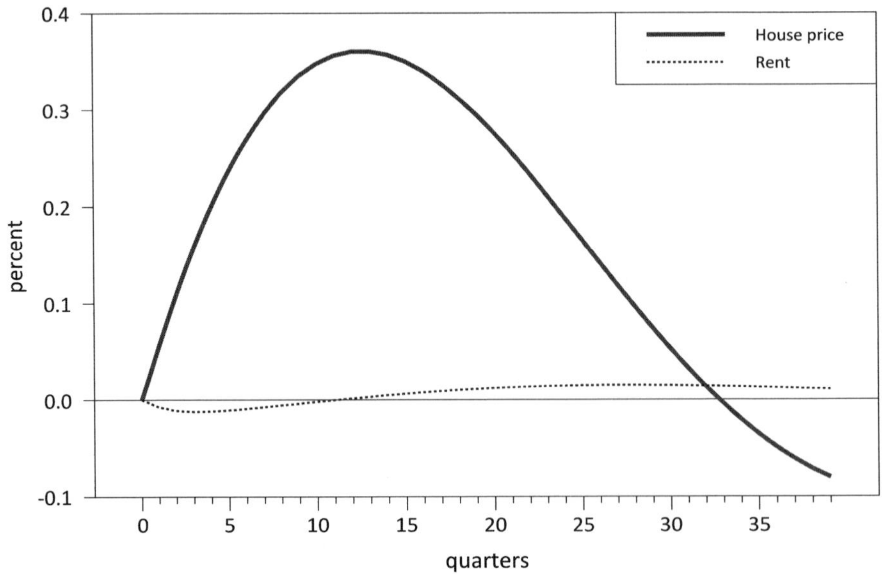

Figure 3. The Estimated Effect of a −10 Basis Point Real UC Shock on House Prices and Rents.

No attempt is made to identify structural features other than the long-run relationship implied by the user cost model, so it would be hazardous to attach economic interpretations to the shocks. The model was estimated with two lags on quarterly U.S. data for the 1984Q1 through 2011Q1 sample period, imposing a cointegrating relationship with coefficients (1,−1) on the house price and rent variables, and ensuring that the rent-to-price ratio reverts to a constant mean. Consistent with the cointegration results, the error correction term is significant in the price (but not the rent) equation; and UC has a negative, statistically significant effect on the house price.

The most interesting results from the standpoint of this paper have to do with the way in which house prices and rents react to changes in UC. Figure 3 plots the responses to a 10 basis point negative real UC innovation: house prices gradually increase, with a maximum response of roughly 0.35 percent at 12 quarters.[4] The effect subsequently diminishes, and by 30 quarters the effects have dissipated. The effect on rent is trivial.

[4]The standard Cholesky decomposition is used, with the user cost ordered last. The effect of the UC shock is roughly one-third smaller when UC is ordered first.

Although it uses a very different econometric specification, these results are comparable to (but on the low end of) those based on the VAR approach. Taken together, the available evidence points to a modest effect of interest rates on property prices. There is therefore no evidence that house prices overreact to interest rates, relative to the user cost benchmark. Rather, these results collectively raise the question of why house prices should be so *insensitive* to interest rates.[5]

4. Interest Rates and the Property Price Boom of the mid-2000s

Turning from the time series evidence on the effects of interest rates on property prices, this section focuses on the behavior of the housing market during the previous decade's boom. One objective is to evaluate informally the plausibility of low interest rates as a cause of significant house price appreciation in the U.S. The second is to determine whether differences in interest rates can explain why the housing boom was large in some countries, but small in others.

4.1 *The U.S. experience*

Figure 4 plots the rent-to-price ratio for the U.S. from 1985 onward, using the FMHPI index and the rent component of the CPI.[6] The spectacular rise in house prices drove the rent-to-price ratio down to just over 0.75 at the late 2006 peak, from roughly 1.1 in 1997. Relative to rents, house prices appreciated by approximately 32 percent over this period, which corresponds to the shaded area in the figure.

Also shown on the plot is real UC, calculated as described in Section 2.1, which was in fact unusually low during much of the boom period. Prior to 2001, real UC fluctuated around a level of just under 6 percent. At about that time, UC fell by roughly 80 basis points, to just over 5 percent, a decline that was associated with the Fed's expansionary policy in the early 2000s. Puzzlingly, real UC remained low even as the Fed raised its funds rate target by 3.25 percent from mid-2004 to mid-2006, a manifestation of Alan Greenspan's (2005) low bond yield "conundrum."

[5]Glaeser *et al.* (2010) showed that the option to refinance, plus labor mobility, reduces the interest rate sensitivity by roughly one-half.

[6]Other house price measures, including the FHFA and Case-Shiller indexes, exhibited similar behavior.

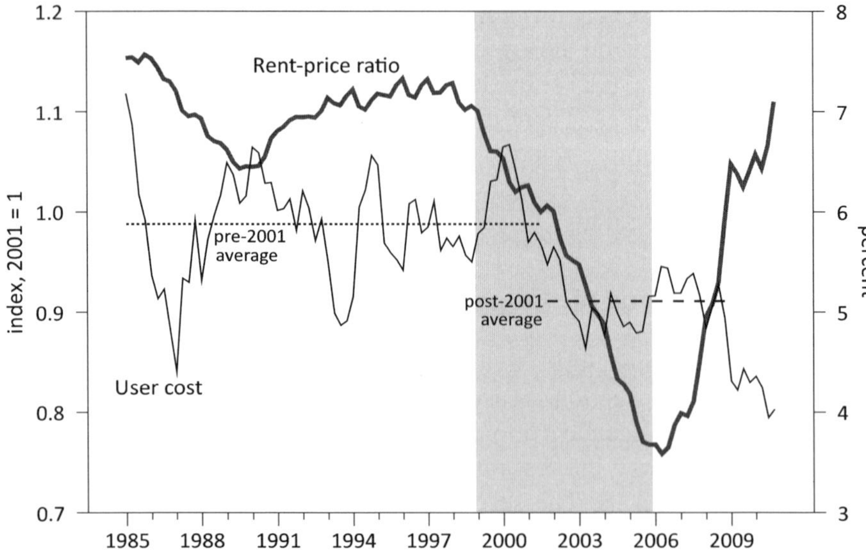

Figure 4. The Rent-to-Price Ratio and Real User Cost in the U.S., 1985–2010.

The drop in real UC by itself cannot fully explain the escalation in house prices, however. For one thing, the timing does not line up. House prices began to appreciate in 1998, three years before the drop in UC, and by 2001 the FMHPI index had already outpaced rents by 10 percent. The initial stages of the boom therefore appear to have had nothing to do with interest rates. It is only after 2001 that low interest rates enter the picture.

Moreover, the size of the boom exceeds the implications of the user cost model, and the VAR estimates summarized in Section 3.1. According to the user cost calculations discussed in Section 2.1, an 80 basis point decline in UC should have led to an increase in the rent-to-price ratio of approximately 10 percent to 13 percent, accounting for roughly half of the post-2001 boom. But if the VAR estimates are taken at face value, it is hard to attribute the boom to expansionary monetary policy. Even if one were to assume that a 25 basis point expansionary shock led to a 1 percent appreciation in house prices — a response that exceeds any of the VARs' estimates — a 20 percent rise in house prices would have required 20 such shocks, and consequently a cumulative 5 percentage point deviation from the interest rate rule embedded in the VAR model.

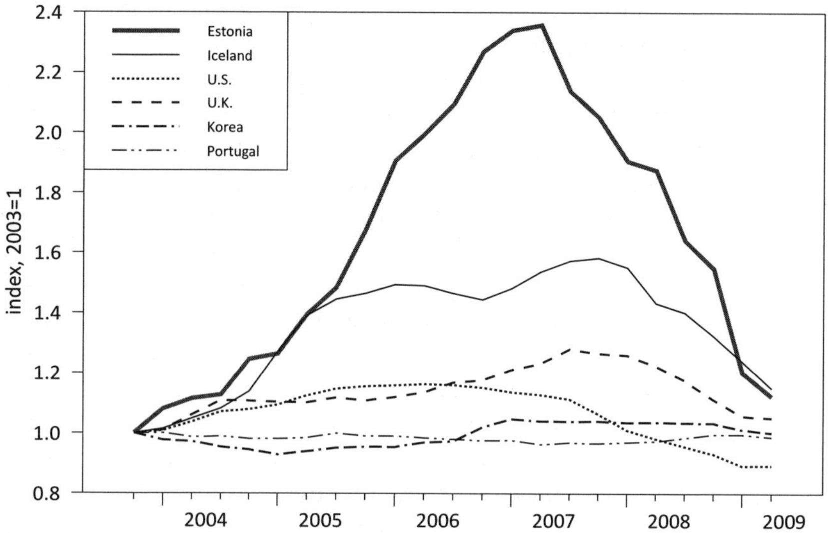

Figure 5. Real House Prices in Selected Countries.

4.2 *A cross-country exploration*

From a global perspective, two observations about the recent real estate boom and bust stand out. First, the boom was a global phenomenon: Most countries experienced rapidly rising real estate prices during the early and middle part of the last decade. The second observation is that the degree of appreciation varied widely across countries. This is vividly illustrated in Figure 5, which plots real house prices for six countries: Estonia, Iceland, the U.S., the U.K., Korea, and Portugal, a set of countries chosen to emphasize the wide variation in the size of the boom. Estonia takes the prize for the most spectacular bubble, with real house prices in that country increasing by a factor of nearly 2.4 between the fourth quarter of 2003 and the second quarter of 2007. In comparison with Estonia, Iceland's 60 percent appreciation seems restrained. Both countries' booms dwarf those of the U.S. and the U.K., which experienced real house price appreciation over a comparable period of 17 percent and 28 percent, respectively.[7] House prices barely appreciated at all in Korea, and actually fell slightly in Portugal.

[7]Note that because these numbers, and Figure 5, only cover 2003Q4 through 2007Q2, they understate the size of the boom, which began earlier in many countries.

Some of the cross-country differences may be due to discrepancies in the definition and construction of the series. Some control for changes in composition (e.g., the repeat sales FMHPI index in the U.S.) whereas others do not. Moreover, some are national averages, while others, like Iceland's, are specific to the capital city. (Details on the house price series used can be found in the Appendix.) It is unlikely that differences in data construction can account for the extreme range of outcomes across countries, however.

A variety of country- and region-specific factors surely account for much of this diversity. But in light of concerns about interest rates' putative contribution to property price bubbles, an important question is the extent to which differences in interest rates across countries can explain the relative sizes of the booms. If low interest rates inflate house prices, then one would expect those countries with lower rates to have experienced more appreciation. And more broadly, if low interest rates were also associated with more relaxed lending standards and greater credit supply, as suggested by the credit and risk-taking channels, then low rates would also give rise to rapid credit growth.

Analogous questions have been examined empirically using the VAR approach surveyed in Section 3.1. Those studies' emphasis was on the comovements over time between interest rates, credit, and house prices, however, rather than on cross-country differences in the average rates of appreciation that are the focus of this section.[8] Here, the aim is to determine the extent to which the prevailing level of real interest rates was an important determinant of the booms' relative sizes.

Perhaps the most difficult part of this exercise is obtaining usable property price data. The primary source of the data used in this analysis is the dataset compiled by the Bank for International Settlements (BIS). One problem is that many countries, especially transition and emerging market economies, have only recently begun collecting property price data, which severely constrains the time series dimension of the analysis. In the end, property price data from 2003Q4 onward were available for only 36 countries. Details on data sources and definitions can be found in the Appendix.

Another problem is, as noted earlier, that there is no standard methodology for constructing house price indexes. It therefore goes without saying

[8]In panel data parlance, one could say that VAR analysis corresponds loosely to a "within" estimator, whereas the cross-sectional analysis of averages can be interpreted as a "between" estimator.

that the property price *levels* are not directly comparable across countries. One has to assume that it is possible to make meaningful comparisons of the growth rates calculated from these series. Methodological differences will surely introduce country-specific measurement error, but since property price growth will be used as the dependent variable in the regressions, the additional noise would increase the regression standard error, but not bias the parameter estimates.

Finding data on housing-related credit presents another challenge. This paper relies on data taken from several sources, including the BIS, CEIC, Datastream, and central banks. Cross-country consistency is again a problem with no clear solution, but as in the case of property prices, there is reason to believe that any measurement error introduced by methodological differences and other data issues would increase the standard errors, but not cause bias. Data availability limits to 33 the number of countries with suitable data from 2003Q4.

Compared with property price and credit data, basic monetary and financial series are relatively easy to find, as they are available from the IMF's International Financial Statistics database. Short-term and lending interest rate series are used, the latter as a proxy for the interest rate that would be relevant for home purchases. Monetary base data are also obtained from the IMF.[9]

Histograms of house price growth, credit growth, and interest rates are shown in Figures 6 and 7, distinguished by country group: Eurozone, emerging market, and an "other" category that includes countries such as U.S., the U.K., Canada, Australia, and New Zealand. All figures are calculated for the 2003Q4–2007Q2 time span, the end date corresponding approximately to the housing market peak.

The distribution of house price growth is shown in the top panel of Figure 6. Over the 2003Q4–2007Q2 period, the majority of countries experienced real property price growth of 5 percent per year or more, with many exceeding 10 percent. Four emerging market economies had real appreciation in excess of 15 percent per year. The bottom panel of Figure 6 shows the distribution of credit growth, expressed as the annualized percentage point change in housing credit as a share of GDP. Outcomes here are similarly varied. The modal growth rates are in the 1–3 percent range (indicating

[9]For Euro area members, the monetary base data reported by the IMF corresponds to the reserves held by the country's banking system.

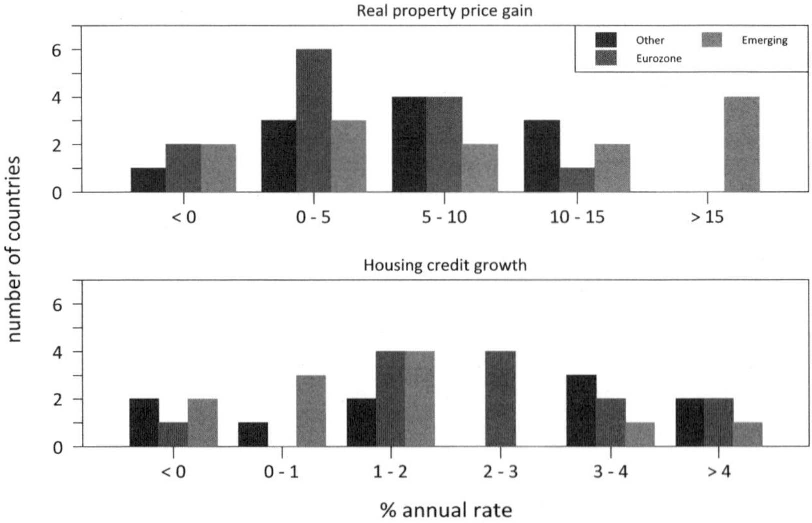

Figure 6. Distribution of Real House Price and Credit Growth.

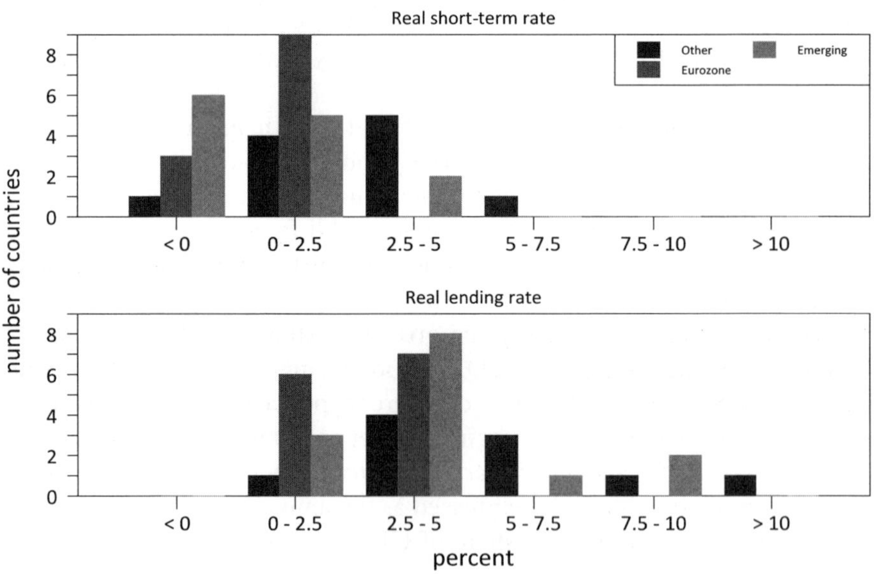

Figure 7. Distribution of Real Short-Term and Lending Interest Rates.

that housing credit grew 1–3 percent more rapidly than GDP), but the rate exceeded 3 percent in a sizable minority of the countries in the sample.

As shown in the top panel of Figure 7, while relatively low, *ex post* real short-term interest rates did not vary much across countries. Most fall in the 0–2.5 percent range, with a few below zero and some exceeding 2.5 percent. Real lending rates, shown in the bottom panel, tended to be higher, and most fall into the 2.5–5 percent range. Some are lower, but still positive, and a few exceed 5 percent. The relatively low dispersion of interest rates alone suggests that they are unlikely to explain much of the cross-country variation in house price appreciation: Property prices would have to be extraordinarily interest-sensitive for changes of one or two percentage points to account for the wildly differing rates of house price appreciation plotted in Figure 6.

A cross-sectional regression model will be used to evaluate the relationship between monetary conditions and the housing market:

$$Y_i = \beta_0 + \beta_1 r_i^S + \beta_2 r_i^L + \beta_3 \%\Delta MB + \beta_4 D_i^{eu} + \beta_5 D_i^{em} + u_i, \qquad (7)$$

where the dependent variable Y represents either the real property price gain or the growth in housing credit. The regressors are r^S, the average real short-term interest rate; r^L, the average real lending rate; and percent change in the monetary base, the annualized average change in the real monetary base. All changes are calculated over the 2003Q4–2007Q2 period. The regression also includes dummies for euro-area and emerging market/transition economies, D^{eu} and D^{em}.

The inclusion of the monetary base term requires some explanation. Strictly speaking, the user cost model has no place for monetary quantities, since in the steady state house prices should be determined solely by rents and interest rates (plus taxes, depreciation, and the risk premium). However in some countries, base money may serve as a proxy for credit conditions, loosely defined. A central bank targeting a short-term interest may find itself in a position of having to accommodate increased credit demand by allowing an expansion in the base, for example. Alternatively, in countries with actively managed exchange rates, base growth may be associated with unsterilized capital inflows. Either way, the monetary base may convey some information about the availability of bank credit beyond that contained in the short-term and lending interest rates.

Many aspects of this regression are problematic, of course. It would be hard to argue that any of the regressors are exogenous. Since it includes the effects of omitted variables, such as GDP, that affect property prices and housing credit, these omitted variables' effects will be subsumed into the error term. If the monetary authority takes GDP into account in setting its short-term interest rate (or if it responds directly to house prices), then the coefficient on the interest rate will be biased. In addition, the lending rate and monetary base growth are endogenously determined. The regression is therefore unable to provide a credible answer to counterfactuals involving the likely effect of an interest rate cut on property prices or credit. At most, it can say something about the expectation of property prices or credit conditional on the observed behavior of interest rates and the monetary base.

With these caveats in mind, Table 2 displays the results from estimating Equation (7). The regression with real property price growth as the dependent variable, shown in the first column, provides only weak evidence of an interest rate effect. Neither of the two interest rate coefficients is statistically significant, nor are they jointly significant. The coefficient on the lending rate does have the correct sign, however, and with a p-value of 0.11 it is *almost* significant at the 10 percent level. Indeed, if the short-term interest rate is dropped, as in the second column of the table, the coefficient on the lending rate becomes significant at the 5 percent level. Even so, the parameter estimate of roughly -1 implies a relatively modest effect: a 1 percentage point increase in the real long-term interest rate is associated with a 1 percentage point reduction in the annualized real rate of house price appreciation. During normal periods with stable property prices, this would represent a sizable effect. And taking the estimate at face value, one could point out that a 1 percentage point increase in the lending rate in the U.S. would have significantly reduced the annualized growth rate of house prices from 3.4 percent to 2.4 percent. But for countries experiencing double-digit annual growth rates, such as Estonia and Iceland, a change in the lending rate of a percentage point or two would not have made a tangible difference.

Interestingly, the coefficient on the monetary base is highly statistically significant, with a 1 percentage point increase in the rate of base growth implying a 0.35 percent increase in house prices. This may seem like a relatively small effect, and, for those countries with modest rates of real base growth, it is. But a significant number of countries experienced spectacular real base growth during this period, including: Iceland (35 percent), New Zealand (31 percent), Ireland (26 percent), Slovenia (24 percent), Russia (18 percent), Estonia (15 percent), and Latvia (12 percent). For these countries, the estimated coefficient on the base growth variable implies quite

Table 2. Results from Cross-Country Regressions.

	Dependent variable		
	Real property price growth		Real housing credit growth
Intercept	9.57***	9.69***	3.33***
	(2.74)	(2.87)	(0.81)
Real short-term interest rate	0.37		−0.11
	(0.89)		(0.24)
Real lending rate	−1.22	−1.07**	−0.43**
	(0.76)	(0.54)	(0.17)
Real monetary base growth	0.35***	0.36***	0.17***
	(0.11)	(0.11)	(0.03)
Emerging market dummy	4.17	2.21	−0.99
	(3.41)	(2.92)	(1.10)
Euro area dummy	−3.95	−4.34*	−0.72
	(2.44)	(2.47)	(0.84)
p-value for interest rates' exclusion	0.14		0.05
Adjusted R-squared	0.21	0.19	0.40
Observations	35	36	33

Notes: The table reports the estimates of Equation (7). Asterisks denote statistical significance: *** for 1%, ** for 5%, and * for 10%. Heteroskedasticity-consistent t-statistics are in parentheses.

large effects on property prices. These extreme observations stand out in Figure 8, which plots real house price growth against real base growth, illustrating how rapid base growth was in some countries accompanied by pronounced house price appreciations.

The third column of Table 2 shows an analogous set of estimates for the regression with housing credit growth (expressed as the percentage point change in the share of housing credit relative to GDP) as the dependent variable. Here, the lending rate is individually significant at the 5 percent level, and the two interest rates are also jointly significant at that level. The −0.43 parameter estimate says that a 1 percentage point increase in the real lending rate is associated with a 0.43 percentage point reduction in credit growth. The effect is not large, but with annualized credit growth rates in the 0–4 percent range, a 1 or 2 percentage point change in the lending rate would make a noticeable difference.

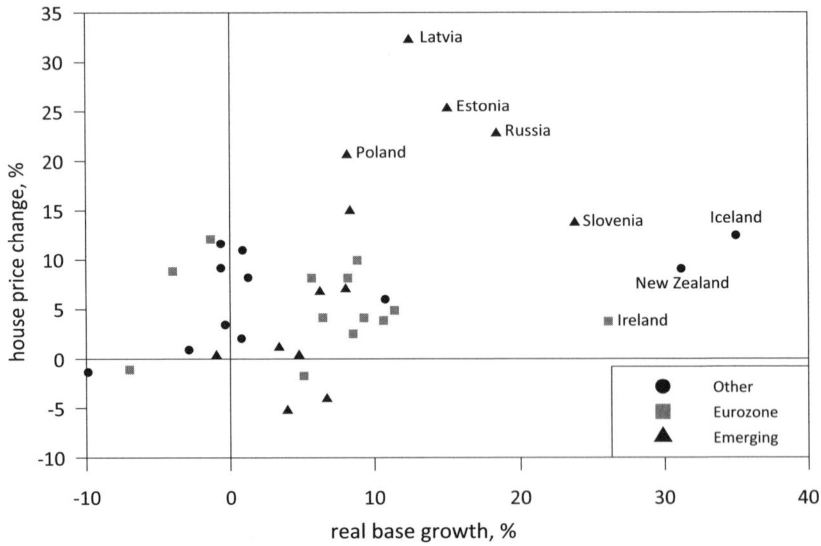

Figure 8. Real Monetary Base and Property Price Growth.

As in the interest rate regression, the monetary base is highly significant. The point estimate of 0.17 says that a 1 percentage point increase in base growth would translate into a 0.17 percentage point increase in credit growth. This would not have been a major contributor to credit growth for those countries with modest rates of base growth. But as with property prices, double-digit growth in the monetary base in some countries seems to have been associated with sizable increases in housing-related credit.

5. Conclusions

This paper's main conclusions are twofold. The first is that all available evidence — existing studies, plus the new findings presented above — points to a rather small effect of interest rates on housing prices. VAR-based estimates of the effect of a 25 basis point expansionary monetary policy shock range from 0.3 percent to 0.9 percent, both in the U.S. and in other industrialized countries. These estimates are broadly consistent with results from other methodologies, including simple OLS regressions and error-correction models. They are also considerably smaller than the effects implied by the standard user cost model. Moreover, they are too small to explain the previous decade's tremendous real estate boom in the U.S. and elsewhere.

This is not to say that low interest rates had nothing to do with the real estate boom. The real user cost of home ownership in the U.S. fell by roughly 0.8 percent after 2001, a change that appears to have been only partly related to monetary policy. If one were to ignore the empirical evidence showing a much smaller interest sensitivity, taken literally the user cost model could account for roughly half of the post-2001 house price appreciation. But given that real UC did not begin to decline until 2001, interest rates could not have been a contributor to the 10 percent appreciation that occurred *before* 2001.

Even if a robust inverse relationship between interest rates and house prices existed, it would not follow that low interest rates caused bubbles. In the context of standard theory, the interest rate, along with rents and tax rates, is a fundamental determinant of valuations. Making the case that low interest rates cause bubbles would require showing that house prices tend to overreact to rate reductions. Although the previous decade's house price boom was out of proportion to the interest rate decline, there is no evidence that this happens systematically. The puzzle is why house prices are *less* sensitive to interest rates than theory says they should be, not more so.

Still lacking is an explanation of why low interest rates sometimes seem to be associated with bubbles, and sometimes not. The user cost model may contain a clue. As noted earlier, the expected rate of house price appreciation is an important if unobserved ingredient in user cost. As such, it is a *deus ex machina* capable of explaining any level of house prices. But it also suggests that the interest sensitivity of house prices depends on the expected rate of appreciation, since the interest semi-elasticity is inversely proportional to user cost. Consequently, in an environment of rapidly rising house prices, interest rate reductions may have a larger effect than when prices are stable. Low interest rates may fan the flames, even if they do not start the fire.

The evidence presented in this paper also indicates that credit conditions, broadly defined, may play a larger role in house price booms than low interest rates *per se*. In market-oriented financial systems, like that of the U.S., a loosening of credit conditions plausibly resulted from financial innovation, such as securitization, and a relaxation of lending standards. In more bank-centric financial systems, like those present in many emerging market and transition economies, loose credit conditions have been associated with the rapid increase of quantitative monetary indicators, such as the monetary base. This suggests that it would be a mistake to focus narrowly on interest rates as the cause of asset price bubbles.

References

Ahearne, Alan, John Ammer, Brian Doyle, Linda Kole, and Robert Martin, 2005, "House prices and monetary policy: A cross-country study," International Finance Discussion Papers Series, Board of Governors of the Federal Reserve System, working paper, No. 841.

Bernanke, Ben S. and Mark Gertler, 1999, "Monetary policy and asset price volatility," in *New Challenges for Monetary Policy*, Federal Reserve Bank of Kansas City, Jackson Hole Symposium, pp. 77–128.

Borio, Claudio and Haibin Zhu, 2008, "Capital regulation, risk-taking and monetary policy: A missing link in the transmission mechanism?," Bank for International Settlements, working paper, No. 268, December.

Campbell, John Y., 1991, "A variance decomposition for stock returns," *The Economic Journal*, Vol. 101, No. 405, pp. 157–179.

Campbell, Sean D., Morris A. Davis, Joshua Gallin, and Robert F. Martin, 2009, "What moves housing markets: A variance decomposition of the rent-price ratio," *Journal of Urban Economics*, Vol. 66, No. 2, pp. 90–102.

Claessens, Stijn, M. Ayhan Kose, and Marco E. Terrones, 2011, "Financial cycles: What? How? When?," International Monetary Fund, working paper, No. 11/76.

Del Negro, Marco and Christopher Otrok, 2007, "99 luftballons: Monetary policy and the house price boom across U.S. states," *Journal of Monetary Economics*, Vol. 54, No. 7, pp. 1962–1985.

Dell'Ariccia, Giovanni, Luc Laeven, and Robert Marquez, 2010, "Monetary policy, leverage, and bank risk-taking," International Monetary Fund, working paper, No. 10/276.

Dokko, Jane, Brian Doyle, Michael Kiley, Jinill Kim, Shane Sherlund, Jae Sim, and Skander Van den Heuvel, 2009, "Monetary policy and the housing bubble," FEDS Working Paper, Board of Governors of the Federal Reserve System, No. 2009-49, December.

Gallin, Joshua, 2008, "The long-run relationship between house prices and rents," *Real Estate Economics*, Vol. 36, No. 4, pp. 635–658.

Gambacorta, Leonardo, 2009, "Monetary policy and the risk-taking channel," *BIS Quarterly Review*, December, pp. 43–53.

Glaeser, Edward L., Joshua D. Gottlieb, and Joseph Gyourko, 2010, "Can cheap credit explain the housing boom?," National Bureau of Economic Research, working paper, No. 16230, July.

Goodhart, Charles and Boris Hofmann, 2008, "House prices, money, credit, and the macroeconomy," *Oxford Review of Economic Policy*, Vol. 24, No. 1, pp. 180–205.

Greenspan, Alan, 2005, "Federal Reserve Board's semiannual monetary policy report to the Congress," testimony before the U.S. Senate, Committee on Banking, Housing, and Urban Affairs, February 16.

Himmelberg, Charles, Christopher Mayer, and Todd Sinai, 2005, "Assessing high house prices: Bubbles, fundamentals and misperceptions," *Journal of Economic Perspectives*, Vol. 19, No. 4, pp. 67–92.

Ioannidou, Vasso, Steven Ongena, and José-Luis Peydró, 2009, "Monetary policy, risk-taking and pricing: Evidence from a quasi-natural experiment," Tilburg University, working paper.

Jarociński, Marek and Frank R. Smets, 2008, "House prices and the stance of monetary policy," *Federal Reserve Bank of St. Louis Review*, Vol. 90, July/August, pp. 339–365.

Kuttner, Kenneth N., 2001, "Monetary policy surprises and interest rates: Evidence from the Fed funds futures market," *Journal of Monetary Economics*, Vol. 47, No. 3, pp. 523–544.

Kuttner, Kenneth N., 2011a, "Monetary policy and asset price volatility: Should we refill the Bernanke–Gertler prescription?," in *New Perspectives on Asset Price Bubbles: Theory, Evidence, and Policy*, forthcoming, Evanoff, Kaufman, and Malliaris (eds.), Oxford University Press.

Kuttner, Kenneth N., 2011b, "Rent, price, and user cost in the U.S.: Do the old rules still apply?," unpublished manuscript, September.

Poterba, James M., 1984, "Tax subsidies to owner-occupied housing: An asset-market approach," *The Quarterly Journal of Economics*, Vol. 99, No. 4, pp. 729–752.

Rajan, Raghuram G., 2005, "Has financial development made the world riskier?," in *The Greenspan Era: Lessons for the Future*, Federal Reserve Bank of Kansas City, Jackson Hole Symposium, pp. 313–369.

Reinhart, Carmen M. and Vincent Reinhart, 2011, "Pride goes before a fall: Federal Reserve policy and asset markets," National Bureau of Economic Research, working paper, No. 16815, February.

Sá, Filipa, Pascal Towbin, and Tomasz Wieladek, 2011, "Low interest rates and housing booms: The role of capital inflows, monetary policy, and financial innovation," Bank of England, working paper, No. 411, February.

Taylor, John B., 2007, "Housing and monetary policy," in *Housing, Housing Finance, and Monetary Policy*, Federal Reserve Bank of Kansas City, Jackson Hole Symposium, December, pp. 463–476.

Taylor, John B., 2009, "The financial crisis and the policy responses: An empirical analysis of what went wrong," National Bureau of Economic Research, working paper, No. 14631, January.

Appendix

The following table lists the countries included in the analysis, details on the property price data, and the data used for the regressions reported in Table 2.

Country	Region	Type	New/ existing	House price growth	Short-term rate	Lending rate	Housing credit growth	Base growth
Austria	Capital	all	all	4.2	2.8	4.9	1.80	6.4
Australia	Big cities	all	existing	2.1	6.0	9.6	4.19	0.8
Belgium	Whole	all	existing	8.2	2.8	5.1	2.38	5.7
Canada[a]	Whole	all	existing	8.2	3.4	5.2	1.84	1.3
Switzerland	Whole	single family	all	0.9	1.0	3.3	1.71	−2.9
Colombia[b]	Whole	all	existing	7.0	7.3	15.3	−0.41	8.0
Czech Rep.	Whole	single family	existing		2.5	6.2	1.47	5.7
Germany[d]	Whole	all	new	−1.7	2.7	5.9	−0.33	5.1
Denmark	Whole	all	all	12.1	2.9	5.1	2.13	−1.3
Estonia	Whole	flats	all	25.3	3.1	5.7	6.70	15.1
Spain	Whole	all	all	8.2	2.7	3.9	6.30	8.2
Finland	Whole	all	existing	4.9	2.8	3.9	2.66	11.4
France	Whole	all	existing	9.9	2.8	5.0	2.58	8.9
Great Britain	Whole	all	all	6.0	5.0	4.9	3.55	10.8
Greece	Capital	flats	all	3.9	2.8	5.3	3.85	10.6
Hong Kong	Whole	all	all	11.6	2.8	7.0	−3.15	−0.6
Indonesia	Big cities	all	new	−5.3	7.4	15.8	0.25	4.0
Ireland	Whole	all	all	3.8	2.8	4.1	6.83	26.1
Israel	Whole	all	all	−1.3	5.1	7.6	−1.24	−9.9
Iceland	Capital	all	all	12.5	10.2	16.4		35.0

(Continued)

(*Continued*)

Country	Region	Type	New/ existing	House price growth	Short-term rate	Lending rate	Housing credit growth	Base growth
Italy[d]	Whole	all	all	4.1	2.8	4.9	1.49	9.3
Korea	Whole	all	all	1.1	4.1	6.3	0.90	3.4
Latvia	Whole	flats	existing	32.2	2.4	5.9		12.4
Lithuania	Whole	all	all	8.8	2.8	4.1	1.78	−4.0
Malaysia	Whole	all	all	0.3	3.2	6.6	1.21	4.8
Netherlands	Whole	all	existing	2.5	2.8	5.2	1.27	8.5
Norway	Whole	all	all	11.0	5.5	4.7	0.31	0.9
New Zealand	Whole	all	all	9.1	7.1	11.1	5.98	31.2
Poland	Big cities	flats	existing	20.6	5.3	7.3	1.47	8.2
Portugal	Whole	all	all	−1.1	2.8	4.3	3.56	−7.0
Russia	Urban areas	all	existing	22.7	3.5	11.6		18.4
Sweden	Whole	all	all	9.2	2.5		3.56	−0.6
Singapore[c]	Whole	all	all	6.8	2.4	5.7	−1.31	6.3
Slovenia	Whole	all	existing	13.7	4.2	7.5		23.8
Thailand[c]	Whole	townhouses	all	0.3	3.1	6.8	0.62	−1.0
United States[a]	Whole	single family	existing	3.4	3.5	6.7	3.69	−0.3
South Africa	Whole	single family	all	14.9	7.8	12.1	4.00	8.4

Notes: Property price data are from the BIS except as noted: *a*, Haver; *b*, Datastream; *c*, CEIC.
Interpolated series are denoted by *d*. Interest rates and growth rates are annualized averages over the 2003Q4–2007Q2 period, and expressed in real terms, adjusted using CPI inflation.

Classic FIT and Lean FIT: Is Inflation-Targeting Guilty of Causing the Financial Instability of 2007–2009?

Takatoshi Ito*

Faculty of Economics, University of Tokyo

1. Introduction

From the mid-1990s to mid-2000s, many central banks have succeeded in keeping the inflation rate within their respective inflation-targeting ranges. More central banks in emerging market economies as well as advanced countries have adopted the inflation-targeting framework, and many central banks improved on communication strategies to stabilize the inflation expectation. Just when many central bank governors felt that they had mastered taming both inflation and deflation, the subprime mortgage crisis occurred in the United States. From 2007 to 2009, major financial institutions in the United States and in Europe were engulfed in a flame of financial crisis. Values of complex securities plummeted as underlying MBS values were lost with increasing default rates all over the United States. Financial institutions that created these securities and those that invested in those securities found themselves in shortage of capital. Deleveraging took place and it turned into panic selling of assets and run-on funds. The world experienced financial crisis of a magnitude comparable to the Great Depression in the 1930s.

The direct cause of the financial panic was the boom and bust of the U.S. housing market. But scholars and policymakers have been divided into two camps: The first camp regards the inflation-targeting framework is to

* Takatoshi Ito is a professor at the Graduate School of Economics, University of Tokyo.

blame, because the central bank narrowly focused on the stability of CPI inflation rate while overlooking the asset price bubble; whereas the second camp blames the greatly inadequate supervision and regulation in the U.S. and Europe for the securities industry and conflict of interest in credit rating agencies.

This paper will argue that flexible inflation targeting is a sound monetary policy framework even after the global financial crisis. Putting a weight on asset prices as a monetary policy objective without adding a policy instrument may cause a serious tradeoff problem. If CPI deflation may have to be tolerated to stop an asset bubble, deflation may cause a serious problem. Also, once a bubble has emerged, a slight increase in the interest rate would not stop it.

The first-best policy is to enhance supervision and regulation on financial institutions to avoid moral hazard and concentration of risk. For example, the following measures may be most effective as a brake on the housing booms. First, the loan-to-value ratio can be adjusted in response to rapid asset price movements. When housing prices are rising fast, the loan-to-value ratio should be lowered. Second, countercyclical capital requirements on financial institutions that lend to borrowers related to the housing market would be a measure to reduce risk of financial instability. Third, direct or indirect measures to limit credits (loans) to the housing-related sector may help stop housing booms. These measures are the first-best.

These measures should be employed when there is reasonable conviction that the housing price increases are out of sync with economic fundamentals, namely a bubble. If supervisory and regulatory agencies fail to react, the central bank (monetary policy) may have to react with higher interest rates to asset price movements much more so than otherwise. The monetary tightening to curb lending to housing markets is a blunt instrument, but when supervisory and regulatory agencies fail to do their jobs, they have to be employed. The "leaning against the wind in the housing market" with the interest rate is only the second-best policy. Provided that regulatory measures were clearly lacking in the process of housing mortgage securitization, the interest rate hike should have been justified.

In sum, adding a new objective to the central bank without giving a new instrument would not enhance performance of financial stabilization policy. It is more important to define and implement macroprudential tools than to choose who would exercise it, the central bank or a supervisory agency, such as FSA. Macroprudential measures include, for example, regulation on the loan-to-value ratio (LTV) for real estate loans, regulation on concentration in particular industries, countercyclical regulation on risk-adjusted capital ratio of banks, and flexible adjustment in risk weights in calculation of risk-adjusted capital ratio. If the central bank is to become in charge of prudential measures, it is important to have a firewall between monetary policy wing and financial stability wing. The financial stability wing should have sanctioning power as well as regulatory power with respect to prudential measures. If a supervisory agency, which is outside of the central bank, is to be in charge of regulation, the agency should be independent from politicians and the regulated, and should be staffed with highly competent people.

2. The Cause of the Global Financial Crisis

A huge housing bubble in the U.S. was formed and collapsed, and the burst bubble pushed the world economy toward the severe global recession in the fourth quarter of 2008 and the first quarter of 2009. Low-quality (subprime) mortgages were originated, securitized, re-securitized, and distributed to the world. When the default rate of the original mortgages soared, prices of those re-securitized products (CDOs) plummeted, and global financial markets were caught by panic-selling. In many financial markets, new buyers simply disappeared, and those institutions that held subprime-related securities with borrowed money were squeezed for liquidity. Large capital losses and lack of liquidity pushed many institutions to eventual insolvency. In the early stage of the crisis, say, 2007 to the spring of 2008, the serious problems were limited to those who held subprime-related mortgages. However, as the financial crises became deeper and more widespread, the globally active financial institutions were affected.

After the failure of Lehman Brothers in September 2008, no financial institutions were deemed safe in the United States and Europe, and the global financial markets ceased to function. Many financial institutions in the United States and Europe failed or were bailed out by the governments. The lender-of-last-resort, like massive liquidity provision and asset purchase by Federal Reserve, Bank of England, and ECB, prevented the meltdown of the world economy.

Consumption, investment, and output activities in the United States and Europe shrank rapidly. Through the financial and trade channels, severe contraction in real and financial activities in the West spread throughout the world. The Japanese and Asian economies were also affected severely, mostly through export collapse.

Although the worst outcome was avoided by global fiscal stimulus, unconventional monetary policy as well as global zero interest rate policy, policy discussions continued regarding the causes and cures of the global financial crisis of 2007–2009 (GFC), and prevention of a future financial crisis. In discussion of prevention, there is a consensus that the asset price movements — in particular, equity prices and housing prices — should be monitored carefully and policies should be adopted in an early stage to prevent a bubble from becoming too big. However, experts are divided over the role of monetary policy in its fight against the financial bubble, i.e., whether and how much the interest rate should be raised in reaction to sharp asset price increases.

2.1 *Causes*[1]

Several possible causes of the GFC were identified, but policymakers have debated over the relative weights of blame among the causes. Three suspected causes of the U.S. subprime crisis and global financial crisis have been identified in the literature: failure of financial supervision; global imbalances; and failure of monetary policy. It is important to review these causes in order to assess the role of monetary policy in prevention of a future housing bubble in some country.

The first suspected cause was the lack of supervision and regulation on securitization and re-securitization of the mortgage loans, reinforced by conflict of interest among credit rating agencies in the United States. Mortgage banks in the United States knew that mortgages they originated would be securitized, so they happily lent to financially weak (subprime) borrowers. This was typical moral hazard. Then, investment banks pooled hundreds and thousands of securitized mortgages and created senior and mezzanine tranches and equities out of the pooled securities. The re-securitization created many AAA securities out of subprime loan securities, with what turned out to be overly optimistic default probabilities and unrealistic assumptions of uncorrelated housing prices over different regions. Moreover, AAA ratings were obtained in consultation with credit rating agencies over how many safe assets should be included in the re-securitizing pool. The credit rating agencies suffered from conflicts of interest. Investment banks sold those AAA securities to final investors, such as pension funds, hedge funds, and commercial banks in the United States and Europe. Very few Asian

[1]The rest of this paper draws on Ito (2010).

investors held these securities. The sales subsidiaries of investment banks, known as conduits (or special investment vehicles, SIVs), were not consolidated in parent banks' balance sheets — and were overlooked by regulators. This accounting practice made the accounting opaque. The Securities and Exchange Commission (SEC) was supposed to be a main supervisory agency for investment banks and their financial products. However, the SEC was not effective, to say the least, in supervision on these financial products and accounting. It became clear that major investment banks and an insurance company, AIG, were underregulated. Some of the problems described above — moral hazard, conflict of interest, and opaque accounting — would be preventable if the supervision and regulatory framework regime is completely revamped.[2]

The second possible cause was the global imbalances, namely large current account deficits of the United States and large current account surpluses of China and oil-producing countries that maintained the *de facto* dollar peg. Undervalued exchange rates of these emerging market economies, which are evident from large amounts of intervention, caused fundamental imbalances in trade and finance in 2005–2008. Huge accumulations of foreign reserves in these countries were held in increased amounts of U.S. Treasuries. Thus, the dollar peg and current account surpluses among emerging market economies made it possible for the U.S. government and Federal Reserve to keep the interest rate in the U.S. artificially low and contributed to fueling the bubble. When the U.S. current account deficits rose from 2001 to 2006, the U.S. dollar was supposed to depreciate, resulting in higher inflation and higher nominal interest rates, which might have slowed down, if not stopped, the housing bubble in the United States.

The Chinese monetary authority intervened heavily to keep the renminbi pegged to the U.S. dollar, and recycled money (surpluses) into the United States. That had kept the Treasury rates relatively low. According to this view, surplus saving and dollar peg of the emerging market countries, especially China, caused the U.S. housing bubble.[3]

During the long process of the interest hike by the Federal Reserve, from 2004 to 2006, the long-term interest rate remained low, despite of

---

[2]See Ito (2009) and Svensson (2009) for this view.

[3]See Portes (2009) for this view, and see Obstfeld and Rogoff (2009) for a view that both global imbalances and housing boom were caused by the common cause. In that sense, the two issues are intimately related.

the rising short-term rates. This prompted Chairman Greenspan to call the phenomenon a "conundrum."[4] Global imbalances and global savings glut seem to explain the conundrum.

The third possible cause is the low interest rate that was justified with the inflation-targeting framework. Taylor (2007, 2009) forcibly argued that the interest rate from 2002 to 2006 was too low (compared to the Taylor rule), so that the increase in housing prices became excessive. The interest rate was lowered sharply in 2001 to help the economy soft-land from the collapse of the dot.com bubble of 1999–2000. The decisions that kept the interest rate low from 2001 to 2003 and that raised the interest rate only very gradually from 2004 to 2006 were based on the fear that the U.S. economy may tumble into a Japan-like post-bubble deflation and stagnation. The skillful soft landing that prevented deflation was generally praised at the time. However, in retrospect, some experts like Taylor argued that the low interest rate (to mitigate the pain of the burst of a bubble) spawned another bubble.[5]

Relative importance of the three causes: The three causes mentioned above are not mutually exclusive, or they may have been even mutually reinforcing. In order to sharpen the views on the relative importance of the three suspected causes, some counterfactual exercises are helpful. First, suppose that supervision and regulation in the U.S. and the UK had been tightened in 2004. Suppose that the SEC in the U.S. and FSA in the UK had adopted macroprudential policies: limiting the loan-to-value ratio of subprime mortgages, conducting stress tests on investment banks on risk concentration, forcing investment banks to consolidate balance sheets of SPVs, and other measures. Would these measures have made differences

[4]In the Congressional testimony, Greenspan (2005) said, "Concurrently, greater integration of financial markets has meant that a larger share of the world's pool of savings is being deployed in cross-border financing of investment. The favorable inflation performance across a broad range of countries resulting from enlarged global goods, services, and financial capacity has doubtless contributed to expectations of lower inflation in the years ahead and lower inflation risk premiums. But none of this is new and hence it is difficult to attribute the long-term interest rate declines of the last nine months to glacially increasing globalization. For the moment, the broadly unanticipated behavior of world bond markets remains a conundrum."

[5]Some Bank of Japan economists have sympathies to Taylor's criticism of the low interest rate for its fuelling the housing bubble, since they hold a view that the low interest rate in the second half of the 1980s was the main cause of the asset price bubble that collapsed in the 1990s to cause widespread financial instability.

in the course of housing prices, the amount of securitized mortgages, and their distribution to the rest of the world? I would answer, "Yes, it would have stopped the housing bubble before 2006." Regardless of the level of the interest rate, these prudential measures would have been effective.

Second, suppose that there had not been global imbalances, that is, U.S. household savings had been higher and/or Chinese RMB had been appreciating to reduce current account surpluses. Would these macro environments have prevented the housing bubble? I would say, "Unlikely, unless regulatory measures were tightened at the same time." Mortgages might have been extended anyway to subprime borrowers, if all the distorted incentive structure — moral hazard among mortgage banks that securitized them and sold them without thinking twice of default probability. The teaser rate (the low mortgage interest rate for the first two years of the mortgage) might have been as low as the actual, even without global imbalances. Once subprime mortgages were created, they would result in AAA securities by investment banks out of a pool of thousands of subprime mortgages in consultation with rating agencies. The moral hazard, conflict of interest, and other failures in the capital markets have nothing to do with global imbalances.

Third, suppose that the policy interest rate had been hiked much earlier than the actual pace in 2004 to 2006 — the thought experiment that Taylor (2007, 2009) conducted. How much difference would it have made on the housing prices? Taylor thinks it must have shaved off the peak of the bubble significantly. The problem of empirics is that it is very difficult to model a bubble process and counterfactual simulations because of a small sample of bubble experiences. When the housing price is increasing, say, at 20 percent a year, even a 4 percent hike in the interest rate, which Bernanke and Gertler (1999) argued for the Japanese case, should not have been enough to dampen the profit expectation.[6] Hence, it is uncertain that the interest rate can be a strong weapon once the bubble had started.

---

[6]Suppose that the property is sold for \$120 million at year t, which is expected to become \$144 million in the following year (a 20 percent increase). Suppose also that the investor buys the property with \$20 million equity and \$100 million bank mortgage loans. If the mortgage rate is 2 percent, the repayment to the bank is \$102 million and the equity enjoys more than 100 percent return (\$20 million to \$42 million). The interest rate hike from 2 percent to 4 percent would make a dent on the return by a mere \$4 million. The expected return is now 90 percent instead of 110 percent.

3. Flexible Inflation Targeting (FIT) and Bubble

Flexible inflation targeting (FIT) is the monetary policy framework that aims at the price stability defined as low but positive inflation rate (typically 1–3 percent, or narrower than that range). Since there is the long and variable lag in the monetary policy transmission channel, the target is only possible as a medium-term objective (i.e., an achievement of the target level/range in two years). Hence, it is sometimes called inflation forecast targeting (see Svensson, 1997).

An early criticism of FIT is that other important macroeconomic variables, such as GDP growth and full employment, are ignored from monetary policy objectives. A standard answer from FIT advocates is that output stability is as important as price stability. The central bank loss function that is used in the FIT literature typically contains two variables: the squared deviation of the inflation rate from the optimal inflation rate, and the squared deviation of output from the potential output. The short-run tradeoff between inflation and output targets is well-recognized in the FIT literature.

One of the most important benefits of the FIT framework is to stabilize the inflation expectation, thus reducing volatility in the shocks arising from expectation variations (position of the New Keynesian supply curve). With inflation expectation anchored at around the targeted inflation rate, the room to maneuver against temporary shocks becomes larger. So, the FIT as best practice among advanced countries and emerging market economies was well-established by the mid-2000s.

In the wake of the global financial crisis of 2007–2009, a new kind of criticism of inflation targeting emerged. According to critics, the FIT disregards financial stability, as it targets inflation (monetary) stability. By allowing the bubble to be formed, while the CPI inflation rate was low and stable, FIT was guilty of eventually causing financial instability when the bubble burst. There are two opposite views to the question posed above[7]:

(A) "Classic FIT": The FIT should not directly react to the asset price increases and decreases, since the asset prices are not the target variable. First, it is very difficult to differentiate a bubble from a fundamentally strong economy. Second, even a bubble can be identified; fighting against

[7] See my earlier writing on this issue: Ito (2006) and Ito and Hayashi (2004). See also Ingves (2007) and Svensson (2009) for slightly different classification and discussions.

it by monetary policy tools (usually, the interest rate) could jeopardize the goal of price stability and less output variability. The main burden of prevention of a banking crisis should be placed on financial supervision policy, a separate entity from monetary policy. In order to prevent hard-landing of the banking system, the regulatory authority can introduce various prudential measures — such as higher and variable capital standards, introducing and tightening regulation on the loan-to-value ratio and the loan-income ratio ceiling, and examination of the internal risk assessment of bank portfolios.

(B) "Lean FIT": The FIT should pay more attention to both the (projected) CPI and the asset prices and react to them. Since the burst of the bubble most likely causes the financial instability, precautionary monetary tightening is recommended to nip the bubble in the bud. The low interest rate is destined to encourage risk-taking activities — more reckless than normal — and the financial supervision policy cannot perfectly prevent risk concentration in some sectors of the economy. Asset prices should be either included in a set of target variables or made a special variable that should be watched carefully in parallel with the CPI inflation rate.

The "Classic FIT" view is most famously told by the then-chairman of the Federal Reserve, Alan Greenspan (2002): "Moreover, it was far from obvious that bubbles, even if identified early, could be preempted short of the central bank inducing a substantial contraction in economic activity — the very outcome we would be seeking to avoid." The reference for the comments was the dot.com bubble in the second half of the 1990s.

In the course of the housing bubble in the United States becoming bigger and bigger from 2004 to 2006, the lending standard became lower and lower, ending up at the state of lending to subprime borrowers. This is clearly a failure of supervision rather than the low interest rate policy. Those institutions that securitize mortgages and market those securities were increasing the leverage ratio. This should have been warned as a risky practice. A direct measure of warning about risk could have been called for, regardless of the level of the interest rate. It is true that the interest rate is a blunt instrument to tame asset bubbles. FIT cannot pursue too many policy goals with only one policy instrument.

The "Lean FIT" view is put forward by Cecchetti, Genberg, Lipsky, and Wadhwani (2000), Borio and White (2003), and White (2009). This view is sometimes called "leaning against the wind" of the housing prices. They argue that the movements of asset prices, namely the stock prices and housing prices, should influence the course of monetary policy.

As a monetary policy rule, the so-called Taylor rule has become very popular. It states that the policy interest rate setting by the central bank (in the original Taylor paper) can be approximated by three factors: the natural interest rate, the difference in the current inflation rate from the target inflation rate, and the GDP gap. It does not include asset prices in the specification.

Many interpret the Taylor rule as a policy reaction function, or the average behavior of the central bank in the past. However, Taylor (2009) tends to interpret the rule as a desirable path. John Taylor (2007, 2009) criticized that the too-low interest rate (compared to the Taylor rule) from 2002 to 2006 is to blame for the subprime bubble. The interest rate was too low for too long. Therefore, he argues, the subprime crisis was caused by too lax monetary policy. Based on the hypothetical (desirable) Taylor rule interest rate path, Taylor estimated the "counterfactual housing starts" that showed much more moderated rise and decline from 2003 to 2006.

The fact that the Taylor rule equation does not include asset prices as an explanatory variable for the policy rate setting is similar to the "classic" view. But both the "lean" view and Taylor (2009) argue that monetary policy from 2003 to 2006 was to blame for the global financial crisis. They differ in understanding the best monetary policy. Taylor (2009) argues that even with the inflation rate gap and the output gap, the monetary policy was too lax during the crucial period. View (B) may include asset prices in the objective function of monetary policy and argue that monetary policy was too lax.

4. Digression: The Japanese Bubble Experience

With respect to the Japanese housing bubble in the second half of the 1980s and its subsequent collapse in the first half of the 1990s, an interesting debate took place back in the Jackson Hole conference in 1999. Bernanke and Gertler (1999) presented a paper in which they heavily criticized the Bank of Japan's monetary policy: "We find that easy monetary policy in Japan actively fueled the increase in stock prices during the 1987–1989 period." They showed that the optimal policy rule they estimated would have suggested an 8 percent interest rate as early as the summer of 1988, when the actual call rate was at around 3 percent. Then-deputy governor of the Bank of Japan, Mr. Yamaguchi, responded that it would have been very difficult to raise the interest rate from 4 percent to 8 percent when the CPI inflation rate was below 1 percent.

Okina, Shirakawa, and Shiratsuka (2001) reflected on the 1999 debate. While they consider that the preemptive hike of the interest rate a la Bernanke and Gertler would have been impossible for political reasons, they also put importance on the role of the interest rate in reducing the magnitude of the bubble by inducing an earlier peaking of the bubble: "If interest rates had been raised early, expectations for the continuation of low interest rates would have receded more quickly than otherwise, and to that extent the timing of the autonomous collapse of the bubble would have been somewhat expedited" (Okina, Shirakawa, and Shiratsuka, 2001, p. 430).

The housing prices and stock prices sometimes exhibit a spectacular price increase followed by a crash. Toward the end of the boom, many investors are lured into the market just to make profits from short-term buying and selling. Traditional fundamental signals, like the price-rental ratio or equivalently the ratio of the purchase price to the theoretical discounted present value of rental revenues, are totally disregarded. The phenomenon of the high price level (relative to the fundamental, intrinsic value) supported only by expectation of further price increase is typically called a bubble.

Can we identify, with reasonable certainty, in real time, a housing market bubble as opposed to fundamentals-driven price increases? Probably yes, but only at the very last stage of the bubble. While the housing price increases improve the economic welfare of many households and firms since they produce wealth effects, a premature end to the price increase would be an economic loss.

On the other hand, the crash brings about hardship. Foreclosures of homes, bankruptcy of firms, and unemployment soar, and when it is severe, the banking system becomes very weak. The banking crisis causes credit crunch, liquidity shortage, and, in the worst-case scenario, the systemic breakdown. Simply put, financial stability is threatened when the bubble bursts. Many cases in history are evidence. The cost to the economy from financial instability could become enormous. The asset price bubble often occurs without CPI inflation rate. That was the case in the U.S. housing boom of 2002–2006, the U.S. dot.com stock boom of 1997–2001, and the Japanese housing (land) boom of 1985–1989.

How should the FIT central bank react to the asset price inflation? Let me first make one point clear. The FIT targets not only the current inflation rate, but the medium-term price stability, that is, the expected inflation rate. Therefore, if the asset price boom is expected to produce overheating, most likely through wealth effects, in the near future, then the FIT will act to stop it. How should the FIT react to the asset price boom when the CPI inflation rate is projected to stay low and stable?

Supervision policy, conducted by the supervision agencies like the FSA and central bank, should pay much more attention to the asset price bubble to ensure the financial institutions' robustness: Capital requirement should be increased in the boom (dynamic capital requirement); the loan-to-value ratio should be adjusted when the asset prices are rising fast; and risk assessment, like stress tests, should be regularly conducted to the large, systemically important institutions. One more important element is to legislate a framework to take over a large, systemically important institution if its capital becomes less than a certain critical level — a resolution mechanism. This avoids moral hazard while systemic stability is maintained.

The inflation-targeting framework should be coordinated with supervision policy. The coordination between the central bank and the supervision agency is critical.

5. Middle Ground: Should the Central Bank Target Asset Prices?

Advocates of "Classic FIT" press the advocates of "Lean FIT" whether asset prices should be included in the central bank loss function along with inflation rate and output gap. If the answer is no, then advocates of "Classic FIT" view would say that the FIT already takes into account asset prices when forming medium-term forecasts of CPI and output. If the answer is yes, then it poses the question whether there are enough instruments to hit multiple targets.

Is there a middle ground? Many central banks operate in some form of compromises — let us say "practical" compromises — between "Classic" and "Lean." Let us explore some of them.

The first compromise is to allow a tolerance band of projected CPI inflation targeting, and lean against asset price inflation within the band. When asset prices are rising quickly, the FIT should be vigilant. The interest hike should happen earlier and the level should be higher within the tolerance band. This includes the so-called Riksbank view: "The paths of asset prices and indebtedness can at times be either difficult to rationalize or unsustainable in the long term. This means that there are risks of sharp corrections in the future which, in turn, affect the real economy and inflation.... In practice, taking risks of this kind into consideration can mean that interest rate changes are made somewhat earlier or later, in relation to what would have been the most suitable according to the forecasts for inflation and the real economy" (Ingves, 2007).

The second compromise is the "two-pillar" approach. The first pillar is more short-term, CPI stability, while the second pillar is the financial stability. As long as the second pillar is not threatened, the first pillar operates with a usual FIT central bank policy rule with CPI price stability and output stability in the objective function. When there are worrying signs — e.g., credit expansion, asset price increases, and the vulnerable bank balance sheets are detected — the first pillar will give way to the second pillar. This follows more lexicographic ordering from financial stability to CPI inflation stability.

The "Classic FIT" advocates may condition their views on the existence of a strong regulatory framework. Dynamic capital ratio, strong power to direct financial institutions avoiding risk concentration, and some sort of resolution authority in case some banks fall into trouble after the burst of a bubble may be important to separate financial stability and monetary policy. In other words, if the country has an effective regulatory regime, the burden on the monetary policy is lessened. So, strengthening the regulatory framework to prevent the bubble and clean up the crash swiftly is always welcome. It is more pressing and important to debate over the issue of the best practice of a supervision and regulatory framework and concrete measures of anti-bubble regulations than to debate how asset prices should be used in monetary policy.

6. Collecting and Calculating Housing Price Data

Having reliable data is key for sound policy decisions. For monetary policy decision for price stability, the reliable general price index is needed. Almost all advanced countries and emerging market economies have adopted similar methods in collecting data and calculating the consumer price index. Although there are some differences in sampling methods (how to define a basket), in statistical treatment of indexes (Laspeyres or chain), and in measuring quality differences (use of hedonic approach), the consumer price index, headline and core, in many countries is reliable and comparable across countries. For better policy judgment, both headline (all goods and services) and core (excluding energy and some fresh food items) should be used.

When we consider asset bubbles, we need asset price information. The stock prices are readily available and mostly reliable.[8] Other financial assets are also readily available and reliable, except for some products with thin markets.

The most serious shortcoming in judging an asset bubble lies in housing price data. Housing price data in many countries are quite unreliable. In principle, all detached houses are different with unique addresses. Even in the same neighborhood, the age of building structures and floor space (square meters) and views may be different. High-rise condominium units have the same street address, similar floor plans, and the same age of the building, but the exact floor space (square meters), the floor number of the building, and the views from the window are different. The point is that we need to standardize "housing" in order to come up with reliable housing price data.

The housing price index calculated without correcting for heterogeneity of houses would be seriously flawed. Calculating the "average prices" of the city would underestimate the price increase during the bubble period.

There are two major ways to standardize the housing price, controlling for heterogeneity. First, a hedonic approach is to correct the quality differences by identifying factors that determine values of housing, and adjusting for them using the so-called hedonic regression. Commonly used factors are floor space (square meters), the age of the structure, distance to the train station, proxy for view and security, and proxy for better/worse school district. Ito and Hirono (1993) attempted such a hedonic regression for the Tokyo condominium market.

The second approach is the "repeated sales" of the same housing unit. Limiting samples to the "same unit" controls for the floor space and location — two important determinants of housing prices. When a unit is sold, it is compared to the past sale prices — whenever it was sold k years ago. Then, the price change for k years is measured. The price change from $t-k$ to $t-1$ is already calculated in $t-1$, so that the price change from $t-1$

[8]There are technical issues, such as the selection of stocks, entry and exit from the selected group of stocks, simple average or weighted average, treatment of stale quotes, and adjustment for dividend payments. However, once the specification is determined, the stock price index is quite reliable since prices are traded and observed in the stock exchange.

to *t* can be extracted. The now widely used Case–Shiller index is based on the repeated sale.[9]

The prerequisite for reacting to the housing prices is to obtain reliable data. Only when the reliable data on housing are available, appropriate policy judgment and policy measures can be made. In many cases, housing price increases start with good fundamental reasons but they transform into a bubble after some sustained period of price increases. When fundamentals-driven housing price increases would turn into a bubble, they have to be carefully analyzed, if a housing bubble should be countered by some policy measures. It is also very helpful in policy decisions to have a database on the housing loan (mortgage) details, including the loan-to-value ratio, how the down payment is financed, whether it is the primary home, second home, or for rental/lease. The information would be relevant to see whether speculative purchases are increasing and whether they pose financial risk to lenders as well as borrowers.

7. Legal Framework to Avoid Too-Big-to-Fail

One of the reasons that the U.S. subprime crisis developed into a full-blown financial crisis was the lack of legal framework to take over large systemically important financial institutions. Since there was no legal framework, the bailout of Bear Stearns in March 2008 was arranged. Then critics criticized the deal for allowing for moral hazard. When the next financial problem became serious at Lehman Brothers, the government had no plan to bail out (with subsidies to an acquirer) the troubled institution. As a result, Lehman Brothers filed for Chapter 11. This caused panic in the global financial markets, causing unprecedented turmoil in interbank markets, derivative markets, mortgage-backed securities, corporate bonds, and commercial papers. Many other financial institutions needed government help in terms of capital injection and liability guarantees. These market reactions, fear of sudden failures of financial institutions, could have been avoided if the United States had introduced a legal framework to resolve systemically important institutions in time.[10] Having a legal framework

---

[9]The Case–Shiller index can be seen at the Standard & Poor's website; available at www.standardandpoors.com/indices/sp-case-shiller-home-price-indices/en/us/?indexId=spusa-cashpidff–p-us—.

[10]The importance of having a legal framework to temporarily nationalize a large financial institution is explained in Ito (2009).

of orderly resolution is the backstop for financial stability (without moral hazard).

For both views, it is necessary to introduce, if not already, a legal framework to take over a troubled large financial institution when the institution is deemed insolvent. For this, the Japanese Deposit Insurance Law, Article 102 (see Financial Services Agency homepage) can be used as a model. It says that financial emergency is determined by the council chaired by the prime minister, and nationalization under this emergency clause is possible. Once a financial institution is identified as undercapitalized but systemically important as mentioned above (Article 102), then the deposit insurance corporation can subscribe the shares — that is, the de facto nationalization. So, the process explicitly involves the government, and the central bank is only in the background.

8. Commitment to FIT with Financial Stability

There is a consensus on the importance of financial supervision among both "Classic" and "Lean" FIT advocates, but there is no consensus on whether the central bank should be in charge of financial supervision, or whether a separate organization like the Financial Services Agency (FSA) should be in charge. Financial supervision is key to examine the macroeconomic impact and systemic risk of a possible early call of a bubble (macroprudence) and introducing prudential policy measures such as requiring to lower the loan-to-value ratio, and to examine the vulnerability of financial institutions that have exposure to the housing sector (microprudence).

Benefits of having financial supervision in the central bank include wide availability of a high caliber of staff and comprehensive judgment of the financial market conditions. However, there may be a concern of conflict of interest. If banks' balance sheets are judged to be weak, the interest rate hike may be hesitated. Having an independent FSA, like in Australia, Canada, Japan, and Korea, among others, may avoid the conflict of interest. The institutional difference between the financial supervision wing and the FSA may not be so important if it is staffed by experts on best practices of supervision and regulation; and if it is endowed with a budget; a legal authority for policy instruments, such as the loan-to-value ratio; and political independence.

When those measures are exhausted or ineffective, the FIT is modified so that the interest rate is hiked to insure that the bubble would not become too large to threaten financial stability. This may cause output declines and deflationary pressure, but the sacrifice may be needed to avoid even bigger sacrifices later. However, this approach is the second-best. The weaker supervision regime would force the central bank (monetary policy department) to deviate from the regular FIT framework. In a country where prudential authority is lacking, it may be necessary that the FIT is sacrificed in favor of financial stability down the road, but this is second-best.

9. Concluding Remarks

This paper examined whether the best-practice monetary policy, namely Classic FIT, has to be modified in light of the global financial crisis of 2007–2009. Several critics of Classic FIT argue that asset prices, in particular housing prices, should be explicitly considered in monetary policy decisions. Some even regard that the FIT framework has been discredited. A standard answer from the Classic FIT camp would be that when it is difficult enough to control CPI inflation and output gap, adding housing prices as a third policy target would make the tradeoff problem almost impossible. The best way to handle the tradeoff is to assign different policy variables to prevent housing prices from getting into a bubble process. The supervision agency or the financial stability wing in the central bank would be able to gather information and use power to introduce prudential measures, while the monetary policy wing of the central bank can concentrate on Classic FIT. When supervision fails, monetary policy may be deviated from the best Classic FIT recommendations.

In sum, flexible inflation targeting remains as a sound monetary policy framework even after experiencing the severe financial crisis that originated in the United States. Putting a weight on asset prices as a monetary policy objective without adding a policy instrument may cause a serious tradeoff problem. It is more important to define and implement macroprudential tools than to decide who would be in charge of those policies. Defining and monitoring an appropriate set of asset prices — some qualitative and some quantitative — is an important first step. Macroprudential measures should be carefully defined and their effectiveness should be examined from the past experiences. If a macroprudential role is given to the central bank, it is important to separate the financial stability function from the monetary policy function so that a compromise to (CPI) inflation stability should be avoided. Political independence of the central bank should be protected even under the increased role. If a macroprudential role is given to an agency outside the central bank, say the FSA, then its independence of political process and of the regulated industry has to be crafted and protected. The orderly resolution process of financial institutions should be created to lessen the burden of both the central bank and the FSA for their proper policy implementation, avoiding the too-big-to-fail principle. Whether all reforms implemented in the United States, Europe and other parts of the world stand up to future challenges of preventing a bubble remains to be seen.

References

Bernanke, Ben and Mark Gertler, 1999, "Monetary Policy and Asset Price Volatility," symposium sponsored by Federal Reserve Bank of Kansas City, p. 107.

Borio, Claudio and William R. White, 2003, "Whither monetary and financial stability? The implications of evolving policy regimes," Federal Reserve Bank of Kansas City, annual conference, *Monetary Policy and Uncertainty: Adapting to a Changing Economy*, pp. 131–211.

Cecchetti, Stephen G., Hans Genberg, John Lipsky, and Sushil Wadhwani, 2000, "Asset prices and central bank policy," Geneva Reports on the World Economy, No. 2, Geneva, Switzerland: International Center for Monetary and Banking Studies.

Greenspan, Alan, 2002, "Economic Volatility," symposium sponsored by the Federal Reserve Bank of Kansas City, Jackson Hole, WY, August 30.

Greenspan, Alan, 2005, "Federal Reserve Board's semiannual Monetary Policy Report to the Congress," testimony before the U.S. Senate, Committee on Banking, Housing, and Urban Affairs, February 16.

Ingves, Stefan, 2007, "Housing and monetary policy: A view from an inflation-targeting central bank," Federal Reserve Bank of Kansas City, annual conference, *Housing, Housing Finance, and Monetary Policy*, pp. 433–443.

Ito, Takatoshi, 2006, "Optimal monetary policy in an environment of low inflation and rising asset prices," in Bank of Korea, Monetary Policy in an Environment of Low Inflation, International Conference 2006, June 16, Korea, pp. 159–177.

Ito, Takatoshi, 2009, "Fire, flood, and lifeboats: Policy responses to the global crisis of 2007–2009," Federal Reserve Bank of San Francisco conference, Asia and the Global Financial Crisis, October 18–19.

Ito, Takatoshi, 2010, "Monetary policy and financial stability: Is inflation-targeting passé?" ADB Economics, working paper, No. 206, July.

Ito, Takatoshi and Tomoko Hayashi, 2004, "Inflation targeting in Asia," Hong Kong Institute for Monetary Research, occasional paper, No. 1, March.

Ito, Takatoshi and Keiko Nosse Hirono, 1993, "The efficiency of the Tokyo housing market," *Bank of Japan, Monetary and Economic Studies*, Vol. 11, No. 1, pp. 1–32.

Ito, Takatoshi and Tokuo Iwaisako, 1996, "Explaining asset bubbles in Japan," *Bank of Japan, Monetary and Economic Studies*, Vol. 14, July, pp. 143–193.

Obstfeld, Maurice and Kenneth Rogoff, 2009, "Global imbalances and the financial crisis: Products of common causes," Federal Reserve Bank of San Francisco conference, Asia and the Global Financial Crisis, October 18–19.

Okina, K., M. Shirakawa, and S. Shiratsuka, 2001, "The asset price bubble and monetary policy: Japan's experience in the late 1980s and the lessons," *Bank of Japan, Monetary and Economic Studies*, special edition, Vol. 19, No. S-1, pp. 395–450.

Portes, Richard, 2009, "Global imbalances," in *Macroeconomic Stability and Financial Regulation: Key Issues for the G20*, Mathias Dewatripont, Xavier Freixas, and Richard Portes (eds.), London: Centre for Economic Policy Research.

Svensson, Lars E.O., 1997, "Inflation forecast targeting: Implementing and monitoring inflation targets," *European Economic Review*, Vol. 41, No. 6, pp. 1111–1146.

Svensson, Lars E.O., 2009, "Flexible inflation targeting: Lessons from the financial crisis," speech, September 21.

Taylor, John, 2007, "Housing and monetary policy," Federal Reserve Bank of Kansas City, annual conference, *Housing, Housing Finance, and Monetary Policy*, pp. 463–476.

Taylor, John, 2009, *Getting Off Track*, Stanford, CA: Hoover Institution.

White, William, 2009, "Should monetary policy 'lean or clean'?", Federal Reserve Bank of Dallas, Globalization and Monetary Policy Institute, working paper, No. 34, available at www.dallasfed.org/institute/wpapers/2009/0034.pdf.

IV. CURRENT, PAST, AND POTENTIAL FUTURE THREATS TO FINANCIAL STABILITY

Bank Capital Regulations: Learning the Right Lessons from the Crisis

Asli Demirgüç-Kunt*

Director of Research, the World Bank

The recent financial crisis demonstrated that existing capital regulations — in design, implementation, or some combination of the two — were completely inadequate to prevent a panic in the financial sector. Needless to say, policymakers and pundits have been making widespread calls to reform bank regulation and supervision.[1] But how best to redesign capital standards? Before joining the calls for reform, it is important to look at how financial institutions performed through the crisis to see if we are learning the right lessons from the crisis. Is capital regulation justified? What type of capital should banks hold to ensure that they can better withstand periods of stress? Should a simple leverage ratio be introduced to reduce regulatory arbitrage and improve transparency? These are some of the questions we addressed in a recent paper I wrote with Enrica Detragiache and Ouarda Merrouche.[2]

Since the first Basel capital accord in 1988, the prevailing approach to bank regulation has put capital front and center: Banks that hold more capital should be better able to absorb losses with their own resources, without becoming insolvent or necessitating a bailout with public funds. In addition, by forcing bank owners to have some "skin in the game,"

---

* The author is the director, Development Policy, and chief economist, Financial and Private Sector Development Network, of the World Bank. The views expressed in this paper are those of the author and should not be attributed to the World Bank.

[1] See Caprio, Demirgüç-Kunt, and Kane (2010), Demirgüç-Kunt and Serven (2010), Viñals *et al.* (2010), Hellwig (2010), Admati *et al.* (2011).

[2] This paper and presentation draws largely on Demirgüç-Kunt, Detragiache, and Merrouche (2010).

minimum capital requirements help counterbalance incentives for excessive risk-taking created by limited liability and amplified by deposit insurance and bailout expectations.[3] However, many of the banks that were rescued in the latest turmoil appeared to be in compliance with minimum capital requirements shortly before and even during the crisis. In the ensuing debate over how to strengthen regulation, capital continues to play an important role. A consensus is being forged around a new set of capital standards (Basel III), with the goal of making capital requirements more stringent.[4]

In my research with Enrica and Ouarda, we investigate whether banks that were better capitalized experienced a smaller decline in their stock market value during the financial crisis. Specifically, we use a panel of quarterly bank data for 12 countries over 2006–2009 to study the impact of bank capital and its various definitions and components on changes in market valuation of banks. If bank capital truly helps in curbing banks' incentives for risk-taking and ability to absorb losses, we would expect that when a large unexpected negative shock to bank value materializes — as was the case with the financial crisis that began in August 2007 — equity market participants would judge better capitalized banks to be in a superior position to withstand the shock, and the stock price of these banks would fall less than that of poorly capitalized banks.

We also investigate which concept of capital was more relevant to stock valuation during the crisis. Existing capital requirements are set as a proportion of risk exposure; but if the risk exposure calculation under Basel rules did not reflect actual risk, capital measures based on cruder risk-exposure proxies, such as total assets, might have been considered as more meaningful by equity traders.

Another issue is the quality of different types of capital used for regulatory purposes. As recognized by the Basel Committee (2009), under current standards some banks were able to demonstrate strong capitalization while holding a limited amount of tangible common equity, which is the component of capital that is available to absorb losses while the bank remains a going concern. So it is important to see whether banks with higher quality capital were really viewed more positively by equity market participants.

---

[3]See Santos (2001) for a review of the literature on bank capital.

[4]See Basel Committee on Banking Supervision (2009).

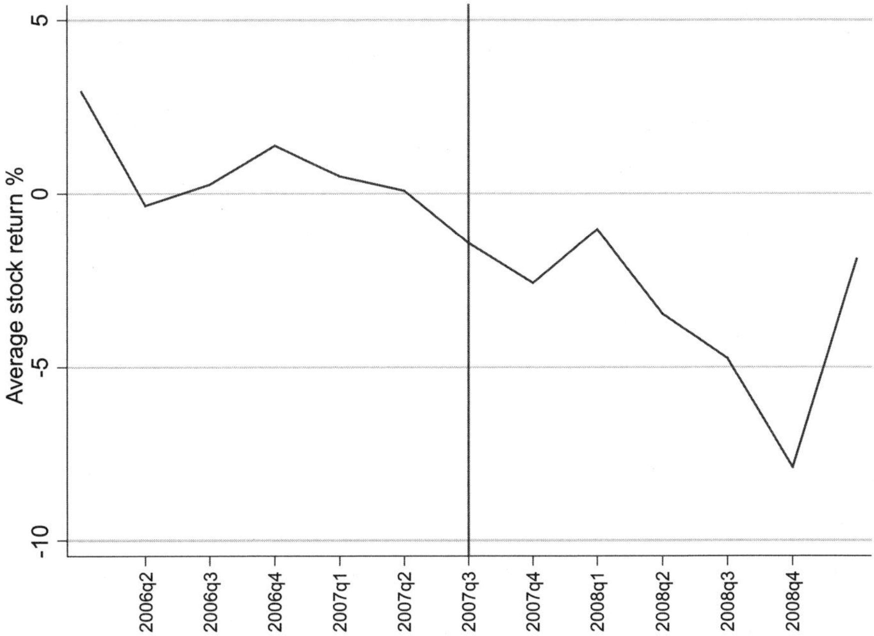

Figure 1. Average Quarterly Bank Stock Returns, in Percent, Q1.2006–Q1.2009.

1. The Analysis and Results

Average quarterly stock returns during the sample period are given in Figure 1. Figure 2 reports these returns for each country in the sample. The returns are positive in the pre-crisis period and as expected become negative in the crisis period. As Table 1 shows, the median returns for the full sample of 381 banks went from 0.4 percent to −3.5 percent. If we focus on the more acute phase of the crisis after Lehman bankruptcy, they are only −5.3 percent. The second panel of the table reports returns for the largest banks, with assets greater than $50 billion. We are interested in looking at the largest banks separately because typically large banks are more sophisticated and operate on a global scale with complex balance sheets. This makes their assets more opaque, and the banks are better able to avoid regulation through regulatory arbitrage. They also tend to be the focus of macroprudential regulation since they are important for systemic stability of the financial systems. Table 1 shows that the largest 91 banks in the sample were doing better before the crisis compared to smaller banks

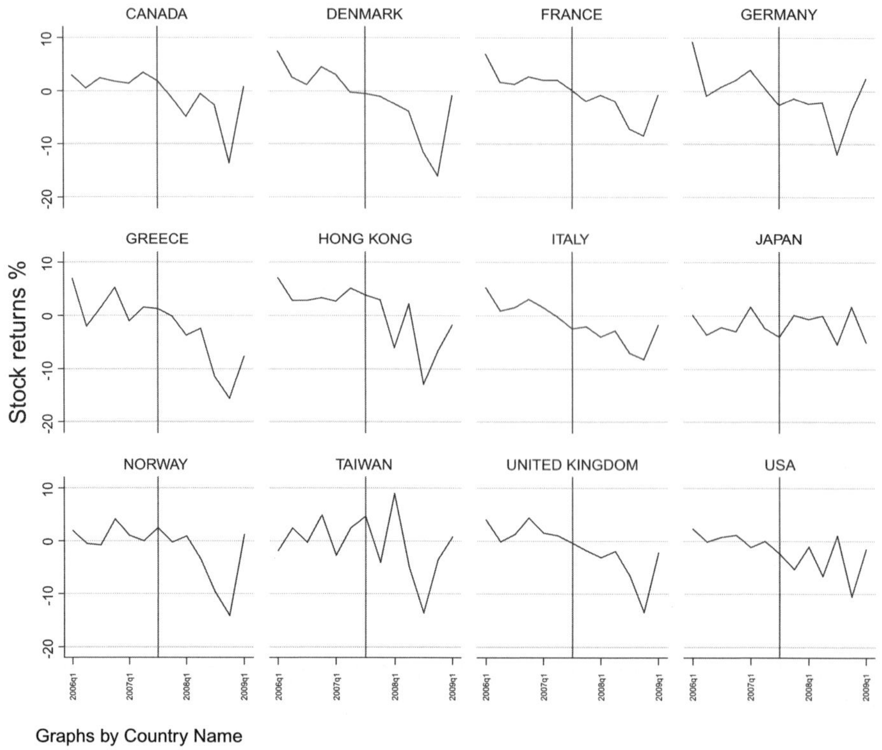

Figure 2. Average Quarterly Bank Stock Returns by Country, in Percent, Q1.2006–Q1.2009.

Table 1. Bank Stock Returns — Before and During the Crisis.

Full sample	Median	Standard deviation
Pre-Crisis Q1-2006 to Q2-2007	0.4	3.6
Crisis Q3-2007 to Q1-2009	−3.5	7.8
Post-Lehman Q3-2008 to Q1-2009	−5.3	9.8
Large Banks		
Pre-Crisis Q1-2006 to Q2-2007	0.8	3.0
Crisis Q3-2007 to Q1-2009	−4.7	8.0
Post-Lehman Q3-2008 to Q1-2009	−6.7	10.3

with returns of 0.8 percent. However, the decline in their returns was also greater: It fell to −4.7 percent in the crisis period and −6.7 percent post-Lehman. The uncertainty around these returns was also greater as can be seen from the higher standard deviations.

The main variable of interest is bank capital. We use a number of alternative definitions of capital, namely the risk-adjusted regulatory capital ratio (calculated according to Basel rules) and leverage ratio (defined as regulatory capital divided by total assets). The numerators for both ratios are calculated as the sum of Tier 1 and Tier 2 capital. Tier 1 capital comprises shareholder funds and perpetual, non-cumulative preference shares. Tier 2 capital comprises hybrid capital, subordinated debt, loan loss reserves, and valuation reserves. In the debate following the crisis, questions about the ability of the risk-adjustment used in the Basel framework to capture bank risk have been raised. More recently with the Greek bailout and the euro crisis, the wisdom of assigning zero risk weights to all government bonds has made this issue of risk-weighing even more questionable.

Looking at capital ratios also reveals interesting differences across large and small banks. For the full sample, the median risk-adjusted capital asset ratio was 11.9 percent (see Table 2), comfortably above the minimum Basel requirement of 8 percent, with a standard deviation of 2.8 percent. The median Tier 1 capital was a seemingly healthy 9.7 percent. The median leverage ratio was 7.8 percent, and the Tier 1 leverage ratio was 6.3 percent. Interestingly, larger banks had lower capital than the full sample as measured by the Tier 1 leverage ratio (a median of just 4.6 percent), or the

Table 2. Summary Statistics — Capital Ratios.

Full sample	Median	Standard deviation
Risk-Weighted Capital	11.9	2.8
Tier 1 Risk-Weighted Capital	9.7	2.8
Leverage Ratio	7.8	2.5
Tier 1 Leverage Ratio	6.3	2.4
Large Banks		
Risk-Weighted Capital	11.7	2.4
Tier 1 Risk-Weighted Capital	8.2	1.9
Leverage Ratio	6.5	2.2
Tier 1 Leverage Ratio	4.6	1.7

Tier 1 risk-adjusted ratio (8.2 percent). The standard Basel capital ratio, on the other hand, barely differed between the two groups of banks. Thus, larger banks were relying more heavily on lower quality capital and had larger "risk-adjustments" of assets than smaller banks. This reliance by large banks on lower quality capital has been criticized after the crisis because this type of capital cannot be used to offset losses in times of distress.

In our regressions, we estimate various versions of basic return equation, regressing dividend-inclusive Datastream return index between the end of quarter $t - 1$ and end of quarter t on lagged values of bank capital, a matrix of bank control variables, and a matrix of country/time dummy variables. Through the interaction term with the crisis dummy, we allow the effect of the various explanatory variables on stock returns to differ during the crisis period. We also estimate a specification where a separate crisis period is identified as the period following the Lehman default. The country/year dummy variables control for any possible omitted effect that operates at the country level, such as macroeconomic shocks, the systemic component of the shock to bank equity prices, the policy response to the crisis, differences in accounting and regulatory definition of capital across countries, and so on. In other words, what our model seeks to explain is just the cross-sectional, within-country dispersion in stock returns in each quarter.

To isolate the effect of capital on this dispersion, we control for other bank-specific characteristics that may affect stock returns. Specifically, we control for bank liquidity using liquid assets/assets, the bank's reliance on deposits for funding (deposits/total assets), asset quality (loans loss provisions/total assets), the banks' business model (net loans/assets), and the bank size (log of total assets). Also, following standard asset pricing models, we include in the regression the stock's beta (computed as the five-year covariance between the bank's monthly stock return and the country stock market return) and the market-to-book value of equity. The price-earnings ratio (PE) measures possible mispricing of bank equity during the boom.

Explanatory variables computed from bank balance sheet information, including the variables measuring bank capital, are available on a yearly basis rather than a quarterly basis, while our dependent variable is quarterly. For these variables, we use the last available (but not contemporaneous) observation. For example, stock returns during each of the four quarters of 2007 are regressed on balance sheet variables at the end of 2006. The model is estimated with OLS, and standard errors are

Table 3. Bank Returns and Capital.

	Full sample		Large bank sample	
	Risk-weighted capital	Leverage ratio	Risk-weighted returns	Leverage ratio
Tier 1 Pre-Crisis	0.024	0.110*	−0.092	0.061
Tier 2 Pre-Crisis	0.074	0.006	−0.106	−0.252
Tier 1 Crisis	0.117	0.154	0.264	0.603***
Tier 2 Crisis	0.051	0.058	0.131	0.415
Controls	x	x	x	x
Country*Year FEs	x	x	x	x
No. of Obs.	4049	3726	827	736
R-squared	0.23	0.23	0.32	0.33

Notes: Table is based on regressions in Demirgüç-Kunt, Detragiache, and Merrouche (2010). The dependent variable is the quarterly stock return including dividends for the period Q1-2006 to Q1-2009. All control variables are lagged one year. Crisis is a dummy variable that takes value one from Q3-2007 to Q1-2009. Tier 1 (Tier 2) is Tier 1 (Tier 2) capital scaled either by risk-weighted assets (RWR) or by total un-weighted assets (LR). Large banks are defined as banks with total assets above US$50 billion. The regressions include country and time fixed-effects. Control variables are not reported for brevity. Standard errors clustered by bank; *, **, *** stand for statistical significance at 10 percent, 5 percent, and 1 percent, respectively.

clustered at the bank level to take into account possible autocorrelation in the residuals.

What do we find? The results are reported in Table 3. Before the crisis, differences in initial capital — whether risk-adjusted or not, however defined — did not consistently affect subsequent bank stock returns. But during the crisis period, the importance of capital for returns became evident, particularly for the largest banks in our sample. These are the banks of systemic importance, as well as those holding capital of lesser quality at the inception of the crisis. Our results also show that during the crisis, the stock returns of large banks were more sensitive to the leverage ratio than to the risk-adjusted capital ratio. This suggests that market participants viewed the risk-adjustment under Basel rules as more subject to manipulation or, at the very least, not reflective of true risk in the case of large banks. Finally, we also find that the positive association with subsequent stock returns is stronger for higher-quality capital, i.e., Tier 1 leverage ratio.

2. Policy Implications

Our results have potential policy implications for the current process of regulatory reform. First, we find support for the view that a stronger capital position is an important asset during a systemic crisis, suggesting that the current emphasis on strengthening capital requirements is broadly appropriate. Second, our results indicate that the introduction of a minimum leverage ratio to supplement minimum risk-adjusted capital requirements is important, as properly measuring risk exposure is very difficult, especially for large and complex financial organizations.

However, our results also question the usefulness of emphasizing risk-weighted concepts of bank capital, and this is important since these still very much remain at the core of Basel regulations. Hence, one interpretation of these findings would be that they also provide support to those proposals that call for completely doing away with risk calibration of capital in favor of focusing completely on leverage ratio in regulating bank capital.[5]

Finally, our study indicates that greater emphasis on "higher-quality capital" in the form of Tier 1 capital or tangible equity is justified. The fact that differences in stock returns among large banks did not reflect expectations about actions by regulators (which would have been the case had regulatory capital mattered for stock returns), but instead on higher-quality leverage ratio, is an indication that capital mattered because of its ability to absorb losses as well as its possible role as a signal of bank asset quality.

References

Admati, Anat R., Peter M. DeMarzo, Martin F. Hellwig, and Paul Pfleiderer, 2011, "Fallacies, irrelevant facts, and myths in the discussion of capital regulation: Why bank equity is not expensive," Max Planck Institute, working paper.

Basel Committee on Banking Supervision, 2009, "Consultative proposals to strengthen the resilience of the banking sector announced by the Basel committee," Bank of International Settlements, available at www.bis.org/press/p091 217.htm.

---

[5] See, for example, Hellwig (2010) and statements of the U.S. Shadow Regulatory Committee on Bank Regulation and Supervision.

Blum, M. Jürg, 2007, "Why Basel II may need a leverage ratio restriction," Swiss National Bank, working paper, No. 2007-4.

Caprio, Gerard, Asli Demirgüç-Kunt, and Edward Kane, 2010, "The 2007 meltdown in structured securitization: Searching for lessons, not scapegoats," *The World Bank Research Observer*, Vol. 25, No. 1, pp. 125–155.

Caprio Jr., Gerard and Patrick Honohan, 1999, "Beyond capital ideas: Restoring banking stability," World Bank, policy research working paper, No. 2235, November.

Demirgüç-Kunt, Asli, Enrica Detragiache, and Ouarda Merrouche, 2010, "Bank capital: Lessons from the financial crisis," World Bank, policy research paper, No. 5473, November; also forthcoming in *Journal of Money, Banking and Credit*.

Demirgüç-Kunt, Asli and Luis Serven, 2010, "Are all sacred cows dead? Implications of the financial crisis for macro and financial policies," *The World Bank Research Observer*, Vol. 25, No. 1, pp. 91–124.

Hellwig, Martin, 2010, "Capital regulation after the crisis: Business as usual?" Max Planck Institute, working paper.

Santos, Joao A. C., 2001, "Bank capital regulation in contemporary banking theory: A review of the literature," *Financial Markets, Institutions, and Instruments*, Vol. 10, pp. 41–84.

Viñals, José, Jonathan Fiechter, Ceyla Pazarbasioglu, Laura Kodres, Aditya Narain, and Marina Moretti, 2010, "Shaping the new financial system," *IMF Staff Position Note*, 10/15.

International Monetary Reform: Exchange Rates or Interest Rates?

Ronald McKinnon*
Stanford University

1. Introduction

In reforming the international monetary system, exchange rates usually get primary attention front and center — such as in numerous meetings of the Group of 20. Nobody wants a replay of the destructive beggar-thy-neighbor exchange rate depreciations of the 1930s.

But at the G-20 meeting in November 2010, President Obama attacked China for not *appreciating*. In the dollar-based world of East Asia, China's monetary policy has been oriented toward keeping the yuan/dollar rate fairly stable since 1994, when it unified its exchange rate system and went to current-account convertibility under the IMF's Article VIII. This policy of exchange rate stability served China well as a nominal anchor for its domestic price level, and to balance exchange relationships with its smaller neighbors (McKinnon and Schnabl, 2011). In addition, the left-hand panel of Figure 1 shows no clear evidence that China's exchange rate is undervalued *vis-à-vis* Europe or the United States relative to their "real" multilateral exchange rates averaged over the past 20 years.

Not finding any agreement on exchange rate practices, the G-20 meetings shifted to trade imbalances. Last November, the United States suggested that countries with trade surpluses cap them at, say, 4 percent of GDP. But trade surpluses simply reflect net saving surpluses: the difference between national saving and investment. And in market economies,

---

*Ronald McKinnon is the William D. Eberle Professor of International Economics at Stanford University. Much of the analysis in this chapter is contained in his new book, *The Unloved Dollar Standard: From Bretton Woods to the Rise of China* (Oxford University Press, 2013).

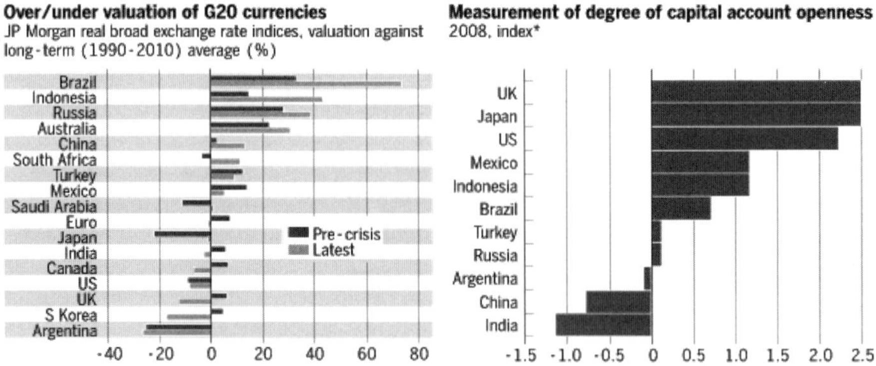

Figure 1. Exchange Rate Valuations.

Source: *Financial Times*, November 11, 2010.

governments do not directly control either. Nor, contrary to popular opinion and the proponents of "China bashing" to appreciate the RMB, can exchange appreciation be used as an instrument to reduce any creditor country's saving (trade) surplus (Qiao, 2007; McKinnon and Schnabl, 2011).

Moreover, the U.S. weakened its position by not following through: It did not pledge to eliminate its saving deficiency, i.e., to reduce its fiscal deficit and to raise the woefully deficient saving of American households. But, *eventually*, for global imbalances to be corrected, surplus countries must consume more while the saving-deficient United States consumes much less. However, in view of the dramatic November impasse of the G-20 and continuing stalemate in 2011 on exchange rate and U.S. fiscal issues, better to let sleeping dogs lie.

2. Interest Differentials, Carry Trades, and Worldwide Inflation

With exchange rates and trade balances off the table for now, what remains for constructive international monetary reform? Almost all emerging markets (EM) at the G-20 meeting in November 2010, and even more now in 2011, complain about ultra-low interest rates at the "center" inducing hot money flows to the "periphery." With today's two-speed world recovery, the slowly growing mature industrial countries — the United States, Europe, and Japan — have cut short-term interest rates very low. Figure 2 shows short-term interbank interest rates in the United States to be near zero since the end of 2008 — and Japan had been stuck in a zero-interest liquidity trap since the mid-1990s. In addition, the U.S. Federal Reserve's "quantitative

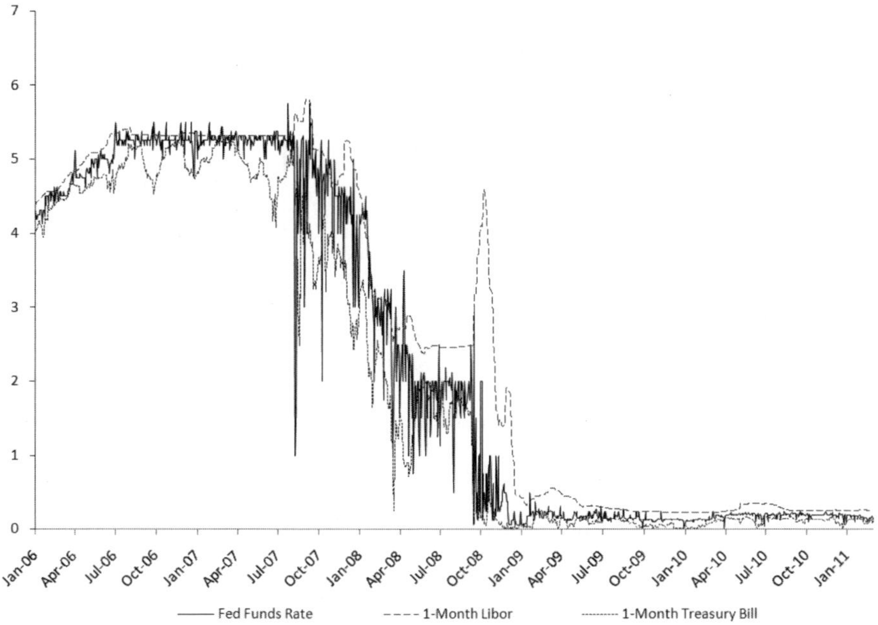

Figure 2. U.S. Short-Term Interest Rate.

Source: Federal Reserve Economic Data and Bloomberg.

easing" for reducing long rates (ending in June 2011) exacerbated the problem. In 2010–2011, the resulting "carry trade" has induced a flood of hot money into emerging markets — which have higher growth and naturally higher interest rates.

Although interrupted by the credit crunch in the last half of 2008 into 2009, when the crisis demand for dollars shot upward, the dollar's trade-weighted nominal exchange rate has been depreciating since 2002 through 2011 (Figure 3). The main pressure comes from the Fed keeping interest rates, on average, below those prevailing in most industrial countries, and much below those prevailing in emerging markets. The federal funds rate had been reduced to just 1 percent in 2003–2004 and the Fed was very slow to increase it before the 2008 crisis; since then, the U.S. has had near-zero short-term interest rates from late 2008 onward. For emerging markets only, Figure 4 is the mirror image of Figure 3, and shows their ongoing nominal appreciation since 2002 as the counterpart of the dollar's slow depreciation. Figure 5 shows that China's modest appreciation from 2002 to early 2011 cumulated to be about the same as that of other emerging

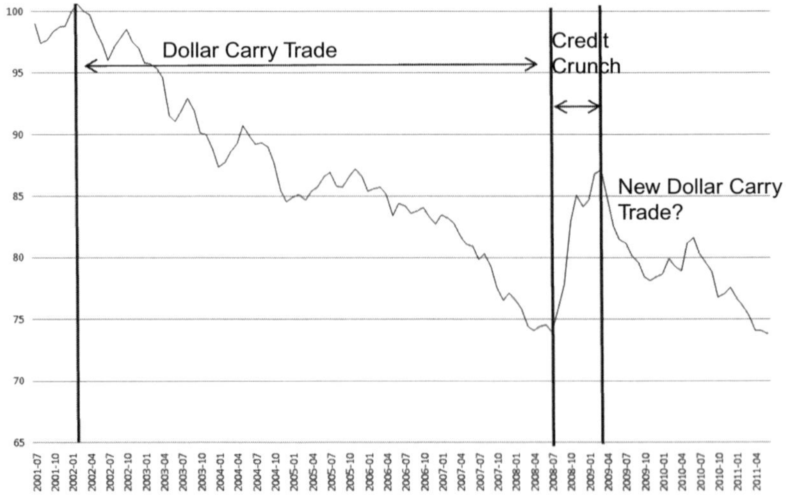

Figure 3. The Nominal Broad Dollar Index Movements (January 2002 = 100).

Source: Federal Reserve Economic Data.

markets — but the upward course of the RMB has been smoother and more predictable.

So the combination of very low American interest rates and a declining dollar has provoked large outflows of financial capital ("hot" money) into EM for almost a decade. When EM exchange rates are not tied down by official parities, their endogenous ongoing appreciation induces even more hot money inflows. Trend-following (chartist) speculators see a double benefit: the higher EM's interest rates combined with their currencies appreciating against the dollar or yen. For 2000–2007, before the global credit crunch in 2008, Table 1 provides illustrative returns to borrowing in dollars, euros, or yen to invest in surrounding EMs. The annual returns to dollar-based carry traders investing in Brazil, Mexico, and Canada were about 7.9 percent.

For emerging markets, therefore, exchange rate flexibility is no protection from foreign interest rate disturbances — as when the Fed reduces its short rates to zero. In the short run, exchange rate flexibility may actually enhance the returns that carry traders see as the target EM currency appreciates against the dollar. To slow the appreciations of EM currencies, EM central banks typically intervene to buy dollars with domestic base money. And these interventions have been truly massive. Figure 6 shows

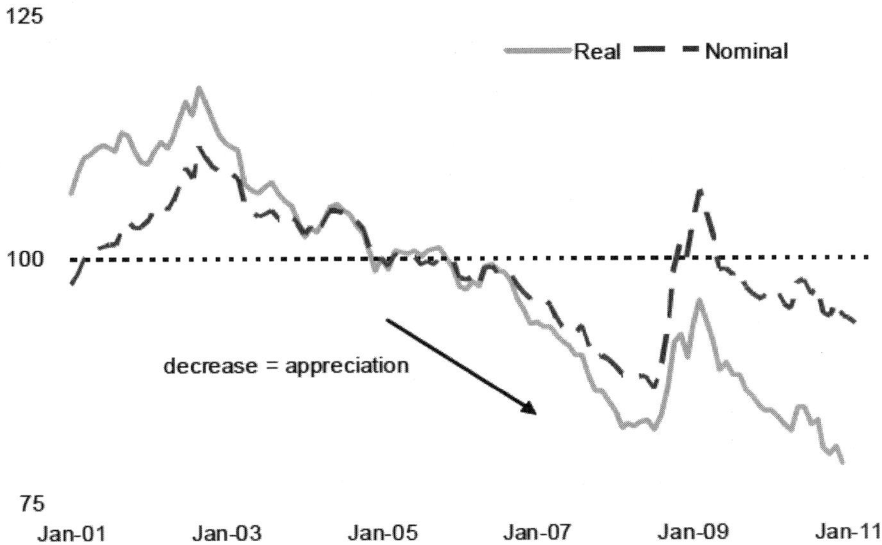

Figure 4. EM Real and Nominal Exchange Rate Appreciation (January 2005 = 100).

Note: Emerging markets (EM) include the following countries: Russia, Poland, Czech Republic, Hungary, Romania, Ukraine, Turkey, Israel, UAE, Saudi Arabia, South Africa, China, India, Hong Kong, Korea, Taiwan, Singapore, Indonesia, Malaysia, Thailand, Brazil, Mexico, Chile, Peru, Colombia, Argentina, and Venezuela.

Source: Haver Analytics, Morgan Stanley Research.

that from the first quarter of 2001 to the first quarter of 2011, the dollar value of EM foreign exchange reserves rose sixfold — from $1 trillion to $6 trillion! Figure 6 also shows that China accounted for about half of this huge buildup — but the collectivity of other EMs was equally important.

Figure 7 shows that this EM buildup of foreign exchange reserves increased much faster than the growth of their nominal GDPs. For the EM group, reserves rose from about 15 percent of GDP at the beginning of 2001 to 34 percent of GDP at the beginning of 2011. For China alone over this same 10-year period, Figure 7 shows that the ratio of FX reserves to GDP increased particularly strongly, from about 13 percent to 50 percent. Some EMs, notably China and Brazil, have re-imposed exchange controls on capital *inflows* — but with limited success.

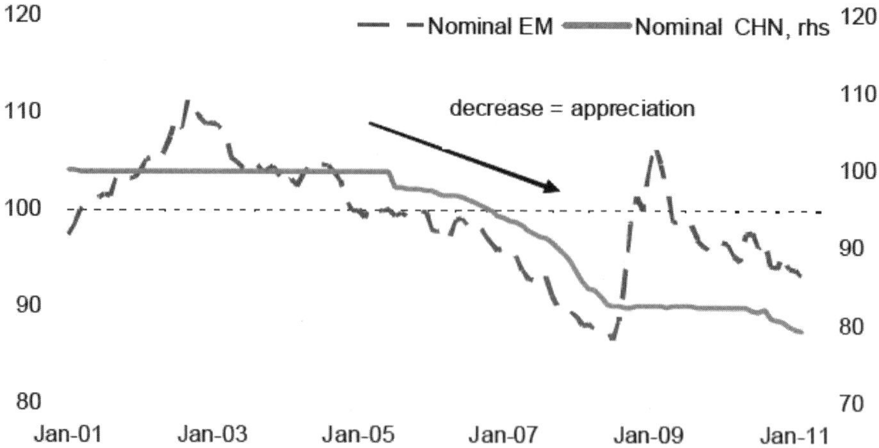

Figure 5. EM and CHN Nominal Exchange Rate Appreciation (January 2005 = 100).

Source: Haver Analytics, Morgan Stanley Research.

Table 1. Returns on Carry Trade (2000–2007).

Funding currency	Interest rates		Returns from appreciation	Returns of carry trades	Investment currencies
	Funding	Investment			
US Dollar	3.4	10.2	1.1	7.9	Brazil, Mexico, and Canada
Euro	3.2	7.4	1.0	5.2	Iceland, Poland, and Czech Republic
Japanese Yen	0.1	5.3	5.2	10.7	Australia, Korea, and New Zealand

Source: IMF.

This sharp buildup of EM foreign exchange reserves has been too big to be fully offset by domestic monetary sterilization operations. The resulting loss of monetary control in the EM led (and leads) to inflation generally higher than that in the developed market economies (DM) — as shown in

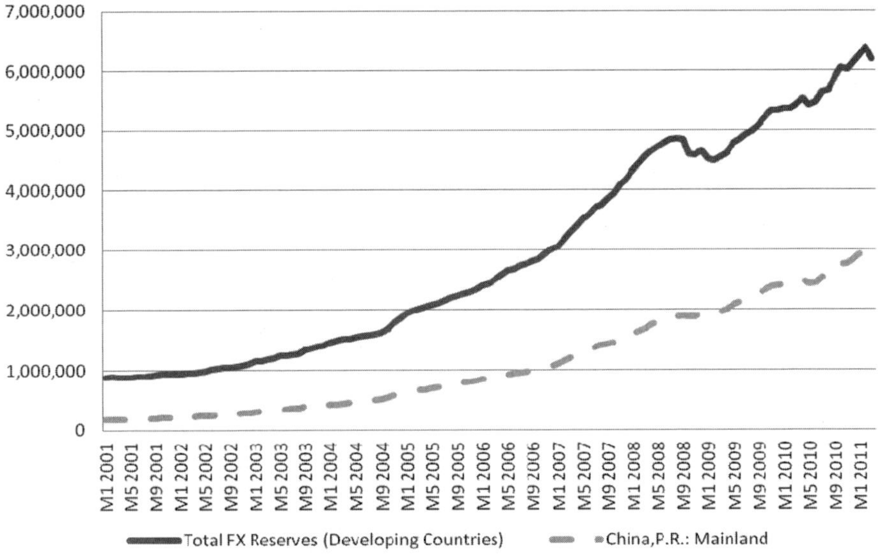

Figure 6. Foreign Exchange Reserves ($MM).

Note: Emerging markets (EM) include the following countries: Russia, Poland, Czech Republic, Hungary, Romania, Ukraine, Turkey, Israel, United Arab Emirates, Saudi Arabia, South Africa, China, India, Hong Kong, Korea, Singapore, Indonesia, Malaysia, Thailand, Brazil, Mexico, Chile, Peru, Colombia, Argentina, and Venezuela.

Source: IFS.

Figure 8. This greater inflation in EMs occurred *despite* the fact that since 2002, EM currencies on average appreciated against the DM currencies — as shown in Figure 4.

More recently, after the interruption of the 2008 global credit crunch, a renewed carry trade began and was led by the now zero short-term interest rates in the United States. From May 2009 into 2011, Table 2 shows the continued rapid buildup of foreign exchange reserves in the largest EMs — China, Russia, Indonesia, India, and Brazil — all of whom have nominal CPIs growing more than 5 percent per year. This is substantially higher than CPI or PPI inflation in Europe, or Japan, or in the United States itself. China's ongoing trade surplus (without any normal offsetting capital outflow) also contributes to its buildup of foreign exchange reserves — but is no longer dominant.

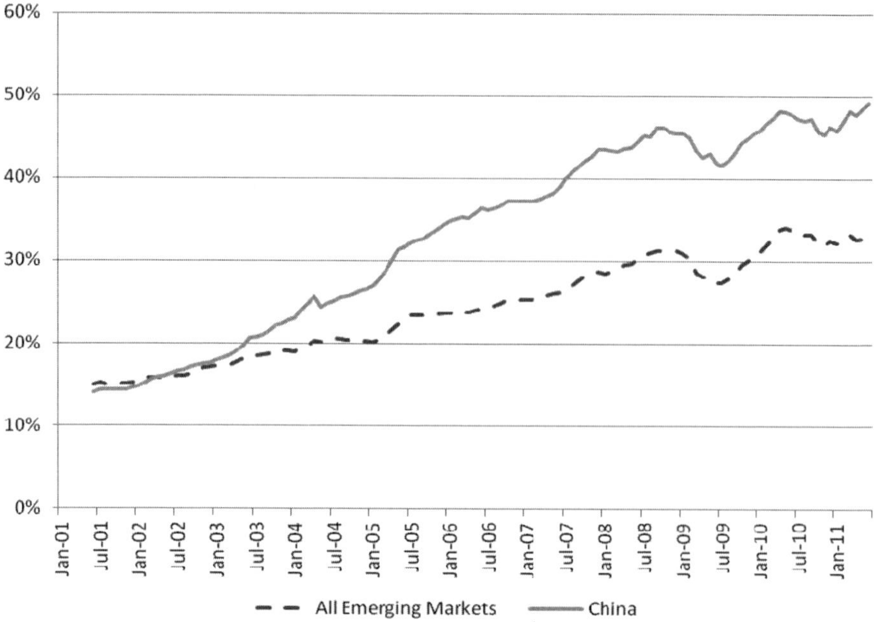

Figure 7. FX Reserve-GDP Ratio.

Notes:

a. The ratio uses annual GDP of the corresponding year in the denominator. The months in 2011 use 2010 GDP in the denominator.
b. Emerging markets (EM) include the following countries: Russia, Poland, Czech Republic, Hungary, Romania, Ukraine, Turkey, Israel, United Arab Emirates, Saudi Arabia, South Africa, China, India, Hong Kong, Korea, Singapore, Indonesia, Malaysia, Thailand, Brazil, Mexico, Chile, Peru, Colombia, Argentina, and Venezuela.

Source: IFS.

Stephen Green of Standard Chartered Bank shows (Figure 9) that net financial inflows into China in the last quarter of 2010 were much bigger than its trade surplus. And in the first quarter of 2011, Green estimates that China's foreign exchange reserves rose by $152 billion even though its trade surplus was negligible. Hot money inflows now seem to be the main source of China's increased foreign exchange reserves — as they were in the first half of 2008 (see Figure 9) before the global credit crunch took hold in the second half.

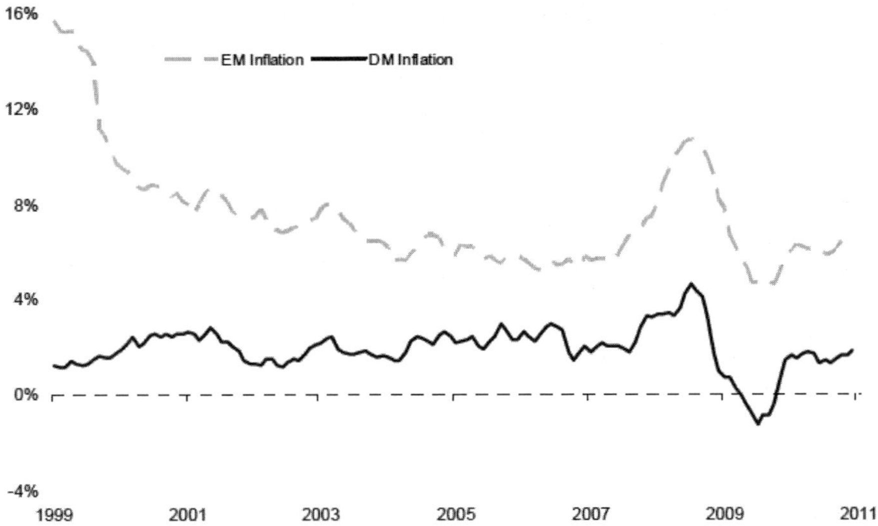

Figure 8. Emerging Markets (EM) and Developed Markets (DM) Inflations.

Note: Developed markets (DM) include the following countries: United States, Germany, France, Italy, Spain, Japan, United Kingdom, Canada, Sweden, and Australia.

Source: Haver Analytics, Morgan Stanley Research.

On a world scale, the most striking inflationary impulse is seen in primary commodity prices. Year-over-year to June 21, 2011, the *Economist's* dollar Commodity Price Index for all items shows an average increase of 38.6 percent, with food prices alone rising 39 percent. For the past decade, Figure 10 gives a longer perspective on various asset price bubbles — including two extraordinary surges in commodity prices before and after the global credit crunch of 2008.

Near-zero interest rates in the mature industrial countries contribute to commodity price inflation in two ways. First, they generate hot money inflows into the emerging market periphery — as analyzed here — and EM demand for primary commodities rises. Secondly, once commodity prices begin to rise, "commodity" carry traders find they can borrow ultra cheaply in New York or Tokyo to fund long positions in commodity futures. Of course, this adds to the upward price momentum, making commodity prices, and asset prices in general, more prone to bubbles — as a glance at Figure 10, "The Greenspan–Bernanke Bubble Economy," would suggest.

Table 2. Foreign Exchange Reserves (Million Dollars).

Date	China	Russian Federation	Indonesia	India	Brazil
M5 2009	2,089,490	385,738	55,430	251,456	194,209
M6 2009	2,131,610	394,186	55,122	254,093	199,900
M7 2009	2,174,620	383,170	54,971	260,631	205,169
M8 2009	2,210,830	383,044	55,440	261,247	209,998
M9 2009	2,272,590	383,578	56,955	264,373	215,336
M10 2009	2,328,270	403,048	59,058	266,768	224,763
M11 2009	2,388,790	413,573	60,034	263,191	230,087
M12 2009	2,399,150	405,825	60,572	258,583	231,888
M1 2010	2,415,220	402,778	64,039	256,362	233,889
M2 2010	2,424,590	402,750	64,220	253,991	234,531
M3 2010	2,447,080	412,834	66,326	254,685	237,029
M4 2010	2,490,510	425,126	72,966	254,773	240,481
M5 2010	2,439,510	418,808	68,940	247,951	242,874
M6 2010	2,454,280	422,778	70,609	249,628	246,025
M7 2010	2,538,890	437,551	73,163	258,551	250,107
M8 2010	2,547,840	436,647	75,540	256,227	254,082
M9 2010	2,648,300	447,567	80,520	265,231	267,717
M10 2010	2,760,900	452,905	85,674	269,093	277,212
M11 2010	2,767,810	438,237	86,653	263,281	277,885
M12 2010	2,847,340	432,949	89,970	267,814	280,570
M1 2011	2,931,670	439,969	89,252	269,893	289,497
M2 2011	2,991,390	447,175	93,333	271,988	299,176
M3 2011	3,044,670	454,223	99,350	274,330	308,578
M4 2011	n.a.	471,725	n.a.	n.a.	319,233
M5 2011	n.a.	n.a.	n.a.	n.a.	n.a.
Percentage Increase from May 2009	46%	22%	79%	9%	59%

Source: IFS.

But also notice from Figure 10 that the U.S. "core" CPI index, which excludes food and energy prices, has yet (in June 2011) to register any of this inflationary pressure. This backward-looking index, which includes the post-bubble downward fall in house prices and rents, is the Fed's favorite inflation target! With the Fed looking the other way, this international inflation will eventually — albeit with a lag of somewhat uncertain duration — come back to the United States and other mature industrial countries,

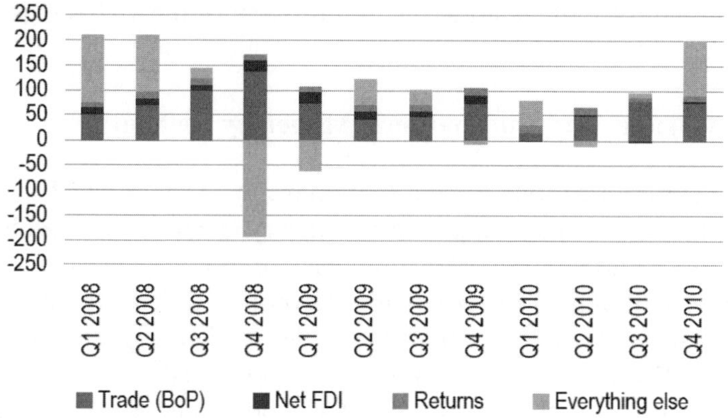

Figure 9. Components of China's Foreign Exchange Reserve Growth.
Source: Standard Chartered.

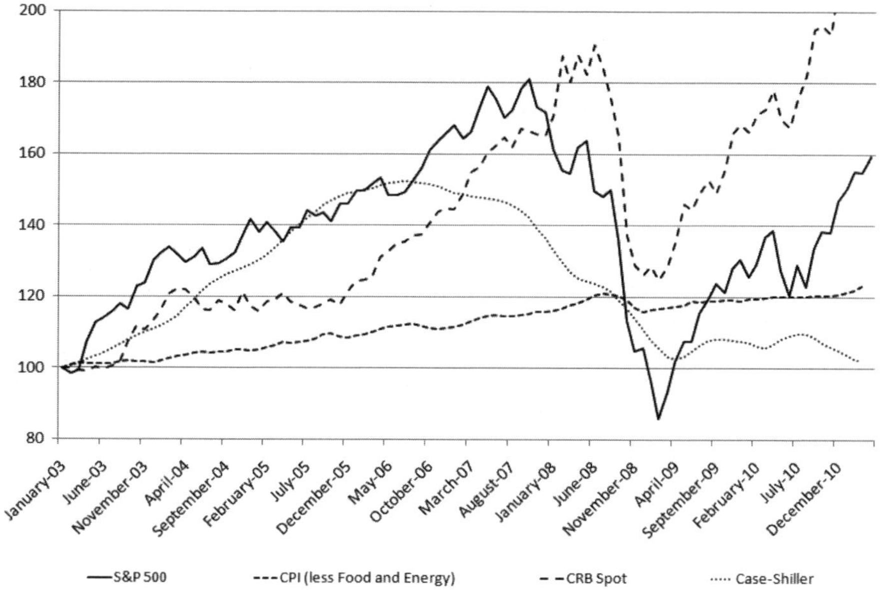

Figure 10. The Greenspan–Bernanke Bubble Economy.
Source: Bloomberg and Federal Reserve Economic Data.

perhaps in the form of "stagflation" reminiscent of the 1970s (McKinnon, 2011).

3. Carry Trades and International Monetary Reform

What are the implications for international monetary reform? In the new millennium, I have argued that world monetary instability has been (and is) provoked by large and persistent interest differentials that induce "carry trades": the willingness of speculators to borrow in low-interest-rate currencies (source currencies) to invest in higher-yield currencies (investment currencies). But what can governments do about this?

First, some economic history. In 1945, the United States was the only industrial country to survive the war with its financial system intact. The dollar was convertible on both current and capital accounts, and inflation was moderate. The Western European countries and Japan had open or repressed inflation — and detailed balance of payments restrictions on both importing and exporting as well as on capital flows. So right away the dollar became the key currency for international transacting.

But initially, the dollar's legal status as key currency was not recognized. In 1944, when the Bretton Woods (BW) agreement was first negotiated, all currencies were defined in terms of gold. The "1944 gold dollar" was the prevailing unit of account. The U.S. par value was .888671 grams or 1/35 ounces, and other currencies were defined similarly. There was complete symmetry in the Articles with respect to exchange rate fixing.

The BW agreement did not really recognize the underlying reality until after the International Monetary Fund had been set up in 1945. Then the Board issued a bylaw, which stated that any country that was keeping a convertible currency within the prescribed limits (one percent margins) *vis-à-vis* any member that was tied to gold would be deemed to be fulfilling its fixed exchange rate obligation under Article IV.[1] Then, virtually all member countries opted to peg to the dollar as the key or central currency. This left the United States without an exchange rate obligation (other than its gold parity, which was suspended in 1971) or target of its own.

And this asymmetry persists to the present day long after official exchange rate parities had been suspended. Other countries may or may not intervene in the foreign exchanges, although today's emerging markets are heavy interveners — as shown by their massive buildup of foreign

[1] I am greatly indebted to Robert Mundell for clarifying these points.

exchange in Figure 6 — while the United States stays passive except in emergencies. Because the U.S. in 1945 had accumulated virtually all the world's monetary gold, nobody then believed that this residual gold parity obligation would ever constrain American behavior.

The new International Monetary Fund provided financial wherewithal to help other countries maintain their dollar parities as they moved toward current-account convertibility and freer multilateral trade. By 1950, the system of fixed (but adjustable) dollar parities, and current-account convertibility under the IMF's Article XIII, was in place. This dollar anchor became the monetary basis for the dramatic post-war economic growth of the industrial countries in the 1950s and 1960s — most unlike the shambolic monetary aftermath of World War I.

But one of the principal designers of Bretton Woods, J.M. Keynes, was adamant that capital controls be retained to minimize cross-currency financial flows. Keynes wanted the new system to be insulated from the hot money flows characteristic of the 1920s and 1930s, which had undermined and then caused the implosion of the inter-war gold standard, leading to worldwide depression. Instead, Keynes wanted *national macroeconomic autonomy* (McKinnon, 1993), where each nation remained free to set its own interest rates and conduct its own fiscal policy to secure full employment without being bound by an international standard. So, to this day, under the IMF Articles of Agreement, any signatory is free to impose exchange restrictions on capital accounts. Although legal for all countries, the United States itself could not possibly impose capital controls. Because the dollar is the key currency, the whole system of clearing international payments multilaterally would collapse.

From 1945 to the late 1960s, most industrial countries and virtually all developing ones kept capital controls in place. But unlike what Keynes wanted or projected, a common international monetary standard was re-established. The stable-valued dollar became the common anchor for keeping national price levels roughly aligned, and the need for dramatically different interest rates was minimal. Although imperfect, the old system of fixed dollar parities eliminated the possibility of prolonged exchange rate movements in one direction on which carry traders now thrive.

Compared to the 1950s and 1960s, today's worldwide carry-trade problem has become more acute because exchange rates are more flexible and because of the relaxation of controls on international movements of financial capital — at least in part at the misguided behest of the IMF as a necessary step toward economic "liberalization." (However, illiquid longer-term direct foreign investments are not a problem.) Fortunately, over the last year, the IMF now seems to have reversed itself and is more tolerant of controls on liquid international capital flows — but only after a lot of damage had been done.

The Asian crisis of 1997–1998 was worsened by an earlier carry trade with Japan. By 1995, Japan had fallen into a near-zero interest rate liquidity trap with a weakening yen. Hot money poured out of Japan and into the Asian Crisis Five: Indonesia, Korea, Malaysia, Philippines, and Thailand. Although Japan was not the only source for overborrowing by the Crisis Five, they became badly over-extended in their foreign-currency indebtedness. Thus, when speculators attacked Thailand in June 1997, the contagion spread to the other four by the end of the year — with capital flight, widespread financial bankruptcies, sharp exchange rate depreciations, and sharp downturns in output and employment. Japan was hurt as its exports to other East Asian countries slumped. Fortunately, China ignored foreign advice to depreciate the renminbi in tandem. Instead, the yuan/dollar rate was kept stable — which made it easier for its five smaller East Asian trading partners (and competitors) and Japan to recover.

Today, the carry-trade story is no better. The prolonged dollar depreciation after 2002 (Figure 3) with ultra-low U.S. interest rates led to the huge buildup of foreign exchange reserves (Figure 6) in the EM. Similarly over the last decade, misdirected pressure on China to continually appreciate the RMB has given carry traders a one-way bet on foreign exchange movements that they really love. Notice that this explanation differs from the common view (Rajan, 2010, p. 82) that Asian countries were so badly burned by the 1997–1998 crisis that they turned conservative and resolved to run large trade surpluses to build up their foreign reserve positions. But today's large size of Asian official exchange reserves is far in excess of any such prudential motivation and much larger than their cumulative trade surpluses.

4. A New International Monetary Agreement?

How best can carry trades be limited? Central bankers from the G-20 could meet continually to monitor each other in order to prevent wide interest differentials from developing. True to its newly professed virtue, the IMF should refrain from criticizing countries who attempt to impose capital controls to stem hot money flows. It could also provide technical advice on how to do so most efficiently.

But if interest spreads are too wide, capital controls will always fail. The first item on the agenda would be to abandon monetary policies by the mature economies that set interest rates near zero, which pressures emerging markets to keep their interest rates low despite the inflationary pressure they now face. The Fed must be the leader in raising interest rates because under the asymmetrical world dollar standard, it has the greatest autonomy in monetary policy.

But American officials point to the stagnant U.S. economy as the reason they want to keep domestic interest rates as low as possible — even zero. Thus, they have to be convinced that this common view is mistaken, and that raising short-term interest rates on dollar assets from zero to modest levels is in America's own best interests — as well as that of the rest of the world.

5. The Supply Constraint on Bank Credit

How do near-zero interest rates in U.S. interbank markets constrict the economy? Since July 2008, the stock of base money in the U.S. banking system has virtually tripled. As part of its rescue mission in the crisis and to drive interest rates down and flood markets with liquidity, the Fed has bought many non-traditional assets (mortgage-backed securities) as well as Treasuries. However, these drastic actions have not stimulated new bank lending. As shown in Figure 11, much of this huge increase in base money is now lodged as excess reserves (cash assets) in large American commercial banks: a *liquidity trap.* In addition, Figure 11 shows that banks have invested heavily in Treasury and Agency securities.

Despite the Fed's strenuous efforts, the supply of ordinary bank credit to firms and households continues to fall. Figure 11 shows outstanding "Commercial and Industrial Loans" falling from $1.54 trillion in May 2008 to just $1.24 trillion in March 2011. Although large corporate enterprises have recovered from the credit crunch of 2008 through their renewed access to bond and equity financing, bank credit is the principal source of finance for working capital for small and medium-sized enterprises (SMEs), enabling them to purchase labor and other supplies. In cyclical upswings, SMEs have traditionally been the main engines for increasing employment; but not in the very weak upswing of 2010–2011, where employment gains have been meager or non-existent.

Why should zero interest rates be causing a credit constraint? After all, conventional thinking has it that the lower the interest rate, the better

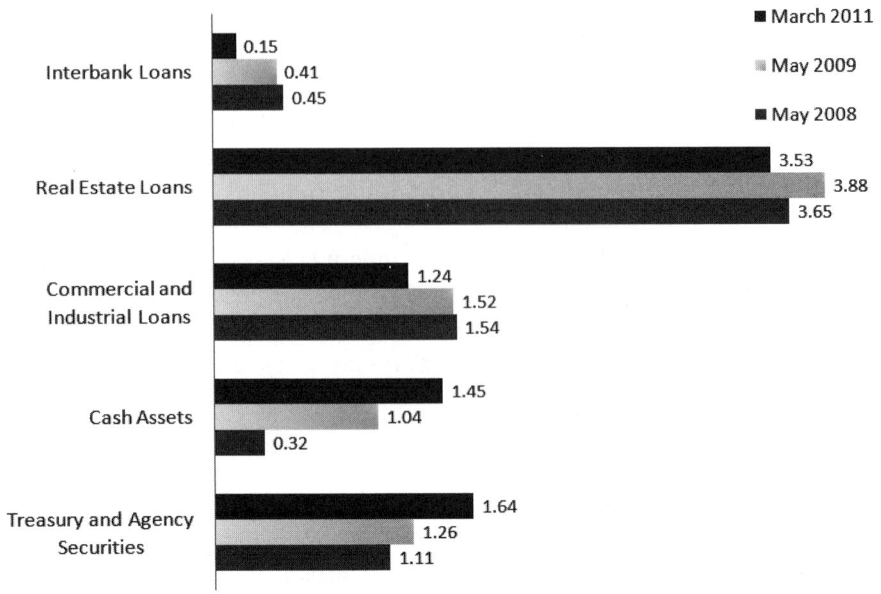

Figure 11. Holdings of Bank Assets at Commercial Banks in the U.S. ($ Trillion).

Source: Federal Reserve Economic Data.

credit can expand. But this is only true when interest rates — particularly interbank interest rates — are comfortably above zero. Banks with good retail lending opportunities typically lend by opening credit lines to non-bank customers. But these credit lines are open-ended in the sense that the commercial borrower can choose when — and by how much — he will actually draw on his credit line (subject to some maximum limit, of course). This creates uncertainty for the bank in not knowing what its future cash positions will be. An illiquid bank could be in trouble if its customers simultaneously decided to draw down their credit lines.

However, if the "retail" bank has easy access to the "wholesale" interbank market, its liquidity is much improved. To cover unexpected liquidity shortfalls, it can borrow from banks with excess reserves with little or no credit checks. But if the prevailing interbank lending rate is close to zero (as it is now), then large banks with surplus reserves become loath to part with them for a derisory yield. Then smaller banks, which collectively are the biggest lenders to SMEs, cannot easily bid for funds at an interest rate significantly above the prevailing interbank rate without inadvertently signaling that they might be in trouble, i.e., distress borrowers. And indeed, counterparty risk in smaller banks remains substantial as almost 50 have failed so far this year. (Remember that the huge Fed and TARP bailouts of 2008–2009 were limited to large banks deemed too big to fail.)

That the American system of bank intermediation is essentially broken is reflected in the sharp fall in interbank lending: Figure 11 shows that interbank loans outstanding in March 2011 were only one-third of their level in May 2008, just before the crisis hit. How to fix bank intermediation and escape from the liquidity trap is a long story for another time (McKinnon, 2009 and 2010). However, raising short-term interest rates above zero is an important part of the story.

6. A Concluding Note on Stagflation in the United States

The Fed's zero interest rate policy has worsened the situation and made escape to a more normal flow of bank intermediation more difficult. Without more lending to SMEs, domestic economic stagnation will continue even though inflation will take off.

The stagflation of the 1970s was brought on by unduly easy U.S. monetary policy in conjunction with attempts to "talk" the dollar down (the Nixon shock of August 1971), leading to massive outflows of hot money that destabilized the monetary systems of America's trading partners (McKinnon, 1982) and generated worldwide inflation. Although today's stagflation is not identical, the similarities would seem to be more important than the differences.

Today's "shock" is the Fed's overreaction to the global downturn of 2008 by setting the short-term federal funds rate close to zero. So the solution is more straightforward. The Fed should announce a program for gradually increasing the Fed Funds rate to some modest target, say 2 percent. This should be accompanied by a definite program for reducing the counterparty risk in interbank lending to all banks, but particularly small ones, possibly by allowing them to pledge loans to SMEs as collateral.

To better preserve financial and exchange rate stability in the transition, the big four central banks — Fed, ECB, Bank of England, and Bank of Japan — should move jointly and smoothly to phase in a common minimum target (say, 2 percent) for their basic short-term interbank rates. By escaping from liquidity traps which so impair the efficiency of domestic bank intermediation and lessening the bubbles problem, the mature center would benefit along with the periphery.

Reducing the spread in interest rates between the center and the periphery would dampen carry trades and hot money flows in an important way. But it may not be sufficient to end them altogether. So acknowledging the legitimacy of emerging markets using capital controls and other devices to dampen hot money inflows should be an important part of the new G-20 discussion. Indeed, central banks in the mature center could monitor their own commercial banks to help central banks on the periphery enforce their controls.

But there is an important asymmetry here. Capital controls are not for everybody. In particular, the United States at the center of the world dollar standard cannot itself impose capital controls without destroying the world's system for clearing international payments multilaterally. Thus, everybody has a vested interest in rehabilitating the unloved dollar standard with open U.S. financial markets. The first of many necessary steps in the rehabilitation process is for the Fed to abandon any thought of a QE3 while phasing out its policy of keeping short rates near zero.

References

Green, Stephen, 2011, "China, in, out, shake it about," *Global Research*, Standard Chartered, May 5.

McKinnon, Ronald, 1982, "Currency substitution and instability in the world dollar standard," *American Economic Review*, June, pp. 320–333.

______, 1993, "The rules of the game: International money in historical perspective," *Journal of Economic Literature*, March, pp. 1–44.

______, 2009, "Zero interest rates and the fall in U.S. bank lending," *The Journal of Economic Asymmetries*, October.

______, 2010, "Beggar-thy-neighbor interest rate policies," Stanford Center for International Development, November.

______, 2011, "The Return of Stagflation," *The Wall Street Journal*, May 24.

______, 2013, *The Unloved Dollar Standard: From Bretton Woods to the Rise of China*, Oxford University Press.

McKinnon, Ronald and Gunther Schnabl, 2009, "The case for stabilizing China's exchange rate: Setting the stage for fiscal expansion," *China & World Economy*, Vol. 17, January–February.

______, 2011, "China and its dollar exchange rate: A worldwide stabilizing influence?," CESifo, Working Paper, No. 3449, May.

Qiao, Hong (Helen), 2007, "Exchange rate changes and trade balances under the dollar standard," *Journal of Policy Modeling*, Vol. 29, pp. 765–782.

Rajan, Raghuram G., 2010, *Fault Lines: How Hidden Fractures Still Threaten the World Economy*, Princeton University Press.

Threats to Financial Stability in Emerging Markets: The New and Very Active Role of Central Banks

Liliana Rojas-Suarez*

Center for Global Development

1. Introduction

This paper focuses on the threats to financial stability in emerging markets posed by the recent episode of large and highly volatile capital flows; a problem which, to a large extent, is the product of the ongoing difficulties in the developed world. It argues that the monetary policy responses to low growth in the United States and to the debt crisis in Europe have significantly complicated the role of central banks in emerging markets. In this regard, this paper complements that of Ronald McKinnon in this volume.

The task of maintaining price and financial stability in the context of large and highly volatile capital flows has forced many central banks from emerging markets to actively utilize an increasing variety of tools. The simultaneous use of these tools, however, has not been free of trade-offs and raises the question of how effective market-friendly central bank policies can continue to be if the turbulences in developed countries continue.

The rest of the paper is organized as follows. Section 2 analyzes the recent evolution of capital inflows to emerging markets and shows how these inflows are highly correlated with economic activity in this group of countries. The section also argues that the recent fluctuations in capital flows are driven more by the weak fundamentals/low assets' yields in developed countries than by the strong economic performance of emerging markets. Section 3 argues that in spite of the different growth models followed by emerging market economies, all emerging market regions in the world are

*Liliana Rojas-Suarez is a senior fellow at the Center for Global Development. The author acknowledges the valuable research assistance support of Maria Alejandra Amado and Amaka Okechukwu. Any remaining mistakes are those of the author.

affected by the vagaries of the international capital markets. This central claim rests on the close and growing interrelationship between trade and finance. Section 4 discusses the new and very active role that central banks in emerging markets have adopted to deal with the capital flows problem. The section illustrates the variety of tools available to central banks and the dilemmas posed by the simultaneous use of these tools. Section 5 concludes the paper.

2. Capital Flow Volatility in the 2000s: The Dominance of Events in Advanced Economies

The problem of large and highly volatile capital flows to emerging markets is not new. The severe financial difficulties associated with a sudden and sharp reversal of capital inflows have been extensively documented in theoretical and empirical literature.[1] A recent phenomenon, however, is that for a number of emerging market economies, the effects of the huge contraction of capital flows that followed the eruption of the global financial crisis of 2008–2009 sharply contrasted with those that occurred in the episodes of capital flow reversals in the 1980s and the 1990s. While the local effects of capital flow reversals in the 1980s and 1990s can be largely attributed to economic and financial fragilities in emerging markets, the lion's share of the local *adverse* effects generated by the eruption of the global financial crisis can be ascribed to contagion from financial disruptions in advanced economies.

During the 1980s and the 1990s, the typical evolution of events was as follows: After a period of large capital inflows, sudden changes in international investors' perceptions regarding the risk/return characteristics of a country/region (often triggered by an external shock, such as an increase in the policy interest rate in the U.S.) exposed existing macroeconomic and financial vulnerabilities in that country/region. Major sources of financial vulnerabilities included large stocks of debt (public and/or private), unsustainable exchange rates, large asset–liability currency mismatches, and weak regulatory and supervisory financial frameworks. As international capital flows declined sharply, available sources of finance also fell significantly, leading to increases in real interest rates and output growth contractions. These circumstances exposed faulty bank lending (especially in the real-estate sector) and accounting practices. Not surprisingly,

[1] See, for example, Calvo and Reinhart (2000).

non-performing loans mounted and banks' capital vanished, resulting in severe banking crises. Albeit important differences among regions, this characterization applies to the numerous Latin American crises and to the mid-1990's East Asian crisis.

Having learned from past experiences, however, the reversal of capital flows that took place during the 2008–2009 global crisis found many emerging market economies, especially those in Asia and Latin America, on a much better footing. These economies had put in place sound macroeconomic policies and improved their financial regulations by the time the crisis erupted. While the adverse external shock hit local financial systems through large reductions in the supply of credit, this time around no financial crises ensued in most emerging market regions of the world and the adverse effects on credit were (relatively) short-lived. The exception was a number of countries in Emerging Europe that were already facing severe financial difficulties at the time the global crisis erupted. Regrettably for this set of countries, their inclusion into the European Union in the early and mid-2000s gave policymakers a false sense of security. As a result, they did not learn from the experiences of Asia and Latin America.

Thus, in sharp contrast with past experiences, the effects of highly volatile international capital flows on a large number of emerging markets during the global crisis cannot be attributed to *existing profound vulnerabilities in this group of countries*.[2] However, being better prepared does not necessarily insulate countries from external shocks. In line with past experiences, the fortunes of emerging market economies continue to be linked, to a large extent, to the behavior of international capital flows. As proved by the global financial crisis, decoupling is just a myth. To illustrate this point, Figure 1 shows the evolution of net private capital inflows to emerging markets and the behavior of economic activity since the mid-1990s.

As can be observed from Figure 1, there is an important correlation between net private capital inflows to emerging markets and output growth: The periods of increasing real GDP growth (1999–2000, 2003–2007, and 2010) are all associated with increasing net capital inflows to emerging markets. Likewise, the large contractions in real economic growth (1998, 2001, and 2009) are all associated with sharp reductions in net capital inflows. In addition, as the sheer size of the private flows has dramatically

---

[2]This does not mean, of course, that emerging market economies are free from economic and financial weaknesses. The emphasis is only on the dominant impact of events in the North affecting emerging market economies relative to conditions in this latter set of countries.

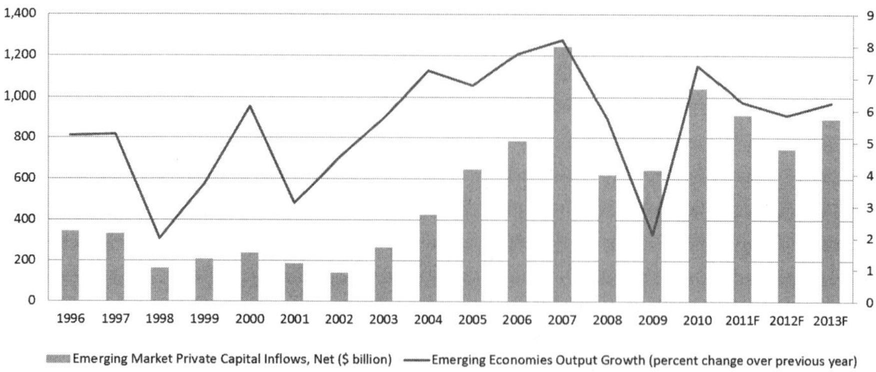

Figure 1. Economic Growth and Net Inflows of Private Capital to Emerging Markets.

Sources: Institute of International Finance; International Monetary Fund, World Economic Outlook.

increased over time, so has the (weighted) average real GDP growth rate. For example, while emerging market economies were growing at an average rate of 5 percent in the pre-East Asian crisis period (1994–1997), they grew at an average rate of 7.4 percent in the pre-global crisis period (2004–2007).[3]

An analysis of the period surrounding the global financial crisis of 2008–2009 and its aftermath provides further insights. While many factors contributed to the eruption of the crisis (and there is still a debate on the relative importance of those factors), a well-documented fact is that since the early 2000s, developed countries in general, and the United States in particular, followed a loose monetary policy stance that incentivized a sharp increase in capital inflows to emerging markets.[4] The combination of ample global liquidity, high yields in *emerging* markets, and the perception of low risks in these countries due to improved macroeconomic fundamentals was behind the acceleration of capital inflows. The liquidity squeeze that followed the bankruptcy of Lehman's led to an overall increase in risk perceptions and a reversal of capital inflows to emerging markets. The

[3]While China and India play a key role in explaining the increase in the weighted average real rate of growth, a number of Latin American countries and other Asian countries have also experienced very high growth rates in the 2000s.

[4]The so-called *carry trade*, by which investors borrowed at low interest rates in developed countries to invest in emerging market instruments yielding higher returns, played an important role in the acceleration of capital inflows.

reversal of capital inflows was, however, short-lived for two reasons. The first was the resilience of the financial systems of emerging markets to the shock and the effective policy responses, especially from their central banks. The second reason was the protracted resolution of financial difficulties in the United States and the implementation of the Fed's *Quantitative Easing*, a policy that increased the availability of liquidity (through purchases of long-term Treasury bonds and other financial assets) for the purpose of reducing long-term interest rates and facilitating credit expansion.[5] The combination of these factors led investors to once again flood many emerging markets with funds directed toward purchasing local assets, including government bonds and equities in local stock exchanges. By 2010, net capital inflows to emerging markets reached levels close to those attained in the pre-crisis period in 2007.

There is a question of which of the two factors (the good economic performance of emerging markets or the weak fundamentals/low assets' yields in developed countries) had the dominant effect on the behavior of capital inflows. While an appropriate response to this question requires in-depth econometric analysis, well beyond the scope of this paper, events in Europe in the second half of 2011 support my view that the recent influx of capital flows to emerging markets largely reflects events in developed countries. Indeed, as the European debt crisis deteriorated and concerns about solvency issues in Italy and Spain mounted, investors flew to the safety of U.S. Treasury bonds — considered the most liquid global asset. Capital inflows to emerging markets declined significantly in the latter part of 2011, more than offsetting the increase in the first part of the year. Consistent with our premisé, real GDP growth declined in 2011 relative to 2010.

As will be discussed in Section 4, central banks in emerging markets have faced enormous challenges in the conduct of monetary policy as a result of the volatile capital flows during the 2000s, which, as discussed above, are determined mainly by events in developed countries. All central banks from emerging markets face this problem in spite of their alternative growth models and this is the subject of the next section.

[5]As discussed in Rojas-Suarez (2011), the Quantitative Easing programs (QE1 and QE2) did not have the intended effect of increasing bank credit in the United States. The central reason is that more liquidity cannot generate more credit in the context of a large problem in the mortgage market, where excessive bad debt in banks' balance sheets still persists.

3. The Capital Inflow Problem: A Common Concern Under Different Growth Models

Growth models differ significantly between regions of the world. While there are many ways to characterize the main features of a growth paradigm, here we follow Montoro and Rojas-Suarez (2012) and Rojas-Suarez (2012a) and distinguish between growth models by the way in which investment and growth are financed.[6] Growth in emerging markets can be financed through foreign capital flows, proceeds from net exports, and domestic savings. Although all emerging market regions in the world use these three sources of funding, their different growth models imply that a region's reliance on alternative sources of finance is also very diverse. For example, Emerging Asia is well-known for its export-oriented growth model, while Latin America's reliance on foreign capital flows is compatible with the region's low savings ratios.

Table 1, which updates data from Montoro and Rojas-Suarez (2012), serves to illustrate this point. For three emerging market regions — Emerging Asia, Latin America, and Emerging Europe — the table presents three indicators. The first is an index of financial openness which, by construction, takes on larger values as restrictions on cross-border capital

Table 1. Financial Openness, Trade Openness and Savings Ratios in Emerging Markets (Regional Percentage Average).

	Financial Openness Index 2008	Trade Openness Indicator (X+M)/GDP 2009	Savings/GDP (average 2009–2010)
Latin America	1.1	48	22
Emerging Asia	0.6	163	34
Emerging Europe	2.2	113	21

Sources: Chinn and Ito (2008); World Bank, World Development Indicators; and International Monetary Fund, World Economic Outlook.

[6]This is, of course, a simple characterization that does not take into account the very complex social and political differences between growth models. Our chosen simplification, however, is sufficient to illustrate the issues at hand.

transactions are reduced (see Chinn and Ito, 2008[7]). The second is an indicator of trade openness: the sum of exports and imports as a percentage of GDP. The third indicator is the ratio of savings to GDP.

Comparing the regions in the table, Emerging Asia and Latin America contrast each other. Emerging Asia is the least financially open region; it is also the most open in trade flows and has the highest savings rate. Conversely, Latin America stands out as a highly financially open region, the least open region in trade flows and has an extremely low savings rate. Emerging Europe is more similar to Latin America in its degree of financial openness and very low savings ratio, but it is closer to Emerging Asia in terms of trade openness.

On first glance — and as claimed by some analysts — these indicators might lead to the conclusion that Asian countries are much more insulated from capital flow volatility than the more financially open countries in Latin America and Emerging Europe. While it is true that some forms of capital flows — especially portfolio flows — may be quite sensitive to capital controls, and, therefore, could potentially display lower volatility in lower-financially open economies, there are two reasons to expect that Emerging Asia has been and will continue to be highly affected by global volatile capital flows, even if this region is the least financially open region in the developing world.

The first reason derives from an important lesson learned from the 2008–2009 global crisis, namely, that there are strong linkages between trade and finance, which are the two central channels of transmission of external adverse shocks. This is because the integration of emerging markets to the global economy through trade in goods and services is highly related to trade finance. During the global crisis, trade finance was the most affected among credit flows, according to reports by the International Monetary Fund and the Bankers Association for Finance and Trade. As a result of large external uncertainties, huge capital flow volatility and the drying up of global liquidity, banking systems around the world reduced the growth rate of credit, including trade finance. Therefore, even if the majority of credit is locally supplied, a sharp external financial shock, and increased capital flow volatility, will have an adverse effect on the financing of exports. While we do not have specific figures on the behavior of trade finance in Asian

[7]The most updated values of the Chinn and Ito index can be found at http://web.pdx.edu/~ito/Chinn-Ito_website.htm. By construction, the index fluctuates between –2.5 and 2.5.

countries, data from Montoro and Rojas-Suarez (2012) indicate that, with the exception of China, domestic real credit growth declined significantly during the crisis.[8]

The second reason is straightforward: The existence of certain constraints to the movement of cross-border capital in Emerging Asia *does not imply that capital flows are unimportant in this region*. Indeed, according to data from the Institute of International Finance (IIF), net capital inflows to Asia account for over 40 percent of total net inflows to emerging markets. Moreover, during the financial turmoil in the second half of 2011, associated with the escalation of Europe's debt problems, capital inflows to Emerging Asia declined significantly. According to the IIF, Asia's vulnerability was due to the large role played by European banks in this region and the large inflows that took place in 2010 and the first half of 2011.

The evidence, therefore, supports our view that all emerging market economies are highly vulnerable to the capital inflows problem regardless of their growth model. Albeit with important differences in the transmission mechanism of external financial shocks across regions, the high interrelation between trade and finance implies that no country/region is insulated from the vagaries of the international capital markets. Central banks in emerging markets are well aware of this fact and have taken a leading role in dealing with the capital inflows problem. We now turn to discussing their recent use of instruments.

4. Central Bank Responses in Emerging Markets: Can There be Enough Instruments in Countries that Do Not Issue Hard Currency?

The discussion above suggests that in spite of important differences in their growth models, an important similarity across emerging market economies is that their central banks face the challenge of minimizing the adverse impact of high capital flow volatility. Another important similarity, insufficiently recognized in international discussions, is that, *in contrast to developed countries, no emerging markets' central bank can issue hard currency; that is, currency that is internationally traded* (see Rojas-Suarez, 2003 and 2012b).

[8]However, the decline in real credit growth during the crisis was not uniform. While this variable fell by over 15 percent in Indonesia, it only declined by 1 percent in Thailand.

Key events during the U.S. recent financial crisis highlight the importance of having the ability to issue hard currency. A central reason that prevented massive bank runs in the United States in the midst of its financial crisis was the credibility of its deposit insurance scheme. But what makes the U.S. deposit insurance credible? In my view, it is the ability of the U.S. government to issue bonds in a currency that is widely accepted internationally and that is very liquid. Likewise, holders of U.S. dollars (both in the U.S. and internationally) can confidently expect that the *market* for U.S. dollars will not dry up if the Fed were to significantly increase the supply of U.S. dollars.[9]

In contrast, no emerging market currency in the world enjoys the high levels of liquidity described above. Bank runs in emerging markets were a common occurrence in the 1980s and 1990s partly because, in the presence of financial difficulties, deposit insurance schemes could not be credibly financed by the large issuance of governments bonds or by the printing of local currency. Without liquid currencies, these types of actions very often simply resulted in speculative attacks against the currency.

Recognition of this problem led central banks in emerging markets around the world to significantly increase their holdings of international reserves; i.e., holdings of currencies that they cannot issue. A major lesson learned by emerging markets from past crises is that being solvent is not sufficient; it is also necessary to be liquid at all times. Interestingly enough, this lesson has only begun to be understood by regulators in developed countries.[10]

Moreover, in the presence of highly volatile capital flows, it becomes imperative to show *proof of liquidity* in the form of large holdings of hard currencies; that is, large stocks of international reserves. Abundant liquidity can decrease a country's vulnerability to sudden shifts in investors' sentiments as well as to contagion in international capital markets.[11] *Proof of liquidity* does not depend on the exchange regime.

[9]Of course, large increases in the supply of dollars will press for a depreciation of the currency and for increases in the inflation rate. The point advanced here is that, at least in the foreseeable future, there will be buyers and sellers of U.S. dollars (a market for the currency). Holders of U.S. dollars might find themselves facing losses in real terms, but not to the extreme of facing a 100% loss in the value of their holdings.

[10]The inclusion of liquidity requirements in Basel III is an example of the recent recognition of these issues in developed countries.

[11]See Guidotti and Rojas-Suarez (2011) for further discussion of these issues in the Latin American context.

Significant *ex-ante* accumulation of foreign exchange reserves is needed even where countries have floating exchange rate regimes. The reason is that if inflows were to suddenly cease, a sharp depreciation of the exchange rate would not be able to generate resources quickly enough to meet due external payments.[12] Without sufficient accumulation of foreign exchange reserves, both in the public and private sectors, sudden reversals of capital inflows can lead to severe financial difficulties. As a result, even those emerging market economies that have moved toward greater exchange rate flexibility (such as those in Latin America) do not display *pure* exchange rate flexibility and have chosen instead to follow *managed floating* regimes.

In this context, there is a question of the appropriate response from emerging markets' central banks in the face of the ongoing capital market turbulences derived from financial difficulties in developed countries. As discussed above, ample global liquidity resulting from loose monetary policies in developed countries and investors' perception of improved fundamentals in emerging economies have led to large inflows of capital to the latter set of countries, albeit with a high degree of volatility. What should central banks do?

To answer this question, it is first necessary to identify the objectives of most central banks in emerging markets. Albeit with important differences, most central banks in emerging markets have three main objectives: to maintain acceptable levels of inflation, to avoid excessive currency appreciation (in countries where there is a significant amount of exchange rate flexibility), and to avoid asset price bubbles and credit booms.

While there is no simple answer to the question of how to reach desired objectives in the presence of large capital inflows, an analysis of the experience suggests that central banks need to simultaneously use a variety of tools. In particular, in periods of large capital inflows (which have the potential of a sudden reversal), an adequate policy response would include: (a) changes in the policy rate to control inflationary (deflationary) pressures, (b) interventions in the foreign exchange markets to limit currency appreciation, and (c) macroprudential regulations to limit the formation of asset price bubbles and credit booms.

I reached this conclusion by examining the multiple dilemmas that central banks from emerging markets have faced in the most recent period

---

[12]I made this point in Rojas-Suarez (2003).

of capital inflows (2010–2012). These dilemmas, which are elaborated in Rojas-Suarez (2012b), are as follows:

- If, due to internal or external factors, inflation is above desirable levels, the central bank has the option of increasing interest rates. However, such increases might attract further capital inflows.
- If, to contain excessive capital inflows and pressures on currency appreciation, the central bank follows a loose monetary policy, inflationary pressures may exacerbate. Moreover, in countries with low development of domestic capital markets — which is the case in most emerging market economies — the formation of asset bubbles and credit booms may be encouraged.
- If, to contain pressures for currency appreciation, the central bank intervenes in the foreign exchange market, the resulting monetary expansion may increase inflationary pressures and, if large enough, these interventions may encourage speculative positions in which market participants bet in favor of an exchange rate appreciation.
- If, to avoid the dilemmas above, the central banks impose capital controls, there is the risk of entering a pattern of continuously increasing the controls to retain their effectiveness. This is because experience shows that controls lose their effectiveness as market participants find ways to avoid them.

These dilemmas imply that no single tool will be enough to achieve the desired goals. In the ever-changing global environment, the importance of alternative goals will also be evolving continuously. This means that the relative usage of alternative tools will also need to be modified over time. In a nutshell, *discretion in the usage of rules* seems to be the most appropriate response of emerging markets' central banks to large and volatile capital flows.

Have central banks in emerging markets been actively using the alternative policy tools at their disposal? A review of the recent experience yields a positive response and this can be illustrated by analyzing: (a) the use of interest rate policy, (b) interventions in the foreign exchange markets, and (c) the use of reserve requirements during the most recent period of capital inflows.

Figure 2 shows the behavior of inflation and the changes in policy rates in five emerging market economies: three in Latin America — Brazil, Colombia, and Chile — and two in Asia — South Korea and Malaysia.

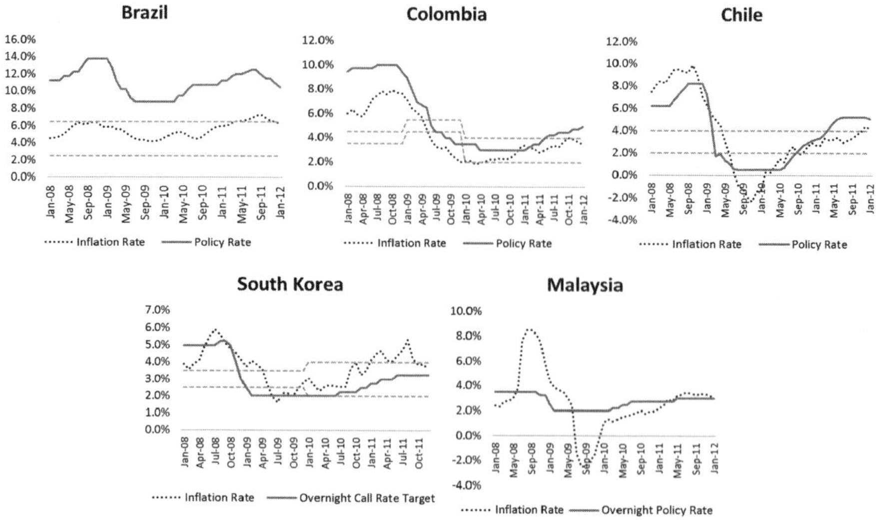

Figure 2. Inflation and Monetary Policy Interest Rate in Selected Emerging Market Economies.

Source: Central banks.

Most central banks change the policy rate based on expected, rather than actual, inflation. However, in this case, we use actual inflation as a proxy for expected inflation since we do not have information on the latter variable. Overall, there is a clear relationship between changes in policy rates and changes in inflation (although that relationship is less apparent in Malaysia). In the period surrounding the sharp decline in global liquidity resulting from the international financial crisis, all emerging markets in the sample reduced their policy rates significantly as they faced deflationary pressures. In addition, they allowed their currencies to depreciate and used their accumulated foreign exchange reserves to offset the loss of liquidity from international capital markets. Given that the effects of the crisis on many emerging market economies were short-lived, capital inflows started to recover in late 2009 and, albeit with high volatility, increased until mid-2011. The exacerbation of the problems in Europe led to a decline in capital inflows in the second half of 2011. However, at the time of writing this paper, capital inflows had once again recovered.

The resurgence of capital inflows to emerging markets has led to pressures for currency appreciation. In addition to the short-run decline in international competitiveness resulting from real exchange rate appreciations, central banks fear that capital flows might significantly reverse once the problems in developed countries have been resolved. In other words, based on past experiences, central banks from emerging markets fear that there is a significant *transitory* component to the capital inflows. As a result of this view, the policy decision of these central banks has been to intervene in the foreign exchange markets to limit currency appreciations and to renew the accumulation of international reserves. Indeed, by the end of 2011, the holdings of international reserves by a large number of emerging market economies surpassed their holdings in the pre-crisis period. The degree of intervention has, of course, varied significantly across countries, with some countries allowing for greater appreciation of their currencies than others.

How have central banks made compatible their objectives of maintaining acceptable levels of inflation (defined by targets in some countries) and limiting currency appreciation? After all, intervention in the foreign exchange markets might result in a loss of control over monetary policy, at least for those countries with more open capital accounts.[13] The decisions of central banks have been made on the basis of international developments, which in turn have influenced inflationary/deflationary pressures in emerging market economies. To understand these policy decisions, we will analyze two sub-periods of the recent capital inflows episode.

The first sub-period of capital inflows can be defined from late 2009 to the beginning of 2010. At that time, the developed world was in a *deflationary* period and, therefore, pressures for currency appreciation in emerging markets took place in a context where inflationary pressures were absent. It was, therefore, relatively less costly for emerging markets to lose a certain amount of control over monetary policy by means of intervention in the foreign exchange markets. During that period, a large number of central banks in emerging markets continued to reduce their policy rate (or kept it constant at low levels) without the fear of an eruption of inflation.

The second sub-period, running from mid-2010 to mid-2011, involved greater challenges for central banks since not only capital inflows accelerated but also inflationary pressures increased. The central banks' perceptions that inflationary pressures were basically a response to domestic demand factors (fed by capital inflows) led authorities to increase interest

[13]This, of course, refers to the so-called *Impossible Trinity*, by which it is not possible to simultaneously maintain open capital accounts, independence in determining monetary policy interest rates, and fixed exchange rates.

rates.[14] As shown in Figure 2, all countries in the sample started a process of gradual increases to the policy rate. To many emerging market economies, this process also reflected a move toward the *normalization* of interest rates; i.e., a move toward the interest rates that prevailed in the pre-crisis period. This process, however, was interrupted in mid-2011 when the problems in Europe exacerbated and capital inflows declined, albeit temporarily. Since then, increased uncertainties in the global economy have led most emerging market economies to either keep interest rate policies constant (on hold) or even reduce them.[15]

It was during this second sub-period that central banks in emerging markets made use of a large variety of policy tools to deal with the challenges of large capital inflows. As mentioned above, the policy rate was used to control inflation. Moreover, interventions in foreign exchange markets continued to contain currency appreciation. But as increases in interest rates further encouraged capital inflows, central banks resorted to the use of macroprudential regulations to limit the formation of credit booms and asset price bubbles.

One of the most popular macroprudential measures has been the use of reserve requirements on bank deposits, which as long as they are not remunerated at market rates, constitute a tax on financial intermediation. The attraction of central banks to the use of reserve requirements rests on the fact that this policy instrument directly affects the expansion of domestic credit and can, therefore, control the formation of credit booms. Moreover, as is well-known, the effectiveness of this instrument is greater in countries with limited development in the local financial markets and where there are no adequate substitutes for bank deposits (which makes it extremely difficult to avoid this tax).

Figure 3 shows the use of reserve requirements by a sample of emerging market economies during the most recent periods of capital inflows. Notwithstanding significant differences between countries, reserve requirements have increased significantly. Other macroprudential policies, such as

[14]External factors, such as food and fuel inflation, also contributed to the increase in inflationary pressures in emerging markets. These pressures, however, were deemed to have transitory effects on inflation (not on the price level) as they were considered to reflect structural changes in the global economy, especially greater demand from China for this type of products.

[15]Among countries in Figure 2, Colombia is an exception since it continued to increase the policy rate.

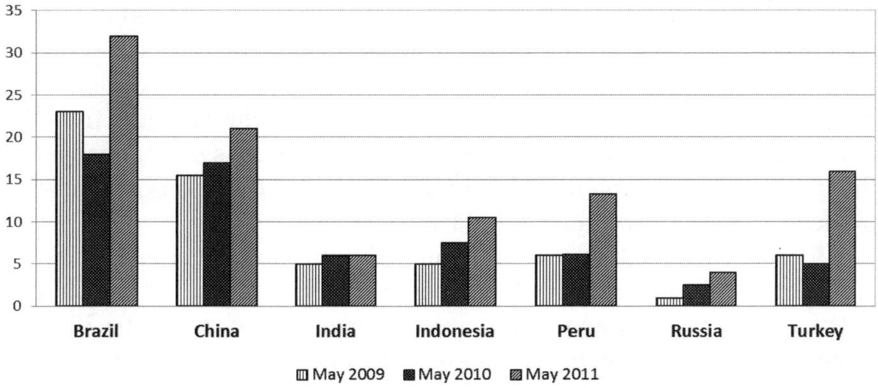

Figure 3. Reserve Requirements in Selected Emerging Market Economies (in Percentage).

Source: IIF Research Note, June 1, 2011.

countercyclical provisions and limits to the indebtedness of domestic banks with short-term foreign lines of credit, are also being increasingly used by emerging market economies.

But in spite of the intention of many central banks to utilize market-friendly policies to deal with the capital inflows problem and despite their apparent success so far, it is not yet clear how long this large set of instruments will remain effective. The discretionary use of capital controls in countries like Brazil and Colombia is a clear indicator that maintaining financial stability in emerging markets in the presence of large capital inflows might eventually become a task that surpasses the confines of market-friendly central bank policies. At a time when emerging markets are the world's *motor of growth*, it is unfortunate that events in developed countries — the source of highly volatile capital flows — are the major threat for the financial stability of emerging markets.

5. Concluding Remarks

This paper has dealt with the increased challenges that central banks in emerging markets face as a result of large and highly volatile capital flows. The paper has shown that the recent episode of large capital inflows resulted more from the financial disturbances in developed countries than from the good economic performance in emerging markets. It has also shown that no emerging market region of the world can be insulated from sharp and sudden variations in capital flows, even in the case of countries that restrict the cross-border movement of capital. Through a number of examples, the paper has illustrated the very active role that central banks have adopted to deal with threats to the stability of their financial systems resulting from the volatility of capital flows. In particular, the simultaneous use of changes in the policy rate, intervention in the foreign exchange markets and macro-prudential regulations was highlighted.

To date, financial systems remain stable in most emerging markets. Although this is a great accomplishment by central banks, if financial turbulences in advanced economies were to continue, it would be illusory to believe that the monetary authorities could continue to use the variety of market-friendly tools without these policies losing their effectiveness. Indeed, over the last year there were episodes of increasing use of capital controls by central banks that are mainly market-friendly otherwise.

In light of the progress achieved by emerging market economies in terms of economic growth and financial stability, it is scary to think that the unresolved problems in developed countries may indeed aggravate the capital inflows problem and potentially lead to the extensive use of capital controls by emerging markets. The widespread use of this type of policy can result in what is known as the fallacy of composition — where policies that might be good for each individual country are bad for the system as a whole. In the end, if carried out, such a policy would come to haunt all countries and would significantly reverse the gains already achieved through globalization. The plea for a prompt resolution to the problems in advanced economies, including increased interventions by multilateral organizations such as the International Monetary Fund, might be supported more broadly if international policymakers increase their awareness of the heavy burden that the current crisis imposes on the central banks of emerging economies.

References

Calvo, Guillermo and Carmen Reinhart, 2000, "When capital inflows come to a sudden stop: Consequences and policy options," in *Reforming the International Monetary and Financial System*, Peter Kenen and Alexandre Swoboda (eds.), Washington, DC: International Monetary Fund, pp. 175–201.

Chinn, Menzie D. and Hiro Ito, 2008, "A new measure of financial openness," *Journal of Comparative Policy Analysis*, Vol. 10, No. 3, pp. 309–322.

Guidotti, Pablo and Liliana Rojas-Suarez, 2011, "Learning from past mistakes: The key to Latin America's financial system's resilience to the global financial crisis," in *World in Crisis: Insights from Six Shadow Financial Regulatory Committees from Around the World*, Robert Litan (ed.), Philadelphia, PA: FIC Press, Wharton Financial Institutions Center.

Montoro, Carlos and Liliana Rojas-Suarez, 2012, "Credit at times of stress: Latin American lessons from the global financial crisis," Bank for International Settlements, working paper, No. 370, February.

Rojas-Suarez, Liliana, 2003, "Monetary policy and exchange rates: Guiding principles for a sustainable regime," in *After the Washington Consensus: Restarting Growth and Reforms in Latin America*, Pedro-Pablo Kuczynski and John Williamson (eds.), Washington, DC: Institute for International Economics, pp. 123–155.

Rojas-Suarez, Liliana, 2011, "Advanced economies pose three financial risks to developing countries," Center for Global Development, essay, January.

Rojas-Suarez, Liliana, 2012a, forthcoming, *Same Global Crisis, Different Regional Experiences*, Washington, DC: IFPRI.

Rojas-Suarez, Liliana, 2012b, forthcoming, *Capital Flow Volatility and the Central Banks of Latin America: New Solutions for Old Dilemmas?*, Washington, DC: Center for Global Development.

V. THE SOCIAL PRODUCTIVITY OF THE FINANCIAL SECTOR

In Defense of Wall Street: The Social Productivity of the Financial System

Ross Levine*

Haas School of Business at University of California-Berkeley,
Milken Institute, and National Bureau of Economic Research

1. Introduction

Finance is powerful. It mobilizes savings, allocates those savings, monitors the use of funds provided to firms and individuals, pools and diversifies risks, and organizes trade in goods, services, and securities.

When financial systems perform these functions well, they tend to promote growth and expand economic opportunities. For example, when banks screen borrowers effectively and identify firms with the most promising prospects, this is a first step in boosting productivity growth. When financial markets and institutions mobilize savings from disparate households to invest in these promising projects, this represents a second crucial step in fostering growth. When financial institutions monitor the use of investments and scrutinize managerial performance, this is an additional, essential ingredient in boosting the operational efficiency of corporations and reducing waste, fraud, and the extraction of private rents by corporate insiders. But that is not all. When securities markets ease the diversification of risk, this encourages investment in higher-return projects that might be shunned without effective risk management vehicles. And when financial systems

---

*Ross Levine is affiliated with Haas School of Business at the University of California-Berkeley, the Milken Institute, and the National Bureau of Economic Research. This paper draws from "Regulating finance and regulators to promote growth," which was presented at the Federal Reserve Bank of Kansas City's Symposium, *Achieving Maximum Long-Run Growth*, held in Jackson Hole, Wyoming, on August 25–27, 2011, and will be published in the proceedings of that symposium. The author thanks David Glancy and Tim Squires for excellent research assistance and bears full responsibility for the views expressed in this paper.

lower transaction costs, this facilitates trade and specialization, which are fundamental inputs into technological innovation and economic growth.

But when financial systems perform these functions poorly, they tend to hinder economic growth and curtail economic opportunities. For example, if financial systems simply collect funds with one hand and pass them along to cronies, the wealthy, and the politically-connected with the other hand, this produces a less efficient allocation of resources, implying slower economic growth. If financial institutions fail to exert sound corporate governance, this makes it easier for managers to pursue projects that benefit themselves rather than the firm and the overall economy. Thus, poorly functioning financial systems can become an effective tool for restricting credit — and hence opportunity — to the already rich and powerful rather than a mechanism for financing the best projects and entrepreneurial ideas. And when financial institutions create new-fangled financial instruments and fob them off onto unsophisticated investors, this might boost the bonuses of financial engineers and executives, but it might be socially destructive, distort credit allocation and attract talented individuals into these socially unproductive activities.

This paper uses evidence from cross-country studies and from research on the states of the United States to assess the impact of the financial system on economic growth and inequality. Many have criticized "Wall Street" — which I use as a shorthand phrase for the financial services industry in general — for its role in the recent global economic crisis and in fostering greater income inequality. Many suggest that the financial system has little to do with encouraging "creative destruction," whereby financial systems fund the initiation and expansion of new and better products and production processes, and has more to do with "destructive creations," whereby financial institutions invent new ways to extract ever-larger bonuses for financial institution executives with potentially detrimental effects on the overall economy.[1] Indeed, such critiques of Wall Street are not new. The second President of the United States, John Adams, argued that "... banks have done more harm to the morality, tranquillity, and even wealth of this nation than they have done or ever will do good." In this paper, I take a

[1] In private conversations, the Brown University political scientist, Mark Blyth, has emphasized to me this distinction between the Schumpeterian notion of "creative destruction," which is a key factor in many models of economic growth, and the view that "destructive creations" by financial institutions have exerted deleterious effects on most individuals.

step back from recent and past rhetoric to re-evaluate the evidence on the socially productive role of the financial system.

The first major finding emerging from the literature is that the financial system exerts a powerful influence over the economy primarily by affecting the quality of capital allocation, not the quantity of investment — a result that is summarized in Levine (1997, 2005). Thus, finance should not be viewed as a plumbing system, where pouring more credit in one end yields more growth at the other. Rather, finance is like an economy's central nervous system, *choosing* where to allocate resources. It is the incentives shaping these choices that influence economic prosperity — by which I mean economic growth and the economic opportunities available to all individuals. Thus, when regulations incentivize financial systems to allocate credit to those with the best entrepreneurial ideas and abilities and not simply to those with the most wealth and political connections, this boosts growth and expands economic opportunities.

Second, a growing and diverse body of empirical research produces a remarkably consistent, though by no means unanimous, narrative: The services provided by the financial system exert a first-order impact on (1) the rate of long-run economic growth and (2) the distribution of income, primarily by affecting the earnings of lower-income individuals. Improvements in the functioning of the financial system are associated with disproportionately large increases in the incomes of those at the lower end of the income distribution, accelerations in total factor productivity growth, and sustained improvements in income per capita. As I emphasize below, these same findings emerge from cross-country analyses and detailed analyses of the individual states of the United States, which had distinct banking systems until the last decades of the 20th century.

Finally, this paper considers the dynamics of financial development — financial innovation. Due to the roles of credit default swaps (CDSs) and collateralized debt obligations (CDOs) in the crisis of 2007–2009, many analysts criticize financial innovation and question its role in promoting economic growth (Stiglitz, 2010). They argue that financial innovations are often used to fool investors, circumvent regulations, and facilitate the extraction of large bonuses by financial executives. In fact, the former chairman of the Federal Reserve, Paul Volcker, made the following skeptical request in a *Wall Street Journal* (2009) interview: "I wish that somebody would give me some shred of neutral evidence about the relationship between financial innovation recently and the growth of the economy, just one shred of information." While it is impossible to evaluate the long-run growth effects of such recent financial innovations as CDSs and CDOs, recent research addresses Mr. Volcker's general skepticism of financial innovation.

Historical evidence and cross-country empirical findings indicate that financial innovation is *necessary* for sustaining technological change and economic growth (Levine, 2010). The very nature of economic growth involves greater specialization and technological complexity. Thus, growth itself makes the "old" financial system less effective at screening and monitoring the new, more complex technologies. Without commensurate improvements in financial systems, economies become less effective at identifying and financing growth-inducing endeavors. Laeven, Levine, and Michalopoulos (2011) show that financial systems that rapidly adopt and adapt improved screening methodologies exert a positive effect on growth, while more stagnant financial systems slow economic progress.

These findings, of course, do not mean that *all* — or even most — financial innovations are socially productive. Just as some medical innovations have proven to be harmful to the public, some financial innovations are destructive. But, just as it is difficult to imagine broad-based increases in longevity and the quality of human life without medical innovation, it is difficult to imagine enduring technological innovations that boost living standards without the financial innovations necessary for funding new, opaque technological advances.

Before continuing, I want to defend and clarify this paper's title, "In Defense of Wall Street." Clearly, I do not defend all of its actions. For example, I do not defend the ability of financial institutions to manipulate politicians into passing laws that favor those institutions. I do not defend the ability of financial firms to manipulate financial regulators into designing and interpreting laws in ways that boost the profits of financial institutions at the expense of the public at large. And, I do not defend the ability of financiers to influence supervisors charged with overseeing financial markets and institutions on behalf of the public. Rather, this paper defends the view that the functioning of the financial system materially influences economic prosperity. It is only in this narrow sense that I title the paper, "In Defense of Wall Street."

The remainder of this paper is organized as follows. Section 2 reviews the cross-country evidence on linkages between the functioning of the financial system and both economic growth and the distribution of income. I provide information both from cross-country comparisons and from studies of the United States. Section 3 discusses the evidence on the connection between financial innovation and economic growth. In this section,

I primarily discuss anecdotal evidence from across history, but also review recent cross-country regressions on the financial innovation and growth nexus. Section 4 concludes.

2. Finance and Growth, Inequality, and Poverty

This section presents evidence that the operation of the financial system exerts a powerful effect on national rates of long-run economic growth, the distribution of income, and the proportion of people living in poverty. Moreover, the evidence shows that financial institutions and markets affect the economy primarily by influencing the allocation of resources, not by altering the aggregate savings rate. Therefore, financial regulation can materially influence economic prosperity by shaping the operation of the financial system and hence the economy's capital allocation choices. Rather than reviewing the entire empirical literature on finance and growth as in Levine (1997, 2005), I illustrate the literature's major findings first by using cross-country comparisons and then by presenting evidence from the United States. Although I use simple ordinary least squares regressions and figures to illustrate the results, an extensive body of research confirms these findings when using instrumental variables and other techniques to identify the causal impact of financial development on economic performance.

2.1 *Banks, growth, inequality, and the poor*

2.1.1 *Cross-country evidence*

Broad cross-country evaluations of the impact of financial development on growth use one observation per country, where the data are typically averaged over 30 or 40 years. The studies control for many other possible determinants of economic growth such as initial income, educational attainment, inflation, government spending, openness to trade, and political instability (King and Levine, 1993; Levine, 1998 and 1999; Levine, Loayza, and Beck, 2000; Beck, Levine, and Loayza, 2000). These studies also examine whether financial development is associated with productivity growth and capital accumulation, which are two channels through which the operation of the financial system can influence growth.

To measure financial development, cross-country studies typically use *private credit*, which equals banks' credit to the private sector as a share of gross domestic product. This is a problem. We would like to measure the quality of the financial services available in an economy. But *private credit* does not directly measure the effectiveness of the financial system in mobilizing savings, allocating capital, monitoring the use of that capital, providing risk management services, and easing transactions. Rather, *private credit* measures the size of the financial intermediary sector. Another problem is that private credit focuses on banks and does not consider the broader array of financial institutions and markets. In its defense, *private credit* excludes loans to the government and state-owned enterprises and therefore gauges the intermediation of private credit. Furthermore the same results hold when using a broader measure that includes credits issues by non-bank financial institutions (not just bank credit) and when incorporating measures of stock market development.

Figure 1 illustrates that countries with better-developed financial systems grow faster. Based on Levine, Loayza, and Beck (2000), this partial scatter plot shows the relationship between growth and *private credit* over the 35 years between 1960 and 1995 while controlling for some of the other potential growth determinants noted above. Furthermore, Beck, Levine, and Loayza (2000) show that financial development boosts growth primarily by enhancing the efficiency of capital allocation. The connection between financial development and the savings rate is weaker. Thus, it is the choices that the financial system makes in allocating society's resources that shape national growth rates.

The operation of the financial system can also influence the distribution of income in a variety of ways, some of which disproportionately help the poor and others primarily boosting the incomes of the rich. First, better-functioning banks focus more on a person's ideas and abilities than on family wealth and political connections when allocating credit. Second, by enhancing the quality of financial services, financial development will naturally benefit heavy users of financial services, which are primarily wealthy families and large firms. Finally, finance can also affect the distribution of income through its effects on labor markets. For example, improvements in finance that boost the demand for low-skilled workers will tend to tighten the distribution of income. And the financial system helps determine whether people live in a dynamic, growing economy or whether they must find work in a more stagnant environment.

Figure 2 illustrates that countries with better-developed financial systems tend to experience reductions in income inequality, as measured by the growth rate of the Gini coefficient of income inequality. Critically,

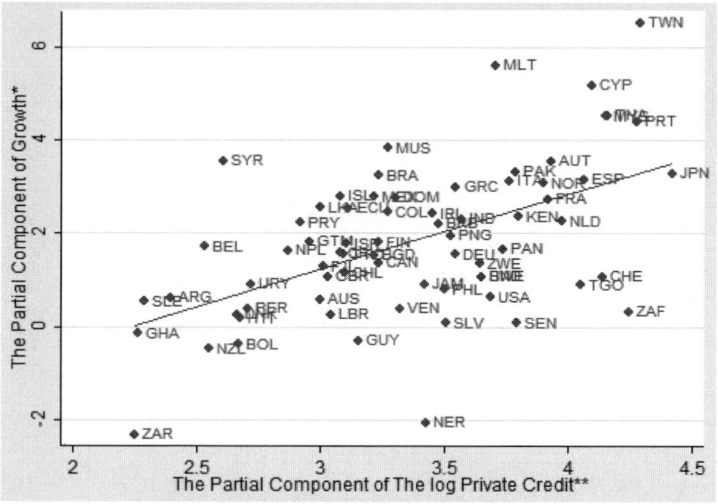

Figure 1. Growth in GDP Per Capita and the Log of Private Credit.

Notes: This is a partial scatter plot of the regression:

$$Growth = \beta_0 + \beta_1 Log(Private\ Credit) + \beta_2 X + \varepsilon,$$

where *Growth* is average real GDP per capita growth over the 1960 to 1995 period, *Private Credit* is the claims on the private sector by banks and other financial institutions as a share of GDP, and X is a vector of the following control variables: log of initial GDP, and secondary schooling attainment in 1960. The regression includes 71 observations and the estimated coefficient, β_1, equals 1.77, with a p-value of 0.00. To construct the figure, first regress *Growth* on X and collect the residuals. These residuals are called the *Partial Component of Growth*. Second, regress *Private Credit* on X and collect the residuals. These residuals are called the *Partial Component of Private Credit*. Finally, plot the *Partial Component of Growth* against the *Partial Component of Private Credit*. This represents the two-dimensional representation of the regression plane in Growth–Private Credit space while conditioning on X.

Source: Levine, Loayza, and Beck (2000) in the spirit of Table 3 Regression Set 1, which is available at http://www.econ.brown.edu/fac/Ross_Levine/Publications.htm.

this result holds when controlling for the economy's aggregate growth rate and the level of overall economic development, as well as a wide array of other country-specific characteristics (Beck, Demirgüç-Kunt, and Levine, 2007). Thus, financial development tightens the distribution of income

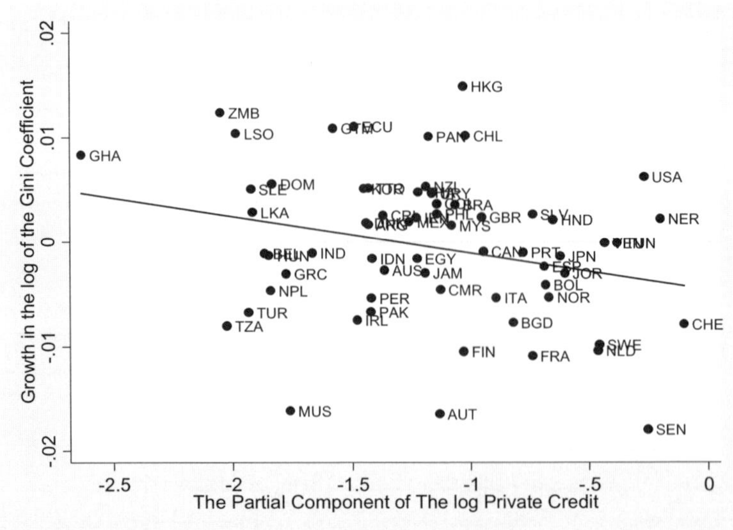

Figure 2. Growth in the Log of the Gini Coefficient and the Log of Private Credit.

Notes: This is a partial scatter plot of the regression:

$$Growth\ in\ the\ Gini\ Coefficient = \beta_0 + \beta_1 Log\,(Private\ Credit) + \beta_2 X + \varepsilon,$$

where *Growth in the Gini Coefficient* is the ratio of the area below the Lorenz Curve, which plots share of population against income share received, to the area below the diagonal from 1960 to 2005, *Private Credit* is the claims on the private sector by banks and other financial institutions as a share of GDP, and X is a vector of the following control variables: inflation, the log of exports as a fraction of GDP, government consumption as a share of GDP, log of initial Gini Coefficient, GDP per capita growth, and secondary schooling attainment in 1960. The regression includes 65 observations and the estimated coefficient, β_1, equals -0.005, with a p-value of 0.014. To construct the figure, first regress *Growth in the Gini Coefficient* on X and collect the residuals. These residuals are called the *Partial Component of Growth in the Gini Coefficient*. Second, regress *Private Credit* on X and collect the residuals. These residuals are called the *Partial Component of Private Credit*. Finally, plot the *Partial Component of Growth in the Gini Coefficient* against the *Partial Component of Private Credit*. This represents the two-dimensional representation of the regression plane in Growth in the Gini Coefficient–Private Credit space while conditioning on X.

Source: Beck, Demirgüç-Kunt, and Levine (2007) Table 2 Regression 3, which is available at http://www.econ.brown.edu/fac/Ross_Levine/Publications.htm.

above and beyond any effect running through economic growth on the level of economic development.

Figures 3 and 4 show that financial development disproportionately boosts the incomes of those at the lower end of the distribution of income, including the incomes of the extremely poor. As illustrated in Figure 3, *private credit* boosts the income growth of the poorest quintile, even after controlling for many other country characteristics, including the rate of economic growth and the level of economic development (Beck, Demirgüç-Kunt, and Levine, 2007). One can push this further and focus on the extremely poor, i.e., those living on less than two dollars per day.[2] Figure 4 shows that financial development is associated with a reduction in the fraction of the population living in extreme poverty. Critically, these results hold when controlling for average growth. It is not just that finance accelerates economic growth, which trickles down to the poor; finance exerts a *disproportionately* positive influence on lower income individuals.

2.1.2 *U.S. evidence on finance, growth, inequality, and the poor*

The U.S. states provide a unique setting in which to examine further the causal impact of improvements in the quality of banking services on economic growth, the distribution of income, and the poor. From the mid-1970s to the mid-1990s, individual U.S. states removed regulatory restrictions on opening banks' branches within its boundaries. States changed their regulatory policies in different years. The reforms intensified competition and triggered improvements in banking services, reducing interest rates on loans, raising them on deposits, lowering overhead costs, spurring the development of better techniques for screening and monitoring firms, and reducing the proportion of bad loans on the books of banks (Jayaratne and Strahan, 1998).

The driving forces behind the financial reforms that enhanced the quality of financial services were largely independent of state-specific changes in growth, income inequality, and labor market conditions. Kroszner and Strahan (1999) show that technological, legal, and financial innovations diminished the economic and political power of banks benefiting from geographic restrictions on banking. The invention of automatic teller machines (ATMs), in conjunction with court rulings that ATMs are not

[2] Data on the fraction of the population living on less than \$2.00/day is limited to less-developed countries over the period from 1980 to 2005.

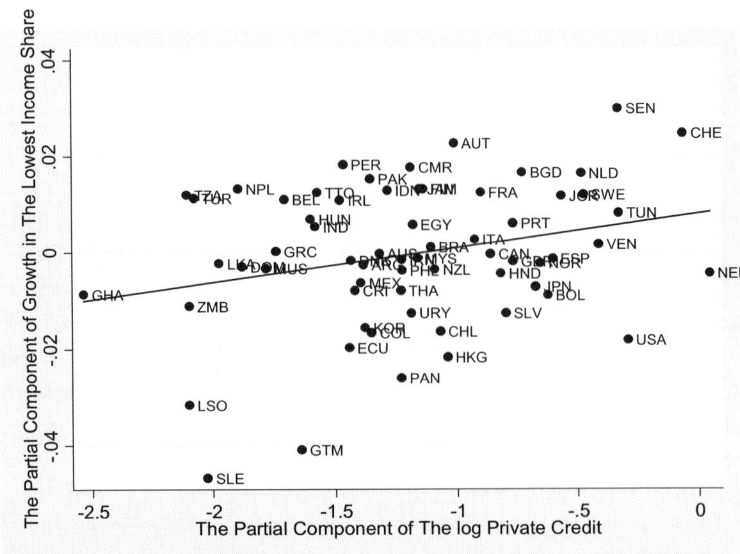

Figure 3. Growth in the Log of the Lowest Income and the Log of Private Credit.

Notes: This is a partial scatter plot of the regression:

$$\textit{Growth in the Lowest Income} = \beta_0 + \beta_1 \textit{Log (Private Credit)} + \beta_2 X + \varepsilon,$$

where *Growth in the Lowest Income* is the log of the average annual growth of the income share of the poorest quintile computed as a log difference between 1960 and 2005, *Private Credit* is the claims on the private sector by banks and other financial institutions as a share of GDP, and X is a vector of the following control variables: inflation, the log of exports as a fraction of GDP, log of initial Lowest Income, GDP per capita growth, and secondary schooling attainment in 1960. The regression includes 65 observations and the estimated coefficient, β_1, equals 0.009, with a p-value of 0.014. To construct the figure, first regress *Growth in the Lowest Income* on X and collect the residuals. These residuals are called the *Partial Component of Growth in the Lowest Income*. Second, regress *Private Credit* on X and collect the residuals. These residuals are called the *Partial Component of Private Credit*. Finally, plot the *Partial Component of Growth in the Lowest Income* against the *Partial Component of Private Credit*. This represents the two-dimensional representation of the regression plane in Growth in the Lowest Income–Private Credit space while conditioning on X.

Source: Beck, Demirgüç-Kunt, and Levine (2007) Table 3 Regression 3, which is available at http://www.econ.brown.edu/fac/Ross_Levine/Publications.htm.

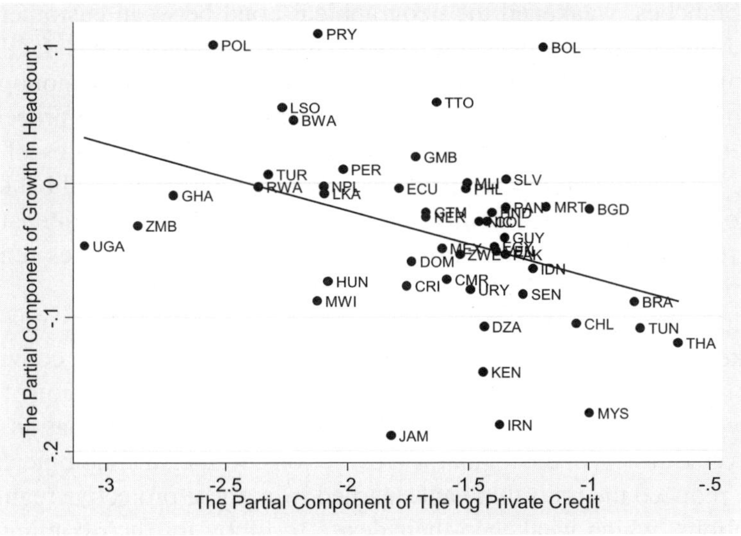

Figure 4. Growth in Headcount and the Log of Private Credit.

Notes: This is a partial scatter plot of the regression:

$$Growth\ in\ Headcount = \beta_0 + \beta_1 Log\,(Private\ Credit) + \beta_2 X + \varepsilon,$$

where *Growth in Headcount* is the growth rate of the percentage of the population living below $1 per day, *Private Credit* is the claims on the private sector by banks and other financial institutions as a share of GDP, and *X* is a vector of the following control variables: inflation, the log of exports as a fraction of GDP, government effectiveness, initial Poverty Gap, Population Growth, Growth in mean income and secondary schooling attainment in 1960. The regression includes 51 observations and the estimated coefficient, β_1, equals -0.050, with a p-value of 0.009. To construct the figure, first regress *Growth in Headcount* on *X* and collect the residuals. These residuals are called the *Partial Component of Growth in Headcount*. Second, regress *Private Credit* on *X* and collect the residuals. These residuals are called the *Partial Component of Private Credit*. Finally, plot the *Partial Component of Growth in Headcount* against the *Partial Component of Private Credit*. This represents the two-dimensional representation of the regression plane in Growth in the Poverty Gap–Private Credit space while conditioning on *X*.

Source: Beck, Demirgüç-Kunt, and Levine (2007) Table 4 Regression 3, which is available at http://www.econ.brown.edu/fac/Ross_Levine/Publications.htm.

bank branches, weakened the geographical bond between customers and banks. Furthermore, checkable money market mutual funds facilitated banking by mail and telephone, which weakened local bank monopolies. And, improvements in credit scoring techniques, information processing, and telecommunications reduced the informational advantages of local banks. These innovations reduced the monopoly power of local banks and therefore weakened their ability and desire to fight for the maintenance of these restrictions on competition. State by state, the authorities removed these restrictions over the last quarter of the 20th century.

Although a slight digression, it is valuable to recognize that policymakers did not remove these regulations because of new, convincing information that they were hindering competition and the provision of high-quality financial services. There was already plenty of information about the adverse effects of the regulatory restrictions. Rather, technological innovation reduced the rents that banks earned from these protective regulatory restrictions, which weakened their desire to lobby for their continuation. Perhaps if the regulatory institutions had better represented the interests of the public, these growth-retarding policies would have been removed earlier. As I will emphasize below, effective governance of financial regulatory institutions can materially influence growth.

To examine growth, I trace out the year-by-year effects of the removal of geographic restrictions on intrastate bank branching on the logarithm of Gross State Product per capita (*GSP*). I plot *GSP* during the decade before a state deregulated and then plot what happens after a state removed restrictions on competition. *GSP* in each year is measured relative to *GSP* in the year of deregulation. Figure 5 plots the results and the 95% confidence intervals. In the figure, the zero date is the year in which a state removed these restrictions on competition, which differs across the states because they deregulated in different years.

Figure 5 illustrates that the removal of geographic restrictions on intrastate banking — which improved the quality of banking services — boosted economic growth. There is a significant increase in *GSP* immediately after deregulation and this impact grows over time.

Figures 6–8 demonstrate that easing restrictions on intrastate banking (1) reduced income inequality by increasing the incomes of those at the lower end of the distribution of income, and (2) lowered the unemployment rate (Beck, Levine, and Levkov, 2010). Figure 6 illustrates that the impact of deregulation on inequality grows for about eight years and then the effect levels off. Ultimately, there is a drop in the Gini coefficient of income

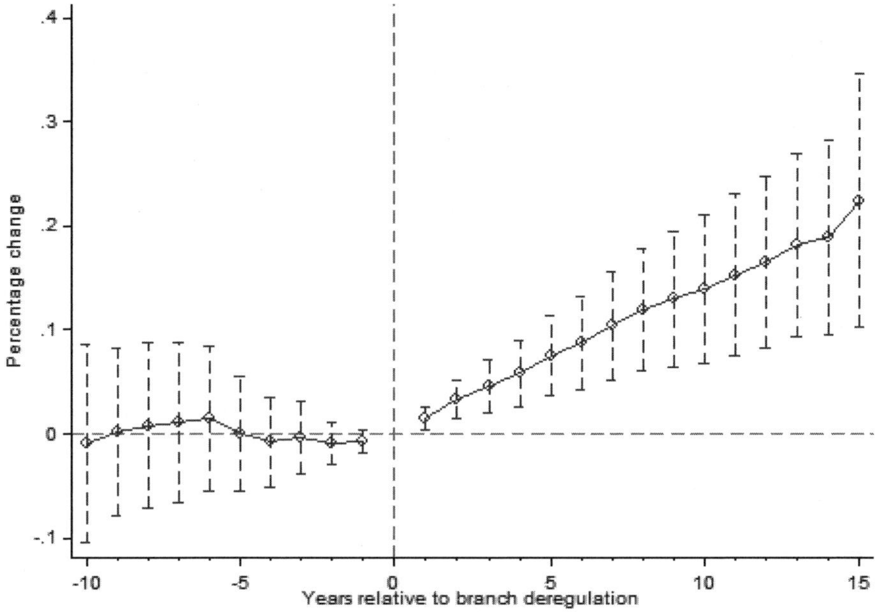

Figure 5. The Dynamic Impact of Deregulation on the Gross State Product.
Notes: The figure plots the impact of intrastate bank deregulation on per capita Gross State Product ($2,000). First we de-trend the Gross State Product per capita data by subtracting out the mean and time trend before deregulation. We then consider a 25-year window, spanning from 10 years before deregulation until 15 years after deregulation. The dashed lines represent 95% confidence intervals, adjusted for state-level clustering. Specifically, we report estimated coefficients from the following regression:

$$\log(\text{GSP})_{\text{st}} = \alpha + \beta_1 \text{D}_{\text{st}}^{-10} + \beta_2 \text{D}_{\text{st}}^{-9} + \cdots + \beta_{25} \text{D}_{\text{st}}^{+15} + \mathbf{A}_{\text{s}} + \mathbf{B}_{\text{t}} + \varepsilon_{\text{st}}.$$

The D's equal zero, except as follows: $\text{D}^{-\text{j}}$ equals one for states in the jth year before deregulation, while $\text{D}^{+\text{j}}$ equals one for states in the jth year after deregulation. We exclude the year of deregulation, thus estimating the dynamic effect of deregulation on the Gross State Product relative to the year of deregulation. $\mathbf{A}_{\text{s}}$ and $\mathbf{B}_{\text{t}}$ are vectors of state and year dummy variables that account for state and year fixed effects, respectively.
Source: Beck, Levine, and Levkov (2010), which is available at http://www.econ.brown.edu/fac/Ross_Levine/Publications.htm.

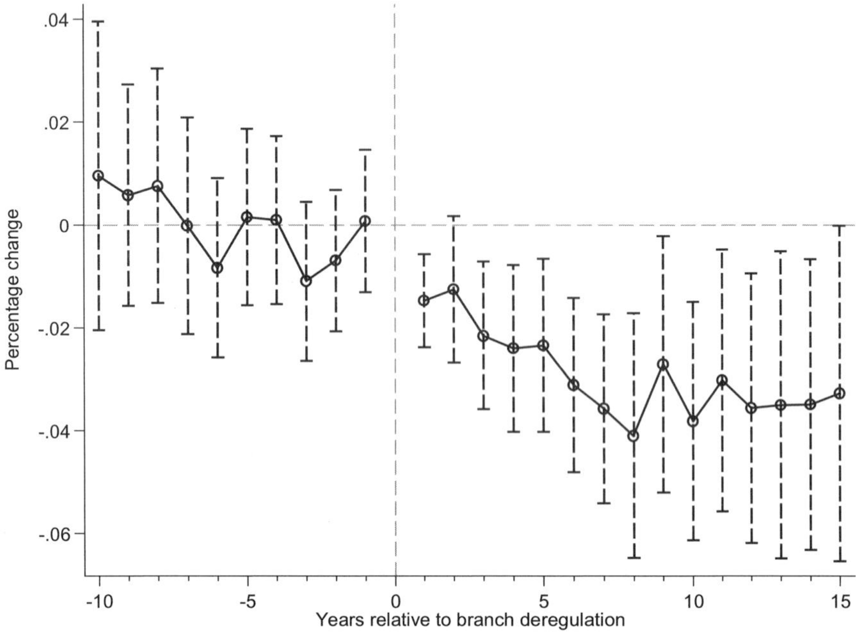

Figure 6. The Dynamic Impact of Deregulation on Gini Coefficient of Income Inequality.

Notes: The figure plots the impact of intrastate bank deregulation on the natural logarithm of the Gini coefficient of income inequality. We consider a 25-year window, spanning from 10 years before deregulation until 15 years after deregulation. The dashed lines represent 95% confidence intervals, adjusted for state-level clustering. Specifically, we report estimated coefficients from the following regression:

$$\log(\text{Gini})_{\text{st}} = \alpha + \beta_1 \text{D}_{\text{st}}^{-10} + \beta_2 \text{D}_{\text{st}}^{-9} + \cdots + \beta_{25} \text{D}_{\text{st}}^{+15} + \mathbf{A}_{\text{s}} + \mathbf{B}_{\text{t}} + \varepsilon_{\text{st}}.$$

The D's equal zero, except as follows: $\text{D}^{-\text{j}}$ equals one for states in the jth year before deregulation, while $\text{D}^{+\text{j}}$ equals one for states in the jth year after deregulation. We exclude the year of deregulation, thus estimating the dynamic effect of deregulation on the different percentiles of income distribution relative to the year of deregulation. $\mathbf{A}_{\text{s}}$ and $\mathbf{B}_{\text{t}}$ are vectors of state and year dummy variables that account for state and year fixed effects, respectively.

Source: Beck, Levine, and Levkov (2010), which is available at http://www.econ.brown.edu/fac/Ross_Levine/Publications.htm.

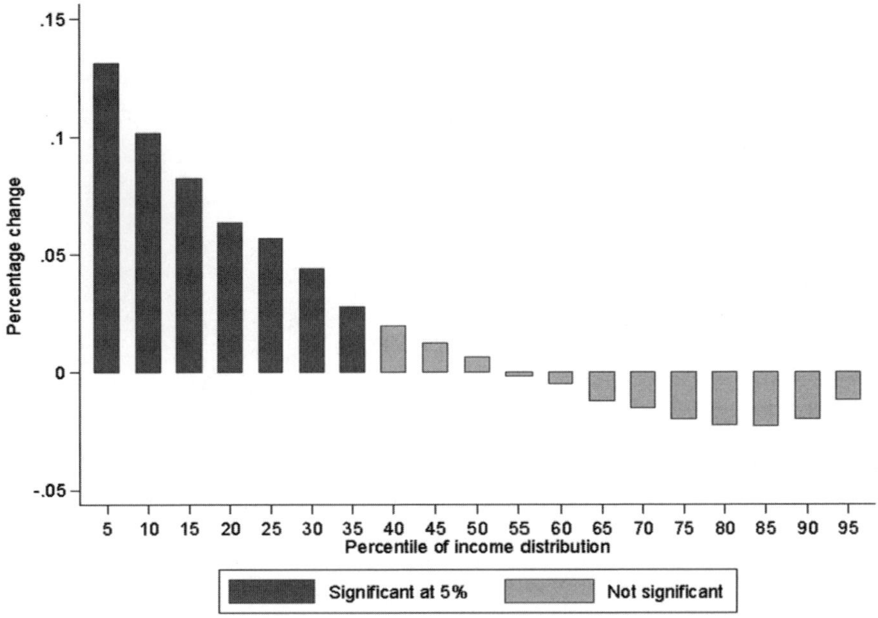

Figure 7. The Impact of Deregulation on Different Percentiles of Income Distribution.

Notes: Each bar in the figure represents the estimated impact of bank deregulation on a natural logarithm of a specific percentile of income distribution. Dark bars represent estimates significant at 5% after adjusting the standard errors for clustering. Light bars represent statistically insignificant estimates. Specifically, we report the estimates of γ from 19 separate regressions of the following form:

$$Y(i)_{st} = \alpha + \gamma D_{st} + A_s + B_t + \varepsilon_{st},$$

where $Y(i)_{st}$ is the natural logarithm of ith percentile of income distribution in state s and year t. D_{st} is a dummy variable which equals to zero prior to bank deregulation and equals to one afterwards. A_s and B_t are vectors of state and year dummy variables that account for state and year fixed effects, respectively. Each of the 19 regressions has 1,519 observations corresponding to 49 states, including the District of Columbia (we exclude Delaware and South Dakota), times 31 years between 1976 and 2006.

Source: Beck, Levine, and Levkov (2010) Figure 2, which is available at http://www.econ.brown.edu/fac/Ross_Levine/Publications.htm.

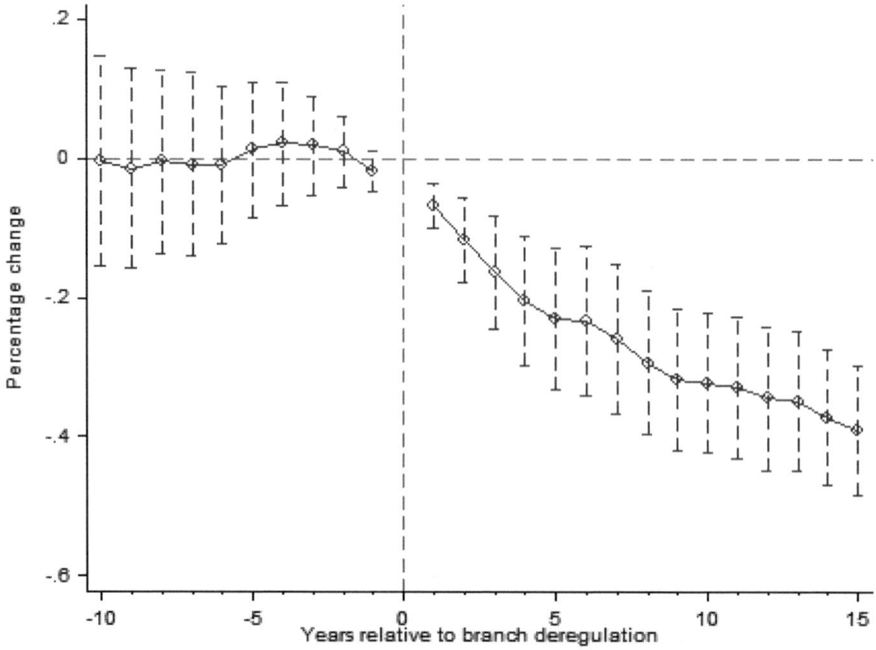

Figure 8. The Dynamic Impact of Deregulation on the Unemployment Rate.

Notes: The figure plots the impact of intrastate bank deregulation on Unemployment. At first we de-trend Unemployment by subtracting out the mean and time trend before deregulation. We then consider a 25-year window, spanning from 10 years before deregulation until 15 years after deregulation. The dashed lines represent 95% confidence intervals, adjusted for state-level clustering. Specifically, we report estimated coefficients from the following regression:

$$\log(\text{Unemployment})_{st} = \alpha + \beta_1 D_{st}^{-10} + \beta_2 D_{st}^{-9} + \cdots + \beta_{25} D_{st}^{+15} + \mathbf{A}_s + \mathbf{B}_t + \varepsilon_{st}.$$

The D's equal zero, except as follows: D^{-j} equals one for states in the jth year before deregulation, while D^{+j} equals one for states in the jth year after deregulation. We exclude the year of deregulation, thus estimating the dynamic effect of deregulation on Unemployment relative to the year of deregulation. $\mathbf{A}_s$ and $\mathbf{B}_t$ are vectors of state and year dummy variables that account for state and year fixed effects, respectively.

Source: Beck, Levine, and Levkov (2010), which is available at http://www.econ.brown.edu/fac/Ross_Levine/Publications.htm.

inequality of about 4%. Figure 7 shows that intrastate branch deregulation tightened the distribution of income by disproportionately raising incomes in the lower part of the income distribution. Finally, Figure 8 shows that the removal of restrictions on intrastate branching was associated with a significant drop in the unemployment rate, with a cumulative effect of more than two percentage points after 15 years.

2.2 *Banks, markets, and growth*

While the evidence above indicates that the functioning of banks influences economic growth and the distribution of income, this ignores equity and bond markets. Are securities markets simply casinos where the rich come to place their bets, or do the services provided by financial markets also affect the allocation of capital and long-run rates of economic growth? A considerable body of theoretical and empirical research tackles this question.

Theory suggests that financial markets matter for growth, too (Levine, 1991). For example, as securities markets become larger and more liquid, it is easier for an investor who has acquired information to profit by quickly trading in the market based on that information (Holmstrom and Tirole, 1993). Thus, larger, more liquid markets will increase the incentives of investors to expend resources researching firms, enhancing the efficiency of resource allocation and fostering growth. As another example, liquid, well-functioning stock markets can improve corporate governance. For example, public trading of shares in stock markets that efficiently reflect information about firms allows owners to align the interests of managers with those of owners by linking managerial compensation to stock prices (Jensen and Murphy, 1990). Similarly, if takeovers are easier in well-developed stock markets and if managers of under-performing firms are fired following a takeover, then better stock markets can promote better corporate control. The threat of a takeover will also help align managerial incentives with those of the owners (Scharfstein, 1988).

The empirical evidence indicates that better-developed securities markets encourage economic growth by boosting the efficiency of resource allocation (Levine and Zervos, 1998; Beck and Levine, 2002). Measures of stock market liquidity — how much trading occurs in the market — are closely associated with economic growth. However, simple measures of the size of the market, as measured by stock market capitalization, are not robustly linked with economic performance.

Furthermore, both bank and stock market development are independently associated with growth, suggesting that the policy debate about whether to promote a bank-based system or a market-based financial system misses the big point. Banks *and* markets matter for growth. This does not imply that banks and markets play the same roles in all economies. Indeed, as countries become more developed, new research indicates that markets become increasingly important for promoting economic activity (Demirgüç-Kunt, Feyen, and Levine, 2013). While still requiring additional work, this suggests that poor bank regulations are particularly costly in countries at low levels of economic development, while regulations impeding market development have larger adverse effect in richer countries.

3. Financial Innovation and Growth

So far, I have ignored the dynamics of financial development: How does financial innovation fit into the process of economic growth? Given the roles of credit default swaps, collateralized debt obligations, and other new financial instruments in the recent financial crisis, financial innovation has gotten a bad reputation. From this perspective, financial innovations are mechanisms for fooling investors, circumventing regulatory intent, and boosting the bonuses of financiers without enhancing the quality of the services provided by the financial services industry. But, such a perspective is too narrow.

A broader, long-run consideration of financial development suggests that financial innovation is *essential* for growth. Adam Smith argued that economic growth is a process in which production becomes increasingly specialized and technologies more complex. As firms become more complex, however, the "old" financial system becomes less effective at screening and monitoring firms. Therefore, without corresponding innovations in finance that match the increases in complexity associated with economic growth, the quality of the financial services diminishes, slowing future growth.

Several examples from history illustrate the crucial role of financial innovation in sustaining economic growth. Consider first the financial impediments to railroad expansion in the 19th century. The novelty and complexity of railroads made pre-existing financial systems ineffective at screening and monitoring them. Although prominent local investors with close ties to those operating the railroad were the primary sources of capital for railroads during the early decades of this new technology, this reliance on local finance restricted growth.

So, financiers innovated. Specialized financiers and investment banks emerged to mobilize capital from individuals, screen and invest in railroads, and monitor the use of those investments, often by serving on the boards of directors of railroad corporations (Carosso, 1970). Based on their expertise and reputation, these investment banks mobilized funds from wealthy investors, evaluated proposals from railroads, allocated capital, and governed the operations of railroad companies for investors. And, since the geographical size and complexity of railroads made it difficult for investors to collect, organize, and assess price, usage, breakdown, and repair information, financiers developed new accounting and financial reporting methods.

Next, consider the information technology revolution of the 20th century, which could not have been financed with the financial system that fueled the railroad revolution of the 19th century. Indeed, as nascent high-tech information and communication firms struggled to emerge in the 1970s and 1980s, traditional commercial banks were reluctant to finance them because these new firms did not yet generate sufficient cash flows to cover loan payments and the firms were run by scientists with little experience in operating profitable companies (Gompers and Lerner, 2001). Conventional debt and equity markets were also wary because the technologies were too complex for investors to evaluate.

Again, financiers innovated. Venture capital firms arose to screen entrepreneurs and provide technical, managerial, and financial advice to new high-technology firms. In many cases, venture capitalists had become wealthy through their own successful high-tech innovations, which provided a basis of expertise for evaluating and guiding new entrepreneurs. In terms of funding, venture capitalists typically took large, private equity stakes that established a long-term commitment to the enterprise, and they generally became active investors, taking seats on the board of directors and helping to solve managerial and financial problems.

Finally, consider the biotechnology revolution of the 21st century, for which the venture capital modality did not work well. Venture capitalists could not effectively screen biotech firms because of the scientific breadth of biotechnologies, which frequently require inputs from biologists, chemists, geneticists, engineers, bioroboticists, as well as experts on the myriad of laws, regulations, and commercial barriers associated with successfully bringing new medical products to market. It was unfeasible to house all of this expertise in banks or venture capital firms. Again, a new technology promised growth, but the existing financial system could not fuel it.

Yet again, financiers innovated. They formed new financial partnerships with the one kind of organization with the breadth of skills to screen biotech firms: large pharmaceutical companies. Pharmaceutical companies employ, or are in regular contact with, a large assortment of scientists and engineers, have close connections with those delivering medical products to customers, and employ lawyers well-versed in drug regulations. Furthermore, when an expert pharmaceutical company invests in a biotech firm, this encourages others to invest in the firm as well. Without financial innovation, improvements in diagnostic and surgical procedures, prosthetic devices, parasite-resistant crops, and other innovations linked to biotechnology would almost certainly be occurring at a far slower pace.

By focusing on the co-evolution of financial and economic systems, two policy implications emerge. First, without denying the potentially harmful effects of some forms of financial innovation, these historical examples and new cross-country empirical findings by Laeven, Levine, and Michalopoulos (2011) suggest that financial innovation is necessary for fostering technological innovations and sustaining economic growth. Thus, financial regulations that stymie healthy financial innovation could slow, or even stop, economic growth.

Second, regulation should focus on *maintaining* sound incentives in a dynamic economy. Regulation influences the degree to which the financial system has incentives to create and use new financial products to avoid the intent of regulatory policies, facilitate excessive risk-taking, and make it easier for executives to extract large bonuses to the detriment of the financial institutions, or whether the financial system is primarily motivated to develop and use financial innovations to enhance the screening and monitoring of investments, managing risk, and easing transactions.

4. Conclusions

While it has recently become popular to demonize Wall Street, considerable evidence suggests that a well-functioning financial system is vital for fostering economic growth and expanding economic opportunities, especially for those at the lower end of the distribution of income. The financial system exerts a profound impact on economic prosperity. This evidence does not imply that the social productivity of all financial systems is everywhere and always positive. But, it does suggest that sustained improvements in living standards are much less likely when financial systems are underdeveloped. Finance is not just about crises; it is about defining the contours of economic possibilities available to individuals and about long-run economic growth.

Although this paper does not make policy recommendations, the findings have relevance for policymaking. Since (1) finance exerts a first-order impact on economic prosperity and (2) finance primarily exerts this impact by *choosing* where to allocate capital, the financial policies, regulations, and supervisory practices shaping the incentives underlying those capital allocation choices are critically important for human welfare. The design and implementation of financial policies matter. Thus, as argued by Barth, Caprio, and Levine (2006, 2012), the institutions and governance systems that actually design and implement financial policies are *the* decisive ingredients in determining the social productivity of the financial sector.

References

Barth, James R., Gerard Caprio, Jr., and Ross Levine, 2006, *Rethinking Bank Regulation: Till Angels Govern*, New York: Cambridge University Press.

Barth, James R., Gerard Caprio, Jr., and Ross Levine, 2012, *Guardians of Finance: Making Regulators Work for Us*, Cambridge, MA: MIT Press.

Beck, Thorsten, Asli Demirgüç-Kunt, and Ross Levine, 2007, "Finance, inequality and the poor," *Journal of Economic Growth*, Vol. 12, pp. 27–49.

Beck, Thorsten and Ross Levine, 2002, "Industry growth and capital allocation: does having a market- or bank-based system matter?" *Journal of Financial Economics*, Vol. 64, pp. 147–180.

Beck, Thorsten and Ross Levine, 2004, "Stock markets, banks, and growth: Panel evidence," *Journal of Banking and Finance*, Vol. 28, pp. 423–442.

Beck, Thorsten, Ross Levine, and Alexey Levkov, 2010, "Big bad banks? The winners and losers from bank deregulation in the United States," *Journal of Finance*, Vol. 65, pp. 1637–1667.

Beck, Thorsten, Ross Levine, and Norman Loayza, 2000, "Finance and the sources of growth," *Journal of Financial Economics*, Vol. 58, pp. 261–300.

Carosso, Vincent P., 1970, *Investment Banking in America: A History*, Cambridge, MA: Harvard University Press.

Demirgüç-Kunt, Asli, Erik Feyen, and Ross Levine, 2013, "The evolving importance of banks and markets in economic development," *World Bank Economic Review*, forthcoming.

Dow Jones and Co., 2009, "Paul Volcker: Think more boldly," *Wall Street Journal*, December 14, available at http://online.wsj.com/article/SB10001424052748704825504574586330960597134.html.

Gompers, Paul A. and Josh Lerner, 2001, "The venture capital revolution," *Journal of Economic Perspectives*, Vol. 15, pp. 145–168.

Holmstrom, Bengt and Jean Tirole, 1993, "Market liquidity and performance monitoring," *Journal of Political Economy*, Vol. 101, pp. 678–709.

Jayaratne, Jith and Philip E. Strahan, 1996, "The Finance–Growth nexus: Evidence from bank branch deregulation," *Quarterly Journal of Economics*, Vol. 111, pp. 639–670.

Jayaratne, Jith and Philip E. Strahan, 1998, "Entry restrictions, industry evolution, and dynamic efficiency: Evidence from commercial banking," *Journal of Law and Economics*, Vol. 41, pp. 239–273.

Jensen, Michael and William Meckling, 1976, "Theory of the firm: Managerial behavior, agency costs, and ownership structure," *Journal of Financial Economics*, Vol. 3, pp. 305–360.

Jensen, Michael and Kevin Murphy, 1990, "Performance pay and top management incentives," *Journal of Political Economy*, Vol. 98, pp. 225–263.

King, Robert G. and Ross Levine, 1993, "Finance and growth: Schumpeter might be right," *Quarterly Journal of Economics*, Vol. 108, pp. 717–738.

Kroszner, Randall S., 1998, "The political economy of banking and financial regulatory reform in emerging markets," *Research in Financial Services*, Vol. 10, pp. 33–51.

Kroszner, Randall S. and Philip E. Strahan, 1999, "What drives deregulation? Economics and politics of the relaxation of bank branching restrictions," *Quarterly Journal of Economics*, Vol. 114, pp. 1437–1467.

Kroszner, Randall S. and Thomas Stratmann, 1998, "Interest group competition and the organization of Congress: Theory and evidence from financial services political action committees," *American Economic Review*, Vol. 48, pp. 1163–1187.

Laeven, Luc, Ross Levine, and Stelios Michalopoulos, 2011, "Financial and technological innovation: Implications for growth," Brown University, mimeo.

Levine, Ross, 1991, "Stock markets, growth, and tax policy," *Journal of Finance*, Vol. 46, pp. 1445–1465.

Levine, Ross, 1997, "Financial development and economic growth: Views and agenda," *Journal of Economic Literature*, Vol. 35, pp. 688–726.

Levine, Ross, 1998, "The legal environment, banks, and long-run economic growth," *Journal of Money, Credit and Banking*, Vol. 30, pp. 596–613.

Levine, Ross, 1999, "Law, finance, and economic growth," *Journal of Financial Intermediation*, Vol. 8, pp. 36–67.

Levine, Ross, 2005, "Finance and growth: Theory and evidence," in *Handbook of Economic Growth*, Vol. 1A, P. Aghion and S. Durlauf (eds.), pp. 865–934, Amsterdam: Elsevier/North-Holland.

Levine, Ross, 2010, "Financial innovation: For the motion that financial innovation boosts economic growth," *The Economist*, February 23–March 3, available at www.economist.com/debate/days/view/471.

Levine, Ross, Norman Loayza, and Thorsten Beck, 2000, "Financial intermediation and growth: Causality and causes," *Journal of Monetary Economics*, Vol. 46, pp. 31–77.

Levine, Ross and Sara Zervos, 1998, "Stock markets, banks, and economic growth," *American Economic Review*, Vol. 88, pp. 537–558.

Scharfstein, David, 1988, "The disciplinary role of takeovers," *Review of Economic Studies*, Vol. 55, pp. 185–199.

Stiglitz, Joseph E., 2010, "Financial innovation: Against the motion that financial innovation boosts economic growth," *The Economist*, February 23–March 3, available at www.economist.com/debate/days/view/471.

Output Growth Variability: The Role of Financial Markets

Alexander Popov*

European Central Bank

1. Introduction

Over the past two decades, a large body of empirical work has documented a robust causal effect of the financial sector on output growth.[1] But is the cost of higher growth a higher variability of the growth process? There is a strong perception that foreign capital increases volatility both in the financial markets and in the real economy (Stiglitz, 2000). Some authors have argued that financial development sharpens the incentives of financial intermediaries to take on risk by intensifying competition (Hellmann *et al.*, 2000). Kaminsky and Reinhart (1999) provide some evidence by demonstrating that crises are usually preceded by rapid growth in financial aggregates. The recent global financial crisis has only served to strengthen this view.

Understanding the effect of financial development on the variability of the growth process is crucial if we are to draw implications about its welfare consequences. Nevertheless, considerably less attention was devoted in the past to this link than to the finance-and-growth nexus. One simple explanation for this discrepancy is that the favorite measure of variability is

*Alexander Popov is an economist in the Financial Research Division of the European Central Bank.

[1]The idea to link finance and growth in a causal way is usually attributed to Schumpeter (1911), with later contributions by Goldsmith (1969) and McKinnon (1973). The roots of the modern empirical finance-and-growth literature can be traced to the seminal contributions of King and Levine (1993a,b). Various scholars have subsequently studied the effect on economic growth of credit markets (e.g., Rajan and Zingales, 1998; Beck *et al.*, 2000; Beck and Levine, 2002), of equity markets (e.g., Levine and Zervos, 1998), and of financial liberalization (e.g., Bekaert *et al.*, 2005), among others. For a recent survey, see Levine (2005).

the *volatility* of the growth process, and while the welfare implications of higher growth are obvious, the welfare benefits of removing all of the business cycle volatility are miniscule (see Lucas, 1987). At the same time, Barro (2006, 2009) has recently demonstrated that within a class of models that replicate how asset markets price consumption uncertainty, individuals are willing to pay a high premium in exchange for eliminating all chances for rare, large, and abrupt macroeconomic contractions. To the extent that output risk cannot be fully insured, the same increase in volatility would have considerably larger negative implications for consumer welfare if it came from one single large contraction than if it came from a series of small, symmetric deviations from a stable growth path. To address this consideration properly, one would need to look at the effect of financial openness on the *skewness* of output growth, which captures such asymmetric and abnormal distributional patterns and is thus related to the concept of tail risk.

In this article, I will review some recent empirical work linking financial development and financial openness to the volatility and the skewness of the growth process and discuss the social welfare implications of these results.

2. Finance, Output Growth, and Output Volatility

A growing empirical literature has investigated the effect of financial intermediation on volatility independent of its growth impact. To begin with, theory has made ambiguous predictions on the direction of this effect. For example, Aghion *et al.* (1999) argue that a more developed financial system may provide borrowers with tools to deal with information asymmetries arising in financial relations. Thus, financial development lowers the dependence of financial contracts on a borrower's net worth, reducing their role in the amplification of shocks. Similarly, financial development may lower volatility by helping firms facing temporary cash flow or net worth problems to obtain the necessary working capital to finance their operations (see Caballero and Krishnamurthy, 2001). At the same time, financial development may fuel competition and erode banks' franchise value, thus incentivizing banks to take on more risk (Hellmann *et al.*, 2000). Since governments cannot commit not to provide bailouts in times of crises, banks have incentives to gamble for resurrection, exacerbating the business cycle. The effect of finance on output volatility is also expected to vary depending on whether monetary or real shocks are at play and on whether the real shocks are due to shifts in credit demand or in credit supply (Morgan *et al.*, 2004). Finally, the effect of financial development on volatility may be non-linear, and so with strategic complementarities and market imperfections, the introduction of a financial technology may affect positively the growth rate of the economy and at the same time be a source of higher volatility.

Empirical work using various sample periods and proxies for financial development has generally produced conflicted evidence. For instance, Easterly *et al.* (2000) find that financial development lowers the volatility of output, while Kaminsky and Reinhart (1999) demonstrate the opposite effect, and Beck *et al.* (2006) find no correlation between financial development and long-term volatility. In an attempt to resolve this controversy, various authors have presented evidence that financial development lowers output volatility in manufacturing industries with high external dependence and liquidity needs, but not necessarily in other industries (e.g., Braun and Larrain, 2005). However, conclusions about aggregate volatility cannot be easily derived from sectoral studies as they entirely neglect the evolution of the sector shares and the correlations across sectors. The existing literature thus provides no clear empirical answers to the question of the effect of finance on volatility, despite its policy relevance.

In addition, there is very little work studying the effect of financial development on the growth-volatility profile of the economy in a more unified framework in an international context. While Levchenko *et al.* (2009) show that financial liberalization increases both the rate and the volatility of output growth at the industry level, their conclusions about the effect of finance on aggregate volatility are based on the strong assumptions about the composition of output and the correlations across sectors. To address this issue, in a recent paper Acharya *et al.* (2011) apply a mean-variance efficiency framework to study how branching deregulation in the U.S. has affected state business cycle volatility through reallocation of output across sectors. They show that reallocation of output from suboptimally large to suboptimally small sectors is faster in U.S. states that deregulated their banking sector. Mechanically, the empirical test amounts to testing whether banking deregulation affects significantly the speed with which the actual distribution of the economy's sector sizes converges to an optimal distribution implied by the minimization of long-term volatility for a given level of long-term growth.[2] This approach has the intrinsic appeal of addressing the

[2]The idea is based on the mean-variance framework first suggested by Markowitz (1952).

question of the *simultaneous* effect of financial intermediation on growth and volatility. In essence, what one can get from this framework is an answer to the question: What is the effect of financial development on output growth volatility, *holding long-term output growth constant*?

In a recent paper entitled "Finance and diversification" (Manganelli and Popov, 2010), Simone Manganelli and I address this question by using the same framework as Acharya *et al.* (2011), but in an international context. Our approach differs in that we study the effect of financial deepening rather than of competition-enhancing policies. In addition, we look at how financial deepening affects the distribution of output across sectors, in a mean-variance sense, for 28 OECD countries over the period 1971–2009.

Before one looks at the role of finance in this process, it might be informative to simply study the evolution of the actual sectoral diversification of a number of economies relative to the "benchmark," or "optimal" one. This should also better illustrate the mechanics of the methodology involved. Figures 1–3 summarize this evolution for three different countries. As the figures demonstrate, between 1971 and 2007, the U.S. experienced a Pareto-improvement, with its economy achieving both a higher growth and a lower volatility in the mean-variance metric. Japan experienced an improvement only in the dimension of growth, which may well

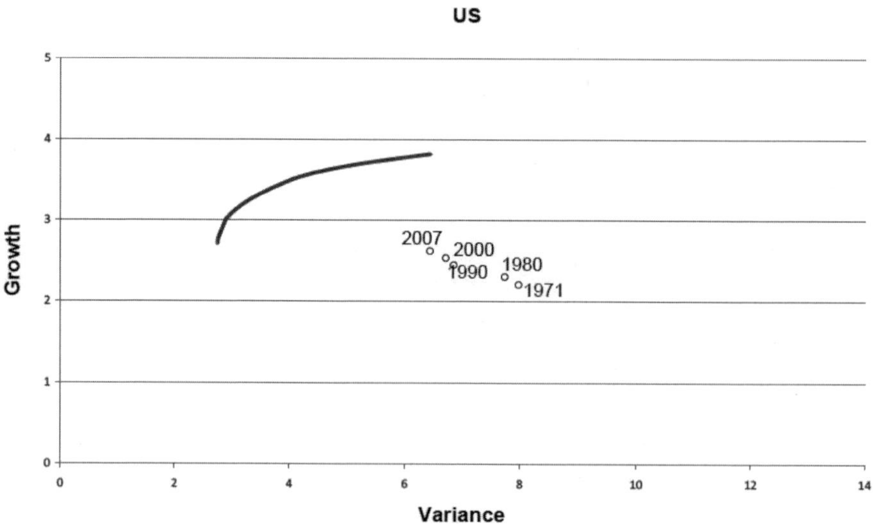

Figure 1. Actual Industrial Composition and the Mean-Variance Efficient Frontier, US 1971–2006.

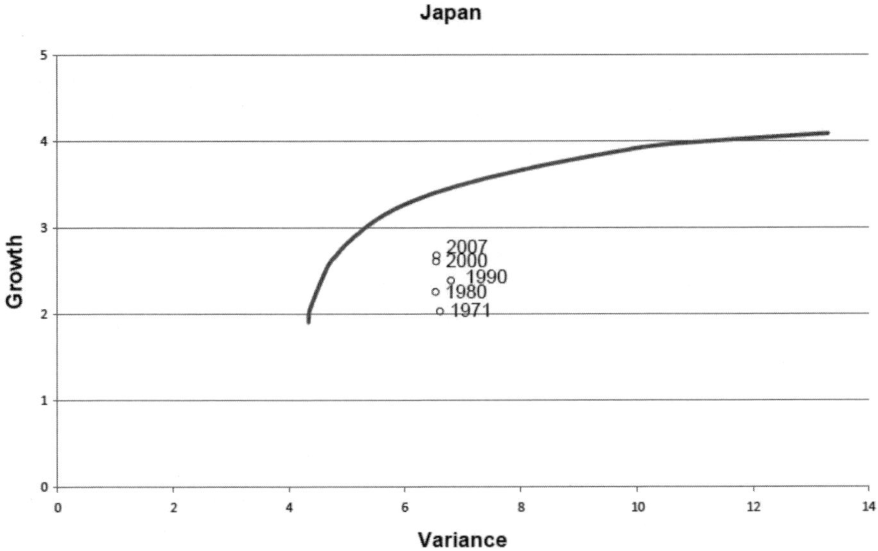

Figure 2. Actual Industrial Composition and the Mean-Variance Efficient Frontier, Japan 1971–2006.

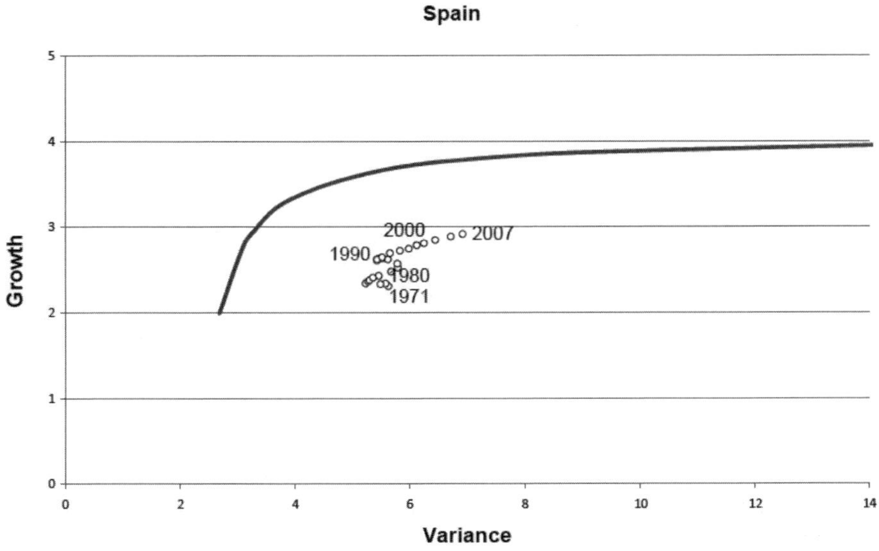

Figure 3. Actual Industrial Composition and the Mean-Variance Efficient Frontier, Spain 1971–2006.

be a mechanical result: As fast-growth sectors become larger over time, the economy converges in the dimension of growth for reasons unrelated to reallocation of output. The most interesting case is Spain, whose industrial composition in 2007 was characterized by an overall higher growth than in 1971, but also by higher growth volatility.

Clearly, different countries have had different types of experience with the evolution of optimal diversification in a mean-variance sense. What is the role of finance in that process?

The answer is — on average, positive. Our paper provides robust empirical evidence that the development of the financial system has a significant, causal, Pareto-improving effect on the economy's growth-volatility trade-off. More specifically, we find that developed financial markets are associated with a higher speed of convergence of the economy to the efficient benchmark. This point is captured by Figure 4, which shows that countries that had deeper credit markets in 1970 experienced a much faster convergence toward the optimal industrial composition of the economy, implied by mean-variance efficiency, in the next almost 40 years. Numerically, a two-standard deviation increase in financial development results in up to 3.5 percent higher annual speed of convergence toward the efficient industrial composition. By means of illustration, if in 1970 Greece had as deep

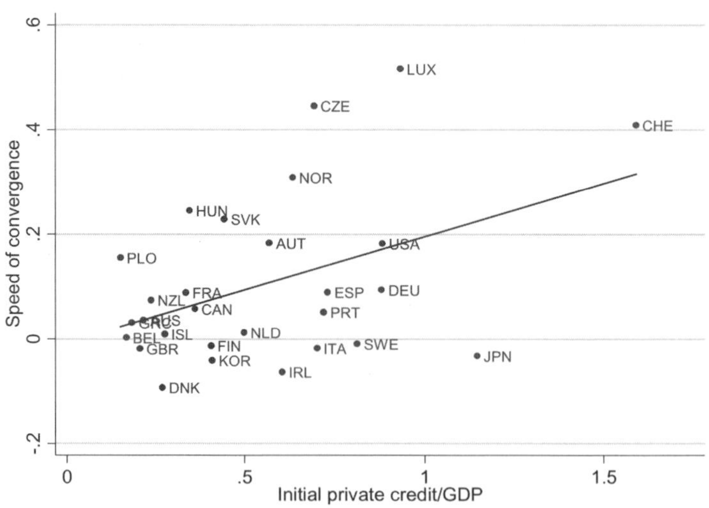

Figure 4. Financial Markets and Speed of Convergence to Mean-Variance Efficient Frontier, 1971–2006.

credit markets as the U.S., in 2007 its economy would have exhibited a sectoral composition associated with 18 percent lower volatility than the realized one, for the same level of realized growth.

Our second main result is that financial development reduces long-term volatility by exploiting the sectoral correlation, rather than by mechanically increasing the weight of low-volatility sectors. In fact, when in the construction of the efficient benchmark the correlations across sectors are artificially set to zero, the effect of financial development on the speed of convergence disappears. This result sheds new light on how financial development affects the economy. While Wurgler (2000) shows that financially developed economies' booming sectors grow faster by generating higher investment, and while Imbs (2007) demonstrates that high-growth sectors tend to have higher volatility, Manganelli and Popov (2010) illustrate that these results are compatible with lower long-term volatility of the economy thanks to the effect that financial development has on aggregate volatility through the sectoral correlations. Importantly, albeit the effect declines when we look at the 1970–2009 instead of at the 1970–2007 period — implying that a large and rare global finance-driven crisis can erase much of the long-term contribution of financial markets to lower aggregate volatility — it does not go away.

3. Finance, Output Growth, and Output Skewness

The empirical evidence linking financial markets to growth has been so abundant that in 2003, in a discussion of a survey on the subject, one author was prompted to conclude that "[...] In 1993 many people doubted that there was a relation between finance and growth; now very few do."[3] At the same time, however, large-scale recessions driven by financial crises, like the one we just experienced, seem to imply that financial markets have a destabilizing potential. Many of the banking crises experienced by various countries in the past several decades have been associated with large drops in GDP, as well as with huge fiscal costs, both in terms of foregone revenues and in terms of direct expenses on recapitalizing the country's financial sector (see Laeven and Valencia, 2010). Such large crises can erase much of the pre-crisis gains in terms of higher economic growth, as the experience of, for example, Chile during the banking crisis of 1981–1985 demonstrates.

[3]Zingales, L., 2003, commentary on "More on finance and growth: More finance, more growth?," Federal Reserve Bank of St. Louis, *Review*, Vol. 85, pp. 47–52.

Does financial development really increase the likelihood of crises? There are a number of theoretical arguments pointing to the fact that large and complex financial systems tend to be associated with higher economic fragility. One identified channel of this process is risk-taking. For example, in recent work, increased risk-taking before the 2007–2008 crisis has been linked to the growth of the financial industry resulting from "excess world saving" in the context of persistent global imbalances. In the wake of the dot-com bubble, the story goes, excess world savings by unsophisticated world investors looking for assets to store value turned to safe debt investments. In order to accommodate this increased demand, the U.S. financial sector manufactured debt claims out of all kinds of products, explaining the wave of pre-crisis securitization (see Caballero and Krishnamurthy, 2009). Another theoretical perspective into the same issue offers the following argument: In a financially liberalized economy with limited contract enforcement, systemic risk-taking reduces the effective cost of capital and relaxes borrowing constraints. This allows greater investment and generates higher long-term growth, but it raises the probability of a sudden collapse in financial intermediation when a crash occurs. Systemic risk thus increases mean growth even if crises have arbitrarily large output and financial distress costs, implying the co-existence of higher-level growth and more frequent crises (Rancière *et al.*, 2008). Biais *et al.* (2009) develop a model in which higher relative productivity in the financial sector can endogenously, through the channel of risk-taking, generate excessive rents and boom-bust episodes.

The literature on finance and volatility, some of which I summarized above, does a poor job in estimating the impact of finance on macroeconomic busts. Under various classes of consumer preferences, the volatility of growth underestimates the welfare consequences of growth variability by positing that economic agents care about the upside as much as they care about the downside. To illustrate this point, consider the growth pattern of two hypothetical countries A and B. Country A's GDP growth is normally distributed, with a mean of 0.01 and a standard deviation of 0.024. Country B exhibits a steady annual growth rate of 0.0126, with arbitrarily small symmetric deviations from that average, but once every century its GDP declines by 25 percent. Over a period of 100 years, country B attains the same mean growth rate and the same standard deviation of output growth as country A. However, with Epstein–Zin–Weil preferences[4] and values for

[4]The main feature of the preference specification developed by Epstein and Zin (1989) and Weil (1990) is that it delinks the IES from the coefficient of relative risk aversion.

the intertemporal elasticity of substitution and the coefficient of relative risk aversion as in Barro (2009), society in the second country would willingly reduce GDP by around 10 percent each year to replace the country's long-term growth profile with that of country A (assuming that the government can insure none of the output risk away).

Addressing this point requires the recognition that the third moment of growth (the *skewness*) captures better economic agents' aversion to the downside than the second moment of growth (the *volatility*). This is the point in a recent paper of mine ("Output fluctuations and growth: The role of financial openness," 2011), in which I use data on sector-level value-added for a wide cross-section of countries over the past 45 years to study the impact of financial liberalization on output growth, volatility, and skewness. The main finding of the paper is that financial liberalization is followed by an increase in industry output growth and by an increase in the negative skewness of the output growth process. At the same time, the data suggest no statistical effect of financial openness on output volatility. These results are consistent with the view that financial constraints are reduced and investment is aligned with growth opportunities when financial markets are liberalized, as well as with the view that financial openness raises the probability of a collapse in industrial output following, for example, a sudden stop in capital flows. I also find that these effects are stronger in industries that are more externally dependent and that face better growth opportunities. The results are remarkably robust to a wide variety of alternative experiments, including accounting for the endogeneity of liberalization, controlling for the channels through which concurrent policy reforms and macroeconomic developments affect the rate and the variability of the growth process, using different subsets of countries, and alternating between *de jure* and *de facto* measures of financial openness.

Figure 5 illustrates these results by comparing the output growth pattern of Argentina and Panama. These two countries are not that different in terms of per capita wealth, are a part of the same economic area, and exhibit similar trade patterns. By the definition of financial liberalization used in the paper, Argentina became fully open in 1991, while Panama did not. Table 1 indicates that Argentina grew at a rate almost four times higher after 1991 (2.6 percent vs. 0.7 percent), while annual growth rates in Panama declined somewhat after 1991, from 3.8 percent to 2.9 percent. Aggregate volatility declined in Panama while it remained steady in Argentina. Finally, while the distribution of growth rates became more positively skewed in Panama, it went from symmetric to negatively skewed in Argentina (–0.666 post-liberalization vs. –0.118 pre-liberalization). Thus, relative to

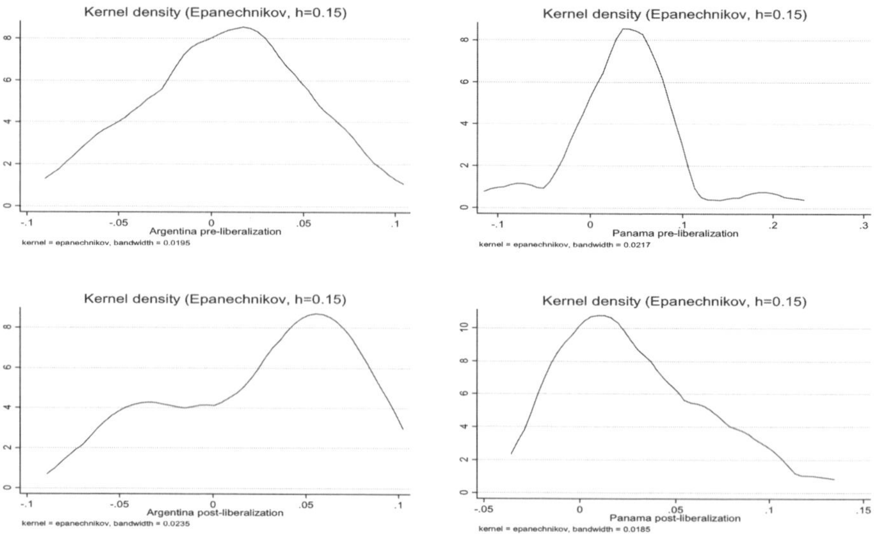

Figure 5. Kernel Distribution of Real GDP Growth, Pre- and Post-Liberalization: Argentina vs. Panama.

Table 1. Moments of Real Growth, Pre- vs. Post-Liberalization Event.

	Argentina		Panama	
Moments of output growth	Pre-	Post-	Pre-	Post-
Mean	0.007	0.026	0.038	0.029
St. dev.	0.042	0.043	0.059	0.034
Skewness	−0.118	−0.666	0.365	0.863

non-liberalized Panama, liberalized Argentina experienced higher growth, and its growth distribution became more negatively skewed indicating the incidence of a large and abrupt macroeconomic contraction in the early 2000s.

The second novelty in the paper is that the effect of financial liberalization on growth and risk is estimated jointly, allowing to separate the direct from the indirect effect of financial openness. It turns out that higher growth is associated with a more positively skewed distribution of growth rates. Therefore, while financial openness has a negative direct effect on skewness, this is offset by an indirect positive effect through the growth channel.

This implies that liberalization increases the risk of rare large contractions more in the short run than in the long run.

The evidence further suggests that countries with deeper domestic credit markets and with more developed institutions, as well as Latin American economies, have benefited more from financial liberalization, both in terms of higher growth and in terms of lower tail risk. Finally, the negative effect of financial openness on skewness holds in the macro-level data as well, implying that it is not a feature of sectoral data which is averaged away in aggregation.

Of course, deriving conclusions about social welfare requires several further steps. First, one needs to show that the pattern suggested by data on output holds in aggregate consumption data too. In particular, Rodrik (1998) argues that in countries open to trade, the government sector expands in order to insure the additional volatility away, and the same may hold in the case of financial liberalization. Second, one needs to estimate a proper welfare function in order to know whether the welfare loss of higher negative skewness is not fully outweighed by the welfare gains from higher growth. Preliminary evidence indicates that the governments of financially open countries are not able to mitigate the impact of large economic crises on consumption. It also tentatively suggests that in a world where agents are willing to pay high premia to avoid rare disasters, financial openness may be associated with a welfare cost that has not been identified before.[5]

How does this combined evidence relate to the existing literature? Actual evidence suggesting that deeper and more dynamic financial markets are causally linked to financial crises was relatively sparse before the 2007–2008 crisis. While Easterly *et al.* (2000) find that domestic financial development has a marginally positive effect on the probability of recessions, Acemoglu *et al.* (2002) have countered that the measured positive effect of finance on economic downturns disappears once institutional factors are controlled for. Raddatz (2006) exploits industry-level data and finds that credit markets' development decreases the magnitude of output declines in sectors with high natural liquidity needs. On the other hand, a large literature on early-warning signals had, even before the crisis, utilized simple statistical methods to link the probability of, for example, banking crises to the size of the financial sector, measured, for example, by credit

[5]Bekaert, G. and A. Popov, 2011, "Openness and risk," ECB mimeo.

growth. In hindsight, such studies did a fairly good job in "predicting" the events from 2007–2008.[6]

4. Conclusion

During the decades-long debate on the link between financial markets and the real economy, academics have tended to side either with Joseph Schumpeter's view of the ability of well-developed financial systems to stimulate economic growth, or with Joan Robinson's (1952) observation that "where enterprise leads, finance follows." The experience from the past several decades from emerging as well as from industrialized countries has mostly confirmed the first claim, namely, that deeper domestic financial markets, as well as international financial integration, improve economic efficiency, lead to better allocation of productive capital, and increase long-term economic growth.

At the same time, the frequent financial shocks associated with more dynamic financial industries and with more integrated financial markets — especially in view of the recent global crisis — also highlight the contribution of financial markets to macroeconomic risk. I have argued that from a social welfare perspective, the implications for rare output disasters are more important than the implications for higher volatility. Moreover, while the evidence is not strong that financial markets increase macroeconomic volatility, the evidence seems to be fairly strong that financial markets may be conducive to the realization of rare economic disasters. While we do not understand yet the full social welfare implications of this process, doing so has never seemed like a more timely venue of research.

References

Acemoglu, D., S. Johnson, J. Robinson, and Y. Thaicharoen, 2002, "Institutional causes, macroeconomic symptoms: Volatility, crises, and growth," *Journal of Monetary Economics*, Vol. 50, pp. 49–123.

Acharya, V., J. Imbs, and J. Sturgess, 2011, "Finance and efficiency: Do bank regulations matter?," *Review of Finance*, Vol. 15, pp. 135–172.

Aghion, P., A. Banerjee, and T. Piketty, 1999, "Dualism and macroeconomic volatility," *Quarterly Journal of Economics*, Vol. 114, pp. 1359–1397.

[6] See, for example, Borio and Drehmann (2009), and Alessi and Detken (2009).

Alessi, L. and C. Detken, 2009, "'Real time' early warning indicators for costly boom/bust cycles — A role for global liquidity," European Central Bank, working paper, No. 1039.

Barro, R., 2006, "Rare disasters and asset markets in the twentieth century," *Quarterly Journal of Economics*, Vol. 121, pp. 823–866.

Barro, R., 2009, "Rare disasters, asset prices, and welfare costs," *American Economic Review*, Vol. 99, pp. 243–264.

Beck, T. and R. Levine, 2002, "Industry growth and capital allocation: Does having a market- or bank-based system matter?," *Journal of Financial Economics*, Vol. 64, pp. 147–180.

Beck, T., R. Levine, and N. Loayza, 2000, "Finance and the sources of growth," *Journal of Financial Economics*, Vol. 58, pp. 261–300.

Beck, T., M. Lundberg, and G. Majnoni, 2006, "Financial intermediary development and growth volatility: Do intermediaries dampen or magnify shocks?," *Journal of International Money and Finance*, Vol. 25, pp. 1146–1167.

Bekaert, G., C. Harvey, and C. Lundblad, 2005, "Does financial liberalization spur growth?," *Journal of Financial Economics*, Vol. 77, pp. 3–55.

Bekaert, G. and A. Popov, 2011, "Openness and risk," European Central Bank, mimeo.

Biais, B., J.-C. Rochet, and P. Wooley, 2009, "Rents, learning and risk in the financial sector and other innovative industries," FMG discussion paper, No. 632.

Borio, C. and M. Drehmann, 2009, "Assessing the risk of banking crises — Revisited," *BIS Quarterly Review*, March, pp. 29–46.

Braun, M. and B. Larrain, 2005, "Finance and the business cycle: International, inter-industry evidence," *Journal of Finance*, Vol. 50, pp. 1097–1128.

Caballero, R. and A. Krishnamurthy, 2001, "International and domestic collateral constraints in a model of emerging market crises," *Journal of Monetary Economics*, Vol. 48, pp. 513–548.

Caballero, R. and A. Krishnamurthy, 2009, "Global imbalances and financial fragility," *American Economic Review*, Vol. 99, pp. 584–588.

Easterly, W., R. Islam, and J. Stiglitz, 2000, "Shaken and stirred: Explaining growth volatility," B. Pleskovic and J. E. Stiglitz, Annual Bank Conference on Development Economics, Washington, DC.

Epstein, L. and S. Zin, 1989, "Substitution, risk aversion, and the temporal behavior of consumption and asset returns: A theoretical framework," *Econometrica*, Vol. 57, pp. 937–969.

Goldsmith, R., 1969, *Financial Structure and Development*, New Haven, CT: Yale University Press.

Hellmann, T., K. Murdock, and J. Stiglitz, 2000, "Liberalization, moral hazard in banking, and prudential regulation: Are capital requirements enough?," *American Economic Review*, Vol. 90, pp. 147–165.

Imbs, J., 2007, "Growth and volatility," *Journal of Monetary Economics*, Vol. 54, pp. 1848–1862.

Kaminsky, G. and C. Reinhart, 1999, "The twin crises: The causes of banking and balance-of-payment problems," *American Economic Review*, Vol. 89, pp. 473–500.

King, R. and R. Levine, 1993a, "Finance and growth: Schumpeter might be right," *Quarterly Journal of Economics*, Vol. 108, pp. 717–737.

King, R. and R. Levine, 1993b, "Finance, entrepreneurship, and growth: Theory and evidence," *Journal of Monetary Economics*, Vol. 32, pp. 513–542.

Laeven, L. and F. Valencia, 2010, "Resolution of banking crises: The good, the bad, and the ugly," International Monetary Fund, working paper, No. WP/10/146.

Levchenko, A., R. Rancière, and M. Thoenig, 2009, "Growth and risk at the industry level: The real effects of financial liberalization," *Journal of Development Economics*, Vol. 89, pp. 210–222.

Levine, R., 2005, "Finance and growth: Theory, evidence, and mechanisms," in *The Handbook of Economic Growth*, Philippe Aghion and Steve Durlauf (eds.), Amsterdam: Elsevier/North-Holland.

Levine, R. and S. Zervos, 1998, "Stock markets, banks, and economic growth," *American Economic Review*, Vol. 88, pp. 537–558.

Lucas, R., 1987, *Models of Business Cycles*, New York: Basil Blackwell.

Manganelli, S. and A. Popov, 2010, "Finance and diversification," European Central Bank, working paper, No. 1259.

Markowitz, H., 1952, "Portfolio selection," *Journal of Finance*, Vol. 7, pp. 77–91.

McKinnon, R., 1973, *Money and Capital in Economic Development*, Washington, DC: Brookings Institution Press.

Morgan, D., B. Rime, and P. Strahan, 2004, "Bank integration and state business cycles," *Quarterly Journal of Economics*, Vol. 119, pp. 1555–1584.

Popov, A., 2011, "Output growth and fluctuations: The role of financial openness," European Central Bank, Working paper, No. 1386.

Raddatz, C., 2006, "Liquidity needs and vulnerability to financial underdevelopment," *Journal of Financial Economics*, Vol. 80, pp. 677–722.

Rajan, R. and L. Zingales, 1998, "Financial dependence and growth," *American Economic Review*, Vol. 88, pp. 559–586.

Rancière, R., A. Tornell, and F. Westermann, 2008, "Systemic crises and growth," *Quarterly Journal of Economics*, Vol. 123, pp. 359–406.

Robinson, J., 1952, "The generalization of the general theory," in *The Rate of Interest and Other Essays*, London: Macmillan, pp. 67–142.

Rodrik, D., 1998, "Why do more open economies have bigger governments?," *Journal of Political Economy*, Vol. 106, pp. 997–1032.

Schumpeter, J., 1911, *The Theory of Economic Development*, Cambridge, MA: Harvard University Press.

Stiglitz, J., 2000, "Capital market liberalization, economic growth and instability," *World Development*, Vol. 28, pp. 1075–1086.

Weil, P., 1990, "Nonexpected utility in macroeconomics," *Quarterly Journal of Economics*, Vol. 105, pp. 29–42.

Wurgler, J., 2000, "Financial markets and the allocation of capital," *Journal of Financial Economics*, Vol. 58, pp. 187–214.

Zingales, L., 2003, commentary on "More on finance and growth: More finance, more growth?," Federal Reserve Bank of St. Louis, *Review*, Vol. 85, pp. 47–52.

Occupying the Wrong Street? The Social Productivity of the Financial Sector: Some Comments*

Gerard Caprio, Jr.†

Williams College

We have before us in the session three different and yet complementary "takes" on what is meant by the social productivity of the financial sector, and three calls, directly or indirectly, for further research. Ross Levine looks at the ways that finance adds to social welfare by contributing to growth and income equality and analyzes the evidence. Alexander Popov adds another variable of possible concern, the volatility of the growth process, surely an important issue in the tumultuous wake of one of the worst financial crises of all time. Josh Lerner, in his paper with Peter Tufano, is concerned about the role of financial innovation and whether it makes our lives better or worse. All three papers are worth your attention.

Certainly in light of the most recent crisis, some, including those in the Occupy Wall Street movement, might paraphrase Milton Friedman and say that there is much in finance that is both new and good, but that unfortunately that which is good is not new and that which is new is not good. Finance appeared to play a role in a very few getting very rich, and not just in the fortunes made in the crisis by those who shorted CDOs, but as Philippon and Reshef (2009) showed us, a generalized rise in compensation in the sector occurred in the 15–20 years leading up to the crisis. And academics, government officials, and others interested in American society had better sit up and take notice. New research by a colleague at Williams College,

*Prepared for the Chicago Fed–European Central Bank conference, "The Role of Central Banks in Financial Stability: How Has It Changed?", November 10–11, 2011.

†Gerard Caprio, Jr. is the William Brough Professor of Economics and chair of the Center for Development Economics at Williams College.

Steve Nafziger, puts together income distribution data for pre-Soviet Russia and the results are bracing: As measured by the Gini coefficient, income inequality in the U.S. as of the early 2000s was worse — more unequal — than in Russia on the eve of their revolution (Nafziger *et al.*, 2011). So I certainly understand why the protestors are out there. But in my discussion of the social productivity of the financial sector, the message that comes out is very much that finance can be a force for good or for ill, and that what determines this outcome also has a powerful lesson for the demonstrators, namely that they are demonstrating on the wrong street. My message also ties in with the theme of this conference on the role of central banks, because they have so much to do with the impact of finance on the economy and society.

In reading these three papers, I was very much conscious that this year is the tenth anniversary of a book that Patrick Honohan and I wrote, *Finance for Growth: Policy Choices in a Volatile World.*[1] One of the goals of that study was to review, especially for readers in developing countries, the impressive evidence on the links between finance and growth and the then-still limited evidence that finance is pro-poor. What is interesting is that there has been no credible empirical assault on these findings; they have only increased in strength. We now have aggregate cross-country, panel, industry, and firm-level studies supporting the positive impact of finance on growth, as well as on income equality. There are even case studies, such as those on Italy (Guiso, Sapienza, and Zingales, 2004) and the United States (beginning with Jayaratne and Strahan, 1997, and continuing with some of the work Ross cited), that show the positive impact of finance on growth within a single country's institutional setting, and others that Ross referenced in his paper. Importantly, at least in his draft, Ross omitted a recent but very important contribution of his, with Alexey Levkov and Yona Rubenstein (2011), that shows that bank deregulation in the U.S., by helping to increase competition among non-financial firms, lessened their ability to indulge in their "taste for discrimination." So finance not only lessens inequality but counters racism!

The research on the growth and distributional impact of finance is now voluminous and in addition to Ross, Asli Demirgüç-Kunt, both personally and through her research team at the World Bank, have added to this literature in such a large number of ways that a full JEL article could easily be devoted to their contributions alone. And of course, there are the financial

[1] I am very grateful that we kept the subtitle!

historians, a number of whom view this literature with some puzzlement, because they thought the impact of financial growth had long ago been demonstrated. After all, the growth leaders of their day, such as Renaissance Italy; 17th and 18th century Netherlands (which was able to defend itself from the armies of much larger countries, thanks in large part to its financial system and ability to issue long-term government debt); 18th century England (which borrowed a financial system, which they further improved, and a king from the Dutch); and the 19th century cases of the United States, and later Germany and Japan, all had their financial revolution and then their happier experiences with economic growth.

Even though no one has overturned these results, there are of course some who disagree and/or bemoan the fact that progress is slow in getting into the black box that hides the channels through which finance contributes to growth and poverty reduction. Now I understand those who can brush off results, saying, "Well, those are just from cross-country regressions, or those are just case studies," etc.[2] But what is striking, notwithstanding the weaknesses of any single methodology, is that a very similar message emerges, namely that finance can be a powerful engine of growth and equality, from all of these avenues of investigation. I do at least understand the impatience to get at some more specific channels. It would be useful to be able to go beyond the advice of "improve your functions of finance" and "develop your financial infrastructure" in discussions of developing country officials. So I agree with Ross that to the extent that anyone in the Occupy Wall Street movement is out there because they think that finance only benefits the rich, then they are terribly misinformed, even though they understand well what happened to the income distribution in recent years. It would of course help if we had detailed evidence of the channels through which finance in the long run contributes to growth and poverty alleviation, as I am sure that Ross would agree.

---

[2]However, it is difficult to understand those who embrace other cross-sectional empirical work and yet deride cross-country analysis. Apparently they are convinced that the differences between, say, the U.S. and Chad, are so great that they do not belong in the same sample, but that, for example, it is fine to do a cross-sectional study of Habit X in New York, because after all they are all New Yorkers. I can only assume that this reasoning is the result of sustained consumption of pastrami on white bread with mayonnaise. In other words, that there are some New Yorkers who like the aforementioned deli combination is consistent with the belief that there is incredible variation in micro data sets, and neither I nor anyone else can judge how these differences compare with variations at the country level.

The idea underlying *The Guardians of Finance*, a forthcoming book with Ross and Jim Barth, is that how finance functions, whether it works for the few or the many, and how effective it is in promoting growth, depends very much on the incentive system in place. A bad incentive system can easily pervert the many positive effects of finance, as we saw so well in the recent crisis. What surprised many was that they thought the United States and other industrial countries had achieved a high level of financial development and that these countries had "good institutions." Indeed, more than a few from these countries lectured the rest of the world that they needed to adopt the rich countries' institutions or even some of the specifics of our approach to regulation. The problem of course is that an institutional environment can be changed over time and that financial development in all countries is a dynamic game. As we all know, finance is all about information asymmetries, and financial intermediaries throughout history have tried to profit from their informational advantages. At times their efforts to make profits have been distasteful, to say the least. When I read about the efforts of Magnetar to short the CDO market, and the use of synthetic CDOs, the first thing that came to mind was the episode of Daniel Drew, when he bought up virtually every printing press in the New York City area to print enough stock to be able to prevent "Commodore" Vanderbilt from taking over the Erie Railroad (Gordon, 2004, Chapter 11). The important point is, this is not the first unsavory episode in the history of finance, and it surely will not be its last, but what matters is learning from these breakdowns and having a regulatory regime that adjusts and pushes back toward a system that benefits all members of society.

That perhaps is where the paper by Alexander Popov fits in. This paper also is a call for more research, but this time on this issue of the link between finance and volatility. Mostly accepting that finance causes growth, the author reviews the literature on growth and volatility. Until the recent crisis, the consensus was that any link, to the extent it existed, was insignificant. However, the real issue, in light of the crisis, is whether financial development, while good for growth much of the time, is conducive to tail events that blow up the economy. It is clear that traditional econometric methods will not do a good job picking up rare events, even if we were blessed to have detailed financial and non-financial sector data going back several centuries — although that certainly would be nice — because many will argue that the economic structure has changed so much as to make comparisons unreliable. My guess is that the type of counterfactual analysis proposed by Josh Lerner will be one of the ways that extreme tail events are studied.

And again, my view is that pursuing such studies without a consideration of the incentive environment misses what is important, and in discussing the next paper I will give an example as to why this is so. To be sure, incentives depend greatly on the regulatory environment, meaning both the regulations and how they are enforced. Unilateral disarmament, as for example practiced by the SEC in the run-up to the crisis, when they failed to fill vacancies and did away with whole divisions (such as that charged with overseeing systemic risk), renders regulation nugatory. Regulators of course proceed as if they knew what worked; as Alexander's paper notes, they assume that stricter capital requirements help to rein in risk when research shows that the effect is ambiguous.

What about the impact of financial innovation? The Lerner–Tufano paper tackles this difficult question and really reads like an introduction to a very large National Science Foundation research proposal. In my view, the right decision is to give them the money! I doubt that counterfactual analysis is going to become the new "gold standard" for research on finance, but those who conclude that it does not add much make a grave mistake. We would — or should — like to have as many different research strategies as possible to analyze the role of finance, and as the authors explain, counterfactual analysis is particularly suitable to the study of innovation. I have to echo the point that I just made above, namely that incentives will have a huge effect on the impact of financial innovations.

Consider a simple thought experiment, which also applies to the study of volatility: Suppose that all the things that encouraged securitization of mortgages had occurred, with one exception, namely that all of the regulations that required or encouraged banks, pension funds, and other entities to hold highly rated securities had disappeared. So there would be no Nationally Recognized Statistical Rating Organization (NRSRO) classification by the SEC, and no risk weights in Basel (I would get carried away and say imagine a world with no Basel Committee at all; but however attractive this option is, I want to limit the thought experiment as narrowly as possible). What would have happened in this alternative universe? Any purchaser of a complex package of securities would only have done so if their institution had the capacity to make informed judgments about the quality of the components and their correlations. Why is that the case? Because in the universe in which we unfortunately live, purchasers of highly rated securities are legally protected against accusations that they failed in their fiduciary duties when there are regulatory requirements mandating or encouraging that they be held. In my alternative universe, without that legal protection, fund managers could face lawsuits and would have to answer questions such as "What did you know about the securities you were buying?" In that universe, there would have been much less securitization.

Or consider a world in which the financial regulators actually stepped in when informed by the FBI that there was widespread fraud in the mortgage industry. Even where the mortgage origination business was conducted by entities that the regulators did not control, they surely could have clamped down on the commercial banks' and investment banks' activities in the sector tremendously, such as by limiting their ability to continue securitizing such paper or by forcing them to consolidate their off-balance sheet entities when calculating capital requirements. Not to mention of course the possibility of freezing activities of Fannie Mae and Freddie Mac at that time. Or more heroically, imagine a world in which regulators understood the Broughton Bridge story. In this episode of history, a British company, by marching in unison across the Broughton Bridge in 1831, caused its collapse, and the British army command absorbed the lesson after that collapse and always required its troops to break cadence when they came to a bridge. Unfortunately, the French army did not learn this lesson, and in 1850 over 200 French soldiers perished in a bridge collapse. If financial regulators internalized this lesson, they would in effect have learned about the fallacy of composition, namely that what may be true at the individual level (holding more safe assets is good) is not only not necessarily true at the global level, but might actually be dangerous. That is, by blessing or endorsing any kind of exposure, the ensuing stampede by financial intermediaries into that asset class in and of itself renders that asset class no longer as safe as it once was. Please excuse me if it seems as though I am speaking Greek (pun intended). A counterfactual in which that lesson was absorbed would be an interesting one indeed.

The key point is that innovation and incentives have to be inherently linked. Notwithstanding their role in contributing to global warming, most would concede that automobiles and other forms of transportation have been a tremendous innovation that have had a positive impact on society, but most also understand that the combination of automobiles and alcohol is a dangerous one indeed. If we lived in a world in which law enforcement officials no longer prosecuted those driving while under the influence, many people having a friend or relative killed by a drunk driver would be convinced that automobiles were a horrible invention. But if the counterfactual examined included lax enforcement of blood-alcohol levels in a world with exceptionally low (e.g., 5 mph) speed limits that were enforced rigorously, we might miss the impact of alcohol on driving. I have belabored this point because I think it is critical. As the authors acknowledge, much care would have to be put into the creation of useful counterfactual.

My only complaint about the paper, other than wanting to see some detailed counterfactual studies, is that the authors try to invent a new functional framework for finance that does not quite add up. Their categories (see their Table 1) are pooling, moving money across time and space, payments, managing risk, resolving information asymmetries, and extracting information from markets. This classification is not very satisfactory. Since finance is all about giving up control of money today in the hope of getting it back, with a positive rate of return in the future, it is hard to conceive of any instrument that does not involve "moving money across time and space." Similarly, if there were no information asymmetries, there would be no intermediaries, so this category should include everything. I would urge the authors instead to adopt the five-way categorization that Ross came up with in his 1997 JEL paper, which is:

- Mobilizing savings,
- Allocating capital,
- Exerting corporate control (a.k.a. monitoring),
- Facilitating risk management, and
- Easing the trading of goods, services, and contracts.

Those who have not worked in this area might think that this difference is not important, but I beg to differ. Financial economics is decades behind the rest of the discipline (okay, except for macro) because finance was "assumed away" and so our measures of what finance does are so poor; we have to rely on measures of depth, turnover ratio on stock markets, etc. The functional approach focuses on what finance does, and until we agree on this, we are unlikely to come up with better measures of finance's real value added. So I ask that the authors put aside their attempt to come up with a new classification and use what has been accepted in the field. Since they want to get an understanding of the impact of financial innovation, they will be much better off with such measures than without them, and their paper already adds much value without attempting a new categorization of the functions of finance.

So the challenges laid out by these papers are great. Our knowledge of finance has advanced significantly since the dark years when financial markets were not even present in most economic models.

One last item. I established a tradition at the conference several years ago when I suggested that every conference ought to have a movie that illustrates the main theme and context of the event. At the 2006 conference I proposed the movie, *A Wing and a Prayer*; such was my optimism on the world being able to avoid a crisis. At the 2007 conference, and this was in early October before the market peaked, I suggested *Jaws*, and said, "For its theme song, which should be playing in central banks around the world, the music that lets them know that the beast is out there, and is hungry." I also evoked that movie's image of a young woman swimming on an otherwise nice day while the shark was getting ready to devour her — and I gather that there was a correspondent from *The Economist* present, because a few months later they used that image on their cover, without of course any attribution.

For this year's conference (and if anyone from *The Economist* is in the room, I would like credit for this one, though it is not quite as striking for a cover), I suggest the movie *Groundhog Day*, the film in which the main character, a reporter covering the ceremony on the eponymous day in Punxsutawney, PA, keeps almost endlessly repeating the same day and then realizes what is happening. We at this conference are reconsidering the role for the central bank in light of a recent crisis. It has been done before — that is after all why Bagehot wrote *Lombard Street* — and I trust that it will be done again. The guardians of finance — those who regulate the financial system — did not distinguish themselves in the recent crisis, and until they are held accountable and more information is revealed about what they know on a timely basis, we will be repeating this lesson over and over again. The movie *Groundhog Day* had a happy ending, eventually. Will any of us live long enough to see a happy ending in the world of financial regulation?

Fortunately, there is a way to hasten the arrival of that day. While it is easy to understand why the occupiers of Wall Street are so upset with the world of finance, their wrath is misdirected. Jamie Dimon and Lloyd Blankfein do not work for us or for the people in the street, and while the demonstrators might like the behavior of those in the sector to be different, I doubt that the present demonstrations are having much effect. Instead, they should be camped out at both ends of Pennsylvania Avenue, near the officials who could adopt rules that would encourage finance in ways that would focus it on carrying out the functions of finance identified here for the benefit of the many, and not the few, and on ways to hold regulators accountable. But that is the subject of another conference.

References

Barth, James, Gerard Caprio, Jr., and Ross Levine, 2012, *The Guardians of Finance: Making Them Work for Us*, Cambridge, MA: MIT Press.

Gordon, John Steele, 2004, *An Empire of Wealth: The Epic History of American Economic Power*, New York: Harper.

Guiso, Luigi, Paolo Sapienza, and Luigi Zingales, 2004, "Does local financial development matter?," *Quarterly Journal of Economics*, Vol. 119, No. 3, pp. 929–969.

Jayaratne, Jith and Philip Strahan, 1997, "The benefits of branching deregulation," *Economic Policy Review*, Vol. 3, No. 4.

Levine, Ross, Alexey Levkov, and Yona Rubenstein, 2011, "Racial discrimination and competition," Brown University, mimeo.

Nafziger, Steven, Tracy Dennison, Igor Fedyukin, and Peter Lindert, 2011, "Inequality in Russian history," Williams College, mimeo.

Philippon, Thomas and Ariel Reshef, 2009, "Wages and human capital in the U.S. financial industry: 1909–2006," National Bureau of Economic Research, working paper, No. 14644.

VI. OPEN ISSUES IN THE REGULATORY DEBATE: FAILURE RESOLUTIONS, BAILOUTS, MORAL HAZARD, AND MARKET DISCIPLINE

Bankers and Brokers First: Loose Ends in the Theory of Central Bank Policymaking

Edward J. Kane*
Boston College

"It is not the horse that draws the cart, but the oats."
— Russian proverb

Representative democracy espouses the principle that all men and women are equal under the law: "Liberté! Égalité! Fraternité!" Nevertheless, throughout the housing bubble and the long-lasting economic slowdown that the bursting of this bubble brought about, governments in the U.S. and Europe have put the interests of elite financial institutions far ahead of the interests of society as a whole.

Taxpayer interests were and are poorly represented because of regulatory hubris and regulatory capture. Influence-driven incentive conflict is a phenomenon that mainstream models of optimal macroeconomic and financial stabilization (e.g., Benigno and Woodford, 2003) studiously ignore. This paper seeks to demonstrate that this modeling failure has helped the financial industry to sow misconceptions, non-transparencies, and outright loopholes into the capital standards and regulatory definitions of capital and risk that — then and now — are supposed to keep financial instability in check.

*Edward J. Kane is a professor of finance at Boston College. This paper expands testimony given before the U.S. Senate Banking, Housing, and Urban Affairs Financial Institutions and Consumer Protection Subcommittee on August 3, 2011. The author wishes to thank Richard Aspinwall, Stephen Buser, Robert Dickler, Rex DuPont, Steve Hanke, Martin Hellwig, Richard Herring, James Moser, Michael Pomerleano, Reinhard Schmidt, Matt Stoller, Stephen Kane, and James Thomson for valuable comments on earlier drafts of this analysis.

1. Misconceptions about Crises and Crisis Response

The strategies of financial stabilization embodied in the Dodd–Frank Act (DFA) and Basel III ignore the economic efficiency and distributional issues raised by back-door bailouts. They presume that central banks can "print" enough money to keep insolvent financial institutions afloat forever and that questions about the economic justice, efficiency, and time consistency of this strategy can safely be ignored. Neither DFA nor Basel tries to define systemic risk operationally or to decide onto just which taxpayers' balance sheets the implicit debt created by U.S. and European central-bank credit support will finally settle.

Because insolvency and unemployment are hard to cure, they may be compared to a pair of grievous plagues. To alleviate the nasty side effects of would-be therapies, authorities must prescribe a *sustainable* cocktail of interacting reforms. In the U.S., strategies for dealing with regulation-induced innovation and for disciplining the institutions that recklessly spawned these plagues have been assigned to teams of incentive-conflicted and understaffed regulators to work out. Scandals such as the Keating 5 or Abscam episodes document the willingness of legislators to transmit lobbyist pressure to regulatory personnel. Regulatory clienteles are using Congress to fan the flames of incentive conflict as the rule-making that the DFA requires creeps forward. For example, Congress is refusing to give the agencies charged with implementing the DFA the funds needed to carry out their assignments and has held up political appointments at safety-and-soundness and consumer regulatory establishments. In the end, U.S. regulators are unlikely to devise and enforce rules or policies that crack down heavily on politically influential firms. Sadly, even more stressful political biases, turf issues, and budgetary pressures undermine efforts to resolve bank and sovereign insolvencies in the European Union as well.

Distressed institutions continue to shift accumulated losses and the downsides of still-expanding risk exposures to taxpayers and other counterparties. Bankers understand the financial safety net *not* as something external to their economic balance sheet, but as a politically enforceable *implicit contract* that they have negotiated with national governments. This contract allows a government to impose capital requirements in exchange for committing itself to bail out large portions of the financial industry in crisis circumstances. But it has proved counterproductive to impose requirements as complex and politically driven as those devised in Basel. The absence of cross-country accountability for individual-country rules and enforcement encourages forum shopping. This and other kinds of regulatory arbitrage enhance firms' ability to hide risk-taking and to misrepresent the depth and timing of actual losses in ways that vaporize the social benefits of capital requirements.

Financial crises are battles over loss distribution. If they want to fight these battles more effectively, governments around the world need to sharpen the risk-control missions of regulatory agencies and rework bureaucratic incentives at these agencies. They also need to refocus reporting responsibilities for regulators *and protected institutions* on changes in the value of taxpayer safety-net support.

In principle, "capital" is a measure of a firm's ability to sustain losses as a going concern (Hellwig, 1995). Acting in concert, market and regulatory discipline force a firm to carry a capital position that outsiders regard as large enough to support the risks it takes. When institutions are protected by the safety net, not all of this capital comes from shareholders. Taxpayers become enmeshed in supplying equity capital to such firms because creditors and other counterparties regard the conjectural value of government guarantees as a valuable option — a "taxpayer put." The value of the government-contributed capital supplied by a firm's taxpayer put serves as a substitute for ordinary on-balance-sheet capital supplied by the firm's shareholders. It frees up opportunities for managers to dividend out capital that shareholders would otherwise have to leave in the firm.

Differences in the protections afforded to stakeholders in Bear Stearns, Lehman, and Goldman Sachs clarify that creditors of some institutions are more fully protected than others. What we can call an "elite institution" is one that possesses political clout as well as economic importance.

Given that financial safety nets transform taxpayers into unwitting *equity investors of last resort*, regulators and financiers owe taxpayer-investors duties of loyalty, competence, and care in return for their stakes in financial firms. The duties of care and competence imply three specific duties:

(1) *A duty of vision*: Supervisors should continually adapt their surveillance systems to discover and neutralize innovative regulatee efforts to disguise their rule-breaking;
(2) *A duty of prompt corrective action*: Supervisors should stand ready to propose new rules and to discipline regulatees whenever a problem is observed; and

(3) *A duty of efficient operation*: Supervisors should strive to produce their insurance, loss-detection, and loss-resolution services at minimum cost.

In turn, the duty of loyalty entails both:

(1) *A duty of conscientious representation*: Supervisors should be prepared to put the interests of the community they serve ahead of their own loyalty; and
(2) *A duty of accountability*: Implicit in the other duties is an obligation for safety-net managers to embrace political accountability by bonding themselves to disclose enough information about their decision-making to render themselves answerable for mishandling their responsibilities.

Unless these duties are honored on political battlefields and enforced in operational and accountable ways, it is unreasonable to believe that authorities can or will adequately measure and contain systemic risk as the next round of boom and bust unfolds.

A critical step would be to strengthen training and recruitment procedures for top regulators. Specialized educational programs are only beginning to emerge. For example, Macquarie University in Australia is planning a Master's degree in financial regulation and is targeting it as an executive course for candidates currently employed as regulators. The most ambitious program is the European Supervisor Education Initiative (ESE). The ESE was formed in 2009 as a confederation of European supervisory authorities, central banks, and academic institutions. It seeks to promote "the concept of a joint supervisory culture in Europe." It organizes its curriculum in a modular fashion. Table 1 lists the subjects to be covered in 2012.

Except for including segments on negotiating and communication skills, the ESE program focuses on techniques of supervisory risk assessment and control. Missing from the curriculum is explicit training in the ethics of regulation and in how to prevent bureaucratic incentives from being distorted by the industry's revolving door and its participation in the patronage process. Incentive conflict is the number-one problem in regulatory and supervisory enforcement, and placing political patronage rather than competence and character at the center of the appointment process amplifies incentive conflict.

One's ability to handle incentive conflict is shaped in large part by one's personal sense of honor and duty. In areas of public service that require individuals to put their lives on the line, a candidate's sense of honor and duty is honed by morale-centered training programs. Although helpful, it is

Table 1. European Supervision Education Initiative Seminar Program for 2012.

Topics	Number of times offered	Planned dates	Length	Host/venue
Interest rate risk and asset-liability management (ALM) in banks (Advanced Basel III Seminars)	Two	14–16.02.2012 19–21.09.2012	2.5 days 2.5 days	Eltville Eltville
Stress testing and capital management in banks (Advanced Basel III Seminars)	Two	30.01–01.02.2012 25–27.04.2012	2.5 days 2.5 days	Eltville Vienna
IFRS vs. Basel requirements for banks (Advanced Basel III Seminars)	Two	20–22.06.2012 14–16.11.2012	2.5 days 2.5 days	Vienna Vienna
Negotiating skills for European supervisors	Six	12–13.01.2012 02–03.02.2012 22–23.03.2012 03–04.05.2012 06–07.09.2012 18–19.10.2012	2 days 2 days 2 days 2 days 2 days 2 days	Eltville Eltville Eltville Eltville Eltville Eltville
Case studies on the development and review of IRB models	Two	30.05–01.06.2012 23–25.10.2012	2.5 days 2.5 days	Eltville Luxembourg
Importance of the liquidity risk management for the stability of individual banks and the financial system	Two	24–26.04.2012 15–17.10.2012	2.5 days 2.5 days	Luxembourg Frankfurt
Risk models in banks	One	07–09.05.2012	2.5 days	Frankfurt
Supervisory colleges	Two	08–09.03.2012 04–05.10.2012	1 day 1 day	Berlin Frankfurt
Supervision of credit rating firms	Two	26–27.04.2012 26–27.04.2012	1 day 1 day	Frankfurt Bonn
English & communication skills for supervisory functions	One	23–25.05.2012	3 days	Prague

not enough for consortiums of individual agencies or universities to offer specialized instruction in the theory and practice of financial regulation for existing staff.

Between them, the Federal Reserve and the European Central Bank have used risky forms of collateralized lending and swap facilities to support troubled institutions all over the globe. As a long-run way to give European and U.S. taxpayer interests the primacy they deserve, I believe that we need to establish a high-profile academy for training financial regulators modeled on West Point and admit cadets from around the world. This would forge connections between graduates at supervisory agencies in different countries and pave the way for more effective information flows and cross-border regulatory cooperation. Besides studying principles of financial engineering and the ways in which past crises have unfolded, students need to be drilled in the duties they owe the citizenry and in how to overcome the political pressures that elite institutions exert when and as they become undercapitalized. It is striking how effectively training for crises prepares police officers, firemen, and nuclear personnel to head without hesitation *toward* — rather than *away from* — danger when emergencies arise.

2. Central Bank and Government Rescue Programs

When regulators pander to the expedient interests of loss-making institutions, they increase expected tax burdens on households and small businesses. The failure to perform triage prolongs economic malaise rather than cures it. Figure 1 summarizes the depth and breadth of the subsidized credit support that the Fed supplied during 2007–2010. The voting and taxpaying public recognizes that central bank and government rescue programs have placed heavy — and not yet fully acknowledged — burdens on the citizenry of the U.S. and EU. Evaluating bailout programs only against a totally irresponsible standard of doing nothing at all, high officials characterize financial crises as generating ruinous external diseconomies for viable financial firms, and go on to make two self-serving claims: (1) that the indiscriminate use of government credit support is *necessary* to save us from worldwide depression, and (2) that bailout arrangements actually *make money* for the taxpayer. Both claims are false, but in different ways.

Bailing out firms without conducting triage and taking control of zombie firms is not a reliable or efficient way to restore financial stability (Kane and Klingebiel, 2004). It wastes taxpayer resources by expanding the opportunity set of previously mismanaged firms, and these firms' attraction to

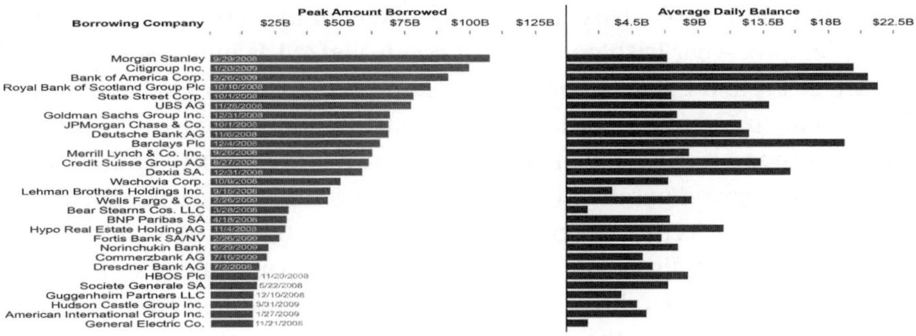

Figure 1. The Fed, Showing Great Creativity, Used Its Last-Resort Lending Powers to Fund Many of the Largest Banks in the World (Fed Loans 8/2007–4/2010).

Source: Bradley Keoun and Phil Kuntz, 2011, "Wall Street aristocracy got $1.2 trillion in secret loans," Bloomberg.com, August 22 (transmitted to me by Richard Herring).

longshot uses of funds undermines rather than promotes economic recovery. Leaving zombie firms in private hands evokes reckless gambles for resurrection and creates uncertainty about who will finally bear bailout costs and about when and how triage will — as it must eventually — be accomplished. The U.S. S&L mess shows that until these issues are resolved, gambles and uncertainties will continue to disrupt the flow of credit and real investment necessary to trigger and sustain a robust economic recovery (Kane, 1989; Kane and Yu, 1995).

In the U.S., the claim that the Fed and TARP programs actually "made money" for the taxpayer is half-true. The true part of the proposition is that, thanks to the heavily subsidized terms these programs offered, most institutions will be able to service the formal obligations they incurred. But the other half of the story is that U.S. citizens had better ways to deploy bailout funds. Blanket rescue programs forced taxpayers to provide undercompensated equity funds to deeply troubled institutions, and the largest and most politically influential of these firms were allowed to gamble for resurrection. Government backing permitted insolvent financial firms to avoid having their debt explicitly downgraded to the junk status it deserved. It also allowed some of the largest zombies to absorb the assets of other troubled firms, making them even bigger and harder to fail.

The payoff structures of lifelines provided to an underwater firm are not those of a loan. They are those of a longshot equity investment whose substantial downside easily justifies a 15 percent to 20 percent return. For example, three-year Irish government bonds yielded as much as 14 percent in July 2011, and the yield on three-year bonds issued by Greece reached 25 percent in October. Hull, Predescu, and White (2005) calculate that during the non-crisis period of 1996–2003, the risk premium over Treasuries appropriate for comparably low-rated bonds averaged 13.21 percent.

Unbridled government credit support runs a tab for past and future losses at protected firms and puts the bill on taxpayers' account. Running such a tab is demonstrably a short-run path of political and administrative least resistance. But in the long run, this strategy creates hard-to-contain social unrest. U.S. and EU authorities chose this path without weighing the full range of out-of-pocket and implicit costs of indiscriminate rescues against the costs and benefits of alternative programs, such as prepackaged bankruptcy or temporary nationalization, and without documenting differences in the way each deal would distribute benefits and costs across the populace over time.

3. Rethinking Systemic Risk

This paper's title metaphor of "loose ends in central bank policymaking" puts one in mind of a figurative cable whose individual strands need to be fused and joined to a nation's (or region's) real economic system. Regulators' operative problem is to conceptualize the connection realistically and to assess the risk that it might unravel in particular ways.

The root problem in supervisory conceptions of capital and systemic risk is that they shield government and industry officials from accountability for the roles they play in generating adverse movements in the true value of each variable. Politicians and regulators are reluctant to acknowledge regulation-induced elements in innovative forms of risk-taking and loss deferral undertaken by client firms, or to report publicly on the ways in which the industry exerts perverse lobbying pressure upon them. The primary task of so-called Wall Street lobbyists is to foster among politicians and regulators an inordinate fear of letting either the reliability of industry accounting standards or the health of major industry segments be called into serious question. These fears cement the taxpayer put and feed an expectation that officials will absorb losses and loss exposures in crisis situations. Despite the numerous changes promulgated in the DFA and Basel III, this expectation remains strong (see, e.g., Figure 2). These fears and proclivities encourage opportunistic firms to cultivate

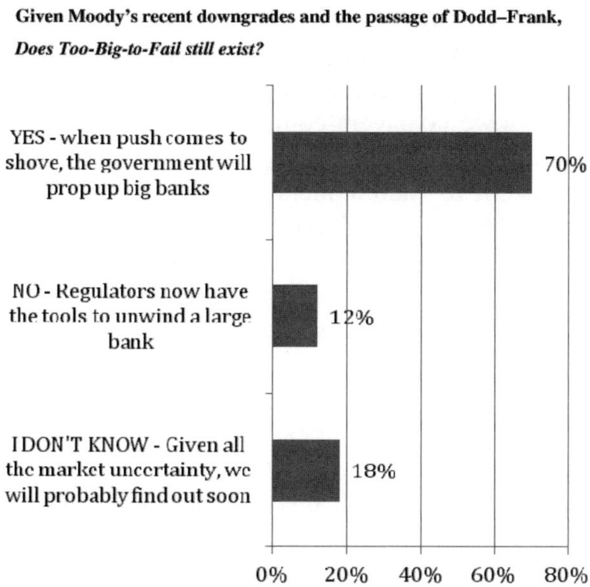

Figure 2. Survey Evidence About the Credibility of Financial Reforms.
Source: American Banker On-Line Subscriber Survey. The survey questionnaire was posted online from 9/25/11 through 10/2/11.

turf battles and exploit incentive conflicts within the supervisory sector to make sure that tough decisions favor industry interests over those of other citizens.

Definitions of systemic risk used by the Basel Committee and other policymakers focus on contagion: i.e., a concern for avoiding potential spillovers of institutional defaults across important firms in the financial sector and from this sector, to employment and asset values in the real economy. This perspective conceives of safety-net costs simply as negative externalities and fails to acknowledge that safety-net arrangements are rooted in an implicit political contract. In crisis circumstances, legislators and regulators renegotiate the terms of this contract and its enforcement with their counterparties, with little input from taxpayers. The understanding that this will occur helps to complete financial markets by credibly segregating downside risk in protected institutions and assigning the deepest tail-risk exposures to taxpayers. If tail events do not materialize, the institution reaps most of the gains. But when and if things go disastrously sour, the management "puts" substantial losses to taxpayers.

This two-piece contractual conception of systemic risk clarifies that it comes from an option-like equity investment that government officials make in protected firms. As agents, government officials and the managers of protected firms owe taxpayers complementary duties of loyalty, competence, and care. Taxpayers' position in each protected firm provides an insurance-like benefit to shareholders and creditors that, in competitive markets, firms would be required to either surrender or pay for. The value of this benefit can be shown to vary inversely with the risk that an institution might sustain a series of losses that exceed its ownership capital (i.e., with the expected value of a firm's deepest downside risks) and with the percentage of a firm's tail risk that the government is likely to absorb if this were to occur.

Research indicates that bond, stock, and swap markets reward elite institutions for increases in asset size and tail risk. See, for example, Brewer and Jagtiani (2009), Penas and Unal (2004), and Völz and Wedow (2009). Hence, empirical research supports the common-sense view that implicit and explicit government guarantees distort the ways in which banks conduct and report their risk-taking. This is why policymakers should interpret taxpayer exposure to tail risk at systemically important firms as an implicit market-completing contract rather than as an external diseconomy. The taxpayer put makes taxpayers unacknowledged equity investors in major firms. The value of their stake can and should be measured jointly by managers and regulators and be supported by an appropriate annual or quarterly dividend. As contracting structures for other stakeholders routinely require, taxpayers deserve to have their stake in financial firms monitored and serviced fairly.

4. Usefulness of Capital Requirements has been Oversold

Regulation may be likened to medicine and systemic risk to a disease. Medicines and other kinds of therapeutic treatments are bundles of good and bad side effects. Therapies seldom prove beneficial for all *intervals of time* or for all *types of patients*. In the financial sector, treatment protocols should be judged by their ability to create net value for patients and society through time.

To evaluate regulatory treatments properly, one must look beyond their immediate palliative effects. One must also worry about both the long-term comprehensiveness of the diagnosis regulatory "doctors" have adopted and the limitations of the therapy they prescribe. In the laboratory in which global regulatory strategies are crafted today (the Basel Committee on

Banking Supervision), the diagnosis that regulators are pursuing is misconceived. They acknowledge that financial crises are socially costly to cure, but pretend that they can be avoided by aligning what turns out to be a firm's understated leverage with politically negotiated conceptions of its exposure to risk. But their treatment plans misperceive capital and misweight risk. Regulators seem to believe it is sufficient to force protected institutions to accept a marked increase in their equilibrium ratio of *accounting net worth* to total assets. But games that can be played with loan-loss reserves and other discretionary items make accounting net worth a loophole-ridden concept whose value is ultimately driven by an institution's appetite for risk. In practice, a firm whose books make a show of higher capital is often more risky than a firm whose books show less.

Hence, the preventive leg of the Basel diagnosis is overly hopeful and not supported by empirical research. On the contrary, financial crises seem **inevitable**. Where data exist, they show that every country's financial sector passes through a succession of three-stage sequences: a pre-crisis bubble in credit, an actual crisis, and a post-crisis period of creative destruction and healthy recovery (Kindleberger, 1978; Reinhart and Rogoff, 2009). Of course, the durations of the different stages vary across countries and across time, and transitions from one stage to another become clear only in retrospect.

Historical data do support a less sweeping hypothesis: namely that bubbles and crises can be amplified by weaknesses in insolvency detection and by subsidies to risk generated by zombie firms' ability to battle for bailouts. In practice, crises and subsidies arise dialectically from path-dependent collisions of efforts by: (1) regulators in their supervisory capacity to control leverage and other forms of risk-taking, with (2) disruptive efforts by regulated and "shadow" financial institutions to expand risks in non-transparent ways and to shift responsibility for ruinous outcomes onto national safety nets. Bank managers face a threefold incentive: to lobby for lenient standards, to hide and understate risk exposures, and to overstate accounting net worth. This set of incentives makes risk and stockholder-contributed net worth hard to measure accurately and reliable standards by which to judge improvements in incentive alignment difficult to set and enforce.

5. Undone by the Regulatory Dialectic

Because regulators have relatively short terms in office, they are attracted to temporary, rather than lasting, fixes. The costs and benefits of capital requirements extend far into the future and are by no means fixed or exogenous. Regulatees search tirelessly for ways to reduce the burdens of regulation. Value maximization leads bankers to devise progressively lower-cost ways to exercise political clout, to adjust and report their asset and funding structures, and to choose the jurisdictions in which they book particular pieces of business.

This kind of financial engineering resembles what happens on a "makeover" television show. Top managers deploy the equivalents of fashionistas, cosmeticians, and hairdressers to revamp their firm's external appearance without changing the underlying character of the risk exposures that they expect taxpayers to support.

The endogeneity of regulatory burdens leads us to view: (1) ongoing negotiations in the Basel Committee on Banking Supervision that seek to establish global risk-based capital rules and (2) disruptive bank objections to — and circumvention of — emerging rules as **conflicting forces** in a dialectical evolutionary process:

> **Regulation** (e.g., Basel I) immediately begets and subsequently perfects patterns of **avoidance**.
> **Avoidance** begets (after a long delay) **re-regulation** (Basel II & III), often in response to **crisis pressures** and a **credit "crunch."**
> **Re-regulation** spawns further rounds of **avoidance**.

Weaknesses in the way U.S. and EU regulators chose to implement Basel standards create differences in the costs of loophole mining that help explain why the crisis hit their financial systems harder than those of Canada, Asia, Latin America, and Oceania (see *Shadow Financial Committee Report* [2011], posted at aei.org). Although Basel II ties risk weights for sovereign debt to credit ratings, it permits national authorities to go below those weights for central-government debt (or debt guaranteed by a central government) that is issued and funded in the currency of the country in question. For political reasons, U.S. regulators assigned unrealistically low weights to mortgage-backed securities and EU officials set zero risk weights for member-state debt. The European Central Bank (ECB) contributed to the process by accepting the sovereign debt of all Eurozone countries at par value when posted as collateral for ECB loans. When and as the debt of the "GIPSI" nations of Greece, Ireland, Portugal, Spain, and Italy began to be downgraded, the EU and the ECB failed to "haircut" their treatment of these countries' increasingly risky debt.

All this was part of a larger strategy of cross-country denial and concealment. EU stress tests and Basel's risk-weighted capital ratios (Demirgüç-Kunt, Detragiache, and Merrouche, 2011) failed demonstrably to distinguish between failing and viable banks. The fundamental weakness in Basel arrangements is their contractual incompleteness. Basel accords fail to make credit-rating organizations and individual-country regulators accountable either to the Basel Committee or to banking regulators in other member countries.

My Hegelian perspective dramatizes the incentive conflicts that regulators and regulatees face. Crises and subsidies arise in a path-dependent manner from prior tensions between efforts by *regulators* in their supervisory capacity to control leverage and other forms of risk-taking and efforts by *regulated and "shadow" financial institutions* to *expand* risks in non-transparent ways and to *shift* responsibility for ruinous outcomes onto national safety nets.

Loopholes make lobbyists' disinformational claim that tougher capital requirements will make banks pass up profitable, but socially risky financial opportunities seem distressingly dishonest. Hopefully, the crisis is teaching the public some important lessons about the game regulators and regulatees have been playing on them. Accounting ratios are not difficult to overstate and bankers do not accept high statutory burdens passively. Other things being equal, higher capital requirements lead banks to choose riskier strategies and to conceal the resulting loss exposures from regulators' losses so as to minimize adverse effects on bank profits and stock prices.

This perspective clarifies that the Dodd–Frank Act and the Basel III framework are using stress tests and higher capital requirements to treat only a subset of the problem: the extent to which institutions expose themselves in *directly observable ways* to credit risks that transmit exposures to default across a chain of possibly fragile counterparties. But to be effective, the medicine of capital requirements must be adapted to take fuller account than Basel does of a firm's asset-liability maturity mismatch and to treat a second and more subtle source of subsidies. This second problem is the ease with which regulatory arrangements continue to allow actual or potential zombie institutions to use financial accounting tricks and innovative instruments to hide risk exposures and to accumulate fresh losses until their insolvency becomes so immense that they can panic regulators and stampede them into providing life support indiscriminately to insolvent firms.

Without the taxpayer put, creditors of a weak bank would face haircuts and excessively risky banks would have risk retrenchment forced on them by market and regulatory discipline. This disciplinary pressure is likely to lead to a "credit crunch" at troubled firms, but so does forbearance. The problem is that *indiscriminate* bailouts are the opposite of discipline. They lead banks to eschew healthy positive net-present-value lending programs to business in favor of negative-NPV "gambling for resurrection."

In good times and in bad, the "taxpayer put" allows elite private institutions to issue the equivalent of government debt and makes ordinary citizens uncompensated equity investors in such firms. Offering endless credit support to zombie firms impedes macroeconomic recovery by making crippled institutions look stronger than they are and turns a blind eye to the ways in which their underlying weakness creates additional damage by incentivizing managers of such firms to waste taxpayer resources by undertaking reckless longshot investments instead of fostering flows of healthy business and consumer credit.

6. Recommendations for Reform

My recommendations for regulatory reform are rooted in the straightforward ethical contention that protected institutions and regulatory officials owe the same fiduciary duties to taxpayers — as implicit equity investors — that corporations owe to stockholders. The existence of a safety net makes taxpayers silent equity partners in major financial firms. As *de facto* investors, taxpayers deserve to be informed by institutions and regulators at regular intervals about the value of their side of the taxpayer put. Consistent with U.S. and European securities laws, managers of important financial firms should measure and report — under penalties for fecklessness, deception, and negligence — the value of taxpayers' stake in their firm on the same quarterly frequency that they report to stockholders. Estimates prepared by individual institutions ought to be vetted by regulators and aggregated within and across countries. To make regulators more accountable for their performance as supervisors, government officials *should be required to examine, challenge, and publicize* any concerns they may have about the assumptions used by different firms and regulators and to expose themselves to sanctions for defects in the ways in which they acquit these tasks.

Defining systemic risk as taxpayers' side of an unfavorably structured option claim also provides a metric for tracking systemic risk over time. Requiring authorities to calculate and disclose fluctuations in the aggregate value of the taxpayer puts enjoyed by elite institutions would make regulatory authorities operationally accountable for the quality of their supervisory performance in booms and recessions alike.

Considerable disagreement exists about how to define and measure systemic risk. In reviewing the literature, Bisias, Flood, Lo, and Valavanis (2012) distinguish 31 different ways of measuring this variable. Still, nearly everyone agrees that it arises from mixing leverage with loan and investment strategies that create volatility in financial institution returns. Most existing measurement strategies incorporate the pioneering perspective of Nobel Laureate Robert Merton (1977, 1978). Studies using his approach show that regulators could have tracked the growing correlation of institutional risk exposures and used it as an early warning system with which to track the increase in systemic risk that resulted in the current crisis. For example, research by Carbó-Valverde, Kane, and Rodríguez-Fernández (2013) indicates that at large U.S. and EU banks during 2004–2008, safety-net benefits per dollar, euro, or pound of assets averaged about 15 basis points and that in the years leading up to the crisis, estimated benefits were significantly higher at banks that eventually received bailout assistance.

The most difficult part of calculating the taxpayer put is to track the changing volatility of a firm's returns on assets. Expanding the format for collecting information from covered institutions in individual countries to include estimates of the actual and future variability of their returns (i.e., the "volatility" of their positions over different horizons) and the value of the taxpayer put could improve the precision of systemic-risk estimates and officials' accountability for regulatory and supervisory performance.

7. Traditional Reporting and Incentive Frameworks are Inadequate

Metrics are important. Accounting standards for recognizing emerging losses make evidence of an institution's insolvency inefficiently slow to surface. Moreover, during this and other crises, officials have proved reluctant to prepare and publicize timely estimates of the financial and distributional costs of bailing out firms that benefited from open-bank assistance.

By engaging in regulation-induced innovation, nurturing clout, and exerting lobbying pressure, a country's systemically important financial institutions (SIFIs) have kept their pursuit of tail risks from being adequately monitored and disciplined. The non-transparent role of political, bureaucratic, and career interests in regulatory decision-making is dangerous. It encourages elite firms to demand the right to screen regulatory appointments, to distort regulatory protocols, and to undermine strategies of enforcement.

In a world of derivatives transactions, top regulators need special training to understand — and considerable mental toughness to discipline abuses of — the incremental taxpayer exposures to risk that innovative instruments and portfolio strategies might entail. Efficient safety-net management requires a more sophisticated informational framework than current methods of bank accounting and examination provide. To protect taxpayers and to enhance financial stability, examinations and bank accounting reports should *not* focus narrowly on measures of tangible capital. They should also develop and report explicit estimates of the *intangible* value of an institution's evolving claim on taxpayer resources. To hold themselves accountable for carrying out these tasks conscientiously, regulators and protected institutions must accept a system of ethical constraints that would make them reveal and defend the forward-looking assumptions they use in calculating their enterprise's share of the taxpayer put.

Summarizing, regulators need to measure and publicize the costs taxpayers incur in supporting national and international safety nets. To help authorities to do this skillfully and conscientiously, governments need to change the way regulators are trained, recruited, and incentivized. I believe that a national or international academy for financial regulators could assist in these tasks.

References

Benigno, Pierpaolo and Michael Woodford, 2003, "Optimal monetary and fiscal policy: A linear quadratic approach," *NBER Macroeconomics Annual*, Vol. 18, pp. 271–333.

Bisias, Dimitrios, Mark Flood, Andrew Lo, and Stavros Valavanis, 2012, "A survey of systemic risk analytics," U.S. Department of the Treasury, Office of Financial Research, available at www.treasury.gov/ofr.

Brewer, Elijah and Julapa Jagtiani, 2009, "How much did banks pay to become too-big-to-fail and to become systematically important?," Federal Reserve Bank of Philadelphia, working paper, No. 09–34, December 3.

Carbó-Valverde, Santiago, Edward Kane, and Francisco Rodríguez-Fernández, 2013, "Safety-net benefits conferred on difficult-to-fail-and-unwind banks in the US and EU before and during the Great Recession," *Journal of Banking and Finance*, Vol. 37, pp. 1845–1859.

Demirgüç-Kunt, Aslı, Enrica Detragiache, and Ouarda Merrouche, 2011, "Bank capital: Lessons from the financial crisis," World Bank, working paper, October 16.

Hellwig, Martin, 1995, "Systemic aspects of risk management in banking and finance," *Swiss Journal of Economics and Statistics*, Vol. 131, pp. 723–737.
Hull, John, Mirela Predescu, and Alan White, 2005, "Bond prices, default probabilities and risk premiums," published online.
Kane, Edward J., 1989, *The S&L Insurance Mess: How Did It Happen?*, Washington, DC: Urban Institute Press.
Kane, Edward J. and Min-Teh Yu, 1995, "Measuring the true profile of taxpayer losses in the S&L insurance mess," *Journal of Banking and Finance*, Vol. 19, November, pp. 1459–1478.
Kane, Edward J. and Daniela Klingebiel, 2004, "Alternatives to blanket guarantees for containing a systemic crisis," *Journal of Financial Stability*, Vol. 1, September, pp. 31–63.
Kindleberger, Charles P., 1978, *Manias, Panics, and Crashes: A History of Financial Crises*, New York: Basic Books (first edition).
Merton, Robert C., 1977, "An analytic derivation of the cost of deposit insurance and loan guarantees," *Journal of Banking and Finance*, Vol. 1, pp. 3–11.
———, 1978, "On the cost of deposit insurance when there are surveillance costs," *Journal of Business*, Vol. 51, pp. 439–452.
Penas, María F. and Haluk Unal, 2004, "Gains in bank mergers: Evidence from the bond markets," *Journal of Financial Economics*, Vol. 74, No. 1, pp. 149–179.
Reinhart, Carmen M. and Kenneth S. Rogoff, 2009, *This Time is Different: Eight Centuries of Financial Folly*, Princeton, NJ: Princeton University Press.
Völz, Manja and Michael Wedow, 2009, "Does banks' size distort market prices? Evidence of too-big-to-fail in the CDS market," Series 2, Deutsche Bundesbank, discussion paper, No. 06/2009, March 24.

The Elusive Scale Economies of the Largest Banks and Their Implications for Global Competitiveness

Joseph P. Hughes*

Rutgers University

1. Introduction

In the wake of the financial crisis that began in 2007, policymakers have focused again on the largest financial firms to consider the association of their size with systemic risk. An equally important question examines whether their size benefits the economy. In particular, is the size of the largest financial institutions the result of technological cost advantages that improve the efficiency of their capital allocation and liquidity and enhance their international competitiveness? Or is their large size the result, not of technological cost advantages, but of safety-net subsidies that confer too-big-to-fail cost advantages and foster moral hazard in investment decisions? The answers to these questions help focus and balance the debate on regulating the size of the largest financial institutions to manage systemic risk.

In a recent speech at the Conference on the Regulation of Systemic Risk at Federal Reserve Board in Washington, Federal Reserve Governor Daniel Tarullo noted the relative dearth of empirical work on the degree of scale and scope economies in large financial firms: "Generally, though, even where intuition suggests economies in some other areas — such as the breadth of securities distribution networks and the ability to provide all forms of financing in significant amounts — evidence for the existence of such economies is limited and mixed. Moreover, even where significant scale is necessary to achieve certain economies, an important question will be what the minimum efficient scale — or, perhaps more realistically, the

*Joseph P. Hughes is professor of economics at Rutgers University, New Brunswick, New Jersey.

minimum feasible scale — actually is. It is possible that a firm would need to be quite large and diversified to achieve these economies, but still not as large and diversified as some of today's firms have become."

Governor Tarullo poses two fundamental questions. Why is the evidence of scale economies limited and mixed — are they illusive or elusive? And if such economies exist, is it possible that they can be achieved by smaller institutions than the largest we observe today? My research in collaboration with Loretta Mester, Choon-Geol Moon, and William Lang has sought to answer these two questions.[1] We have consistently found evidence of large scale economies that increase with size — the largest financial institutions experience the largest scale economies — and we have shown why this evidence eludes the standard investigation. In recent work, Loretta Mester and I have found no evidence that too-big-to-fail subsidies in the cost of funds explain the cost advantages of the largest financial institutions, and we have found that restricting the size of the largest institutions would significantly increase the cost of producing their current menu of financial products and services, an increase which would likely compromise their global competitiveness.[2] The following sections address each of these points. Section 2 reviews the evidence of large scale economies that increase with size. Section 3 considers details of how scale economies are measured and why evidence of scale economies eludes many investigations. Section 4 outlines a method of estimating scale economies that distinguishes the underlying scale effects on cost from the effects on costs of size-related changes in risk-taking. Section 5 describes evidence that technology, not too-big-to-fail subsidies, accounts for the cost advantage of the largest financial institutions. Section 6 considers the implications of scale economies for scaling back the operations of the largest financial institutions and for the global competitiveness of smaller institutions. Finally, Section 7 concludes.

2. Evidence of Scale Economies at the Largest Financial Institutions

The term "economies of scale" describes how cost varies with a measure of firm size, which characterizes the financial products and services produced

---

[1]Hughes, Lang, Mester, and Moon (1996, 2000); Hughes and Mester (1998); Hughes, Mester, and Moon (2001).

[2]Hughes and Mester (2011).

by the institutions. When cost increases less than proportionately with size, economies of scale prevail. When cost varies in the same proportion as size, constant returns to scale obtains. And, when cost increases more than proportionately with size, diseconomies of scale prevail.

Using a variety of recently developed methods of modeling the relationship of cost to financial outputs, a number of studies have found evidence of economically and statistically significant scale economies even at the largest financial institutions. These studies are described briefly below and in more detail in Hughes and Mester (2010). Hughes, Lang, Mester, and Moon (1996) use 1994 data consisting of 443 highest-level U.S. bank holding companies ranging in size from $33 million to $250 billion in consolidated assets. They find that the cost elasticity, 0.89, of the smallest banks (assets less than $300 million) decreases continuously as bank size increases up to a mean of 0.80 for banks whose assets exceed $50 billion.[3] A value of 0.89 for the cost elasticity implies that a 10 percent increase in output would result in an 8.9 percent increase in cost, and for 0.80, an 8.0 percent increase in cost. The less than proportional response of cost to an increase in output implies that economies of scale characterize technology. This study finds the largest scale economies at the largest financial institutions.

Berger and Mester (1997) use U.S. data on commercial banks during the period 1990–1995 and find that in each size class from banks with assets less than $50 million to those with assets that exceed $10 billion, over 90 percent of banks in each size group experience scale economies. The typical bank in each size class would need to be two to three times larger to maximize scale efficiency.

Hughes and Mester (1998) examine U.S. commercial banks with assets that exceed $1 billion during the period 1989–1990 and find significant scale economies for banks in all size groups. For the smallest banks with assets less than $1.8 billion, a 10 percent increase in output implied a 9.4 percent increase in cost, while for the largest banks with assets between $7 billion and $74 billion, an 8.7 percent increase in cost. Hughes, Lang, Mester, and Moon (2000) consider the same sample but employ a more innovative technique to model banking technology, and they find that a 10 percent

[3]The measure of scale economies is often stated as the inverse of the cost elasticity. The cost elasticity of 0.89 implies a measure, 1.12, of scale economies. The cost elasticity of 0.80 implies scale economies of 1.25. Thus, scale economies increase with size as the cost elasticity decreases.

increase in output implies a 9.1 percent increase in cost for the smallest banks and an 8.3 percent increase for the largest banks.

DeYoung, Hughes, and Moon (2001) use the method of Hughes, Lang, Mester, and Moon (1996) to study the relationship of Camels ratings to efficiency. Their sample consists of 356 national banks in the U.S. in 1994. Total assets range from $83.6 billion to $120 billion. In results not reported in the paper, they find a mean cost elasticity for the full sample of 0.893, which ranges from 0.926 for the smallest quartile to 0.826 for the largest quartile.

Bossone and Lee (2004) also apply the method of Hughes, Lang, Mester, and Moon (1996) to data on 875 commercial banks from 75 countries. They find significant scale economies that increase with the size of the country's financial system. They term these economies "systemic scale economies."

Wheelock and Wilson (2010) also use another innovative approach to measure scale economies at all U.S. banks over the period 1986–2004. They find that over the entire period, most banks experienced scale economies.

Feng and Serletis (2010) examine U.S. banks with assets greater than $1 billion over the period 2000–2005 and find scale economies at all sizes. On average, a 10 percent increase in output is associated with a 9.5 percent increase in cost.

Hughes and Mester (2011) employ 2007 data on 842 highest-level U.S. bank holding companies to estimate the production model developed by Hughes, Lang, Mester, and Moon (1996). The companies in their sample range in size from $72 million in total assets to $2.2 trillion. For institutions with less than $0.8 billion in total assets, they find that a 10 percent increase in output is associated with an 8.8 percent increase in cost. For larger institutions with assets between $50 billion and $100 billion, the increase in cost is 8.1 percent. For the 17 institutions whose assets exceed $100 billion — a category they term "too-big-to-fail" — the increase in cost is 7.5 percent.[4] They also test and reject the proposition that too-big-to-fail subsidies generate these scale economies of the largest institutions.

[4]Brewer and Jagtiani (2009) list three definitions of too-big-to-fail: (1) institutions whose book value of consolidated assets exceeds $100 billion; (2) one of the 11 largest banks, a definition offered by the Comptroller of the Currency in 1984 (currently the eleventh-largest has $290 billion in assets); and (3) banks with market value of equity of $20 billion.

3. How are Economies of Scale Typically Measured and Why Do They Elude Many Investigations?

The simplicity of the definition of scale economies — how cost varies with output — obscures some important complications. First, how is cost defined? Second, how is output or size defined? Third, how is the evidence of their association uncovered?

Cost is usually defined as the sum of interest and non-interest expenses, which represent the costs associated with the factors of production — borrowed funds, labor, and physical capital. Hughes and Mester (2011) define six inputs: labor, physical capital, uninsured time deposits, all other deposits, all other borrowed funds (foreign deposits, federal funds purchased, reverse repos, trading account liabilities, mandatory convertible securities, mortgage indebtedness, commercial paper, and all other borrowed funds), and equity capital. The measure of cost sums the expenditures on all inputs for which a price can be computed. The cost function includes these input prices to account for differences in prices among financial institutions. In the case of too-big-to-fail institutions, any advantage they enjoy in their funding costs is taken into account by the prices of their borrowed funds so that, in principle, the cost playing field is leveled. The expense of equity capital is usually excluded since most financial institutions are not publicly traded and, hence, this expense cannot practically be computed. The theoretically correct step to take in such cases requires the inclusion of the quantity of equity capital in lieu of the required return and cost of capital. Including the quantity of equity permits the calculation of a shadow required return and cost of capital for all financial institutions.[5]

Total assets and total earning assets constitute naïve measures of size. Two problems with these measures require a less aggregated characterization of size. First, off-balance-sheet activities represent an important part of many financial institutions' output. Second, the costs of two banks with the same total assets and off-balance-sheet activities might differ substantially because their asset allocations differ — say, because one allocates a larger

[5]Loan losses as well as the cost of equity capital are usually excluded from the measure of total costs used to estimate the cost function. Hughes and Mester (2010, 2011) explain the role of the quantities of equity capital and non-performing loans in the cost function by reference to the standard theoretical result that the quantity of a factor of production can substitute in the cost function for the price of the factor and the associated expense. See also Hughes, Mester, and Moon (2001).

proportion to loans and less to liquid assets. Liquid assets are inexpensive to obtain relative to information-intensive loans. Defining disaggregated outputs must balance the benefits of detail against the costs of statistical complexity that result when the number of outputs is increased. This balance involves some degree of aggregation. However, it should contain sufficient detail that the types of output span the differences in investment strategies across institutions of all sizes. Hughes and Mester (2011) define five outputs: liquid assets (including cash, repos, federal funds sold, and interest-bearing deposits due from banks), securities (including U.S. Treasury and U.S. government agency securities as well as mortgage-backed securities), loans, trading assets, and the credit equivalent amount of off-balance-sheet activities. The differences among small and large banks in their mix of these five types of outputs facilitate the statistical estimation of the relationship of cost to output for banks of all sizes when a sufficiently flexible functional form is used to model the relationship.

Building on these ingredients, the standard study employs statistical analysis to estimate the relationship of measured cost to the characterization of input prices and outputs and, if correctly specified, the quantity of equity capital and non-performing loans. It usually finds evidence of economies of scale at smaller institutions and either constant returns to scale or diseconomies of scale at larger institutions. At least three considerations call these findings of little or no scale economies into question: First, textbook explanations of why larger institutions should enjoy scale economies; second, the historically growing size of the largest financial institutions; and, third, mergers that create large institutions. Of course, these large institutions may have sought their large scale to achieve the status of too-big-to-fail — a potential advantage that might offset any scale diseconomies. Nevertheless, my coauthors and I have consistently found evidence that scale economies at the largest financial institutions are elusive, not illusive.[6]

What makes scale economies so elusive? The standard investigation estimates the relationship of cost to financial outputs using a characterization of cost and output similar to the ones described above. The details of the relationship to be estimated follow from a mathematical model of cost minimization. Given the interest rates of the various sources of funding, the prices of labor and physical capital, and the quantity of equity capital — the

[6]Hughes, Lang, Mester, and Moon (1996, 2000); Hughes and Mester (1998); Hughes, Mester, and Moon (2001).

inputs in the production process — the cost of producing any given quantities of the outputs at their quality measured by non-performing loans is assumed to be minimized, and the resulting cost function is fitted to the data statistically with a flexible functional form.

While this procedure may work well in explaining the costs of many non-financial industries, it misses a key ingredient in the production of financial products and services — ***risk***. In particular, the size of the financial institution influences the institution's diversification of liquidity and credit risk. Textbooks assert that larger, better diversified institutions experience relatively lower costs of risk management than smaller, less diversified institutions. Consequently, larger institutions can economize on holdings of liquid assets without increasing their liquidity risk and on equity capital without increasing their insolvency risk. This assertion implies that, other things being equal, cost increases less than proportionately with output — that is, better size-related diversification tends to generate scale economies. Hughes, Mester, and Moon (2001) estimate a variant of the standard cost function and find diseconomies of scale at smaller banks and constant returns at the largest banks. As hypothesized, they show that its measure of scale economies is positively correlated with asset size and, more to the point, positively correlated with a measure of the geographic diversification of macroeconomic risk. Why, then, do scale economies elude the standard investigation?

They elude the investigations that ignore risk because other things are not equal — in particular, risk. Consider how better diversification influences the investment decisions of larger institutions. *Is the larger, better diversified institution less risky? Not necessarily — better diversification improves the larger institution's risk-expected-return frontier. It does not imply that the larger institution chooses a risk exposure on the improved frontier, which is lower than on the less diversified frontier.* Hughes (1999) describes how the effect of additional risk-taking on cost may obscure inherent scale economies due to better diversification. The better risk-return menu and lower marginal cost of risk management may encourage the larger financial institution to choose a riskier investment strategy and, consequently, incur potentially higher costs of risk management. To the extent that any higher costs occasioned by the additional risk-taking offset or overtake any cost reductions due to better diversification, the naïve estimation of the relationship of cost to output that ignores endogenous risk-taking might find, not that cost increases less than proportionately with output, but that cost increases proportionately or more than proportionately. In such a case, *the scale economies that are occasioned by better diversification are obscured by extra costs of additional risk-taking*. The finding of no economies or even diseconomies of scale at larger institutions is a typical research finding.[7] Hughes, Mester, and Moon (2001) label these two effects of better scale-related diversification the *diversification effect* and the *risk-taking effect*.

Hughes and Mester (2011) illustrate the diversification and risk-taking effects identified in Hughes (1999) and Hughes, Mester, and Moon (2001) in a figure with investment choices on two risk-expected-return frontiers, reproduced here as Figure 1. The lower frontier reflects the trade-off of a smaller, less diversified scale of operations. Assume the smaller institution chooses a mix of financial products and services, asset quality, and funding strategies that implies the trade-off at point A. Now consider a

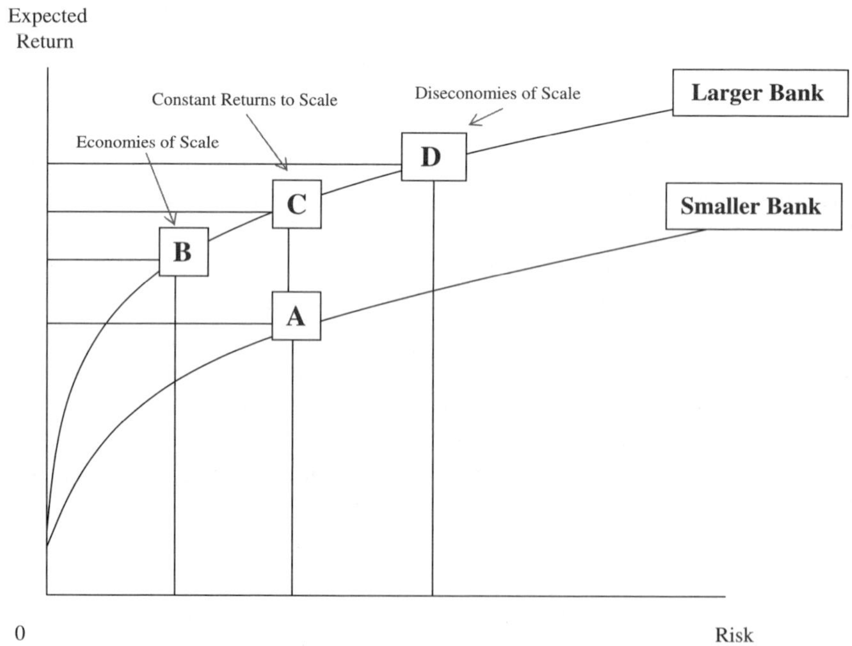

Figure 1. Risk-Expected-Return Frontiers for Smaller and Larger, Better Diversified Banks.
Source: Hughes and Mester (2011).

[7]See Greenspan (2010), Financial Oversight Council (2011), and Tarullo (2011).

proportionately larger institution whose scale-related better diversification gives it the improved risk-return frontier. As the scale of the mix of financial products and services is increased, does cost increase less than proportionately, proportionately, or more than proportionately? If the larger institution takes no additional risks compared to the smaller institution at point A, the better diversification reduces its risk and improves its expected return, which is reflected by point B. Consequently, *cost at point B increases less than proportionately compared to cost at point A, which implies economies of scale.* These scale economies reflect the better diversification of the underlying larger scale of operations.

How might these economies elude detection? Suppose the larger institution takes advantage of the reduced marginal cost of risk management and incurs additional risk for a higher expected return — say, point C. At point C, the risk of the larger institution equals that of the smaller one, but its expected return is higher. For example, point C might result from a reduction in asset quality or an increase in financial leverage. To the extent that the additional risk-taking results in higher costs than at point B, *cost at point C may increase proportionately or even more than proportionately compared to point A.* If cost increases in proportion with the increase in output from the lower to the higher frontier, the standard estimation of scale economies would obtain constant returns to scale. Thus, the additional risk-taking obscures the inherent scale economies and gives the appearance of constant returns to scale. At point D, the larger institution takes more risk than the smaller institution so that the *cost at point D is likely to increase more than proportionately compared to point A as output increases from the lower to the higher frontier, which gives the misleading appearance of diseconomies of scale.*

4. How are Scale Economies Measured While Accounting for Endogenous Risk-Taking?

In measuring scale economies, accounting for endogenous risk-taking is essential. Larger institutions generally have the incentive to take more risk — to operate toward point D rather than point B — which tends to obscure their inherent scale economies from the standard analysis. Marcus (1984) has shown that managers of financial institutions face dichotomous risk-taking strategies for maximizing the value of their firms that result from limitations on entry into banking and from safety-net subsidies. Entry restrictions create market power, which is especially valuable in markets with high-valued investment opportunities. Managers whose institutions operate in such markets enhance value by pursuing less risky investment strategies to reduce the risk of financial distress and the potential loss of the valuable charter to operate in these markets. On the other hand, managers whose institutions operate in more competitive markets with lower valued investment opportunities enhance value by pursuing higher-risk investment strategies to exploit the mispriced safety net. Marcus (1984) pointed out that these incentives are dichotomous: mid-range risk-taking strategies do not maximize value. Hughes, Lang, Moon, and Pagano (1997) provide evidence of these dichotomous investment strategies. Grossman (1992) documents the risk-taking encouraged by mispriced deposit insurance. Keeley (1990) provides evidence that increased competition among U.S. banks in the period 1971–1986 reduced the value of banks' investment opportunities and encouraged additional risk-taking. Tufano (1996) contends that when there is the potential for financial distress and, by extension, when the mispriced safety net subsidizes risk-taking, managing risk is a risk-neutral strategy to maximize value.

Larger institutions typically exploit the safety-net subsidies while smaller institutions typically pursue a less risky investment strategy to protect their valuable charter (Hughes, Lang, Moon, and Pagano, 1997). This pattern suggests that to the extent the extra risk-taking of the larger institutions involves more costs that offset the reduction in cost due to their better diversification, the extra costs due to risk-taking may obscure their scale economies when endogenous risk-taking is not taken into account in estimating the cost-output relationship.[8]

The standard analysis of cost assumes that given the prices of the inputs, the mix of financial products and services is produced with the lowest cost mix of inputs. This mix of inputs includes various funding sources of differing maturities as well as labor and physical capital. Differences among mixes involving liquidity risk, credit risk, and other risk exposures are not taken into account in this analysis. Note, too, that these different risk exposures involve different expected returns. Thus, when value-maximizing firms choose more costly input mixes because they are managing their risk

[8]Some additional risk-taking may be less costly. For example, a bank may skimp on the resources it devotes to credit analysis. Its risk and expected return increase due to this particular cost saving. However, if banks generally responded to better scale-related diversification by skimping, the standard cost analysis that does not account for risk should find economies of scale rather than constant returns or diseconomies of scale.

exposure to achieve higher expected returns, the standard analysis of cost is likely to confuse the extra cost that may result from additional risk-taking with a lack of inherent scale economies and fail to identify the underlying economies.

In a series of papers beginning with Hughes, Lang, Mester, and Moon (1996), the authors propose a cost function that accounts for endogenous risk-taking and, hence, is able to identify the underlying scale economies that may be obscured when larger financial institutions take extra risk to exploit the safety net.[9] They provide an econometric model which estimates managers' rankings of risk and expected return — their choice along their risk-return frontier. Risk is characterized in terms of the production plan, and cost is inferred from the choice of expected return and the underlying production plan. Unlike the standard approach, cost in this model depends not just on the prices of funding sources, equity, labor, and physical capital, but also on revenue considerations and marginal tax rates. Revenue can drive cost. This model is sufficiently general that it subsumes the standard cost minimization model as a special case. In this special case of cost minimization, revenue, risk, return, and tax rates do not influence production decisions. The authors test the hypothesis that these variables have no influence on production and, in every case, cleanly reject the hypothesis.[10]

They illustrate how underlying scale economies elude the standard analysis by estimating scale economies from their risk-return-driven cost function and from several versions of the standard cost function. Table 1 presents their estimates for the 1994 data (Hughes, Mester, and Moon, 2001). In column 1 of Table 1, the cost elasticities are obtained from the estimation of a cost function that omits the cost of equity capital in the measure of total cost and does not control for the amount of equity, which is theoretically required when the expense is not included in total cost. Thus, this cost function, while a commonly used one, is mis-specified. The full sample and size groups larger than \$0.3 billion and smaller than \$10 billion in consolidated assets show slight scale economies. For the full sample, a 10 percent increase in output would imply a 9.885 percent increase in cost. For institutions between \$10 billion and \$50 billion, the cost elasticity of 0.9924

[9] Other papers of these authors which develop the risk-return-driven cost function include Hughes, Lang, Mester, and Moon (2000); Hughes, Mester, and Moon (2001); DeYoung, Hughes, and Moon (2001); Hughes and Mester (2010); and Hughes and Mester (2011).

[10] See Hughes, Lang, Mester, and Moon (1996, 2000); Hughes, Mester, and Moon (2001); DeYoung, Hughes, and Moon (2001).

Table 1. Estimated Mean Scale Economies for 1994 Reported as a Cost Elasticity.

Total assets	n	(1) Mis-specified cost function Omits level of equity Mean	(2) Economic cost function Includes shadow cost of equity Mean	(3) Risk-return-driven cost function Conditioned on optimal equity Mean
Full sample	441	0.9885**	1.0187*	0.8737***
< $0.3 billion	109	0.9882	1.0230*	0.8949***
$0.3 billion–$2 billion	215	0.9878**	1.0167*	0.8883***
$2 billion–$10 billion	67	0.9887*	1.0183*	0.8537***
$10 billion–$50 billion	35	0.9924	1.0223*	0.8017***
> $50 billion	12	0.9922	1.0130	0.7998***

All estimates of mean cost elasticities are significantly different from 0 at the 1 percent level.
*Significantly different from 1 at the 10 percent level.
**Significantly different from 1 at the 5 percent level.
***Significantly different from 1 at the 1 percent level.

Notes:

a. Hughes, Mester, and Moon (2001) report these results in terms of the measure of scale economies which is the inverse of the cost elasticity. This table reports the cost elasticity instead. The cost elasticity gives the proportional response of cost to a proportional increase in all outputs. If cost increases less than proportionally, production is characterized by economies of scale: the value of cost elasticity in this case is less than one, and the value of scale economies, greater than one.
b. The data are taken from the Y9-C Call Reports filed quarterly with regulators. The sample included 441 top-tier U.S. bank holding companies in 1994.
c. The cost functions that generate the results in columns (1) and (2) are based on cost minimization. In column (1) and (3) cost sums all expenses except the cost of equity capital. The cost function in (2) includes the cost of equity. The function in (1) omits any role for equity capital while the function in (2) correctly includes equity as an argument and derives the shadow cost of equity. The risk-return-driven cost function in (3) accounts for endogenous risk-taking.

is not statistically different from one. Neither is the elasticity, 0.9922, for institutions larger than $50 billion. Thus, the largest U.S. financial institutions in 1994 appear to exhibit constant returns to scale. In column 2, the measured cost includes an estimated expense for equity. The results show that for the full sample and for the size groups up to $50 billion, institutions on average exhibit small diseconomies of scale. For the institutions with more than $50 billion, the mean cost elasticity, 1.0130, is not statistically different from one. Thus, the cost elasticity at the largest banks exhibits constant returns to scale. For both estimations of the standard approach, any underlying economies of scale at the largest financial institutions have eluded measurement.

In column 3 of Table 1, the evidence derived from the risk-return-driven cost function shows a mean cost elasticity of 0.8949 for the smallest group of institutions with consolidated assets less than $0.3 billion — a finding of economies of scale — which decreases continuously to a value of 0.7998 for the largest group with assets exceeding $50 billion. This approach, which accounts for risk-expected-return choices in measuring costs, uncovers evidence of large scale economies, which increase with the size of the institution. The largest financial institutions experience the largest economies.

How typical is the year 1994? Does the evidence of such scale economies from the risk-return-driven cost function and the lack of it from the standard cost functions depend on this particular year? Hughes, Lang, Mester, and Moon (2000) estimated the risk-return-driven cost function for 286 U.S. commercial banks in 1990, whose total assets exceeded $1 billion. The total assets of these banks ranged from $1.025 billion to $69.612 billion. Column 1 of Table 2 reports their mean estimates of cost elasticities from the standard, mis-specified cost function by size groups for these banks. The full sample exhibits a mean cost elasticity of 0.967, while the smallest quartile experiences a mean cost elasticity of 0.979 which decreases to 0.952 for the largest quartile. Hence, the standard, mis-specified cost function exhibits slight cost economies for banks in all size groups.

On the other hand, the estimation of the risk-return-driven cost function for these banks uncovers large scale economies that increase with banks' total assets. Column 2 of Table 2 shows that a 10 percent increase in the output of banks in the smallest quartile would be associated with a 9.08 percent increase in cost, while in the largest quartile, an 8.28 percent increase in cost. Thus, banks of all sizes experience, on average, large economies of scale that increase with size. Column 3 reports the mean cost elasticities

Table 2. Estimated Mean Scale Economies for 1990 Compared to 1994 Reported as a Cost Elasticity.

Total assets in 1990 dollars	n	(1) 1990 Mis-specified cost function Omits level of equity Mean	(2) 1990 Risk-return-driven cost function Conditioned on optimal equity Mean	1994 BHCs in the size ranges defined by 1990 study n	(3) 1994 Risk-return-driven cost function Conditioned on optimal equity Mean
Full sample	286	0.967***	0.877***	151	0.856***
$1.00 billion–$1.75 billion	72	0.979***	0.908***	40	0.895***
$1.75 billion–$3.00 billion	71	0.972***	0.887***	27	0.883***
$3.00 billion–$6.40 billion	72	0.966***	0.873***	27	0.842***
$6.40 billion–$70.00 billion	71	0.952***	0.828***	57	0.824***

All estimates of mean cost elasticities are significantly different from 0 at the 1 percent level.
*Significantly different from 1 at the 10 percent level.
**Significantly different from 1 at the 5 percent level.
*** Significantly different from 1 at the 1 percent level.

Notes:

a. Hughes, Lang, Mester, and Moon (2000) report the results in columns (1) and (2) for the 286 U.S. commercial banks in 1990 that exceed $1 billion in total assets. Column (3) reports the cost elasticities for U.S. bank holding companies in 1994 derived by Hughes, Mester, and Moon (2001) for the size groups (in 1990 dollars) defined in study using 1990 data. The bank data are obtained from the Consolidated Reports of Condition and Income filed quarterly with regulators. The data from Hughes, Mester, and Moon (2001) are taken from the Y9-C Call Reports filed quarterly with regulators. The full sample included 441 top-tier U.S. bank holding companies in 1994, but there are 151 institutions in the size range defined by the 1990 data.

b. Both studies report the measure of scale economies which is the inverse of the cost elasticity. This table reports the cost elasticity instead. The cost elasticity gives the proportional response of cost to a proportional increase in all outputs. If cost increases less than proportionally, production is characterized by economies of scale: The value of cost elasticity in this case is less than one, and the value of scale economies, greater than one.

c. The cost function that generates the results in column (1) is based on cost minimization. The measure of costs in columns (1), (2), and (3) sums all costs except the cost of equity capital. The risk-return-driven cost function in columns (2) and (3) accounts for endogenous risk-taking.

for the 1994 data from Table 2 organized by the size grouping of the 1990 data and deflated to constant 1990 dollars. A 10 percent increase in output would be associated with an 8.95 percent increase in cost in the smallest asset quartile and an 8.24 percent increase in the largest quartile. The mean cost elasticities in 1990 for commercial banks and in 1994 for bank holding companies are remarkably similar and suggest that banks experience scale economies that increase with their total assets.

Since the period of 1990 to 1994, a number of technological advances, especially advances in information technology, might be expected to augment scale economies. Moreover, financial institutions have grown appreciably in scale. In a recent working paper, Hughes and Mester (2011) report on their investigation of scale economies at 842 top-tier U.S. bank holding companies in 2007. They employ the production model developed by Hughes, Lang, Mester, and Moon (1996). The companies in their sample range in size from $72 million to $2.2 trillion in total consolidated assets. For institutions with less than $0.8 billion in total assets, they find that a 10 percent increase in output is associated with an 8.8 percent increase in cost. For larger institutions with assets between $50 billion and $100 billion, the increase in cost is 8.1 percent. For the 17 too-big-to-fail institutions whose assets exceed $100 billion, the increase in cost is 7.5 percent. They conduct several robustness tests to check first, that institutions with unusual output allocations, and second, that institutions at the smallest and largest ends of the size distribution, do not overly influence the estimation of scale economies. Their findings are robust to these tests.

5. Do Too-Big-to-Fail Subsidies Account for the Estimated Scale Economies at the Largest Institutions?

Since larger institutions may enjoy a cost-of-funds advantage due to the safety net and since input prices vary across institutions for a variety of reasons, the standard cost function and the risk-return-driven cost function both attempt to level the playing field across institutions by controlling for the prices of inputs — in particular, the average interest rates on various types of borrowed funds paid by each institution. Thus, if the largest institutions experience a cost-of-funds subsidy due to their too-big-to-fail status, this advantage is taken into account in the estimation of cost — that is, cost is conditioned on the interest rates paid for borrowed funds to level the price playing field — so that the cost elasticity is estimated *given the prices paid for these funds*. To check that the playing field is indeed leveled, Hughes and Mester (2011) calculate scale economies for the too-big-to-fail institutions by using the prices of borrowed funds paid by the smaller banks and obtain estimates of scale economies that are remarkably similar to those obtained using the largest banks' own prices. Finally, they drop the too-big-to-fail institutions, those whose consolidated assets exceed \$100 billion, and re-estimate the production model. The estimated scale economies for these largest financial institutions, predicted out of sample, are essentially the same as those from the estimation that included these institutions.

They conclude that there is no evidence from these tests that any too-big-to-fail cost advantage of the largest financial institutions generates the estimated economies of scale. Thus, technological factors appear responsible.

6. What are the Implications of the Estimated Scale Economies at the Largest Institutions for Restricting Their Scale and for Their International Competitiveness?

Governor Tarullo (2011) notes that the presence of scale economies at the largest financial institutions creates a trade-off between considerations of systemic risk and efficiency: "An additional concern would arise if some countries made the trade-off by limiting the size or configuration of their financial firms for systemic risk reasons at the cost of realizing genuine economies of scope or scale, while other countries did not. In this case, firms from the first group of countries might well be at a competitive disadvantage in the provision of certain cross-border activities."

Wheelock and Wilson (2010) explore this question by comparing the costs of the four largest financial institutions in the U.S. in 2009, which range in size from \$1.244 trillion to \$2.225 trillion, with the costs of a sufficient number of \$1 trillion institutions whose total assets equal those of the four institutions. They find that the annual costs of these smaller institutions producing the same total assets as the four larger institutions would be about \$20 billion higher per year, which is approximately 9 percent higher than the costs of the four largest institutions. The \$1 trillion size of their smaller institutions still falls into the region considered too big to fail by many observers.

Taking \$100 billion in total assets as the dividing line between too-big-to-fail banks and all others, Hughes and Mester (2011) compare the costs of the 17 institutions whose consolidated assets exceed \$100 billion with a sufficient number of institutions scaled back in size to \$100 billion, so that they produce the same mix of financial products and their combined total assets equal those of the 17 largest ones. The estimated risk-return-driven cost function is used to predict the costs of these scaled-back $100 billion institutions. As a percentage of consolidated assets, their total predicted costs are 10.9 percent higher than the estimated costs of the 17 institutions. Hence, the cost advantage of the 17 largest banks is substantial.

If larger banks are reduced in scale, what mix of products and services will they produce? If they produce the same mix as that of the largest banks observed today, their costs will be considerably higher and potentially uncompetitive in international markets. In a general equilibrium, they are unlikely to produce them if banks in other countries are able to achieve larger scale and proportionately lower costs.

7. Conclusions

Why is the evidence of scale economies limited and mixed — are they illusive or elusive? Investigations of the response of cost to an increase with scale that separate the effect on cost of scale-related technological advantages from the effect on cost of scale-related risk-taking uncover evidence of the elusive scale economies. Additional costs associated with increased risk-taking tend to obscure reduced costs associated with better diversification and other sources of scale economies.

If such economies exist, is it possible that they can be achieved by smaller institutions than the largest we observe today? When the effects of endogenous risk-taking are peeled away, the evidence shows that financial institutions of all sizes experience large scale economies, but the largest financial institutions obtain the largest scale economies.

Is the size of our largest financial institutions the result of technological cost advantages that improve the efficiency of their capital allocation and liquidity and enhance their international competitiveness? Or is their large size the result, not of technological cost advantages, but of safety-net subsidies that confer too-big-to-fail cost advantages and foster moral hazard in investment decisions? The estimated scale economies of the largest financial institutions are robust to the substitution of the interest rates paid on borrowed funds by smaller institutions, which are not deemed too big to fail. Moreover, the deletion of the too-big-to-fail institutions from the estimation of the cost function and the prediction of their scale economies out of sample, from the smaller sample not subject to the too-big-to-fail doctrine, yield essentially the same large measured scale economies as the estimation from the full sample. These tests suggest that technological factors account for the scale economies of the largest banks.

The evidence of the role of technological factors in generating the largest scale economies at the largest financial institutions suggests that the trade-off between considerations of systemic risk and efficiency is genuine: The efficiency gains from large scale are not the result of cost advantages due to explicit and implicit safety-net subsidies. Consequently, proposals to restrict the size of the largest institutions must account for the implications of such restrictions on the international competitiveness of these institutions.

References

Berger, A.N. and L.J. Mester, 1997, "Inside the black box: What explains differences in the efficiencies of financial institutions," *Journal of Banking and Finance*, Vol. 21, pp. 895–947.

Bossone, B. and J.-K. Lee, 2004, "In finance, size matters: The 'systemic scale economies' hypothesis," *IMF Staff Papers*, Vol. 51, No. 1.

Brewer, E. and J. Jagtiani, 2009, "How much did banks pay to become too-big-to-fail and to become systemically important?," Federal Reserve Bank of Philadelphia, working paper, No. 09-34.

DeYoung, R.E., J.P. Hughes, and C.-G. Moon, 2001, "Efficient risk-taking and regulatory covenant enforcement in a deregulated banking industry," *Journal of Economics and Business*, Vol. 53, pp. 255–282.

Feng, G. and A. Serletis, 2010, "Efficiency, technical change, and returns to scale in large US banks: Panel data evidence from an output distance function satisfying theoretical regularity," *Journal of Banking and Finance*, Vol. 34, pp. 127–138.

Financial Oversight Council, 2011, *Study of the Effects of Size and Complexity of Financial Institutions on Capital Market Efficiency and Economic Growth.*

Greenspan, A., 2010, "The crisis," *Brookings Papers on Economic Activity*, Spring, pp. 201–246.

Grossman, R.S., 1992, "Deposit insurance, regulations, and moral hazard in the thrift industry: Evidence from the 1930's," *American Economic Review*, Vol. 82, pp. 800–821.

Hughes, J.P., 1999, "Incorporating risk into the analysis of production," presidential address, Atlantic Economic Society, *Atlantic Economic Journal*, Vol. 27, pp. 1–23.

Hughes, J.P., W. Lang, L.J. Mester, and C.-G. Moon, 1996, "Efficient banking under interstate branching," *Journal of Money, Credit and Banking*, Vol. 28, pp. 1045–1071.

Hughes, J.P., W. Lang, L.J. Mester, and C.-G. Moon, 2000, "Recovering risky technologies using the almost ideal demand system: An application to U.S. banking," *Journal of Financial Services Research*, Vol. 18, pp. 5–27.

Hughes, J.P., W. Lang, C.-G. Moon, and M. Pagano, 1997, "Measuring the efficiency of capital allocation in commercial banking," Federal Reserve Bank of Philadelphia, working paper, No. 98-2 (revised as Working Paper 2004-1, Rutgers University Economics Department).

Hughes, J.P. and L.J. Mester, 1998, "Bank capitalization and cost: Evidence of scale economies in risk management and signaling," *Review of Economics and Statistics*, Vol. 80, pp. 314–325.

Hughes, J.P. and L.J. Mester, 2010, "Efficiency in banking: Theory, practice, and evidence," in *The Oxford Handbook of Banking*, A.N. Berger, P. Molyneux, and J. Wilson (eds.), New York: Oxford University Press.

Hughes, J.P. and L.J. Mester, 2011, "Who said large banks don't experience scale economies? Evidence from a risk-return-driven cost function," Wharton Financial Institutions, working paper, No. 11–47 [Forthcoming 2013, *Journal of Financial Intermediation*].

Hughes, J.P., L.J. Mester, and C.-G. Moon, 2001, "Are scale economies in banking elusive or illusive? Evidence obtained by incorporating capital structure and risk-taking into models of bank production," *Journal of Banking and Finance*, Vol. 25, pp. 2169–2208.

Keeley, M.C., 1990, "Deposit insurance, risk, and market power in banking," *American Economic Review*, Vol. 80, pp. 1183–1200.

Marcus, A.J., 1984, "Deregulation and bank financial policy," *Journal of Banking and Finance*, Vol. 8, pp. 557–565.

Tarullo, D., 2011, "Industrial organization and systemic risk: An agenda for further research," Conference on the Regulation of Systemic Risk, Federal Reserve Board, Washington, DC.

Tufano, P., 1996, "Who manages risk? An empirical examination of risk management practices in the gold mining industry," *Journal of Finance*, Vol. 50, pp. 1097–1137.

Wheelock, D.C. and P.W. Wilson, 2009 (revised 2010), "Do large banks have lower costs? New estimates of returns to scale for U.S. banks," Federal Reserve Bank of St. Louis, working paper, No. 2009-054C [published 2012, *Journal of Money, Credit and Banking*, Vol. 44, pp. 171–199].

The *Ex Ante* versus *Ex Post* Effect of Public Guarantees

Evren Damar, Reint Gropp, and Adi Mordel*
Bank of Canada and Goethe University Frankfurt

1. Introduction

In the wake of the financial crisis of 2007–2008, many governments extended public guarantees to individual banks or the entire banking system.[1] Government guarantees affect bank risk-taking via two opposing channels. They can exacerbate risk-taking by undermining market discipline (Flannery, 1998; Sironi, 2003; Gropp *et al.*, 2006), while at the same time curb it by enhancing charter values (Keeley, 1990). In addition, public guarantees may affect banks with *ex ante* high charter values differently from those with *ex ante* low charter values (Gropp and Vesala, 2004). If banks have higher charter values and therefore more "skin in the game," they may not suffer from moral hazard. Hence, extending public guarantees to those banks may not affect their risk-taking. Overall, the net effect

*Evren Damar and Adi Mordel are from the Financial Stability Department at the Bank of Canada; Reint Gropp is from the Goethe University Frankfurt. The authors thank seminar participants at the Bank of Canada, Bank of England, the 9th International Industrial Organization conference, the 2011 IBEFA/WEAI Summer Meeting, and the 2011 Federal Reserve Bank of Chicago/European Central Bank conference, "The Role of Central Banks in Financial Stability: How Has It Changed?" Specifically, they would like to thank Jason Allen, John Boyd, Elijah Brewer, Ramdane Djoudad, Marc Fusaro, Ed Kane, David Martinez Miera, Naoaki Minamihashi, and Moez Souissi for their thoughtful and valuable comments. Gropp would like to acknowledge financial support from Loewe Grant "Sustainable Architecture for Europe" (SAFE). Sheisha Kulkarni provided excellent research assistance. All remaining errors are their own. The views expressed in this paper are those of the authors. No responsibility for them should be attributed to the Bank of Canada.

[1]For example, in the U.S.: Indy Mac, Fannie Mae, Freddy Mac; in the UK: Bradford Bingley, Northern Rock, RBS, HBOS, Lloyds; in Germany: IKB, Hypo Real Estate; in Belgium/Netherlands: Dexia, Fortis.

of government guarantees is ambiguous and depends on the interaction of charter value and moral hazard effects (Keeley, 1990; Cordella and Yeyati, 2003; Gropp *et al.*, 2011).

In this study, we take advantage of a unique natural experiment that allows us to identify the net effect of government guarantees. In October 2006, Dominion Bond Rating Service (DBRS) introduced a new support assessment methodology for banks that accounts for the potential of government guarantees. According to the new rating scheme, banks are rated based on the likelihood and predictability of timely external support, which can range from an outright guarantee to a full ownership and control (nationalization). In the rating announcement, DBRS stressed that the rating changes were based on the consequence of the new methodology being applied, and were not a reflection of any changes in the respective banks' credit fundamentals. Furthermore, the new ratings were applied simultaneously to all banks and were not preceded by any news announcement.

Hence, the DBRS announcement represents a natural experiment similar to the one employed by Kliger and Sarig (2000). Kliger and Sarig used the introduction of subcategories for Moody's ratings to identify the information content of ratings. They could use this rating innovation as a clean test of the information content of ratings, as the simultaneous introduction of the subcategories across all firms was not associated with a change in underlying risk of the firms or any pre-announcement news releases.

Our findings suggest a striking difference between the effects of bail-out probabilities during calm times ("*ex ante*") versus during crisis times ("*ex post*"). We show that during calm times, higher bail-out probabilities result in higher risk-taking, consistent with the moral hazard view and much of the empirical literature. However, in crisis times, we find that non-guaranteed banks increase their risk more than guaranteed banks.

Gropp *et al.* (2011) show that during normal times, non-guaranteed banks compete more fiercely with protected banks since the latter benefit from lower refinancing costs, which pushes non-protected banks toward higher risk-taking. To the best of our knowledge, the current paper is the first to document this relationship during a crisis when funding is scarce. We show (relatively weak) evidence that guaranteed banks maintained higher levels of wholesale funding during the crisis. Furthermore, we show that the increase in risk is even smaller if the protected banks have *ex ante* high charter values, consistent with the charter value view of public guarantees. In line with a charter value argument, we conjecture that guaranteed banks may enjoy a funding advantage during the crisis and therefore exhibit lower risk compared to banks that are not guaranteed. At the same time, we cannot rule out other explanations, as our findings would, for example, also be consistent with the idea that guaranteed banks during crisis times are subject to greater scrutiny by supervisors that is effective in reducing risk-taking, as in Berger *et al.* (2001) and Krainer and Lopez (2009).

The paper adds to a voluminous literature on the effects of public guarantees on risk-taking of banks. While the evidence is somewhat mixed, the literature generally tends to conclude that banks increase their risk-taking in the presence of government guarantees. For example, large banks, which may be perceived to be "too big to fail," tend to follow riskier strategies than smaller banks (Boyd and Runkle, 1993; Boyd and Gertler, 1994; Gropp *et al.*, 2013). Public banks, on the other hand, do not appear to follow riskier strategies than private banks (De Nicolo and Loukoianova, 2007). The evidence on the effect of government bailout guarantees on overall banking system stability is also mixed. Demirgüç-Kunt and Detragiache (2002) show that more generous deposit insurance may increase the probability of banking crises. However, Barth *et al.* (2004) show that government ownership has no robust impact on bank fragility, once one controls for banking regulation and supervisory practices.

The interaction between charter values and public guarantees has not been extensively examined in the literature, since Keeley (1990) argued that the introduction of deposit insurance in the U.S. did not have a large effect on bank risk-taking, because banks in the U.S. were heavily regulated and therefore enjoyed local market power. He argued that local market power creates higher charter values, which in turn mitigate the moral hazard effect. Indirect evidence is presented in Beck *et al.* (2006), who find that systemic banking crises are less likely in countries with more concentrated banking sectors. If charter values arise from higher market power in more concentrated banking systems, this would support the hypothesis that charter values mitigate moral hazard. Most closely related to the evidence in this paper is the evidence in Gropp and Vesala (2004), who show that the introduction of deposit insurance in some EU countries had no effect on the risk-taking of banks with higher charter values.

2. The Event

On October 6, 2006, DBRS implemented a new methodology for bank credit ratings that makes references to support assessments (SA) and intrinsic assessments (IA).[2] By using a four-notch scale for the SA ratings, DBRS aimed to provide more transparency and clarity on its analytical process. Based on the new methodology, ratings were assigned to each banking entity to reflect the possibility of external support for various debt instruments. According to DBRS:

> ...An SA-1 [rating] reflects very strong to good likelihood and predictability of timely external support, ranging from an outright guarantee to ownership and control. An SA-2 reflects the expectation of some form of systemic external support, which can be either [provided for] national institutions or local and regional banks with an important local market position and which are part of well-defined sectoral associations. An SA-3 reflects that there is no expectation of any form of timely external support, which means that the most senior debt of the bank is equivalent to DBRS's intrinsic assessment. [...], an SA-4 is the opposite of support enhancement, where the rating of the entity in question is in fact pressured by an external third party.

Finally, it is important to note that the implementation of the new ratings was done simultaneously for all banks, and resulted in upgrades for some of the securities issued by the banks designated as SA-1/SA-2. In its announcement, DBRS stated that the rating changes were not a reflection of any change in the affected banks' credit fundamentals, and were purely driven by the introduction of the SA methodology. With that respect, the rating announcement represents a natural experiment, allowing us to study the moral hazard consequences of government guarantees.

Appendix 1 lists the publically traded financial institutions implicated by the DBRS rating, which constitutes the sample for the empirical analysis to come. The group of banks that can potentially benefit from a guarantee (SA-1/SA-2) includes four banks from Australia, one from Belgium, six from Canada, two from Ireland, and four from the UK. The list of banks that received an SA-3 rating from DBRS and are less likely to receive

[2]An intrinsic assessment reflects DBRS's opinion of a bank's intrinsic fundamentals — market position, franchise value, governance, ownership, management strength, strategy and its implementation, financial strength and earnings capacity as reflected in key ratios and qualitative parameters, risk profile and risk management (credit, market, liquidity, asset liability management, operational, etc.) — in terms of the strength and predictability of the operating and regulatory environment. Thus, the intrinsic assessment of a bank is the result of a comprehensive and multi-faceted analysis of its fundamentals, including both qualitative and quantitative elements.

external support is mainly made up of U.S. banks (41). It also includes one Canadian, one Irish, and two UK banks.

A legitimate concern is that the DBRS ratings do not accurately reflect market expectations, as some U.S. banks might still be considered TBTF even if rated SA-3. If true, markets may have disregarded the ratings and we should not find any significant impact of the rating on bank behavior. In addition, DBRS's SA ratings were in full agreement with Fitch's Support ratings, indicating that as of 2006, none of the U.S. banks were likely to be bailed out.

3. Methodology

We use several risk measures that are derived from financial statements and market variables. Following the literature standard, we calculate:

$$Z = \frac{(\text{AROA} + \text{ACAP})}{\sigma(\text{ROA})}, \tag{1}$$

such that AROA is the average return on assets during the period, σ(ROA) is the standard deviation of ROA, and ACAP is the average of (Total Equity/Total Assets) during the period. A lower Z-score indicates more risk-taking by the bank. We also consider σ(ROA) by itself as another measure of risk-taking.

Market-based risk indicators are calculated using weekly stock return data. We define bank *Total Risk* as the standard deviation of stock returns during the period. In addition, bank *Specific Risk* is the standard deviation of the error term from the following market model regression:

$$R_i = \alpha_i + \beta_i R_m + \varepsilon_i, \tag{2}$$

where R_i is the stock return of Bank i, and R_m is the return on the value-weighted market portfolio of each bank's respective country.

We construct a window period around the event and calculate the banks' riskiness within this window. For banks reporting on a quarterly basis (Canadian and U.S.), the pre-event period is from Q2 2005 to Q3 2006, while the post-event period is from Q4 2006 to Q1 2008. For banks reporting on a semi-annual basis, the pre-event period is from H4 2004 to H1 2006, while the post-event period is from H2 2006 to H1 2008.

The balance sheet, income statement, and stock return data used in the analysis come from a variety of sources. Data on Canadian banks was obtained from the Tri-Agency Database System (TDS) of the Bank of Canada, Office of the Superintendant of Financial Institutions (OSFI), and the Canadian Deposit Insurance Corporate (CDIC). TDS contains the monthly balance sheet and quarterly income statements of all deposit-taking institutions in Canada, except credit unions. U.S. bank data came from the "FR 9-Y: Consolidated Financial Statements for Bank Holding Companies" available from the Federal Reserve Bank of Chicago. Stock return data is from CRSP. Data for all other banks were obtained from Bloomberg. We supplemented this information using annual reports and financial results obtained from the Internet when necessary.

4. Guarantees and Risk-Taking

We report the mean and median risk measures during the post period in Table 1. The banks are categorized according to whether they benefit or not

Table 1. Mean [Median] Comparison.

	Banks with gov. guarantee (n = 17)	Banks without gov. guarantee (n = 45)	*p-value* difference between groups
Post Ln.(Z)	3.26 [3.27]	3.11 [3.32]	0.602 [0.352]
Post σ(ROA)	0.0027 [0.0022]	0.0065 [0.0039]	0.002 [0.001]
Bank Total Risk	0.0337 [0.0300]	0.0445 [0.0412]	0.001 [0.003]
Bank Specific Risk	0.0252 [0.0244]	0.0415 [0.0383]	0.000 [0.000]

Notes: The sample includes 17 banks identified by DBRS on October 6, 2006, as potentially benefiting from a government guarantee and 45 that do not. Risk proxied by Z-score is defined as (AROA + ACAP)/σ(ROA). AROA is the average return on assets during the period, σ(ROA) is the standard deviation of ROA, and ACAP is the average of (Total Equity/Total Assets) during the period. Total Risk is the standard deviation of weekly stock returns. Specific Risk is the standard deviation of the error term from a market model regression of firm on market returns. All risk measures are obtained in the Post period. For quarterly banks, the period is 12/2006 to 3/2008; and for semi-annual banks, the Post period is 12/2006 to 6/2008. Median significance based on Wilcoxon test statistics.

from a government guarantee according to DBRS. The mean and median comparison tests show that the guaranteed banks exhibit significantly lower risk (significant at the 1% level) after the DBRS announcement for all but the Z-score risk measures. This result is surprising since most of the empirical literature concludes that guarantees increase risk-taking.

In order to check risk-taking developments for the banks in our sample before and after the rating change and for banks with and without guarantees, we calculate six-month rolling risk measures for 14 periods (i.e., period 1 — Jan. 1, 2005, to June 30, 2005; period 2 — March 1, 2005, to Sept. 30, 2005; . . . ; period 14 — Jan. 1, 2008, to June 30, 2008). Figure 1 plots these rolling risk measures and exhibits a number of important characteristics. Before the rating introduction, the risk profiles of guaranteed and non-guaranteed banks are almost indistinguishable. After the introduction of the support rating, guaranteed and non-guaranteed banks' risk starts to increase (presumably reflecting the onset of the crisis), but the increase seems significantly more pronounced for non-guaranteed banks compared to guaranteed banks. This tends to contradict the moral hazard view of public guarantees and lends some support to the charter value view (Cordella and Yeyati, 2003).

The evidence in Table 1 and in Figure 1 is univariate. In particular, there may be important heterogeneity across countries that may account for some of the patterns due to differences in accounting, the business cycle,

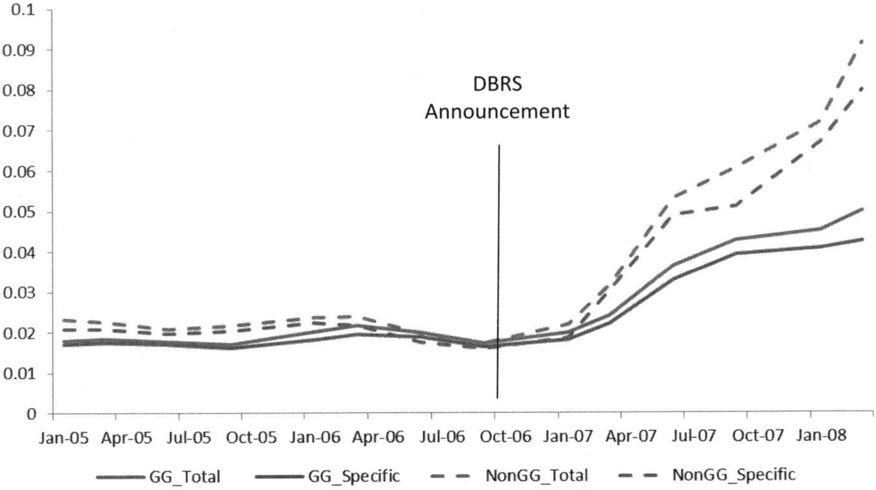

Figure 1. Six-Month Rolling Risk by Category.

or institutional differences. Our next step is to estimate the relationship between risk-taking and government guarantees in a series of regressions. The nature of the introduction of the new rating by DBRS lends itself to a difference-in-differences specification. The advantage of this model is that under some conditions, it permits a causal interpretation of the coefficients as in a random treatment experiment. The treatment in our case is the news that DBRS considers some banks (and not others) "too big to fail" or otherwise explicitly or implicitly insured. Hence, we estimate the following "difference-in-differences" specification:

$$Y_{it} = \alpha + \beta_1 Post + \beta_2 GG_i + \beta_3 Post * GG_i + \delta_k + \varepsilon_i, \qquad (3)$$

where we use each of the risk measures as the dependent variables (Y_{it}). A lower Z-score or a higher σ(ROA), *Total Risk* or *Specific Risk* reflect increased risk-taking by banks. *Post* = 1 for the post-event period. *GG* = 1 for banks that DBRS designates as SA-1/SA-2 (i.e., benefiting from a government guarantee). Finally, δ_k represents country fixed-effects.

The results of the first set of regressions are reported in Table 2. The *Post* dummy indicates that all banks increased risk-taking. This is expected since our post window overlaps with the 2007–2008 financial crisis and is consistent with Figure 1. For our purposes, the most interesting result is that the univariate results from Figure 1 seem to hold up, as guaranteed banks increased their risk-taking less during the post-event period compared to banks without a guarantee. The *Post*GG* coefficient is negative and significant (at the 1% level) in the σ(ROA), *Total Risk* and *Specific Risk* regressions. It is, however, insignificant for Z-score.

This stands in sharp contrast to most of the empirical findings on the effect of government guarantees (see, for example, Boyd and Runkle, 1993; Boyd and Gertler, 1994; and Gropp *et al.*, 2013), which largely finds that public guarantees result in higher risk-taking. It also contradicts theory, which maintains that public guarantees reduce market discipline because creditors anticipate their bank's bailout and therefore have lower incentives to monitor the bank's risk-taking or to demand risk premiums for higher observed risk-taking (Flannery, 1998; Sironi, 2003; Gropp *et al.*, 2006). The effect is similar to that discussed in the deposit insurance literature (Merton, 1977). If depositors are protected by a guarantee, they will punish their bank less for risk-taking, thus reducing market discipline. However, it is consistent with theoretical literature assigning an important role for charter values in the risk decision of banks (Keeley, 1990; Cordella and Yeyati, 2003) and consistent with some evidence in Gropp and Vesala (2004) and Gropp *et al.* (2011). Hence, we next explicitly include charter values in the regressions.

Table 2. Baseline Difference-in-Differences.

	Ln.Z	σ(ROA)	Total risk	Specific risk
Post (=1)	−1.0221***	0.0038***	0.0175***	0.0156***
	[0.192]	[0.001]	[0.002]	[0.002]
GG (=1)	0.5483	0.0008	−0.0049	−0.0067
	[0.493]	[0.002]	[0.005]	[0.004]
Post*GG	0.3285	−0.0034***	−0.0070***	−0.0089***
	[0.365]	[0.001]	[0.002]	[0.002]
Constant	3.3602***	0.0023	0.0175***	0.0195***
	[0.561]	[0.002]	[0.004]	[0.005]
Observations	124	124	124	124
F	6.70	3.98	30.84	28.18
Adjusted R^2	0.21	0.092	0.50	0.51

Notes: The sample includes 17 banks identified by DBRS on October 6, 2006, as potentially benefiting from a government guarantee and 45 that do not. Risk proxied by Z-score is defined as (AROA + ACAP)/σ(ROA). AROA is the average return on assets during the period, σ(ROA) is the standard deviation of ROA, and ACAP is the average of (Total Equity/Total Assets) during the period. Total Risk is the standard deviation of weekly stock returns. Specific Risk is the standard deviation of the error term from a market model regression of firm on market returns. For quarterly banks, the period is 6/2005 to 9/2006 (pre-event) and 12/2006 to 3/2008 (i.e., Post = 1). For semi-annual banks, the period is 12/2004 to 6/2006 and 12/2006 to 6/2008 (i.e., Post = 1). GG = 1 for guaranteed banks. Robust standard errors clustered at the bank level are reported in brackets. Regressions include unreported country fixed-effects. ***, **, * Significance at the 1%, 5%, and 10% level, respectively.

5. The Net Effect of Guarantees — The Role of Charter Values

One way to reconcile the surprising results in Table 2 is to consider the interaction between government guarantees and bank charter value. Keeley (1990) was the first to show that higher charter values decrease the incentives for excessive risk-taking, because the threat of losing future rents acts as a deterrent to risk-taking. Government bailout guarantees result in higher charter values for protected banks due to lower refinancing costs. This tends to *reduce* the protected banks' risk-taking. Hence, as argued theoretically by Cordella and Yeyati (2003) and by Hakenes and Schnabel (2010), the net effect of government guarantees on the risk-taking of protected banks is ambiguous and depends on the relative impact of the two channels, i.e., the reduction in market discipline versus the increase in charter value.

To disentangle the two channels, we follow the literature standard and use Tobin's Q as a proxy for a bank's charter value such that:

$$Tobin's\ Q = \frac{BVA + MVE - BVE}{BVA}. \tag{4}$$

Each component of Tobin's Q is measured as its average over the pre-event window.[3] For Canadian and U.S. banks, whose financial reports are quarterly, the "pre-event" window is Q2 2005 to Q3 2006. For the banks in Australia, Belgium, Ireland, and the UK, all of whom report semi-annually, the window is H2 2004 to H1 2006. BVA is book value of assets, while MVE and BVE are the market and book values of equity, respectively.

We therefore next estimate the following difference-in-differences specification such that:

$$\begin{aligned} Y_{it} = \alpha + \beta_1 Post + \beta_2 GG_i + \beta_3 Post * GG_i + \beta_4 HighQ_i \\ + \beta_5 Post_t * GG_i * HighQ_i + \delta_k + \varepsilon_i, \end{aligned} \tag{5}$$

where *Post* represents the post-event period and *GG* equals one if the bank is recognized by DBRS as benefiting from a guarantee. *Post*GG* takes the value of one for guaranteed banks in the post-event period; *HighQ* is a dummy that equals to one for banks that are above the median charter value for their country. The term *Post*GG*HighQ* captures the impact of the pre-event charter value on the post-event behavior of affected banks. Finally, as in Equation (3), δ_k represents country fixed-effects.

The results for this specification are presented in Table 3. As before, *Post* is highly significant and positively associated with risk. The negative coefficient on *Post*GG* indicates that guaranteed banks had lower risk based on the *Total* or *Specific* risk measures (1% significance). Finally, our variable of interest, *Post*GG*HighQ*, indicates that guaranteed banks with a higher charter value increased their risk *ex post* less compared to guaranteed banks with low charter values, given the positive coefficient in the Z-score regression (5% significance) and the negative coefficient in

[3]An alternative measure of charter value relates a bank's market power with its ratio of demand deposits, since the ability to issue deposits at below-market rates is an important factor of charter value (Keeley, 1990). However, we cannot obtain an accurate measure of demandable deposits since there is not a consistent definition of demand deposits across all of our banks.

Table 3. Difference-in-Differences: Controlling for Charter Value.

	Ln.Z	σ(ROA)	Total risk	Specific risk
Post (=1)	−1.0221***	0.0038***	0.0175***	0.0156***
	[0.194]	[0.001]	[0.002]	[0.002]
GG (=1)	0.5416	0.0008	−0.0047	−0.0066
	[0.560]	[0.002]	[0.005]	[0.005]
Post*GG	−0.1217	−0.0020	−0.0089***	−0.0098***
	[0.396]	[0.002]	[0.003]	[0.003]
High Q (=1)	0.1500	−0.0001	−0.0008	−0.0007
	[0.221]	[0.001]	[0.002]	[0.002]
Post*GG*High Q	0.7654**	−0.0025*	0.0034	0.0016
	[0.366]	[0.001]	[0.003]	[0.003]
Constant	3.2544***	0.0024	0.0177***	0.0198***
	[0.631]	[0.002]	[0.004]	[0.005]
Observations	124	124	124	124
F	5.50	3.96	23.12	21.46
Adjusted R^2	0.22	0.08	0.50	0.50

Notes: The sample includes 17 banks identified by DBRS on October 6, 2006, as potentially benefiting from a government guarantee and 45 that do not. Risk proxied by Z-score is defined as (AROA + ACAP)/σ(ROA). AROA is the average return on assets during the period, σ(ROA) is the standard deviation of ROA, and ACAP is the average of (Total Equity/Total Assets) during the period. Total Risk is the standard deviation of weekly stock returns. Specific Risk is the standard deviation of the error term from a market model regression of firm on market returns. For quarterly banks, the period is 6/2005 to 9/2006 (pre-event) and 12/2006 to 3/2008 (i.e., Post = 1). For semi-annual banks, the period is 12/2004 to 6/2006 and 12/2006 to 6/2008 (i.e., Post = 1). Charter value proxied by Tobin's Q = (book value assets + market value equity − book value equity)/(book value assets). Tobin's Q is the average of its components prior to the DBRS announcement. For quarterly banks, it is calculated between 6/2005 and 9/2006. For semi-annual banks, it is calculated between 12/2004 and 6/2006. GG = 1 for guaranteed banks. High Q = 1 for banks above their country's median Q. Robust standard errors clustered at the bank level are reported in brackets. Regressions include unreported country fixed-effects. ***, **, * Significance at the 1%, 5%, and 10% level, respectively.

the σ(ROA) regression (10% significance). However, for the market risk measures, the *Post*GG*HighQ* coefficient is not significant.

6. Normal Times versus Crisis Times

The above analysis does not provide unambiguous evidence on the relation between charter value, government guarantees, and risk-taking. Furthermore, while the results suggest that charter values are part of the explanation, charter values do not seem to be able to fully explain why guaranteed banks increased risk-taking *ex post* less than banks without guarantees. One particularly interesting feature of our data is that the post-event window overlaps with the 2007–2008 financial crisis. Hence, we can check whether the results are indeed driven by the crisis or hold irrespective of the time period. Hence, our empirical set-up permits a distinction of the effect of guarantees during normal times, i.e., in the center of the risk distribution, versus their effect during crisis times, i.e., in the tail of the distribution.

To address this issue, we define shorter pre- and post-event windows that are identical for all banks. We choose a six-month window around the event such that *pre* is April 1, 2006 to October 5, 2006, and *post* is between October 7, 2006 and March 31, 2007, and therefore before the crisis starts in the summer of 2007. The downside of specifying a shorter window is that we cannot use the Z-score and σ(ROA), as those require a longer period to compute.

The short window results are presented in Table 4. The results tend to confirm the prior empirical evidence in the literature and contradict our earlier finding. Under both market risk measures, guaranteed banks increase risk-taking during the six-month period following the DBRS announcement more than non-guaranteed banks, given the positive and significant *Post*GG* coefficient. This is in sharp contrast with the results in Table 2, in which *Post*GG* is negative and significant for most risk measures. Interestingly for the shorter window, charter values do not have any explanatory power for explaining bank risk-taking as the coefficient on *Post*GG*High Q* is insignificant and also economically small.

One potential explanation for the relatively reduced risk-taking of guaranteed banks during the crisis (*ex post*) may be better access to wholesale funding during the crisis. We check this in Appendix 2. In a difference-in-differences specification similar to the one for risk, we confirm that the wholesale funding (measured as the ratio of non-retail deposits to total liabilities) is higher *ex post* for banks that benefited from a

Table 4. Difference-in-Differences: Shorter Pre and Post Windows.

	Bank total risk		Bank specific risk	
	(1)	(2)	(3)	(4)
Post (=1)	−0.0046***	−0.0046***	−0.0066***	−0.0066***
	[0.001]	[0.001]	[0.001]	[0.001]
GG (=1)	−0.0055	−0.0054	−0.0073**	−0.0073**
	[0.003]	[0.003]	[0.003]	[0.003]
Post*GG	0.0034*	0.0026	0.0054***	0.0063**
	[0.002]	[0.002]	[0.002]	[0.002]
High Q (=1)		0.0000		−0.0004
		[0.002]		[0.002]
Post*GG*High Q		0.0016		−0.0016
		[0.003]		[0.003]
Constant	0.0297***	0.0296***	0.0303***	0.0307***
	[0.004]	[0.004]	[0.003]	[0.004]
Observations	124	124	124	124
F	18.55	15.29	8.66	6.86
Adjusted R^2	0.21	0.20	0.17	0.16

Notes: The sample includes 17 banks identified by DBRS on October 6, 2006, as potentially benefiting from a government guarantee and 45 that do not. Bank Total Risk is the standard deviation of weekly stock returns. Bank Specific Risk is the standard deviation of the error term from a market model regression of firm on market returns. Risk measures are obtained for *all* banks during the same pre-(April 1, 2006–October 5, 2006) and post-periods (October 7, 2006–March 31, 2007). Charter value proxied by Tobin's Q = (book value assets + market value equity − book value equity)/(book value assets). Tobin's Q is the average of its components prior to the DBRS announcement. For quarterly banks, it is calculated between 6/2005 and 9/2006. For semi-annual banks, it is calculated between 12/2004 and 6/2006. GG = 1 for guaranteed banks. High Q = 1 for banks above their country's median Q. Robust standard errors clustered at the bank level are reported in brackets. Regressions include unreported country fixed-effects. ***, **, * Significance at the 1%, 5%, and 10% level, respectively.

guarantee according to DBRS. While the effect is positive, it is only weakly significant.[4]

7. Discussion and Conclusion

In October 2006, Dominion Bond Rating Service (DBRS) introduced a new support rating for banks that accounts for the potential of government guarantees. According to the new rating scheme, banks were rated based on the likelihood and predictability of timely external support. In the rating announcement, DBRS stressed that the rating changes were not a reflection of any changes in the respective banks' credit fundamentals. In addition, the ratings were applied to all banks simultaneously and were not preceded by any news announcement. Hence, the announcement by DBRS represents a natural experiment to evaluate the consequences of bailout expectations for bank behavior.

The results suggest a striking difference between the effects of high bailout probabilities during calm times ("*ex ante*") versus during crisis times ("*ex post*"). Our sample is uniquely suited to distinguish between the two, as we are able to define samples that include and that exclude the 2007–2008 financial crisis. It appears that during normal times, higher bailout probabilities result in higher risk-taking, consistent with the moral hazard view and much of the empirical literature. However, in crisis times, we find that banks with higher bailout probabilities tend to increase their risk-taking less compared to other banks. Gropp *et al.* (2011) show evidence on the competitive distortions introduced by government guarantees during calm periods, which induce non-protected banks to increase risk-taking. Our paper presents consistent evidence for a crisis period. We also show that the increase in risk is even smaller if the banks have *ex ante* high charter values and have better access to wholesale deposit funding during the crisis, although the effect is small and econometrically only weakly significant. This is consistent with the charter value view of public guarantees.

At the same time, the results also suggest that charter values are only part of the explanation and there may be other important reasons for our findings. For example, our evidence is also consistent with the idea that regulators supervise guaranteed banks more closely than non-guaranteed

[4]The analysis excludes Northern Rock (failed in 2007) and DEPFA plc (acquired by Hypo in Sept. 2007) as those do not have valid Post observations. In this context we were concerned about survivorship bias, but found in unreported regressions that guaranteed banks were not more likely to fail *ex post* nor were they more likely to be bailed out.

banks during a crisis. The empirical literature documents that supervisory standards change with respect to economic conditions and that banks experience tighter monitoring during crises versus boom periods (Berger *et al.*, 2001; Krainer and Lopez, 2009).

References

Barth, James R., Gerard Caprio, and Ross Levine, 2004, "Bank regulation and supervision: What works best?," *Journal of Financial Intermediation*, Vol. 13, pp. 205–248.

Beck, Thorsten, Asli Demirgüç-Kunt, and Ross Levine, 2006, "Bank concentration and crises: First results," *Journal of Banking and Finance*, Vol. 30, pp. 1581–1603.

Berger, Allen N., Margaret K. Kyle, and Joseph M. Scalise, 2001, "Did U.S. bank supervisors get tougher during the credit crunch? Did they get easier during the banking boom? Did it matter to bank lending?," in *Prudential Supervision: What Works and What Doesn't*, Frederic Mishkin (ed.), Chicago: University of Chicago Press.

Boyd, John H. and Mark Gertler, 1994, "The role of large banks in the recent U.S. banking crisis," *Federal Reserve Bank of Minneapolis Quarterly Review*, Vol. 18, No. 1, pp. 2–21.

Boyd, John H. and David E. Runkle, 1993, "Size and performance of banking firms: Testing the predictions of theory," *Journal of Monetary Economics*, Vol. 31, No. 1, pp. 47–67.

Cordella, T. and E. L. Yeyati, 2003, "Bank bailouts: Moral hazard vs. value effect," *Journal of Financial Intermediation*, Vol. 12, pp. 300–330.

Demirgüç-Kunt, Asli and Enrica Detragiache, 2002, "Does deposit insurance increase banking system stability? An empirical investigation," *Journal of Monetary Economics*, Vol. 49, No. 7, pp. 1373–1406.

De Nicolo, Gianni and Elena Loukoianova, 2007, "Bank ownership, market structure, and risk," International Monetary Fund, working paper, No. 07/215, Washington, DC.

Dominion Bond Rating Service, 2009, *Enhanced Methodology for Bank Ratings — Intrinsic and Support Assessments*.

Flannery, M., 1998, "Using market information in prudential banking supervision: A review of U.S. evidence," *Journal of Money, Credit and Banking*, Vol. 30, pp. 273–305.

Gropp, R. and J. Vesala, 2004, "Deposit insurance, moral hazard and market monitoring," *Review of Finance*, Vol. 14, pp. 587–622.

Gropp, R., J. Vesala, and G. Vulpes, 2006, "Equity and debt market signals as indicators of bank fragility," *Journal of Money, Credit and Banking*, Vol. 38, pp. 399–428.

Gropp, R., H. Hakenes, and I. Schnabel, 2011, "Competition, risk shifting and public bail-out policies," *Review of Financial Studies*, Vol. 24, pp. 2084–2120.
Gropp, R., C. Gründl, and A. Güttler, 2013, "The impact of public guarantees on bank risk-taking: Evidence from a natural experiment," *Review of Finance*, forthcoming.
Hakenes, H. and I. Schnabel, 2010, "Banks without parachutes — competitive effects of government bail-out policies," *Journal of Financial Stability*, Vol. 6, pp. 156–168.
Keeley, M. C., 1990, "Deposit insurance, risk and market power in banking," *American Economic Review*, Vol. 80, pp. 1183–1200.
Kliger, D. and O. Sarig, 2000, "The information value of bond ratings," *Journal of Finance*, Vol. 55, pp. 2879–2902.
Krainer, John and Jose A. Lopez, 2009, "Do supervisory rating standards change over time?," *Economic Review*, Federal Reserve Bank of San Francisco, pp. 13–24.
Merton, R., 1977, "An analytic derivation of the cost of deposit insurance and loan guarantees," *Journal of Banking and Finance*, Vol. 1, pp. 3–11.
Sironi, A., 2003, "Testing for market discipline in the European banking industry: Evidence from subordinated debt issues," *Journal of Money, Credit and Banking*, Vol. 35, pp. 443–472.

Appendix 1. Listed Banks Implicated by the DBRS Introduction of the SA Methodology on October 6, 2006

Banks with government guarantee	Banks without government guarantee
Australian Banks	*Canadian Banks*
Australia and New Zealand Banking Group	Laurentian Bank
Commonwealth Bank of Australia	
National Australia Bank Limited	*Irish Banks*
Westpac Banking Corporation	DEPFA Bank plc
Canadian Banks	*UK Banks*
Bank of Montreal	Bradford & Bingley plc
Bank of Nova Scotia	Northern Rock plc
Canadian Bank of Imperial Commerce	
National Bank of Canada	*U.S. Banks*
Royal Bank of Canada	Bank of America Corporation
Toronto-Dominion Bank	Bank of Hawaii Corporation
	Bank of New York Company, Inc., The

(*Continued*)

Appendix 1. (*Continued*)

Banks with government guarantee	Banks without government guarantee
Irish Banks	BB&T Corporation
Allied Irish Banks plc	Capital Once Financial Corporation
Governor and Company of the Bank of Ireland	Chittenden Corporation
	Citigroup Inc.
	Citizens Banking Corporation
UK Banks	City National Corporation
HBOS plc	Colonial Bancgroup, Inc., The
HSBC Holdings plc	Comerica Incorporated
Lloyds TSB Bank plc	Compass Bancshares, Inc.
Royal Bank of Scotland plc	Fifth Third Bancorp
	First Merit Corporation
Belgian Banks	Fulton Financial Corporation
Fortis Bank	Greater Bay Bancorp
	Hancock Holding Company
	Huntington Bancshares Incorporated
	IndyMac Bank, F.S.B.
	JPMorgan Chase & Co.
	Keycorp
	M&T Bank Corporation
	Marshall & Ilsley Corporation
	Mellon Financial Corporation
	National City Corporation
	Old National Bancorp
	Pacific Capital Bancorp
	PNC Financial Services Group, Inc., The
	Regions Financial Corporation
	Sky Financial Group, Inc.
	South Financial Group, The
	State Street Corporation
	SunTrust Banks, Inc.
	Susquehanna Bancshares, Inc.
	SVB Financial Group
	U.S. Bancorp
	Wachovia Corporation
	Webster Financial Corporation
	Wells Fargo & Company
	Whitney Holding Corporation
	Zions Bancorporation

Appendix 2. Difference-in-Differences: Wholesale Funding Market Access

	Wholesale funding to total liabilities	
Post (=1)	0.0016	0.0016
	[0.015]	[0.015]
GG (=1)	0.0461	0.0464
	[0.094]	[0.095]
Post*GG	0.0416*	0.0383
	[0.024]	[0.036]
High Q (=1)		−0.0015
		[0.045]
Post*GG*High Q		0.0057
		[0.047]
Constant	0.2891***	0.2895***
	[0.095]	[0.099]
Observations	120	124
F	6.53	33.77
Adjusted R^2	0.09	0.516

Notes: The sample includes 17 banks identified by DBRS on October 6, 2006, as potentially benefiting from a government guarantee and 45 that do not. Wholesale Funding is the year-end ratio of non-retail deposits to total liabilities. The Pre-period is from 12/2004 to 12/2006, while the Post-period is from 12/2007 to 12/2009. Charter value proxied by Tobin's Q = (book value assets + market value equity − book value equity)/(book value assets). Tobin's Q is the average of its components prior to the DBRS announcement. For quarterly banks, it is calculated between 6/2005 and 9/2006. For semi-annual banks, it is calculated between 12/2004 and 6/2006. GG = 1 for guaranteed banks. High Q = 1 for banks above their country's median Q. Robust standard errors clustered at the bank level are reported in brackets. Regressions include unreported country fixed-effects. ***, **, * Significance at the 1%, 5%, and 10% level, respectively.

Real and Imaginary Resolution Options for Large Financial Institutions

David A. Skeel, Jr.*
University of Pennsylvania Law School

1. Introduction

As of 2008, when the financial crisis hit in earnest, there were two principal options if a large financial institution fell into distress in the United States: bankruptcy or some kind of bailout. Specialized administrative resolution rules might govern particular subsidiaries — commercial banks were and are subject to resolution by the FDIC, for instance, and state regulators handle insurance subsidiary failures — but bankruptcy or bailout was the choice for bank holding companies and non-bank financial institutions. After the initial wave of the crisis passed, Federal Reserve Chairman Ben Bernanke, Treasury Secretary Timothy Geithner, and other key regulators called on Congress to put an administrative resolution framework in place. With the enactment of the Dodd–Frank Act of 2010, they got their wish. Title II of the legislation (the Orderly Liquidation Authority, or OLA) gives regulators the power to take over and resolve financial institutions whose failure could cause systemic problems. (See Skeel, 2011, for a full discussion.)

The Dodd–Frank resolution rules were controversial before they were enacted, and their controversy has continued. The FDIC claimed that it might have secured a recovery of 97 cents on the dollar if it had its current resolution powers in the month before Lehman Brothers collapsed (FDIC, 2011). Critics scoffed at these claims, and characterize the new administrative resolution framework as having institutionalized bailouts.

In this paper, I compare the efficacy of administrative resolution under the new Dodd–Frank rules and bankruptcy as mechanisms for resolving

*David A. Skeel, Jr. is the S. Samuel Arsht Professor at the University of Pennsylvania Law School.

the distress of a large financial institution, as well as the bail-in strategies that have gained traction in Europe and the bail-in strategies like "single point of entry" the FDIC has proposed to use under Title II. In my own writings in this area, I have strongly defended bankruptcy as an alternative to either the bailouts of 2008 or to the new Dodd–Frank resolution rules. I continue to defend bankruptcy in this paper, but I nevertheless try to provide a comparatively even-handed assessment of its limitations, as well as the strengths of an administrative approach.

The next section of this paper describes and assesses the new Dodd–Frank resolution rules, and the following section provides an analogous assessment of bankruptcy. In a small concession to my own views, my discussion of Dodd–Frank resolution begins with its problems, whereas I start with the virtues when I turn to bankruptcy. In Section 4, I consider the bail-in proposals that have figured particularly prominently in European discussions. The chief objective of bail-in is assuring that creditors are given haircuts, rather than bailed out as they were in nearly every case in 2008, while channeling regulators' discretion and preserving the institution as an ongoing entity. The benefits and shortcomings of bail-ins parallel those of the Dodd–Frank framework in many respects, but there are also key differences. In Section 5, I advocate two sets of reforms. The first is a simple package of adjustments that would include a stay on derivatives in bankruptcy, as well as several amendments to Dodd–Frank. The second is a proposal for a new Chapter 14 that was drafted by a working group of the Hoover Institution (Jackson *et al.*, 2011). The goal, I argue, should be to make bankruptcy the option of choice, and administrative resolution necessary as seldom as possible. Finally, Section 6 concludes.

2. Dodd–Frank's New Resolution Rules

Resolution under Dodd–Frank begins when "the three keys turn" — Treasury proposes to take over a systemically important financial company that is in or near default, and the Fed and FDIC concur by a two-thirds vote (Dodd–Frank Act § 203). If the company does not agree to the intervention, resolution is commenced by the filing of a petition in the federal district court in Washington, DC. The court has 24 hours to consider the petition (Dodd–Frank Act § 202). Unless the court invalidates the petition as "arbitrary and capricious," the FDIC takes over the company as its receiver, and the managers are kicked out. The FDIC has nearly unfettered discretion to sell the company or any of its parts, either directly or after transferring the assets to a bridge bank.

The resolution rules include a variety of provisions that are designed to counter complaints that the new framework would "institutionalize bailouts." One provision explicitly requires that the financial institution's managers be removed if they were responsible for the financial distress, that shareholders be wiped out, and creditors take losses (Dodd–Frank Act § 206). The framework also instructs regulators to liquidate the institution rather than reorganizing it (Dodd–Frank Act § 214). Although these provisions sound like harsh medicine, the FDIC is also given ample discretion to sidestep them, as we shall see.

The discussion that follows begins by identifying several misleading claims that were used to justify the new resolution framework. I then describe several grounds for serious concern about the framework, and then turn to several benefits it offers.

2.1 *Origin myths and their implications*

The rhetorical justification for the new resolution rules was a misleading analogy promoted by bank regulators during the financial reform debates of 2009 and 2010. According to the Treasury and FDIC, the FDIC has been highly effective in handling the failures of ordinary commercial banks, but these powers did not extend to bank holding companies or non-bank financial institutions. The obvious response to the 2008 crisis, they successfully argued, would be to expand the FDIC's powers to include systemically important financial institutions (see Skeel, 2011, pp. 117–118).

Regulators did encounter serious headwinds in one respect. Although their original blueprint for reform would have given regulators broad rescue powers, popular opinion was extremely hostile to bailouts. In the face of repeated criticism, Dodd–Frank's drafters added a variety of provisions that are designed to make resolution look less like a bailout. Whereas regulators can use a liquidation-like receivership process or a more reorganization-oriented conservatorship process for ordinary banks, Dodd–Frank limits them to the receivership option. The resolution rules also instruct regulators to oust any managers that are responsible for the institution's failure, and to assure that shareholders and creditors take losses. The coup de grace is a provision that was proposed by Senator Barbara Boxer late in the legislative process, which explicitly states that rehabilitation is not permitted;

if regulators take over a troubled financial institution, they must liquidate it (Dodd–Frank Act § 214).

If systemically important banks were indeed like the small and medium-sized banks that the FDIC ordinarily handles, these marching orders would not be problematic. But there are vast differences. With ordinary banks, the FDIC negotiates with one or more healthy banks, and arranges for one to acquire either the troubled bank's deposits or the deposits together with some or all of the troubled bank's assets and other liabilities. Regulators typically descend on the troubled bank on a Friday afternoon, then effect the transfer over the weekend so that the transfer will be complete before the start of business on Monday. This strategy generally will not work with a systemically important financial institution. There often will be very few logical buyers, and the resolution cannot realistically be achieved over a weekend (see Skeel, 2011, pp. 125–126). If these large banks truly were liquidated, the results would be disastrous.

Fortunately, if there ever were a resolution, it is unlikely that regulators would take the command to liquidate seriously. The FDIC's powers in Dodd–Frank resolution can easily be turned to more flexible ends. The FDIC can set up a bridge bank, for instance, and transfer some or all of the bank's assets and liabilities to it. The bridge bank could easily serve as the platform for a restructuring. The FDIC itself has signaled that it intends to use this "single point of entry" strategy in the event of a resolution.

Although Dodd–Frank's liquidation-only rule is unlikely to function the way lawmakers envisioned, it will have two serious costs. First, it will inject uncertainty into the resolution process. The FDIC's use of a bridge bank may be challenged as violating the "thou shalt liquidate" requirement. The second cost is moral and cultural. Many Americans were cynical about claims that the financial reforms would genuinely curb bailouts. The resolution rules were designed to assuage those concerns, but in practice they are more likely to confirm them. To many Americans, the only thing worse than committing to bail out large financial institutions is pretending they will not be bailed out when regulators know they will be.

2.2 *Key problems with Dodd–Frank resolution*

The key shortcomings of administrative resolution are well-known and are handled with varying degrees of effectiveness by the new resolution rules. In the discussion that follows, I focus on four of the most important.

The first difficulty is initiation. Because regulators do not have a financial stake in the institutions they oversee, they do not have an incentive to initiate insolvency proceedings in a timely fashion. Their personal interests are more likely to be served by erring on the side of delay, rather than prompt intervention. After the S&L crisis of the 1980s, Congress addressed this concern in commercial bank resolution by enacting prompt corrective action rules that require regulators to intervene as a bank's financial condition deteriorates. Dodd–Frank, by contrast, gives regulators complete discretion whether and when to intervene. It focuses more on assuring that an intervention is difficult to challenge once regulators decide to take over a large institution. Dodd–Frank's principal strategy for forcing regulators' hands is to make bailouts more difficult outside of resolution by limiting the Fed's 13(3) powers. The new restrictions are unlikely to thwart bailouts, however, which suggests that delayed initiation will continue to be the norm.

The second problem is that administrative resolution is non-transparent and violates rule of law principles, including basic priority rules. In ordinary bank resolution, for instance, the FDIC has almost complete discretion in deciding which assets and liabilities to transfer to a purchaser and which to leave behind. In theory, creditors can challenge the FDIC's determination, but judicial review is severely limited in practice. With most banks, the consequences are not severe, because the vast majority of the bank's liabilities are insured deposits. Nearly 93% of the liabilities of banks with between $100 million and $500 million in assets are deposits (Skeel, 2011, p. 123). Systemically important financial institutions, by contrast, have a far greater range of liabilities. Regulatory discretion is therefore a much more serious concern.

The resolution rules try to address the concern in two ways. First, regulators are not permitted to pick and choose which qualifying financial contracts with a particular party to keep and which to terminate. They must either assume all of the contracts (which ordinarily will mean transferring them to a bridge bank) with a particular counterparty, or terminate all of them. Second, regulators are required to give each creditor at least as much as the creditor would have received if the financial institution had been liquidated and its proceeds distributed in accordance with the absolute priority rule. If creditors receive less than this amount, excess amounts can be clawed back from creditors who received more than their liquidation amount. Because regulators have only one day to make their decision, they will likely assume all of the institution's derivatives. They can preempt other creditors' complaints about this favored treatment by giving them a small recovery and arguing that the creditors would have received little or nothing in a true liquidation. The FDIC already has suggested that it will indeed protect short-term creditors rather than expose them to losses. The cost of this protection will be continued creditor moral hazard. The failure to adequately address creditor moral hazard is the third problem with Dodd–Frank resolution.

The fourth problem is expertise. With ordinary banks, the FDIC has both the experience and the expertise necessary to handle bank failures reasonably well. Under Dodd–Frank resolution, the systemically important financial institutions would be in resolution for well over a weekend — likely a period of months and possibly longer. The FDIC does not have the staff or expertise necessary to run a major bank. Since the Dodd–Frank Act was enacted, the FDIC has been scrambling to scale up its capacity, but it is nowhere near well-positioned to manage a financial institution like Citigroup or Bank of America.

To be sure, several factors may mitigate the expertise deficit to some extent. The first is that the FDIC does not need to have all of the relevant experts in-house. Much as restructuring experts are brought on to help in ordinary corporate bankruptcies, the FDIC could hire managers to run a financial institution in resolution. In addition, if the living wills that are now required by Dodd–Frank are implemented effectively, regulators will not be starting from scratch at the outset of the resolution process. Nevertheless, the FDIC's expertise deficit raises very serious questions about its ability to handle the failure of a systemically important financial institution. And even if the FDIC succeeds in closing some of the expertise deficit in the near term, it is far from clear that it can retain or identify the highly qualified experts it needs over the long haul. The FDIC is likely to be better prepared now than it will be if resolution is first invoked five years from now, or ten.

2.3 *Potential benefits*

As I turn from the problems with Dodd–Frank resolution to its potential benefits, I am reminded of Barack Obama's grudging allowance, during a 2008 debate, that Hillary Clinton was "likeable enough." Although I am not a great deal more enthusiastic about Dodd–Frank resolution than President Obama was about his then-opponent, it does offer several possible benefits.

The first benefit is that the resolution rules give the FDIC the capacity to intervene quickly and with ample funding to support ongoing business operations.[1] This is, of course, the flipside of the propensity for regulators to bail out troubled institutions. The FDIC is authorized to borrow up to 10% of the book value of the institution as of the time it is taken over, and 90% of its value in resolution. (For the largest of banks, this would make over $200 billion available as of the resolution, and far more under an aggressive interpretation of the 90% standard the moment the resolution was underway.) A bridge bank also would presumably have access to the Federal Reserve's discount window. The FDIC should be fully capable of keeping any essential functions operating and paying any counterparties as needed.

A second benefit is the possibility of regulatory coordination. The Dodd–Frank Act itself does not contribute a great deal to the international dimensions of a default of a systemically important financial institution. Its major innovation in this regard is the new requirement that systemically important financial institutions prepare a rapid resolution plan — or "living will." As a result, any coordination on an international level will have to take place on an ad hoc basis. It is possible that regulators will be better able to facilitate this coordination than bankruptcy judges. To some extent, they already interact through international conferences and periodic meetings. Although this is a far cry from a robust solution to the international problems that attended the Lehman default, it may be that a network of regulators will be better able to coordinate an international proceeding than bankruptcy judges are.

3. The Bankruptcy Alternative

Even the most fervent advocates of the new resolution approach have stated that bankruptcy is the presumptive mechanism for resolving the financial distress of all but the most systemically important financial institutions. The question, in a sense, is how big is the set of institutions that requires resolution. I will argue in this section that the benefits of bankruptcy as compared to administrative resolution are considerable, and that lawmakers should seek to make the set of institutions that require administrative resolution as small as possible.

[1]The FDIC also touts its ability to set up a bridge bank.

3.1 *The bankruptcy process*

Although it is quite simple for creditors to file an involuntary bankruptcy case, the overwhelming majority of cases are initiated by the debtor's managers. Once a bankruptcy petition has been filed, the so-called automatic stay prohibits most creditors from grabbing or selling collateral, pursuing litigation against the debtor, or otherwise attempting to collect pre-bankruptcy obligations. Of significant importance for financial institutions, derivatives, repos, and other qualified financial contracts are not subject to the stay (see Skeel and Jackson, 2012, for more detailed analysis). Derivatives' counterparties can therefore terminate their contracts or sell collateral, unobstructed by the automatic stay.

In a traditional bankruptcy, the debtor negotiates with its creditors over the terms of a reorganization plan. When the terms of a plan are in place, the debtor drafts a disclosure statement describing its terms, and the disclosure statement is sent (after court approval) to each creditor or shareholder.[2] The plan is thus submitted to a vote, and if the proper majorities of each class of creditors and shareholders approve the plan, and a number of other requirements are met, the plan is confirmed by the bankruptcy judge. Even if one or more classes object, the plan can still be approved through a non-consensual "cramdown" if, among other things, the plan does not discriminate unfairly and satisfies the absolute priority rule.[3]

One obvious difference between financial institution bankruptcies and a traditional bankruptcy is that a substantial portion of a financial institution's assets are often sold very early in the case, because their value to the debtor will evaporate otherwise. Lehman's brokerage operations were sold four days after Lehman filed for bankruptcy, for instance. Financial institution bankruptcies often involve a prompt sale of time-sensitive assets, followed by a more leisurely decision-making process with the institution's other assets.

3.2 *Benefits of bankruptcy*

The bankruptcy process has three very important benefits as compared to an administrative resolution process. The first can be loosely described

---

[2]11 U.S.C. § 1125 (disclosure and solicitation).

[3]The requirements for consensual and non-consensual reorganization appear in 11 U.S.C. §§ 1129(a) and 1129(b), respectively.

as rule of law virtues. Unlike FDIC resolution of banks, the bankruptcy process is transparent; it is governed by clear priority rules; and it gives creditors a full judicial opportunity to challenge treatment that does not, in their view, honor their entitlements. It is important to acknowledge that bankruptcy is not perfect in this regard. The priority rules are largely but not completely honored. In most courts, courts permit a debtor to pay its "critical vendors" in full, for instance, even though they technically are general creditors. Judicial review is sometimes limited by the difficulty of raising and litigating an issue before it becomes moot. Overall, however, bankruptcy priorities are much firmer and clearer than creditors' treatment in an administrative proceeding. This clarity is likely to enhance credit market efficiency as compared to murkier priority rules.

The second benefit of bankruptcy is that the prospect that shareholders and creditors will take losses curbs moral hazard. In 2008, the government punished the shareholders and managers of firms such as AIG that were bailed out, ousting the managers and diluting shareholders. Creditors, by contrast, were fully protected. Nor is there reason to believe that creditors will be punished in future bailouts. This approach invites creditor moral hazard. If a financial institution is likely to be resolved in bankruptcy, by contrast, creditors cannot assume they will be bailed out and are more likely to screen and monitor their debtors as a result.

Third, in bankruptcy, the principal decisions are made by the parties themselves, rather than by a government regulator. Because the parties have more complete information than even the most vigilant regulator and creditors have a financial stake, the financial distress is more likely to be resolved efficiently (at least if the parties do not have a disincentive to file, an issue I return to in the next section).

3.3 *The limitations of bankruptcy*

Bankruptcy also has three major limitations. I consider the first two here. Because the third — the court and its jurisdiction — may be less familiar and has been less fully explored, I discuss it separately in the next section.

The first criticism of bankruptcy is that it is not well-designed to handle systemic issues. This criticism is often characterized in terms of the limited focus of the bankruptcy process. Bankruptcy is designed to maximize the value of a particular firm, the argument goes; in contrast to bank regulators, the principal players do not consider third-party effects, such as the possibility that a filing will have systemic consequences. The distinction between bankruptcy and administrative resolution is not as sharp as this argument often assumes. Bankruptcy judges do not ignore systemic issues. But neither they nor the parties can take control as fully and effectively at the outset of a case as regulators can under the Dodd–Frank resolution rules. The difficulty is exacerbated by the absence of a stay on derivatives, which are often the most systemically sensitive contracts. These limitations will not prove debilitating in the vast majority of cases — even with Lehman, for instance, no counterparties failed after the company's default — but in a few they might.

Second and related, financing cannot be put in place as quickly in bankruptcy as in administrative resolution. Financing is ordinarily approved through a two-step process — an interim hearing at the outset of the case, and a final hearing a week or two thereafter. If the debtor needs immediate liquidity, even a temporary delay at the beginning of a case could be problematic. The funding limitations should not be overstated. As soon as the debtor files for bankruptcy, the automatic stay goes into effect with most obligations, and the debtor does not have to continue making payments. Derivatives are a major exception to this. But a financial institution could stop payments on other obligations, such as bonds, which would reduce its funding needs somewhat. In addition, bankruptcy does not preclude the government from offering backup funding.

Nevertheless, systemic issues and the timely availability of funding are greater concerns in a bankruptcy case than in administrative resolution.

3.4 *The role and status of bankruptcy judges*

The final major limitation of bankruptcy concerns the status of bankruptcy judges. The status of bankruptcy judges poses two problems. One is inherent in the bankruptcy process; the other is an artifact of the odd, artificial structure of the U.S. bankruptcy courts.

Casual observers of bankruptcy often assume that the bankruptcy judge dictates the terms of a reorganization plan and makes all of the other important decisions in the case. In reality, the bankruptcy judge functions more like an umpire than a player in most respects. The parties themselves decide whether to sell assets or to propose a reorganization, and the judge either approves or disapproves their handiwork. The limited role played by the court, and the wide scope the parties are given to determine the resolution of the case, is part of the genius of bankruptcy. But it also introduces a complication. Because the judge's role is reactive, she has only limited information at the outset of the case. If important decisions need to be made very quickly, as often is the case in large bankruptcies and will almost always be the case if the debtor is a large financial institution, the judge is put in a difficult position. After Lehman filed for bankruptcy, the bankruptcy judge was asked to approve the sale of Lehman's brokerage operations to Barclay's almost immediately, based on relatively limited information. The judge does have the benefit of the debtor's having concluded that the transaction is in its best interests, but many creditors will not be in a position to weigh in effectively, so the judge herself may have to exercise discretion based on much less information than would be ideal.

Bankruptcy judges' other limitation stems from their odd constitutional status. Unlike federal trial judges, circuit court judges, and Supreme Court justices, who are appointed for life under Article III of the Constitution, bankruptcy judges are Article I judges who serve for 14-year terms. This status is the result of a torturous history that came to head when the current bankruptcy laws were put in place in 1978. Although it would have made obvious sense to give bankruptcy judges Article III status, Warren Burger, the Chief Justice of the Supreme Court, and a number of other federal court judges resisted, apparently feeling that the status of the federal trial judges would be diluted if the large number of bankruptcy judges were given equivalent status. Under the structure that was put in place in 1984, after the Supreme Court struck down the 1978 framework, bankruptcy judges were made adjuncts of the federal trial court. Bankruptcy cases technically go to the district court, but every district automatically refers them back to the bankruptcy judges.

Because bankruptcy judges are not appointed for life, some worry that they are not sufficiently "independent" to handle especially sensitive cases. The independence deficit seems minimal at most. Fourteen years is a considerable term — long enough to limit any concerns about job security — and the initial appointment process is less politically charged than with other federal judges, since the circuit court rather than politicians selects bankruptcy judges. Non-Article III status does, however, constrain bankruptcy judges on the margin. The limits were brought home in 2011 when the Supreme Court held that a bankruptcy judge could not handle a dispute involving Anna Nicole Smith. This jurisdictional limitation could easily be remedied, as discussed below. The limitations of an *ex post* overseer are more indigenous to bankruptcy itself.

4. Is Bail-in the Solution?

Since the 2008 crisis, the most popular resolution strategy among European banking experts has not been either bankruptcy or Dodd–Frank style administrative resolution. The word that makes their eyes light up is "bail-in." The best way to earn appreciative nods at a banking conference in 2011 or 2012 was to propose that what we really need is "some kind of bail-in."

Just what is bail-in? The first step toward understanding bail-in and its popularity is to recognize that the bail-in concept predates the recent crisis. The term first came into common usage after the sovereign debt crises of the late 1990s and early 2000s, which culminated with the most recent Argentine default. As unhappiness with the IMF's bailout policies grew, policymakers began talking about bail-in — by which they meant participation by private creditors in any rescue effort.[4] Less euphemistically, bail-in meant that private creditors should be expected to take haircuts.

Under this conception of bail-in, it is easy to understand its initial attraction. The almost uniform protection of creditors in 2008, and the creditor moral hazard this created, has been widely criticized. A genuine bail-in would address this concern. But nothing mentioned thus far would distinguish bail-in from bankruptcy or even Dodd–Frank resolution — at least to the extent Dodd–Frank resolution would not bail out all of the financial institution's creditors. What, then, do bail-in proponents have in mind when they contrast it with bankruptcy and the OLA rules?

The answer seems to be that bail-in would preserve the financial institution as an ongoing entity, rather than liquidating it; and that regulators' discretion would be channeled. Under some of the existing proposals, bail-in would take place outside of the resolution process; under others, its bail-in would occur as a form of regulatory resolution. Lawyers at Clifford Chance have proposed, for instance, that financial institutions be required to issue bail-in eligible senior debt (Clifford Chance, 2011). If bail-in were triggered, the financial institution's stock would be wiped out and the bail-in eligible senior debt would be restructured. Deposits and other obligations would be protected. This, they argue, would more effectively recapitalize the institution than simply wiping out stock and converting some low-priority debt obligations to stock, as contingent capital-based proposals contemplate.

---

[4]Bail-in is described and defended in Roubini and Setser (2005).

The FDIC could achieve essentially the same effect under Dodd–Frank's resolution rules, and after this chapter was first drafted, it began signaling its intent to do so. The FDIC could set up a bridge bank after putting the holding company in resolution, transfer the holding company's assets and any liabilities that the FDIC wishes to protect to the bridge bank, and issue equity to the creditors that have been left behind (see Guynn, 2011). Although this strategy would violate the spirit of the resolution rules, as discussed earlier, it would recapitalize the institution in the same way as the leading bail-in proposals advocate.

As this analogy suggests, bail-ins have many of the same shortcomings as traditional administrative resolution. In particular, most of the recent proposals depend on regulators to decide when to trigger the bail-in and how much of a haircut creditors should receive. The principal European proposals, such as Clifford Chance (2011) and Huertas (2010), contemplate that long-term debt will be subject to bail-in, while regulators will protect short-term obligations. The *extent* of the haircut is left to administrative discretion. In addition, the commitment to bail-out short-term obligations could magnify banks' temptation to rely on these forms of funding, which proved highly fragile in 2008.

There is also something incongruous about the strategy underlying bail-ins. The bail-in proposals assume that systemically important financial institutions must be preserved as going concerns. Not only is this assumption less compelling with financial institutions than with sovereign debtors — the original subject of bail-in proposals — but the bail-in proposals seem to assume that the institution's distress can be solved by making simple adjustments to its balance sheet. In reality, liquidity may be a more important concern for a troubled institution that regulators wish to rescue; bail-in may ease a financial institution's liquidity constraints somewhat, but it does not solve a liquidity problem.

As an alternative to bail-ins that depend on the exercise of administrative discretion, a bail-in also could include automatic, market-based triggers. Contingent capital securities that are converted into equity if the issuer's capital falls below a specified level are, in a sense, a limited version of automatic bail-in. This approach, which is the subject of an extensive legal literature in the corporate bankruptcy context (see, for example, Adler, 1993; Bradley and Rosenzweig, 1992), could be used more fully to provide for automatic haircuts to other classes of securities. The attraction of this approach is that it addresses the problem of regulator delay or inaction. Its limitations are also considerable, however, as is well-known (see, for example, Skeel, 1993). The most obvious triggers — such as capital requirements — could be manipulated by a troubled financial institution. Automatic triggers may also be subject to manipulation by the institution's creditors. As the turmoil in Greece has made clear, regulators may also be reluctant to allow the markets to function in a crisis. Just as regulators have insisted that Greece's obligations must be restructured without technically defaulting, so that the credit default swaps on Greek bonds are not triggered, there is a real risk they would defuse an automatic bail-in.

5. Implications and Potential Reforms

In the wake of Dodd–Frank's enactment, we are no longer writing on a blank slate in the U.S. Contrary to the fond hopes of its most vehement critics, Dodd–Frank and its resolution rules are unlikely to be repealed. For the foreseeable future, the two basic options will be, as they now are, bankruptcy and Dodd–Frank resolution.

The analysis of this paper suggests that the principal focus of reform should be maximizing the effectiveness and likely use of bankruptcy as an alternative to Dodd–Frank resolution, and amending a few of the most problematic provisions in Dodd–Frank. I begin by describing a handful of simple adjustments, then turn to a slightly more elaborate proposal to enact a new bankruptcy chapter for large financial institutions.

5.1 *Next steps for Dodd–Frank and bankruptcy reform*

In my view, four simple reforms would make the current resolution options appreciably more effective. The first is simply to remove the "thou shalt liquidate" provision from Dodd–Frank's resolution rules. As a strident critic of the bailouts of 2008, I am sympathetic to the impulse that led to the provision. But foreclosing the prospect of reorganization is at odds with over a century of American insolvency law, and few believe that regulators will actually honor the liquidation mandate if the resolution rules are ever invoked.

The second and third proposals would establish presumptions that could be implemented by bank regulators, without a need for legislative reform. As it currently stands, nothing in Dodd–Frank requires that either regulators or the financial institution that prepares a "living will" actually follow the blueprint of the living will. If regulators committed to honor its terms — in particular, by not invoking Dodd–Frank's resolution rules if the living will contemplates use of bankruptcy in the event of financial distress — the plans would prove more useful and more firms might use bankruptcy rather than Dodd–Frank resolution. Relatedly, Dodd–Frank gives regulators the power to override a bankruptcy filing, and put a firm that has filed for bankruptcy in resolution (Dodd–Frank Act § 208). This power will create a great deal of uncertainty at the outset of a bankruptcy case. Establishing a strong presumption that regulators will not pluck financial institutions out of bankruptcy would reduce some of the uncertainty.

The last and by far the most important reform would remove the special treatment derivatives and other qualified financial contracts currently receive in bankruptcy. As I have argued in detail elsewhere, subjecting these contracts to a short stay would appreciably enhance the effectiveness of bankruptcy as a resolution mechanism for financial institutions (Skeel and Jackson, 2012; Skeel, 2011). If derivatives were subject to a stay, the managers of AIG might have considered bankruptcy as a plausible option, since it would have enabled them to stop the collateral grabs that began when AIG was downgraded.

5.2 *A more ambitious program: Chapter 14*

A working group at the Hoover Institution has devised a set of proposals for large financial institutions (defined as those with more than $100 billion in assets) that would go still further in making bankruptcy an effective resolution mechanism for nearly any large financial institution (Jackson *et al.*, 2011). Principally authored by Thomas Jackson, Chapter 14 would address several of the limitations of bankruptcy discussed earlier. Of particular note are its proposals for regulator participation, funding in bankruptcy, and the use of Article III judges. The Chapter 14 proposal would marry some of the benefits of administrative resolution with those of bankruptcy.[5]

Start with the role of regulators. In an ordinary Chapter 11 case, regulators' ability to participate is quite constrained. Perhaps most importantly, they cannot initiate the bankruptcy case. The Chapter 14 proposal would explicitly authorize regulators to file an involuntary bankruptcy case against an insolvent financial institution that is covered by the report; and it would give regulators standing to appear and be heard on any issue in the

[5]The proposal is similar to proposals by Robert Bliss and George Kaufman in this regard.

case. Although regulators have traditionally been slow to take action, this proposal would enable them to file a case if managers failed to do so, and it provides a mechanism for tapping the information regulations as a result of their ongoing oversight role.

The second innovation involves funding. Bankruptcy already facilitates financing through its debtor-in-possession financing provision, which gives the court wide latitude to approve new loans. Under the Chapter 14 proposal, the debtor would be explicitly authorized to use some of this financing to make immediate, partial payments to creditors (such as derivatives counterparties) with time-sensitive claims. If the initial payment gives these creditors more than other general creditors eventually receive, the difference could be clawed back. But any clawback would occur much later, after the initial crisis had passed. This should appreciably reduce the risk that the filing would have problematic systemic effects. (For a similar proposal, see Kaufman, 2007.)

One question not fully addressed in the current Chapter 14 proposal is the potential gap between the moment of the filing and the time at which debtor-in-possession financing is put in place. In ordinary Chapter 11 cases, courts approve financing quite quickly, often within a day or two. If the debtor is a financial institution, even a brief delay may be problematic, given the speed at which liquidity can disappear. As noted earlier, the automatic stay relieves a debtor's liquidity needs somewhat, by halting the obligation to make payments on pre-bankruptcy obligations. In addition, the debtor can minimize the gap by arranging its financing prior to filing for bankruptcy. But even a small gap may be problematic. This suggests that it may make sense to give financial institutions automatic access to a government funding facility on terms analogous to those provided in Dodd–Frank's administrative resolution process.

A third innovation of Chapter 14 is its proposed judicial framework. Under Chapter 14, the case would be overseen by a federal trial court judge selected by the chief judge of the federal court of appeals from a panel of judges with financial expertise. This would address any concerns about independence or jurisdictional scope. Chapter 14 also would explicitly authorize the judge to make use of special masters if he wished to bring additional expertise into the case.

If fully implemented, Chapter 14 would make a number of other adjustments as well. It would reshape the existing bankruptcy rules to handle the distinctive challenges posed by the financial distress of one or more of the largest financial institutions.

6. Conclusion

In this paper, I have compared the two principal mechanisms for resolving the distress of a large financial institution — administrative resolution and bankruptcy — in the particular context of the new Dodd–Frank resolution rules and the U.S. bankruptcy laws. I also have considered recent proposals for "bail-in" of large financial institutions, which has turned out to be the strategy of choice even under Dodd–Frank. The principal sticking point with each is the dependence on administrative discretion. In the U.S., at least, the objective should be to make bankruptcy as effective as possible, and to minimize the need for regulators to invoke Dodd–Frank resolution. I have suggested a handful of changes to the Dodd–Frank Act and to the bankruptcy laws that might help further this objective.

References

Adler, Barry E., 1993, "Financial and political theories of American corporate bankruptcy," *Stanford Law Review*, Vol. 45, p. 311.

Bradley, Michael and Michael Rosenzweig, 1992, "The untenable case for Chapter 11," *Yale Law Journal*, Vol. 101, p. 1043.

Clifford Chance, 2011, "Legal aspects of bank bail-ins," Clifford Chance, LLP, May 3, pp. 1–20, available at: www.cliffordchance.com/publicationviews/publications/2011/05/legal_aspects_ofbankbail-ins.html.

Federal Deposit Insurance Corporation, 2011, "The orderly liquidation of Lehman Brothers Holding, Inc. under the Dodd–Frank Act," *FDIC Quarterly*, Vol. 5, pp. 1–19.

Guynn, Randall, 2011, "Are bailouts inevitable?," *Yale Journal on Regulation*, forthcoming.

Huertas, Thomas F., 2010, "The road to better resolution: From bail-out to bail-in," The Euro and The Financial Crisis, Bank of Slovakia, pp. 1–21.

Jackson, Thomas, *et al.*, 2011, "Bankruptcy code Chapter 14: A proposal," Hoover Institution Working Group on Economics, working paper, available at: http://media.hoover.org/sites/default/files/documents/chapter-14-proposal-20101116.pdf.

Kaufman, George G., 2007, "A proposal for efficiently resolving out-of-the-money swap positions at large insolvent banks," *Journal of Banking Regulation*, Vol. 9, pp. 3–13.

Roubini, Nouriel and Brad Setser, 2005, *Bailouts or Bail-ins? Responding to Financial Crises in Emerging Economies*, Washington, DC: Institute for International Economics.

Skeel, David A. Jr., 1993, "Markets, courts, and the brave new world of bankruptcy theory," *Wisconsin Law Review*, pp. 465–521.
Skeel, David A. Jr., 2009, "Bankruptcy boundary games," *Brooklyn Journal of Corporate, Financial & Commercial Law*, Vol. 4, pp. 1–21.
Skeel, David A. Jr., 2011, *The New Financial Deal: Understanding the Dodd–Frank Act and Its (Unintended) Consequences*, Hoboken, NJ: John Wiley & Sons, Inc.
Skeel, David A. Jr. and Thomas Jackson, 2012, "Transaction consistency and the new finance in bankruptcy," *Columbia Law Review*, forthcoming.

VII. POLICY PANEL: WHERE TO FROM HERE?

Is Our Economy's Financial Sector Worth What It Costs Us?

Benjamin M. Friedman*

Harvard University

In 1867, when the American economy was still largely agricultural, Horace Greeley, the editor of the *New York Tribune*, threw out the following challenge in a lecture that he gave in Lower Manhattan: "There are 500,000 farmers, probably, in the State of New York today, who, if you were to ask each of them how much per bushel his corn had cost him to grow for the last twenty years, I doubt if fifty of the 500,000 could tell you. And this is but one instance out of ten thousand. Now, every grower of agricultural products should inquire and ascertain, year after year, 'What does this cost me? What does it bring me?'"[1]

In the United States we no longer live in an agricultural economy. Today we have mostly a service economy, and much of our production of services takes place in the financial sector. Especially in the wake of the recent financial crisis, I think it is important for us to ask ourselves the "Greeley question" — but directed toward our modern financial sector: Do we know what our economy's financial sector is costing us? And do we have a sense of what we are getting for what we pay?

The essential function of the financial sector in a free enterprise, capitalist economy is to allocate the economy's scarce capital investment. In aggregate, the American economy typically invests about one-fifth of what it produces. No central authority makes this so. This determination is

*Benjamin M. Friedman is the William Joseph Maier Professor of Political Economy at Harvard University.

[1]Greeley, Horace, 1867, "Success in business," address delivered before the students of Packard's Bryant and Stratton New York Business College, November 11 (New York: S.S. Packard), p. 27.

made by the financial sector, as is the allocation across countless diverse investment applications, in both respects in a highly decentralized way. The financial sector serves other functions as well, of course, including operating the economy's payments mechanism, providing liquid savings vehicles for individuals, enabling families to save for retirement, and providing insurance of a variety of forms. But there exist successful public utility models for each of those other functions. The one function that is essential to the *private* financial sector in a capitalist economy is allocating the investment of the economy's capital stock.

The fact that this is the financial sector's essential function suggests a logical benchmark for at least beginning to measure what this mechanism costs to run: the share of the total return to the economy's invested capital that is dissipated in the process of allocating that capital. The element of this cost that has attracted the most widespread interest in recent years, as several of the comments at this morning's panel illustrated, is the total profits accruing to the financial sector. As is by now well-known, the share of total profits in the U.S. economy earned by firms in the economy's financial sector rose from 10 percent (on average) from the 1950s through the 1980s, to above 20 percent in the 1990s, and then above 30 percent in the 2000s until the crisis. Given the large increase, it is no surprise that these profits have attracted attention.

But the profits earned by financial firms are only one element, and presumably a small element, of the all-in cost of running the economy's financial sector. There are personnel costs in the form of salaries, benefits, and bonuses. There are real estate costs, including office rentals and rental equivalents for owner-occupied buildings. There are utility bills associated with heating and cooling these premises, there are travel budgets, there are advertising budgets, and the list goes on.

Importantly, referring again to the allocation of the economy's resources, each of these costs is a reflection of real resources absorbed. I teach in a university, and so the aspect of these costs that I see in action on a regular basis is the attraction of so many of our graduates into this line of work. Approximately a quarter of the graduates at my university go into the financial sector. Both at my university and at others too, those who choose to do so include many of our brightest, most energetic, and most highly motivated young people. They could be doing something else. In light of the compensation that they receive, at an individual level no one can question their decision to choose financial-sector careers. At the aggregate level, maybe it is true that their combined talents are actually necessary for allocating our economy's capital stock. If so, then this valuable human resource is an important element in what the economy pays to carry out this function.

Similarly, if we walk outside the door of this Federal Reserve Bank, or in New York if we take a walk up Park Avenue just north of Grand Central Station, we can observe that the use to which our economy puts the choicest real estate in almost every one of America's major cities is likewise the allocation of our capital investment. Here too, maybe our way of allocating the capital stock cannot function without taking up so much of our prime urban real estate. If so, this resource is yet another element in what makes carrying out this key function as we do so expensive.

A different kind of element in this cost, one that we cannot measure directly but that as economists we have ready conceptual means of calculating, is the exposure of our economy to damaging volatility of the form that we have only just experienced in the aftermath of the recent financial crisis. From an economic perspective, the logical approach to assessing this cost is to ask how much of each year's national income we would be willing to pay to buy insurance against such volatility — if that insurance were provided by the market, which of course it is not. Given that it is not, so that we therefore live with the volatility to which our way of allocating the economy's capital subjects us, the shadow price that we would pay for insuring against it is also an element in what this allocation mechanism costs us.

Assessing the benefits that our capital allocation mechanism delivers is conceptually more difficult. The reason is that there is no obvious benchmark for purposes of comparison. We are all aware that the American economy has had a pretty good record of dynamic growth over a very long period of time. It is difficult to imagine firms like Google, or Microsoft, or Apple, having been created in most other economies. It is clear that our financial system has historically played a key role in making this happen.

More recently, however, there is ample room to question how well our capital allocation mechanism is performing. Once again, the fundamental issue is resource allocation. In the wake of the most recent crisis, much of the public conversation was about the losses that firms took on their holdings of mortgage-backed securities, and correspondingly about the difficulties facing households that were (and in many cases still are) under water on their home mortgages. But the important point is that the losses incurred on these securities mean that their price was too high to begin with; and because the price of the securities was too high, the rate paid on the underlying mortgages was too low — with the result that Americans built and bought, and now own, millions of houses that nobody wants. Building those houses was a misuse of the labor and capital resources that went into them.

Nor is the most recent experience unique. When the "dot-com bubble" burst at the end of the 1990s, the public's attention mostly focused on the losses that investors took on their telecom stocks. But once again, those losses were merely the financial reflection of a misallocation of the economy's labor and capital resources. The fact that investors took losses on their telecom holdings means that the price of the securities was too high to begin with — which in turn means that the cost of capital to the firms that issued them was too low, and as a result these firms laid hundreds of millions of miles of fiber optic cable that were never lit.

To repeat, we have no convenient conceptual benchmark for comparing how well our economy's capital allocation mechanism is performing relative to something else. We all know that capital allocation by central planning has been totally discredited — and appropriately so. But this is not an excuse for shying away from questioning the specifics of the capital allocation mechanism that we have. By analogy, it may be worth remembering the concerns that many people expressed a quarter-century or so ago, during the Cold War era, about some European countries' politics (not surprisingly, including many of the countries that are experiencing economic trouble today). At that time, even the supporters of the then-dominant center-right parties in these countries readily acknowledged their sclerotic character, empty programs, and corrupt office holders. But, so the argument went, there was no alternative — because the only alternative was the Communists, and that was no alternative at all. This is not a thought process we should aspire to repeat.

I have no candidate measure to suggest for benchmarking at the aggregate level the benefits we receive from our economy's extremely expensive capital allocation mechanism, although I am optimistic that someone will be able to solve this conceptual problem. But I can also imagine tackling this question on a piecemeal basis — that is, by asking what benefit we get from any given component of our capital allocation mechanism. What would be different, for example, if we did not have the high-speed trading firms whose activity now constitutes well over half of the volume on the New York Stock Exchange? Would we end up allocating our economy's capital stock less efficiently? If so, by how much? Or, to take some examples closer to the causes of the recent crisis, what would be different if we did not have a market for CDSs, or CDOs, or CDO-squareds? More generally, what would be different if we did not have securitization of mortgages at all? An often repeated theme in today's public discussion is that it is now impossible to go back to a world in which mortgages were not securitized. An uninformed visitor, considering the matter from the fundamental perspective of resource allocation, might suppose this means that in the era before mortgage securitization it was impossible for Americans to build and buy houses. But of course that was not so. Americans did build and buy houses, and own them and live in them, in a world in which there was no securitization. Indeed, the American rate of home ownership was among the world's highest long before anyone thought to securitize the first home mortgage.

I propose that the economics profession, including the Federal Reserve System and other key elements of our government's statistical apparatus, ought to play a leading role in undertaking a serious research effort along the lines I have suggested. We should initiate a major project aimed both at measuring the all-in cost of what it takes to run our economy's capital allocation mechanism and, much more difficult because of the conceptual challenge I have outlined, at estimating the benefit we get out of it.

Let me close with an analogy that Horace Greeley's agriculturally grounded listeners would have understood. If a new fertilizer offers a farmer the prospect of a higher yield on his land, it is only common sense that the farmer should compare the incremental economic return from the enhanced harvest to the cost of achieving it. If what it costs him to buy this new fertilizer, and to transport it to his farm and spread it on his fields, exceeds the sale price of the additional crops the fertilizer would enable him to produce, that makes it a poor investment — despite the fact that it does yield additional technical efficiency.

The system that allocates our economy's capital stock is no different. Even if it allocates the economy's capital more efficiently than some alternative, if it costs more to run than the incremental return that the superior allocation produces, then it is only so much overpriced manure.

The Eurozone Crisis: Causes, Remedy, and Misperceptions

Richard C. Koo*
Nomura Research Institute

The creation of the euro is one of humanity's greatest achievements. But as in the initial trials of any modern sophisticated creation such as aircraft, a glitch has been discovered in the structure requiring immediate corrective action. If the necessary modifications are not carried out in time, the euro could crash and plunge the world economy into depression. The glitch has two components, neither of which has been fully recognized in the policy debate up to now. The first is that the Maastricht Treaty never envisioned the kind of turbulence that is afflicting the single-currency area. The second is that the highly procyclical capital flows that are unique to the Eurozone are undermining official efforts to stabilize the plane. Once these two problems are corrected, the Eurozone will be able to function as a viable currency zone and the problems we see today will not be repeated.

1. Eurozone in Balance Sheet Recession

Today, the Eurozone is afflicted with a rare type of recession that occurs only after the collapse of a nationwide asset price bubble financed with debt. It is the same kind of recession that struck Japan 15 years ago and that afflicts the U.S. and UK today.

When a debt-financed bubble bursts, asset prices collapse but liabilities remain, leaving millions of private-sector balance sheets underwater. In order to restore their financial health and credit ratings, businesses and households are forced to repair their balance sheets by increasing savings

* Richard C. Koo is the chief economist of Nomura Research Institute. The general ideas of this paper are put forward and explained in Koo (2008).

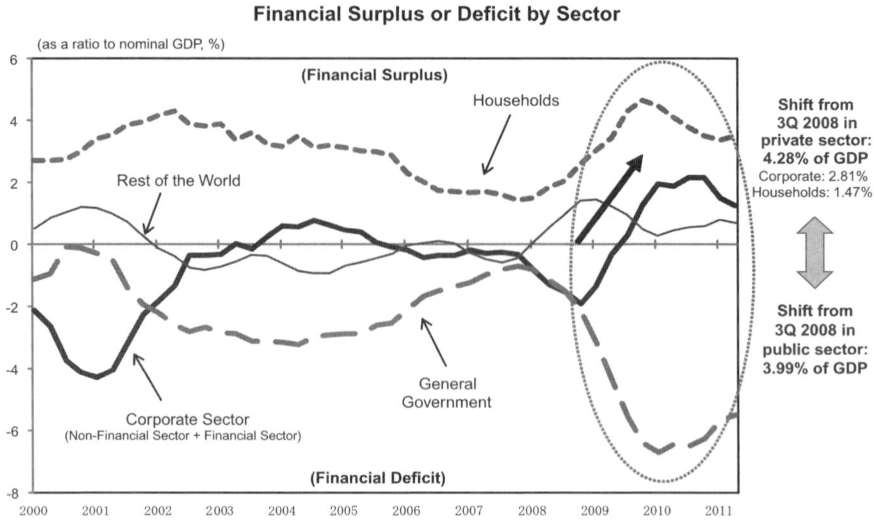

Figure 1. Private Sector in Eurozone is Increasing Savings despite Record Low Interest Rates.

Note: For the latest figures, 4 quarter averages ending with 2Q/11' are used.
Source: ECB.

or paying down debt. The private sector in the Eurozone (Figure 1), like those in the U.S., UK, and Japan, is doing so in spite of record low interest rates, a state of affairs seldom discussed in the economics literature. Shifting from the standard mode of profit maximization to debt minimization is the right course of action for individual businesses and households, but when everyone deleverages at the same time, the economy falls into what is now known as a *balance sheet recession.*

The first casualty of this shift to debt minimization is monetary policy, the traditional remedy for recessions, because people with negative equity are not interested in borrowing more, no matter how low the interest rate. Nor are there many willing lenders to those borrowers, especially when the lenders themselves have balance sheet problems.

That is why the ECB's super-low interest rates have failed to stimulate Eurozone economies suffering from a burst housing bubble. It is also why the near-zero interest rate policies in place in Japan since 1995 and in the U.S. since 2009 have failed to turn those economies around. It is also the reason why the then-record low ECB interest rates failed to stimulate the German economy after the bursting of its telecom bubble in 2000.

More importantly, when the private sector is deleveraging in spite of near-zero interest rates, the economy enters a destructive deflationary spiral because, in the absence of people borrowing and spending money, the economy *continuously* loses demand equal to the sum of savings and net debt repayments. To see this, consider a world in which a household has an income of $1,000 and a saving rate of 10 percent. This household would then spend $900 and save $100. In the usual or textbook world, the $100 that is saved would be taken up by the financial sector and lent to a borrower who can make best use of the money. When that borrower spends the $100, aggregate expenditure totals $1,000 ($900 plus $100) against original income of $1,000, and the economy moves on. When demand for the saved $100 is insufficient, interest rates are lowered, which usually prompts some borrowers to take up the remaining sum. When demand exceeds the amount that has been saved, interest rates are raised, which persuades some borrowers to drop out.

But in a world where the private sector is minimizing debt, there are no borrowers for the saved $100 even at an interest rate of zero, leaving the economy with only $900 in expenditures. That $900 represents someone's income, and if that person saves 10 percent, only $810 will be spent. Since repairing balance sheets after the collapse of a major bubble typically takes a long time — 15 years in Japan's case — the saved $90 will go unborrowed again, and the economy will shrink to $810, and to $730, and so on. This is what happened during the Great Depression, when the U.S. lost 46 percent of its GDP in just four years due mostly to a debt-repayment-induced deflationary spiral.

Because monetary policy is largely ineffective in this type of recession, the only way for the government to stop the deflationary spiral is to borrow and spend the $100 in savings itself. That way, total expenditures will remain at $1,000 and there is no reason for the economy to shrink. By keeping the economy from shrinking, this also provides income to the private sector so that it can pay down debt.

Japanese businesses, which borrowed and invested some 12 percent of GDP during the bubble days, were paying down debt to the tune of 10 percent of GDP by 2003 (Figure 2) in response to a staggering 87 percent decline in nationwide commercial real estate values. In effect, corporate deleveraging resulted in a loss of domestic demand equivalent to 22 percent of GDP. But the Japanese government managed to keep GDP at above the bubble peak throughout this period (Figure 3) by borrowing and spending the aforementioned $100. This fiscal action kept the unemployment rate

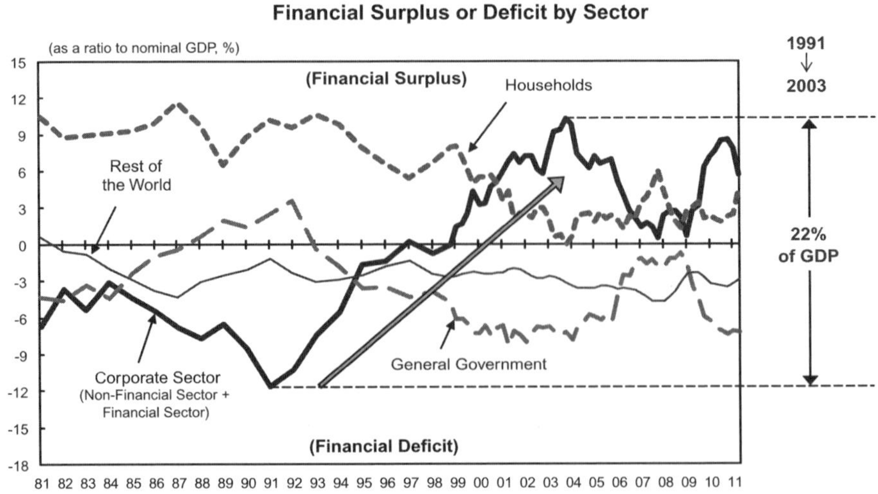

Figure 2. Japan's Corporate Sector Increased Savings Massively after the Bubble.

Note: For the latest figures, 4 quarter averages ending with 2Q/11' are used.
Sources: Bank of Japan, *Flow of Funds Accounts*, and Government of Japan, Cabinet Office, *National Accounts*.

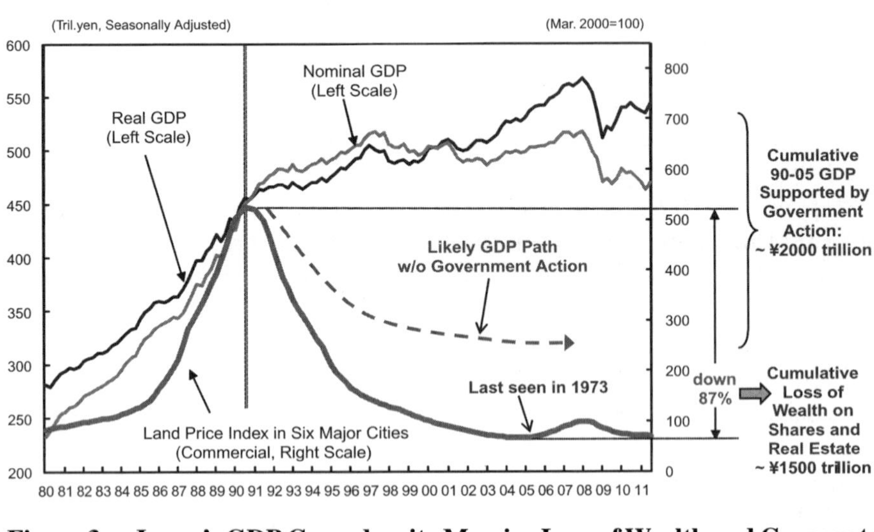

Figure 3. Japan's GDP Grew despite Massive Loss of Wealth and Corporate Deleveraging.

Sources: Cabinet Office, Japan Real Estate Institute.

from rising above 5.5 percent and allowed the private sector to finish paying down debt by 2005. Although this fiscal action increased government debt by 460 trillion yen, or 92 percent of GDP, between 1990 and 2005, it was a tremendous bargain because it managed to sustain over 2,000 trillion yen of GDP compared with a depression scenario.

In the Eurozone, Spain, Ireland, and Portugal are facing serious balance sheet recessions with massive increases in private savings since 2008. Flow-of-funds data show that Spain's private sector has increased savings to the tune of 18 percent of GDP since the Lehman shock (Figure 4). For Ireland, the figure is over 29 percent of GDP (Figure 5), and for Portugal, 8 percent (Figure 6). The corresponding numbers for the U.S. and the UK are 9 percent and 8 percent, respectively. In other words, these countries are no longer low-savings countries. Instead, they are in need of substantial fiscal stimulus to counter deflationary pressures coming from private-sector deleveraging.

But the Maastricht Treaty, which never envisioned a world of balance sheet recessions, capped fiscal deficits at 3 percent of GDP. Although this limit was temporarily suspended in 2009 to address the economic collapse

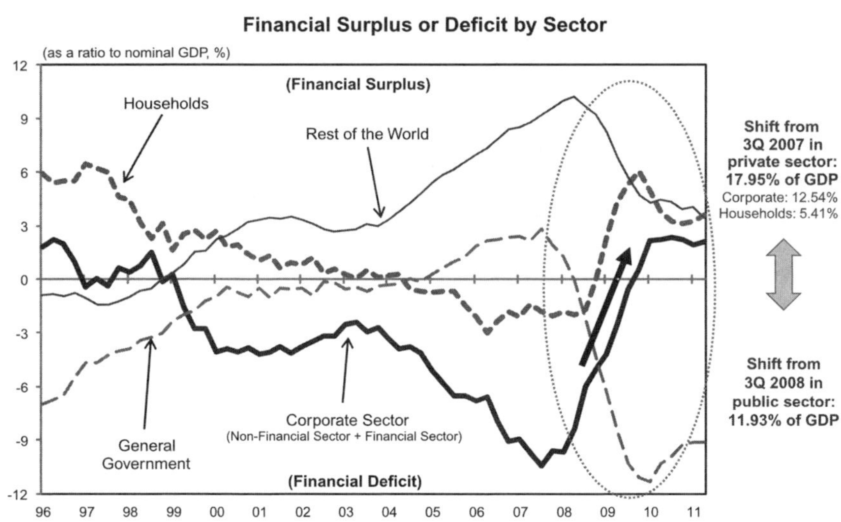

Figure 4. Private Sector in Spain is Increasing Savings despite Record Low Interest Rates.

Note: For the latest figures, 4 quarter averages ending with 2Q/11' are used.
Source: Banco de España.

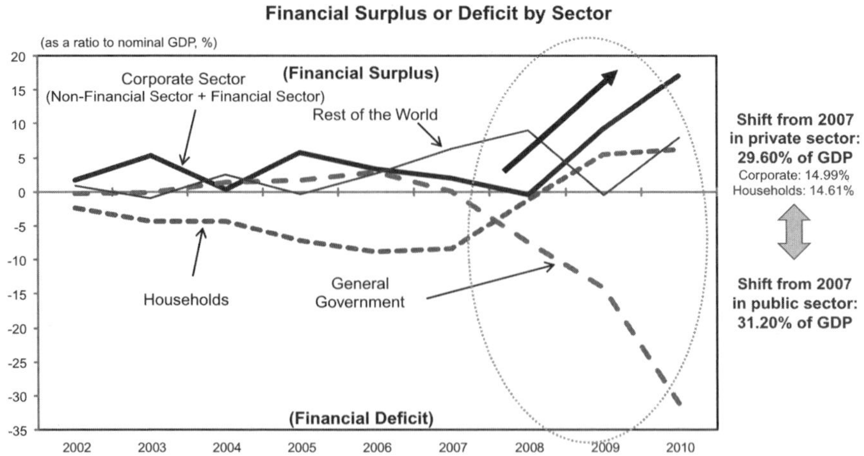

Figure 5. Private Sector in Ireland is Increasing Savings despite Record Low Interest Rates.

Sources: Eurostat, Central Statistics Office, Ireland.

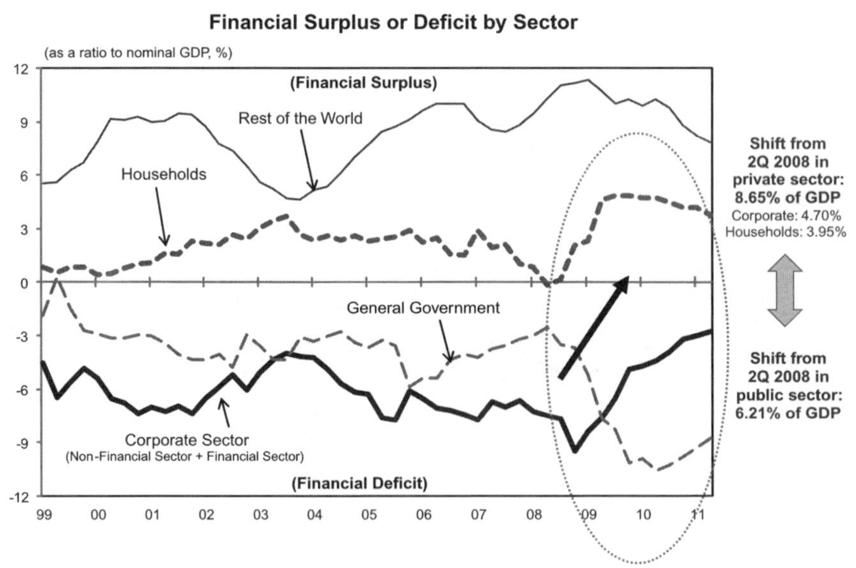

Figure 6. Private Sector in Portugal is Increasing Savings despite Record Low Interest Rates.

Note: For the latest figures, 4 quarter averages ending with 2Q/11' are used.
Source: Banco de Portugal.

triggered by the failure of Lehman Brothers, all countries were forced into fiscal austerity by 2010, triggering deflationary spirals in all of these countries.

Similar attempts by the Japanese government to reduce deficits while the private sector was deleveraging in 1997 and 2001 also precipitated deflationary spirals and ultimately resulted in *larger* deficits. The 1997 policy misstep led to five quarters of negative growth and increased Japan's fiscal deficit by 68 percent, from 22 trillion yen in 1996 to 38 trillion yen in 1999. It took the country 10 years to climb out of the resulting hole (Figure 7). Japan would have come out of its balance sheet recession much faster and at a significantly lower cost than the 460 trillion yen noted above had it not implemented the austerity measures. The U.S. made the same mistake (of premature fiscal consolidation) in 1937, with equally devastating results.

To correct this problem, the Maastricht Treaty must be revised so that countries suffering from balance sheet recessions are allowed, if not encouraged, to implement sufficient fiscal stimulus to stabilize their economies.

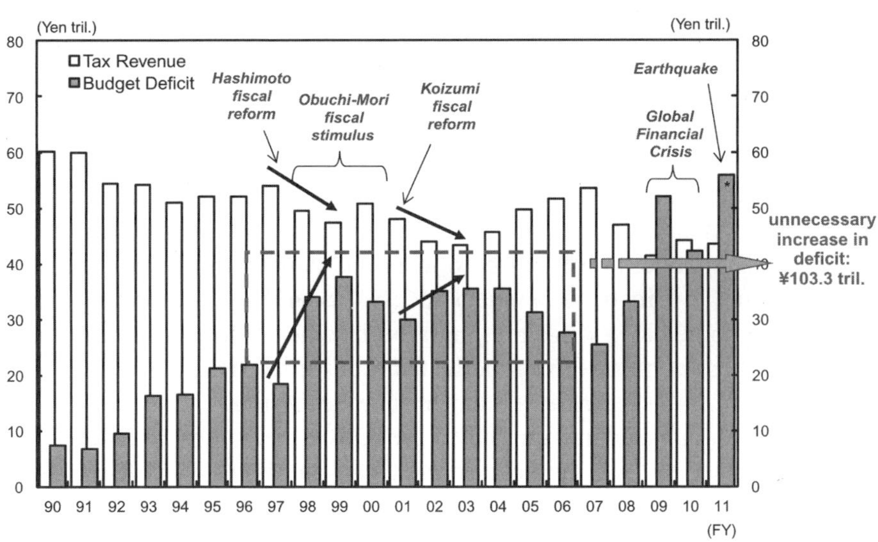

Figure 7. Premature Fiscal Reforms in 1997 and 2001 Weakened Economy, Reduced Tax Revenue and *Increased* Deficit.

Source: Ministry of Finance, Japan.

*estimated by MOF.

2. Destabilizing Intra-Eurozone Capital Flows

The recent crisis has also indicated that one more regulation is needed to make the currency zone work properly — a rule to address the destabilizing capital flows that are unique to the Eurozone.

Contrary to popular belief, there is no sovereign debt crisis; there is only a Eurozone sovereign debt crisis. This can be easily seen from the fact that government bond yields in non-Eurozone countries facing balance sheet recessions with similar budget and current account deficits have dropped to historically low levels. U.S. and UK bond yields, for example, have fallen to record lows in spite of massive current account and budget deficits. Japanese bond yields fell at one point to the lowest in human history even though government debt was approaching 200 percent of GDP and the country's credit rating was for a time lower than that of Botswana.

Once the concept of balance sheet recessions is understood, it is easy to see why ultra-low government bond yields are a natural outcome of this type of recession. During a balance sheet recession, when the private sector is deleveraging despite interest rates close to zero, fund managers entrusted with those deleveraged funds are unable to place them with the private sector since the private sector as a whole is not borrowing money. If the fund managers are also restricted from incurring foreign exchange risk and must buy securities with principal guarantees — meaning no equities or foreign bonds — they have no choice but to buy domestic government bonds. That forces bond yields down to exceptionally low levels, which is the market's way of telling the government that the economy is in a balance sheet recession and that it is no time to try to reduce the budget deficit.

In the Eurozone, however, the opposite is happening. Bond yields in countries that are in balance sheet recessions and are generating large amounts of domestic savings are going up instead of down. That, in turn, has forced these countries to adopt the fiscal austerity measures that should be avoided at all costs during a balance sheet recession.

This funding problem, unique to the Eurozone, stems from the fact that fund managers in a member country can buy bonds issued by *other* Eurozone governments without taking on foreign exchange risk. A Spanish fund manager can buy German government bonds, and an Irish fund manager can buy Dutch government bonds.

When concerns are expressed about a member country's budget deficit, therefore, funds start flowing out of that country to government bonds perceived as being safer, in the present case German and Dutch government bonds. That outflow increases bond yields in the country in question and forces the government to pursue fiscal austerity. But that is the worst possible policy during a balance sheet recession because it triggers the $1,000–$900–$810–$730 deflationary spiral mentioned above.

The deteriorating economy triggers a vicious cycle by making it more difficult for the government to trim the deficit and prompting even more domestic savings to flee the country. In other words, Eurozone countries in balance sheet recessions are unable to tap their own savings needed to finance fiscal stimulus because those savings are fleeing to safer markets. My worst fears were confirmed on a trip to Madrid in mid-November 2011, when I found that almost every fund manager I met was moving funds out of Spain to Germany.

This capital flight would not be a major problem for the broader Eurozone if recipients borrowed and spent those funds to improve their economies. For example, if the German government took advantage of the fund inflows to deliver more fiscal stimulus, that could create a trickle-down effect in the form of German tourists deciding to spend more time in Spain. Unfortunately, the German government is not only pursuing fiscal austerity on its own but is also forcing other countries to add balanced-budget amendments to their constitutions. Similarly, the German private sector has chosen not to borrow and invest more in spite of the lower interest rates brought about by capital inflows (Figure 8). As a result, the entire Eurozone is shuffling towards a contractionary equilibrium.

These highly destabilizing intra-zone capital flows are nothing new, of course. Five to ten years ago, the capital flows were headed in the opposite direction as French and German banks sought higher yields free of foreign exchange risk by lending to Greece and Spain. The German banks *had* to lend to foreigners because the German private sector had increased its savings to nearly 10 percent of GDP since the telecom bubble burst in 2000, but its government refused to borrow beyond the Maastricht-imposed limit of 3 percent of GDP.

At the time, peripheral countries were able to offer higher returns because they were in the midst of real estate bubbles. And the bubble was in response to the ECB bringing interest rates down to the post-War low of 2 percent by 2003 in order to save the German economy. The resulting inflows from France and Germany aggravated those bubbles by keeping interest rates lower than otherwise.

In short, the Eurozone suffers from an unusual pattern of capital flows that contributes to the formation of bubbles during the upswing but hampers

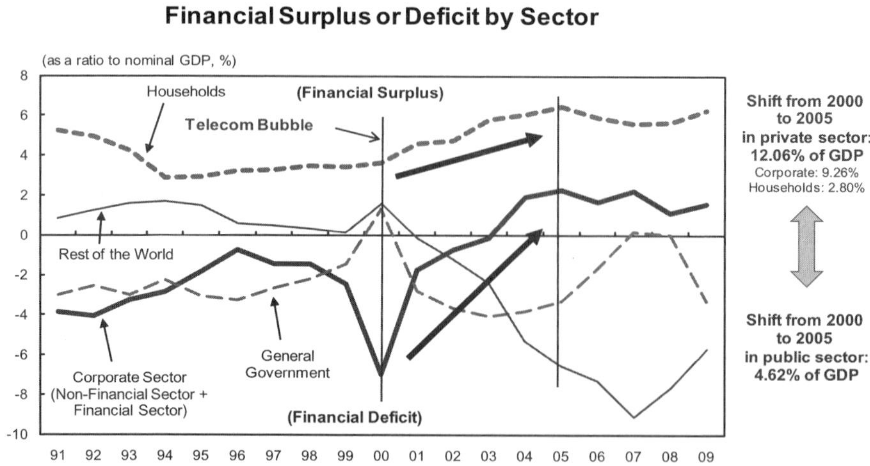

Figure 8. After 2000 Telecom Bubble, German Private Sector Has Been Increasing Savings despite Low Interest Rates.

Note: The assumption of Treuhand agency's debt by the Redemption Fund for Inherited Liabilities in 1995 is adjusted.

Sources: Deutsche Bundesbank, Federal Statistical Office, Germany.

corrective measures — i.e., fiscal stimulus — once the bubble bursts. Measures must be introduced to contain these destructive capital flows if the Eurozone is to be saved.

3. An Endgame Solution

One way to do this would be to announce that, after a transition period of perhaps five to ten years, member governments will be allowed to sell bonds only to their own citizens. For example, Greece would be permitted to sell its debt only to Greek nationals.

Such a rule would provide national governments with both fiscal discipline and fiscal flexibility and prevent a repeat of the kind of problems facing the Eurozone today. It would restore fiscal discipline because governments would not be able to run deficits larger than their citizens tolerate. It would also provide fiscal flexibility by allowing governments to run larger deficits if they could convince their citizens of the need for those deficits. This is of critical importance during a balance sheet recession, when a larger deficit may be necessary to stabilize the economy.

Most importantly, this rule would keep destabilizing capital flows in check by preventing Spanish savings from fleeing to German government bonds because Spanish citizens would no longer be allowed to purchase those bonds. Given the large surplus of private sector savings in Spain, that alone would bring Spanish government bond yields down to levels comparable to those in the U.S. or UK. No one would be talking about a Spanish sovereign debt crisis if yields were at historically low levels.

The same would be true in Ireland. Portuguese yields would also come down, although perhaps not to the extent of Spain or Ireland, because its corporate sector is still borrowing money (albeit much less than during the bubble era).

This rule would also prevent fiscal problems in one nation from threatening the broader currency area by making fiscal policy an internal issue of individual countries. If the Greek government were to default, for example, it would only be a problem for the Greek public and could be considered separately from the health of the Eurozone as a whole. This would free the ECB from having to worry about the fiscal health of member governments and allow it to concentrate on managing monetary policy.

Moreover, this rule would change the tenor of the national political debate. Protesters in the streets of various capitals could no longer blame everything on bureaucrats in Brussels or on the fat, rich bankers of Germany and France. Instead, they will have to redirect their energies to convince their relatives and friends to buy more government bonds of their own countries.

Although this rule would constitute a kind of capital control, limiting the sale of government bonds to citizens represents a minimal constraint on the free movement of capital because Eurozone citizens would still be able to buy corporate paper of other member countries, which is where the efficiency gains from free capital movements really matter. Indeed, it is difficult to see what kind of efficiency gain is obtained by allowing German banks to buy Greek government bonds. On the contrary, German bank purchases of Greek government bonds allowed the latter to run an ever more profligate fiscal policy which, in the end, resulted in diminished economic gains for everyone. Since government bonds always offer the lowest yields, the inability to buy another member nation's bonds will not be a great loss to residents of the Eurozone.

Artificial constraints are required to maintain the artificial currency zone called the Eurozone. The Maastricht Treaty's 3 percent cap on fiscal deficits as a percentage of GDP represented a first attempt at such a constraint. The current crisis, however, has made it clear that this constraint is incapable of addressing a balance sheet recession or destabilizing capital flows. Replacing the 3 percent cap with a rule stating that only domestic investors may buy government bonds would restore fiscal discipline in these countries and enable authorities to respond appropriately to balance sheet recessions.

The ECB, of course, should be able to buy and sell the government bonds of member countries as part of the conduct of monetary policy. Foreign governments and international organizations should also be allowed to purchase member countries' debt. But no private-sector entities should be allowed to buy the government debt of another member country if destabilizing capital flows are to be prevented.

It has been argued that fiscal union is the real answer to the Eurozone crisis. But this will require an enhanced political union that could take years, if not decades, to achieve. If the first-best solution is not realistic at present, policymakers will have to decide among all other options which policy is the second-best. The rule limiting the issuance of government bonds to own citizens is likely to be a strong candidate in this race for the second-best solution because of its simplicity.

4. Navigating the Transition Period

If this rule had been in place from the outset of the euro, none of today's problems would have happened. Unfortunately, the euro operated without such a rule for more than a decade, during which time massive imbalances developed. Foreigners, for example, now hold some 70 percent of Greece's liabilities. Many countries will require time to migrate from the present regime to one in which government bonds are sold only to citizens, hence the need for a transition period.

The first order of business for policymakers in this transition period should be to end forced fiscal consolidation for economies in balance sheet recessions. For Ireland, Spain, and other countries, a new diagnosis must be offered together with a new schedule of treatment. The EU and the ECB should announce that because of massive private sector deleveraging at a time of record low interest rates, these countries are in balance sheet recessions and require large fiscal stimuli to stabilize their economies. This official blessing is absolutely essential because capital flight will only accelerate without it. These institutions should also make it clear that they stand ready to help.

In addition, they should announce that after five years (or longer if necessary), bonds issued by member countries will be sold only to their citizens. Such a commitment should go a long way toward assuring the international financial community that the countries are serious about rebuilding their finances. It would also signal that destabilizing intra-Eurozone capital flows will eventually come to an end and that the current crisis will not be repeated. (If the above segregation of national government bond markets from the rest of the single market is too much of a change, Eurozone could achieve a similar result with an introduction of favorable risk weights for holding domestic government bonds and less favorable risk weights for holding non-domestic government bonds.)

The authorities should also highlight the often overlooked fact that these countries are actually generating huge amounts of private savings as businesses and households deleverage. Like the U.S. and the UK, Spain and Ireland are now experiencing a massive increase in savings that can finance a substantial portion of their government deficits. Indeed, these countries are in recession precisely because their private sectors are increasing savings faster than their governments can borrow and spend.

Unfortunately, raising taxes and cutting spending is the only game in town in Europe today. For countries in balance sheet recessions, that game is resulting in devastatingly vicious cycles: The Spanish unemployment rate has climbed above 21 percent, and Irish GDP is down 10 percent from its peak. As long as fiscal consolidation is the only policy being pursued, bond investors *should* be worried because premature fiscal retrenchment during a balance sheet recession will only make things worse.

Once a different diagnosis is offered, together with a pledge that past mistakes will not be repeated, bond investors are likely to realize that the vicious cycle is finally behind them and that a well-defined endgame is now in sight. That may make yields on some countries' bonds sufficiently attractive for buyers, especially with both the EU and ECB pledging to provide support. That, in turn, should give both markets and individual countries the breathing space they need to make necessary adjustments.

5. ECB Could Buy More Government Bonds to Counter Lender-Side Problems

Given the extent to which the crisis has already torn up the financial fabric of the Eurozone, however, the announcement of a new roadmap and endgame may not be enough to restore order. A "bazooka" may be needed to turn the tide. Current efforts to increase the EFSF's firepower should be continued, but the ECB may have to play a larger role as well.

It was argued above that monetary policy is largely impotent during a balance sheet recession, which is a borrower's problem. But during a financial crisis, which is primarily a lender's problem, monetary policy must be mobilized to the fullest extent possible to prevent a collapse of the financial system.

Financial institutions holding debt issued by Europe's periphery nations are currently seeing their credit suffer and their ratings downgraded, hindering access to market funding and creating an added impetus to sell their sovereign debt holdings. But the more they sell, the higher yields rise. That aggravates both the financial crisis, centering on the banks, and the fiscal crisis, which involves governments. In an emergency like this, the ECB may have to use its balance sheet to intervene, much like the Federal Reserve intervened in the mortgage-backed securities market to restart the flow of money after Lehman Brothers failed.

The question then becomes how much Eurozone government debt the ECB can buy without sparking inflation. The quantitative easing experiences of Japan, the U.S., and the UK suggest the answer is "very much indeed."

When the private sector as a whole is trying to minimize debt (despite ultra-low interest rates) in a balance sheet recession, the money multiplier for the private sector turns negative at the margin. In other words, no amount of quantitative easing by the central bank will increase the money supply. And without growth in the money supply, there can be no inflation.

After Japan's bubble burst, the Bank of Japan increased its supply of liquidity more than 200 percent compared with 1990 by buying Japanese government bonds. In spite of that action, the money supply grew only modestly, and the inflation rate actually turned negative.

In the U.S., the Fed more than tripled its monetary base in the wake of the Lehman collapse with QE1 and QE2. But instead of a 200 percent inflation rate, the result was a barely perceptible increase in the money supply and absolutely no pick-up in inflation.

The Bank of England also responded to the Lehman crisis with a bold program of quantitative easing under which liquidity increased by some 170 percent. As in the U.S. and Japan, however, money supply growth remained depressed and the rate of core inflation increased only marginally.

This experience suggests that no matter how much liquidity the central bank provides during a balance sheet recession by buying government

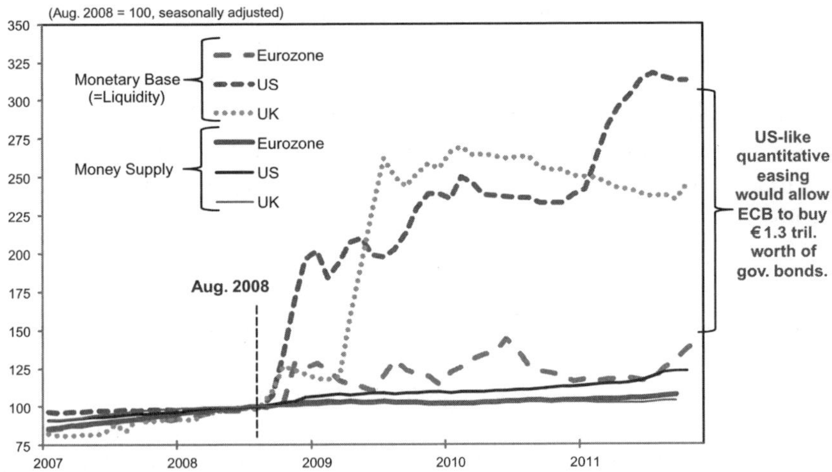

Figure 9. ECB Can Increase Bond Purchases and Liquidity Provision without Increasing Money Supply or Inflation.

Notes: 1. UK's reserve balances data are seasonally unadjusted.
2. UK's money supply and bank lending data exclude intermediate financial institutions.
3. Base money's figures of Eurozone are seasonally adjusted by Nomura Research Institute.

Source: Nomura Research Institute, based on FRB, ECB and Bank of England data.

debt, it will increase neither the money supply nor the inflation rate. There is therefore no reason why the ECB, which also faces a balance sheet recession, cannot follow the lead of central banks in Japan, the U.S., and the UK, and buy more government securities.

The BOJ increased its supply of liquidity by 206 percent between 1990 and 2006, and the corresponding figures for the Fed and the BOE were 217 percent (2008–2011) and 169 percent (2008–2010), respectively. In contrast, the increase in ECB-supplied liquidity between 2008 and 2011 was only 43 percent (Figure 9). It is difficult for the ECB to justify pulling back on the liquidity spigot in the midst of a financial crisis and balance sheet recession with no risk of inflation.

The ECB should embark on a quantitative easing program similar in scale to those undertaken by Japan, the U.S., and the UK. The ECB has provided a total of €1.3 trillion in liquidity since its inception. If the U.S.

experience is any guide, it could buy an additional €1.3 trillion in Eurozone government bonds without having to worry about inflation. That would be seven times the total of €186.8 billion in government debt the ECB had purchased during this crisis as of November 11, 2011. Purchases on that scale would almost certainly be enough to stabilize the government bond market whilst providing sufficient liquidity to relieve the stress in the banking system.

This would effectively be a form of financial stabilization that uses the balance sheet recession to its advantage (if the Eurozone were not in such a recession, such large purchases of government debt by the central bank would spark massive inflation). As long as the ECB is willing, therefore, it has the power to do a great deal to address the lender-side problems.

The German government is currently opposed to an expansion of the ECB's role out of concerns about inflation. But its objections would probably fade if German policymakers studied the examples of Japan, the U.S., and the UK, and realized that in a balance sheet recession there is no reason why central bank purchases of government debt must lead to inflation.

The ECB will have to divest its government bond holdings in order to avoid inflation once private-sector demand for funds returns. However, past balance sheet recessions, such as the Great Depression in the U.S. and the post-1990 recession in Japan, suggest that it may take years before that becomes necessary.

This is because the private sector, having gone through a painful deleveraging process, may not want to borrow money again for a very long time. This kind of debt-induced trauma is what kept U.S. interest rates so low for three decades after the Depression. The same trauma is keeping Japanese interest rates low even though Japanese balance sheets were cleaned up long ago. The Bank of Japan was so worried about inflation that it ended quantitative easing and its zero-interest-rate policy as soon as Japan's private sector repaired its balance sheet in 2006, only to take interest rates back to zero after discovering that the post-deleveraging recovery in funds demand was miniscule. The ECB is likely to find that a large portion of its government bond holdings will mature long before it has to divest those bonds.

There should also be plenty of time to repair government balance sheets once the crisis is behind us because the next balance sheet recession of this magnitude is likely to be decades away. This is because those of us who remember the current recession will not make the same mistake twice, which means the next bubble and balance sheet recession are unlikely to occur in our lifetimes. Balance sheet recessions, like nationwide debt-financed bubbles, are rare. But when they do happen, the government must act decisively with substantial and sustained fiscal stimulus until the private sector returns to health.

6. Conclusion

The original Maastricht Treaty assumed, in line with neoclassical economics taught in schools, that the private sector is healthy and always maximizing profits. As a result, the treaty never considered the possibility of balance sheet recessions. Nor did it anticipate the destabilizing intra-Eurozone capital flows discussed above.

But when the private sector is paying down debt in spite of zero interest rates, a scenario seldom discussed at business schools or in the economics literature, the private sector is very sick and in need of help. That help can come only from the public sector in the form of the aforementioned \$100. The forced removal of that help as mandated by the treaty led to self-destructive policy responses in many member countries.

The Eurozone was not created to offer member governments greater opportunity to run irresponsible deficits. The Eurozone can satisfy this need for more fiscal discipline *and* attain the flexibility needed to fight balance sheet recessions while reining in procyclical capital flows by first announcing that member countries will limit the sale of government bonds to their own citizens after a transition period and then working out a path to get there for individual countries.

For countries in balance sheet recessions, such as Ireland and Spain, it will have to be a two-stage process in which fiscal policy is mobilized until private-sector balance sheets are repaired. Once the private sector resumes maximizing profit instead of minimizing debt, the public sector can begin the fiscal consolidation process. For Greece, where private-sector deleveraging has been minimal, the government will have to reduce its fiscal deficit during the transition period to a level that can be financed domestically.

The EU and ECB should also make it clear that they stand ready to help during the transition. It is essential that these organizations give their blessing to the new roadmap because the destabilizing capital flight out of distressed countries will only accelerate without it. Once the new endgame is announced, with full support from the EU, ECB and, if possible, the IMF, private investors should feel much safer returning to the markets as the risk of an endless vicious cycle is eliminated.

In retrospect, limiting the sales of government bonds to citizens should have been a provision of the Maastricht Treaty from the outset. If all member countries had adopted this rule in 2000 instead of the 3 percent deficit cap, none of the current problems would have happened.

Revising the treaty will not be easy. But given that the alternative could be a breakup of the euro that could have devastating consequences, it is well worth trying to make the treaty more responsive to balance sheet recessions while ending destabilizing capital flows.

Reference

Koo, Richard, 2008, *The Holy Grail of Macroeconomics: Lessons from Japan's Great Recession*, Singapore: John Wiley & Sons.

Macroprudential and Monetary Policies

Frederic S. Mishkin*
Columbia University

1. Introduction

As a result of the global financial crisis from 2007 to 2009, academics and policymakers have been rethinking their approaches to both prudential and monetary policies to avoid the high costs of a financial crisis like the one we have recently experienced. In my remarks here on where policy should head in the future, I first look at the views before the crisis and then I will discuss what lessons we have learned from the crisis. Finally, I will address what these lessons imply for how we should conduct both macroprudential policy and monetary policy.

2. Views Before the Crisis

Even before the crisis, both academics and central bankers were aware that financial disruptions could have a serious negative impact on the economy. Ensuring the safety and soundness of the financial system was therefore viewed as an important policy objective, but the focus was on *microprudential* policies, which focus on the safety and soundness of *individual* institutions, and not the financial system as a whole. Furthermore, the standard view was that there was a dichotomy between monetary and prudential policies. The general equilibrium modelling frameworks used both in academia and at central banks did not incorporate financial frictions as a major source of business cycle fluctuations. This naturally led to the dichotomy between

*Frederic S. Mishkin is the Alfred Lerner Professor of Banking and Financial Institutions at the Graduate School of Business, Columbia University, and a research associate at the National Bureau of Economic Research. The views expressed here are those of the author and not necessarily those of Columbia University or the National Bureau of Economic Research.

monetary policy and financial stability policy, in which these two types of policies were conducted separately. Monetary policy instruments would focus on minimizing inflation and output gaps. It would then be up to prudential regulation and supervision to prevent excessive risk-taking that could promote financial instability.

Although I would say that most of the economics profession and central bankers supported the dichotomy between monetary policy and financial stability policy, there were views that monetary policy should address financial stability issues, particularly as regards responding to potential asset price bubbles.

The clear-cut dangers of asset price bubbles led some economists before the crisis, both inside and outside central banks, to argue that central banks should at times "lean against the wind" by raising interest rates to stop bubbles from getting out of hand (e.g., Borio and Lowe, 2002; Borio and White, 2003; and White, 2004). They argued that raising interest rates to slow a bubble's growth would produce better outcomes because it would either prevent the bubble or result in a less severe bursting of the bubble, with far less damage to the economy.

The opposing view to the "leaning against the wind" view that asset prices should have a special role in the conduct of monetary policy over and above that implied by their foreseeable effect on inflation and employment is often referred to as the "Greenspan doctrine," because, when chairman of the Federal Reserve Board, he strenuously argued that monetary policy should not try to lean against asset price bubbles, but rather should just clean up after they burst (Greenspan, 2002). There are several elements of this argument.

First, bubbles are hard to detect. In order to justify leaning against an asset price bubble, a central bank must assume that it can identify when asset prices have deviated from fundamental values. That assumption was viewed as highly dubious because it is hard to believe that the central bank has such an informational advantage over private markets. If the central bank has no informational advantage, and if it knows that a bubble has developed, the market will almost surely know this too, and the bubble will burst. Thus, any bubble that could be identified with certainty by the central bank would be unlikely ever to develop much further.

A second objection against leaning against bubbles is that raising interest rates may be very ineffective in restraining the bubble, because market participants expect such high rates of return from buying bubble-driven assets.

A third objection is that there are many asset prices, and at any one time a bubble may be present in only a fraction of assets. Monetary policy actions are a very blunt instrument in such a case, as such actions would be likely to affect asset prices in general, rather than solely those in a bubble.

Fourth, although some theoretical models suggested that raising interest rates could diminish the acceleration of asset prices, others suggest that raising interest rates would cause a bubble to burst more severely, thus doing even more damage to the economy (Bernanke, Gertler, and Gilchrist, 1999; Greenspan, 2002; Gruen, Plumb, and Stone, 2005; and Kohn, 2006). This view was supported by historical examples, such as the monetary tightening that occurred in 1928 and 1929 in the United States and 1989 in Japan, suggesting that raising interest rates may cause a bubble to burst more severely, thereby increasing the damage to the economy (Hamilton, 1987; Cargill, Hutchison, and Ito, 1995; Jinushi, Kuroki, and Miyao, 2000; and Posen, 2003). Another way of saying this is that bubbles are departures from normal behavior, and it is unrealistic to expect that the usual tools of monetary policy will be effective in abnormal conditions.

Particularly important was the view that the monetary authorities had the tools to keep the harmful effects of a bursting bubble at a manageable level, as long as they respond in a timely fashion. This was true even if interest rates fell and approached the zero lower bound, and so the conventional tool of lowering the policy interest rate was no longer an option. In this situation, the economy could be stimulated by either: (1) managing expectations so that the policy rate would be viewed as staying low for an extended period, thereby lowering long-term interest rates; (2) risk and term premiums could be lowered by purchasing securities, thereby changing their relative supply; and (3) by exchange rate interventions to lower the value of the domestic currency, thereby increasing foreign demand for domestic production.

The bottom line from this analysis was that the cost of leaning against asset price bubbles was likely to be high, while the costs of a bursting bubble could be kept low. Instead of trying to lean against bubbles, this analysis supported an approach in which central banks just clean up after the bubble afterward. This approach was fully consistent with monetary policy focusing on stabilizing inflation and employment without a special focus on asset price bubbles.

3. Lessons from the Crisis

The global financial crisis undermined one of the key linchpins of the argument for the Greenspan doctrine that the cost of cleaning up after an asset price bubble burst would be low. To the contrary, there is now a recognition that the cost of cleaning up after an asset price bubble bursts can be very high if it is followed by a financial crisis.

Besides the obvious cost of a huge loss of aggregate output as a result of the worldwide recession, the global financial crisis suggests that there are likely to be additional costs that will raise the costs far higher. First, financial crises are typically followed by very slow growth, and second, the budgetary positions of governments sharply deteriorate.

When economies experience deep recessions, the typical experience is that they subsequently have very strong recoveries, often referred to as V-shaped recoveries. However, as Reinhart and Reinhart (2010) document, this V-shaped pattern is not characteristic of recessions that follow financial crises because the deleveraging process takes a long time, resulting in strong headwinds for the economy. We now recognize that the cumulative output of losses from financial crises is massive, and this current crisis is no exception.

As pointed out by Reinhart and Rogoff (2009), the aftermath of financial crises is almost always a sharp increase in government indebtedness. We have seen exactly this situation in the aftermath of the current crisis. The massive bailouts of financial institutions, fiscal stimulus packages, and the sharp economic contractions that reduced tax revenue, which occurred throughout the world, have adversely affected the fiscal situation for many countries. Budget deficits over 10% of GDP in advanced countries like the United States have become common. Furthermore, this rise in indebtedness has the potential to lead to sovereign debt defaults, which has become a serious concern in Europe. The fiscal retrenchments required to put fiscal balances on a sustainable path are likely to not only be contractionary, but also will increase societal stress. Indeed, there is even a possibility that the fiscal problems brought on by the crisis could lead to a demise of the euro.

The high cost of cleaning up after asset price bubble bursts has led to major rethinking on the lean versus clean debate. The lean versus clean debate initially had a lot of its focus on whether monetary policy should react to potential asset price bubbles. However, given the interaction between the housing price bubble and credit markets in the run-up to the global financial crisis, there is now a recognition that we need to distinguish between two different types of asset price bubbles.

As I pointed out in Mishkin (2010), not all asset price bubbles are alike. Financial history and the financial crisis of 2007–2009 indicate that one type of bubble, which is best referred to as a *credit-driven bubble*, can be highly dangerous. With this type of bubble, there is the following typical chain of events: Because of either exuberant expectations about economic prospects or structural changes in financial markets, a credit boom begins, increasing the demand for some assets and thereby raising their prices. The rise in asset values, in turn, encourages further lending against these assets, increasing demand, and hence their prices, even more. This feedback loop can generate a bubble, and the bubble can cause credit standards to ease as lenders become less concerned about the ability of the borrowers to repay loans and instead rely on further appreciation of the asset to shield themselves from losses.

At some point, however, the bubble bursts. The collapse in asset prices then leads to a reversal of the feedback loop, in which loans go sour, lenders cut back on credit supply, the demand for the assets declines further, and prices drop even more. The resulting loan losses and declines in asset prices erode the balance sheets at financial institutions, further diminishing credit and investment across a broad range of assets. The decline in lending depresses business and household spending, which weakens economic activity and increases macroeconomic risk in credit markets. In the extreme, the interaction between asset prices and the health of financial institutions following the collapse of an asset price bubble can endanger the operation of the financial system as a whole.

However, there is a second type of bubble that is far less dangerous, which can be referred to as an *irrational exuberance bubble*. This type of bubble is driven solely by overly optimistic expectations and poses much less risk to the financial system than credit-driven bubbles. For example, the bubble in technology stocks in the late 1990s was not fueled by a feedback loop between bank lending and rising equity values, and so the bursting of the tech stock bubble was not accompanied by a marked deterioration in bank balance sheets. The bursting of the tech stock bubble thus did not have a very severe impact on the economy, and the recession that followed was quite mild.

The recent crisis has clearly demonstrated that the bursting of credit-driven bubbles not only can be extremely costly, but are very hard to clean up after. Furthermore, bubbles of this type can occur even if there is price and output stability in the period leading up to them. Indeed, price and output stability might actually encourage credit-driven bubbles because it leads market participants to underestimate the amount of risk in the economy. The case for leaning against potential bubbles rather than cleaning up afterward has therefore become much stronger.

However, the distinction between the two types of bubbles, one which (credit-driven) is much more costly than the other, suggests that the lean versus clean debate may have been miscast. Rather than leaning against potential asset price bubbles, which would include both credit-driven and irrational exuberance-type bubbles, there is a much stronger case for leaning against credit bubbles that would involve leaning against credit-driven bubbles, but not irrational exuberance bubbles. As White (2009) and Mishkin (2010) have pointed out, it is much easier to identify credit bubbles than it is to identify asset price bubbles. Financial regulators and central banks often have information that lenders have weakened their underwriting standards, that risk premiums appear to be inordinately low, or that credit extension is rising at abnormally high rates. The argument that it is hard to identify asset price bubbles is therefore not a valid argument against leaning against credit bubbles.

4. Macroprudential Policy

Although there is a strong case to lean against credit bubbles, what policies will be most effective? First, it is important to recognize that the key principle for designing effective policies to lean against credit bubbles is whether they fix market failures. Credit extension necessarily involves risk-taking. It is only when this risk-taking is excessive because of market failures that credit bubbles are likely to develop. Recognizing that market failures are the problem, it is natural to look to prudential regulatory measures to constrain credit bubbles.

Some of these regulatory measures are simply the usual elements of a well-functioning prudential regulatory and supervisory system. These elements include adequate disclosure and capital requirements, liquidity requirements, prompt corrective action, careful monitoring of an institution's risk-management procedures, close supervision of financial institutions to enforce compliance with regulations, and sufficient resources and accountability for supervisors.

The standard measures mentioned above focus on promoting the safety and soundness of *individual* firms and fall into the category of what is referred to as *microprudential* policies. However, even if individual firms are operating prudently, there still is a danger of excessive risk-taking because of the interactions between financial firms that promote externalities. An alternative regulatory approach, which deals with these interactions, focuses on what is happening in credit markets in the aggregate, referred to as *macroprudential* policies.

Macroprudential policies can be used to dampen the interaction between asset price bubbles and credit provision. For example, research has shown that the rise in asset values that accompanies a boom results in higher capital buffers at financial institutions, supporting further lending in the context of an unchanging benchmark for capital adequacy; in the bust, the value of this capital can drop precipitously, possibly even necessitating a cut in lending (e.g., Kashyap and Stein, 1994; and Adrian and Shin, 2009). It is important for research to continue to analyze the role of bank capital requirements in promoting financial stability, including whether capital requirements should be adjusted over the business cycle. Other macroprudential policies to constrain credit bubbles include dynamic provisioning by banks, lower ceilings on loan-to-value ratios or higher haircut requirements for repo lending during credit expansions, and Pigouvian-type taxes on certain liabilities of financial institutions (e.g., Bank of England, 2009; and French *et al.*, 2010).

Some policies to address the risks to financial stability from asset price bubbles could be made a standard part of the regulatory system and would be operational at all times — whether a bubble was in progress or not. However, because specific or new types of market failures might be driving a particular credit bubble, there is a case for discretionary prudential policies to limit the market failures in such a case. For example, during certain periods, risks across institutions might become highly correlated and discretionary policy to respond to these higher-stress environments could help reduce systemic risk.

5. Monetary Policy

The fact that the low interest rate policies of the Federal Reserve from 2002 to 2005 were associated with excessive risk-taking suggests to many that overly easy monetary policy might promote financial instability. Using aggregate data, Taylor (2007) has argued that excessively low policy rates led to the housing bubble, while Bernanke (2010); Bean, Paustian, Penalver, and Taylor (2010); Turner (2010); and Posen (2009) have argued otherwise.

Although it is far from clear that the Federal Reserve is to blame for the housing bubble, the explosion of microeconomic research, both theoretical and empirical, suggests that there is a case for monetary policy to play a role in creating credit bubbles. Borio and Zhu (2008) have called this mechanism the "risk-taking channel of monetary policy."

The literature provides two basic reasons why low interest rates might promote excessive risk-taking. First, as Rajan (2005, 2006) points out, low interest rates can increase the incentives for asset managers in financial institutions to search for yield and hence increase risk-taking. A second mechanism for how low interest rates could promote risk-taking operates through income and valuation effects. If financial firms borrow short and lend long, as is often the case, low interest rates increase net interest margins and the value of these firms, thus increasing their capacity to increase their leverage and take on risk (Adrian and Shin, 2009, 2010; and Adrian, Moench, and Shin, 2010). In addition, low interest rates can boost collateral values, again enabling increased lending.

Monetary policy can also encourage risk-taking in two other ways. Although desirable from a viewpoint of establishing credibility and a strong nominal anchor, which helps stabilize the economy, more predictable monetary policy can reduce uncertainty and contribute to asset managers underestimating risk (Gambacorta, 2009). Monetary policy that cleans up after financial disruptions by lowering interest rates, which has been named the "Greenspan put" because this was the actual and stated policy of the Federal Reserve when Alan Greenspan headed the Fed, can lead to a form of moral hazard in which financial institutions expect monetary policy to help them recover from bad investments (e.g., see Tirole and Farhi, 2009; Keister, 2010; and Wilson and Wu, 2010). The Greenspan put can also increase systemic risk because it is only exercised when many financial firms are in trouble simultaneously and so they may be encouraged to pursue similar investment strategies, thereby increasing the correlation of returns.

Micro empirical analysis provides a fair amount of support for the risk-taking channel of monetary policy (e.g., Jiménez, Ongena, Peydró, and Saurina, 2008; Ioannidou, Ongena, and Peydró, 2009; and Delis and Kouretas, 2010), while Adrian and Shin (2010) provide evidence for the risk-taking channel of monetary policy using more aggregate data.

Given the support for the risk-taking channel, does this mean that monetary policy should be used to lean against credit bubbles? Besides some of the previously listed objections, there is the additional objection that if monetary policy is used to lean against credit bubbles, there is a violation of the Tinbergen (1939) principle, because one instrument is being asked to do two jobs: (1) stabilize the financial sector, and (2) stabilize the economy.[1] Because there is another instrument to stabilize the financial sector — macroprudential supervision — wouldn't it be better to use macroprudential supervision to deal with financial stability, leaving monetary policy to focus on price and output stability?

This argument would be quite strong if macroprudential policies were able to do the job. However, there are doubts on this score. Prudential supervision is often subject to more political pressure than is monetary policy because it affects the bottom line of financial institutions more directly. Thus, they will have greater incentives to lobby politicians to discourage macroprudential policies that would rein in credit bubbles. There will also be strong incentives for financial institutions to think of clever ways to get around macroprudential regulations.

The possibility that macroprudential policies may be circumvented, and so might not be able to constrain credit bubbles, suggests that monetary policy may have to be used as well. But this raises another objection to using monetary policy to lean against credit bubbles: it may not work. I am sympathetic to the view discussed earlier that tightening monetary policy may be ineffective in restraining a particular asset bubble because market participants expect such high rates of return from purchasing bubble-driven assets. On the other hand, the evidence on the risk-taking channel of monetary policy suggests that there is a stronger case that raising interest rates would help restrain lending growth and excessive risk-taking. Furthermore, the theoretical analysis discussed immediately above suggests that if the public believes that the central bank will raise interest rates when a credit bubble looks like it is forming, then expectations in credit markets will work to make this policy more effective. The expectation that rates will go up with increased risk-taking will make this kind of activity less profitable and thus make it less likely that it will occur. Furthermore, expectations that rates will rise with increased risk-taking means that interest rates will *not* have to be raised as much to have their intended effect.

[1] Stabilizing the financial sector is not a completely separate objective from stabilizing the economy because financial instability leads to instability in economic activity and inflation. However, because the dynamics of financial instability is so different than the dynamics of inflation and economic activity, for purposes of the Tinbergen principle, promoting financial stability can be viewed as a separate policy objective from stabilizing the economy.

Nonetheless, using monetary policy to lean against credit bubbles is not a monetary policy strategy that can be taken lightly. Doing so could at times result in a weaker economy than the monetary authorities would desire or inflation that falls below its target. This suggests that there is a monetary policy tradeoff between having the inflation forecast at the target and the pursuit of financial stability. Also, having monetary policy focus on financial stability might lead to confusion about the central bank's commitment to the inflation target, with potentially adverse effects on economic outcomes.

Another danger from having monetary policy as a tool to promote financial stability is that it might lead to decisions to tighten monetary policy when it is not needed to constrain credit bubbles. A situation of low interest rates does not necessarily indicate that monetary policy is promoting excessive risk-taking. One lesson from the analysis here is that policymakers, and especially monetary policymakers, will want tools to assess whether credit bubbles are developing. Research is underway (e.g., see Borio and Lowe, 2002; and Adrian and Shin, 2010) to find measures that will signal if credit bubbles are likely to be forming. High credit growth, increasing leverage, low risk spreads, surging asset prices, and surveys to assess if credit underwriting standards are being eased are pieces of data that can help central banks decide if there is imminent danger of credit bubbles. Monitoring of credit market conditions will become an essential activity of central banks in the future, and research on the best ways of doing so will have a high priority in the future.

This danger of considering using monetary policy to promote financial stability is highly relevant today. Some economists are currently calling for the Federal Reserve to raise interest rates because they argue that the current low rates may be encouraging excessive risk-taking. However, the U.S. economy is currently not in a situation of rapid credit growth, low risk premiums, and increasing leverage. Indeed, it still seems to be mired in a deleveraging cycle that is producing serious headwinds for the economy. This does not mean that the situation cannot change. However, at the current juncture, low interest rates do not appear to be creating the next credit bubble in the United States, and justification for raising them to curb risk-taking is lacking.

On the other hand, many emerging market economies and some advanced economies like Israel are currently in a very different environment because they did not go through a deleveraging cycle such as occurred in the United States and Europe. They thus have the potential for a credit bubble to develop, and low U.S. interest rates are a potential danger because they could promote excessive risk-taking. In these countries, however, the option of tightening monetary policy to restrict risk-taking may not be available because raising interest rates would just encourage capital inflows that could also promote a credit boom. For these countries, the only option may be to pursue macroprudential policies to limit credit growth.

Another lesson learned from the financial crisis and the discussion above is that monetary policy and financial stability policy are intrinsically linked to each other, and so the dichotomy between them is a false one. As we have seen, monetary policy can affect financial stability, while macroprudential policies to promote financial stability can have an impact on monetary policy. If macroprudential policies are implemented to restrain a credit bubble, they will slow credit growth and the growth of aggregate demand. In this case, monetary policy may need to be easier in order to offset weaker aggregate demand.

Alternatively, if policy rates are kept low to stimulate the economy, there is a greater risk that a credit bubble might occur. This may require tighter macroprudential policies to ensure that a credit bubble does not develop. Coordination of monetary and macroprudential policies becomes of greater value when all three objectives of price stability, output stability, and financial stability are to be pursued.

I have argued elsewhere (Mishkin, 2009; and in French *et al.*, 2010) that the recent financial crisis provides strong support for a systemic regulator and that central banks are the natural choice for this role. The benefits of coordination between monetary policy and macroprudential policy provide another reason for having central banks take on the systemic regulator role. Coordination of monetary policy and macroprudential policy is more likely to be effective if one government agency is in charge of both. As anyone who has had the pleasure of experiencing the turf battles between different government agencies knows, coordination of policies is extremely difficult when different entities control these policies.

6. Conclusion

The aftermath of the global financial crisis is that our thinking about prudential and monetary policies will never be the same. This makes the job of a central bank that much more complicated because it will not only need to focus on what monetary policy is appropriate to stabilize inflation and economic activity, but will also need to design macroprudential and monetary policies to make financial crises less likely and worry about the interaction between them.

References

Adrian, Tobias and Hyun Shin, 2009, "Money, liquidity and monetary policy," *American Economic Review*, Vol. 99, No. 2, pp. 600–605.

Adrian, Tobias and Hyun Shin, 2010, "Financial intermediation and monetary economics," Federal Reserve Bank of New York, staff report, No. 398, revised May.

Adrian, Tobias, Emanuel Moench, and Hyun S. Shin, 2010, "Macro risk premiums and intermediary balance sheet quantities," Federal Reserve Bank of New York, staff report, No. 428.

Bank of England, 2009, "The role of macroprudential policy," discussion paper, November.

Bean, Charles, Matthias Paustian, Adrian Penalver, and Tim Taylor, 2010, "Monetary Policy After the Fall," Federal Reserve Bank of Kansas City, Jackson Hole Symposium.

Bernanke, Ben S., 2010, "Monetary policy and the housing bubble," speech at the American Economic Association annual meeting, Atlanta, GA, January 3, available at www.federalreserve.gov/newsevents/speech/bernanke-20100103a.htm.

Bernanke, Ben S. and Mark Gertler, 1999, "Monetary policy and asset price volatility," in *New Challenges for Monetary Policy*, Kansas City, MO: Federal Reserve Bank of Kansas City, pp. 77–128, available at: www.kc.frb.org/PUBLICAT/SYMPOS/1999/sym99prg.htm.

Bernanke, Ben S., Mark Gertler, and Simon Gilchrist, 1999, "The financial accelerator in a quantitative business cycle framework," in *Handbook of Macroeconomics*, Vol. 1, Part 3, John B. Taylor and Michael Woodford (eds.), Amsterdam: Elsevier/North-Holland, pp. 1341–1393.

Borio, Claudio and Philip Lowe, 2002, "Asset prices, financial and monetary stability: Exploring the nexus," Bank for International Settlements, working paper, No. 114, July.

Borio, Claudio and William White, 2003, "Whither monetary and financial stability? The implications of evolving policy regimes," in *Monetary Policy and Uncertainty: Adapting to a Changing Economy*, Kansas City, MO: Federal Reserve Bank of Kansas City, pp. 131–211.

Borio, Claudio and Haibin Zhu, 2008, "Capital regulation, risk-taking and monetary policy: A missing link in the transmission mechanism?," Bank for International Settlements, working paper, No. 268, December.

Cargill, T.F., M.M. Hutchison, and T. Ito, 1995, "Lessons from financial crisis: the Japanese case," in *The New Tool Set: Innovations in Banking*, Federal

Reserve Bank of Chicago 31st Bank Structure Conference Proceedings, May, pp. 101–109.

Delis, Menthes D. and Georgiou Kouretas, 2010, "Interest rates and bank risk-taking," Munich Personal RePEc Archive, MRPA paper, No. 20132, January.

French, Kenneth R., *et al.*, 2010, *The Squam Lake Report: Fixing the Financial System*, Princeton, NJ: Princeton University Press.

Gambacorta, Leonardo, 2009, "Monetary policy and the risk-taking channel," *BIS Quarterly Review*, December, pp. 43–53.

Greenspan, Alan, 2002, "Opening remarks," in *Rethinking Stabilization Policy*, Federal Reserve Bank of Kansas City Economic Symposium Proceedings, pp. 1–10.

Gruen, D., M. Plumb, and A. Stone, 2005, "How should monetary policy respond to asset price bubbles?," *International Journal of Central Banking*, Vol. 1, December, pp. 1–31.

Hamilton, James D., 1987, "Monetary factors in the Great Depression," *Journal of Monetary Economics*, Vol. 19, March, pp. 145–169.

Ioannidou, Vasso, Steven Ongena, and José Luis Peydró, 2009, "Monetary policy, risk-taking and pricing: Evidence from a quasi-natural experiment," European Banking Centre, discussion paper, No. 2009-04S.

Jiménez, Gabriel, Steven Ongena, José Luis Peydró, and Jesús Saurina, 2008, "Hazardous times for monetary policy: What do twenty-three million bank loans say about the effects of monetary policy on credit risk-taking?," Bank of Spain, working paper, No. 0833.

Jinushi, T., Y. Kuroki, and R. Miyao, 2000, "Monetary policy in Japan since the late 1980s: Delayed policy actions and some explanations," in *Japan's Financial Crisis and Its Parallels to U.S. Experience*, R. Mikitani and A.S. Posen (eds.), Washington, DC: Institute for International Economics, pp. 115–148.

Kashyap, Anil K. and Jeremy C. Stein, 1994, "Monetary policy and bank lending," in *Monetary Policy*, N. Gregory Mankiw (ed.), National Bureau of Economic Research Studies in Business Cycles, Vol. 29, Chicago: University of Chicago Press, pp. 221–256.

Keister, Todd, 2010, "Bailouts and financial fragility," Federal Reserve Bank of New York, unpublished manuscript.

Kindleberger, Charles P., 1978, *Manias, Panics, and Crashes: A History of Financial Crises*, New York: Basic Books.

Kohn, Donald, 2006, "Monetary policy and asset prices," speech delivered at European Central Bank Colloquium held in honor of Otmar Issing, Monetary Policy: A Journey from Theory to Practice, Frankfurt, Germany, March 16.

Mishkin, F.S., 2009, "The financial crisis and the Federal Reserve," *NBER Macro Annual, 2009*, pp. 495–508.

Mishkin, Frederic S., 2010, "Monetary policy flexibility, risk management, and financial disruptions," *Journal of Asian Economics*, Vol. 23, June, pp. 242–246.

Posen, Adam S., 2003, "It takes more than a bubble to become Japan," in *Asset Prices and Monetary Policy*, Anthony Richards and Tim Robinson (eds.), Sydney: Reserve Bank of Australia, pp. 203–249.

Posen, Adam S., 2009, "Finding the right tool for dealing with asset price booms," speech to the MPR Monetary Policy and the Markets Conference, London, December 1, available at: www.bankofengland.co.uk/publications/speeches/2009/speech415.pdf.

Rajan, Raghuram G., 2005, "Has financial development made the world riskier?," in *The Greenspan Era: Lessons for the Future*, Kansas City, MO: Federal Reserve Bank of Kansas City, pp. 313–369.

Rajan, Raghuram, 2006, "Has finance made the world riskier?," *European Financial Management*, Vol. 12, No. 4, pp. 499–533.

Reinhart, Carmen M. and Vincent R. Reinhart, 2010, "After the fall," paper at the Federal Reserve Bank of Kansas City Economic Symposium, Macroeconomic Challenges: The Decade Ahead, manuscript, available at: www.kansascityfed.org/publicat/sympos/2010/reinhart-paper.pdf.

Reinhart, Carmen M. and Kenneth S. Rogoff, 2009, *This Time Is Different: Eight Centuries of Financial Folly*, Princeton, NJ: Princeton University Press.

Taylor, John, 2007, "Housing and monetary policy," in *Housing, Housing Finance and Monetary Policy*, Kansas City, MO: Federal Reserve Bank of Kansas City, pp. 463–476.

Tinbergen, Jan, 1939, *Business Cycles in the United States of America: 1919–1932*, Statistical Testing of Business Cycle Theories, Vol. 2, Geneva, Switzerland: League of Nations.

Tirole, Jean and Emmanuel Farhi, 2009, "Collective moral hazard, maturity mismatch and systemic bailouts," National Bureau of Economic Research, working paper, No. 15138.

Turner, Phillip, 2010, "Central banks and the financial crisis," Bank for International Settlements, paper, No. 51, pp. 21–25.

White, William, 2004, "Making macroprudential concerns operational," speech at Netherlands Bank Financial Stability Symposium, Amsterdam, Netherlands, October 26, available at: www.bis.org/speeches/sp041026.htm.

White, William R., 2009, "Should monetary policy 'lean or clean'?," Federal Reserve Bank of Dallas, working paper, No. 34, August.

Wilson, L. and Y.W. Wu, 2010, "Common (stock) sense about risk-shifting and bank bailouts," *Financial Markets and Portfolio Management*, Vol. 24, No. 1, pp. 3–29.

The Eurozone Crisis

Richard Portes*

London Business School and CEPR

The Eurozone crisis of autumn 2011 is a sequel to the financial crisis of 2008–2009. It would have been much easier to contain and resolve had there been no global financial crisis, no deep recession in the advanced countries. It is therefore too facile, indeed wrong, to say that the Eurozone crisis is essentially or even mainly due to inherent faults in the monetary union. Nevertheless, the crisis has exposed genuine faults that were neither manifest nor life-threatening before 2008–2009. They might have been remedied with gradual progress toward a deeper economic union. But all that is for the economic historians. We are where we are, and it is not pretty.

Government bond yields for several of the 17 countries in the Economic and Monetary Union (EMU) are now unsustainable. With the ten-year German bond (the Bund) at 2.26, Italy is at 7.28 (with a gross debt of 120 percent of GDP), Spain 6.62, Belgium 5.65, and France at 3.63 shows a spread of 137 basis points over the Bund. That spread was close to zero for most of the period from 1999 to 2008. Of the EMU government bonds, only Germany is now regarded as a risk-free "safe asset" — but even that is not totally clear, since the credit default swap (CDS) premium for Germany has now risen to 110 basis points (it was 40 in July 2011). The CDS market is by no means a reliable guide to default risk, but it does give information about sovereign bond prices,[1] and the message is disturbing: Italy at 535 basis points, Spain at 466, Belgium 344, and France 225.

---

* Richard Portes is a professor of economics at London Business School and president of the Centre for Economic Policy Research (CEPR). This is the text of remarks delivered at the conference on November 10–11, 2011. It has not been amended to reflect subsequent developments, which have however followed the lines suggested in the text.

[1] See Portes (2010) and Palladini and Portes (2011).

There are no buyers in the markets for Eurozone sovereign debt except the European Central Bank (ECB), sporadically, and domestic financial institutions under open or implicit pressure from their governments. There is a liquidity crunch, too: Euribor is rising (though still well below 2008–2009 levels), and banks cannot access market funding, especially in dollars. There are repeated reports of malfunctioning in the repo market. The European Financial Stability Fund (EFSF) could not sell some of an early November bond issue and admits that its leverage possibilities are limited. France is on course to lose its AAA rating, and all Euro-area banks are under rating review. Deposits in Greek banks have been falling steadily for several months, and there are signs of similar but slower "bank walks" in other countries deemed at risk. The sovereign CDS market itself is now in question, since the authorities are seeking to engineer a deep restructuring of Greek debt without triggering the CDS, which would show that the "insurance" provided by CDS is not insurance after all.

There are bits of good news: ECB monetary policy is still "credible," on the evidence of market inflation expectations (1.79 percent at a five-year horizon, 2.04 percent at a ten-year horizon). The underlying bad news there, however, is that the ECB interest rates have been too high. The new prime ministers in Greece and Italy are very experienced, very able, and fully conscious of what their countries must do to restart economic growth. That said, they are not elected politicians, and their legitimacy and authority may be correspondingly limited. Since the necessary measures would be painful and challenging even with a popular mandate, one may question whether technocratic governments can carry them out.

For the countries at the heart of the crisis but at the geographical periphery of the Eurozone, the sources of their predicaments are varied. Importantly, they are not primarily due to membership of the single currency, nor to fiscal profligacy. Greece is, of course, an exception to the latter generalization because its fiscal excesses were both large and duplicitous, partly hidden from the statisticians. But its problems are due also to major structural weaknesses, especially of its institutions;[2] extreme political polarization; and reckless (for the lenders as well as borrowers) capital inflows that for years disguised these underlying flaws. It is wrong to reduce these factors to inadequate "competitiveness" that could be cured by currency devaluation.

[2]See Jacobides, Portes, and Vayanos (2011).

Ireland's woes arise from an extraordinary housing boom (incontestably a housing price bubble), fed by equally reckless capital inflows through its banks into property development and mortgage finance and lubricated by crony capitalism. The original sin which has led Ireland to its penance was not, however, this process itself, but rather the government guarantee of the bank debts thereby incurred. In a stroke, this socialization of private debt transformed a country with one of the lowest ratios of public debt to GDP into one with an exceptionally high debt ratio.

Spain too had its housing boom and capital inflow into construction. These were exacerbated by the foolish behavior of the politically influenced regional banks, the *cajas*, which fell into deep difficulties when the bubble burst. Portugal has many economic ills: poor education, an uncompetitive production structure, and product and labor market rigidities. But its primary mistake was not to use the very large capital inflow during the pre-crisis decade to modernize the economy.

All four of these countries (the GIPS) had sound fiscal positions but were running large current account deficits within the monetary union. These were financed by equally large capital flows from the surplus countries, especially Germany — a capital flow "bonanza"[3] for the periphery, with the usual consequences. The euro area as a whole ran a balanced current account with the rest of the world — the imbalances were internal. Germany played the same role in the Eurozone as China in the global economy. Unlike the United States, however, the GIPS were not "free spenders" — Ireland and Spain had housing booms, but they and Greece all saw a fall in consumption as a share of GDP and a rise in the investment share during 2000–2007 (the investment share fell slightly in Portugal). And unlike China, the capital flows from Germany (and some other countries, like France) came primarily from banks — they were private, not official, flows.

Correspondingly, the macroeconomic problem in EMU now is the fiscal consequence of the financial crisis in bank-based financial systems. Creditor countries have been unwilling to let their banks suffer the consequences of bad loans — rather, they have managed to put the entire burden on the taxpayers of the debtor countries. This may seem clever, but it is short-sighted, not to say hypocritical. It also disregards the EU and Eurozone financial integration that policymakers have promoted — using an American analogy, should Delaware be responsible for Citibank's liabilities?

[3] See Reinhart and Reinhart (2008).

The result is that Greece is insolvent, Ireland's debt is also excessive and should be restructured,[4] and Portugal's IMF program is not feasible. Spain and Italy, however, are solvent, if financial markets return to normal conditions and both countries carry out appropriate macroeconomic and structural policies. But Italy, Spain, and even France are under pressure from the markets. They fear that Spanish banks will suffer further from bad real estate loans, and the state will have to bail them out. Italian political instability and irresolution has reinforced contagion from the weaker countries, so Italy seems to be entering a self-fulfilling vicious spiral: Rising debt-service costs hurt the fiscal position (Italy is close to primary fiscal balance), that hits market confidence, spreads rise, and debt service begins to look unsustainable despite the primary balance. The markets are also losing confidence in French banks despite the protestations of health from the banks and their regulators. Common to all these cases is an interconnected sovereign and banking crisis: The banks hold large amounts of sovereign debt that have become questionable, and the sovereigns are questioned because of the danger that they will have to rescue their banks. Therefore, we have the "doom loops" represented in Figure 1 and exacerbated by elements of Fisherian debt deflation.

The euro (monetary union) is not the cause of this crisis, although the ECB's interpretation of its role has been blocking a solution. The ECB has been "in denial," maintaining as late as May 2011 that it was inconceivable that a Eurozone country could default on its debt. The agreement of July 21, 2011, to restructure Greek debt was, of course, recognition of default, regardless of whether the restructuring would be "voluntary" or not. The ECB told Ireland in autumn 2008 (backed by the threat of withdrawal of repo facilities) that it was not allowed to consider debt default. Where else in the world can a central bank tell a government what it can or cannot do in fiscal matters?

Politicians share responsibility, however, with their indecision and endlessly repeated "too little, too late" measures — such as the agreement of July 21, 2011, which was recognized only three months later to be wholly inadequate. Moreover, the French president and German chancellor have made two egregious errors with disastrous impact on the markets: the Deauville statement of October 2010, introducing in an ill-considered manner the possibility of private sector involvement in dealing with Eurozone

[4]See Portes (2011).

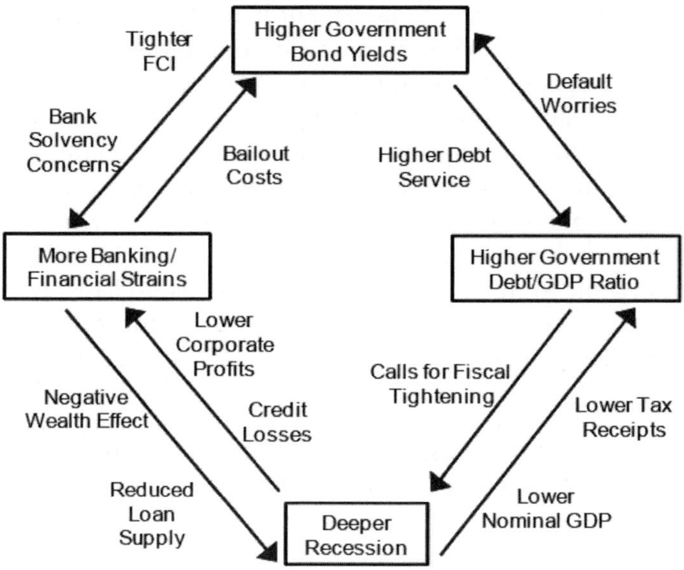

Figure 1. Financial Instability: Doom Loops.

Source: Goldman Sachs, *Global Economics Weekly* 11/38, November 2011.

country debt; and the Cannes statement a year later that explicitly proposed that an EMU member country could exit the euro. There is no legal basis for this, and it had been regarded as a taboo. Some have drawn an analogy with the statement by the president of the Bundesbank in early September 1992 that "devaluations cannot be ruled out" in the EMS — which was followed immediately by the exit of Italy and the UK.

Several ways out have been proposed. If the banks' capital is inadequate, then they should be recapitalized. But with what external funding, if government participation is excluded? Part of the problem is that the markets are denying even short-term funding to the banks. Consequently, the banks are deleveraging by selling assets and not rolling over loans, with dangerous consequences worldwide. What about expanding or "leveraging" the EFSF? Non-euro countries will not contribute, leveraging through borrowing from the ECB is not allowed, and Eurozone countries simply do not want to put up more funds.

The extreme way out is to get out: Might an exit of Greece from the Eurozone end the instability? No, for it would immediately lead to devastating bank runs in all countries that might conceivably be thought of as candidates to follow Greece. What firm or household in Portugal, Ireland, Spain, or Cyprus would not seek to avoid even a low probability that its bank deposits might be devalued overnight? The likely outcome would be multiple exits, quite possibly the breakup of the monetary union. And that would be disastrous not only for the exiting "weak" countries but also for those that would then suffer massive exchange-rate appreciation and the economic dislocation consequent on massive contract uncertainty.

I therefore maintain that the only solution is for the ECB to accept explicitly, in some form, the role of lender of last resort (LLR) for the monetary union. (One might alternatively regard this as a form of quantitative easing.) This does come within the Maastricht Treaty mandate:

> In accordance with Article 105(1) of this Treaty, the primary objective of the ESCB shall be to maintain price stability. Without prejudice to the objective of price stability, it shall support the general economic policies in the Community...
>
> 5. The ESCB shall contribute to the smooth conduct of policies pursued by the competent authorities relating to the prudential supervision of credit institutions and the stability of the financial system.
>
> *Treaty of Maastricht (1992), Article 2 and Protocols Art. 105.5 (numbering changes in Lisbon Treaty, but no change in text).*

It would not violate the "no bailout clause" (which does exclude ECB purchases of Eurozone sovereign debt on the primary market). And in fact, the ECB has been purchasing member state bonds on the secondary market since May 2010, without any successful legal challenge.

To stop self-fulfilling confidence crises, therefore, the ECB should commit to cap yields paid by solvent countries with unlimited purchases in the secondary markets. Arbitrage will then bring primary issue yields down to the capped level. Note "solvent": the then-governor of the Bundesbank was right to oppose such purchases for Greece in May 2010, because it was evidently insolvent.

There is no more inflation risk in such a policy as there is in quantitative easing — and that risk is negligible, as shown by the examples of the U.S., UK, and Japan. The ECB can always tighten as and when necessary. The risk preoccupying the ECB is that of moral hazard: It clearly views "market discipline" as the only way to bring about the macroeconomic policies it favors. The evidence? Berlusconi's departure and replacement by Monti; and a technocratic government in Greece led by the former ECB vice president, willing to accept the harsh austerity policies demanded by the IMF-ECB-EC troika. Financial market pressures are consciously used to drive governments to implement austerity and reforms.

Thus, the ECB does only ad hoc government debt purchases under its Secondary Market Program, in the guise of "normalizing the monetary transmission mechanism" that is impaired by debt market instability. This is a version of the "constructive ambiguity" beloved of central bankers — but in this case, it is manifestly destructive rather than constructive. The piecemeal approach, acting only under pressure and with delay, has proved very costly. In effect, the ECB is playing a game of "chicken" with the politicians and the markets. It is particularly dangerous both because there are three players, of which two have no single decision-maker; and because the parameters defining the game are not well-defined, since no one can tell when a vicious spiral may turn into an overwhelming confidence crisis that the authorities will be unable to control.

On the other hand, the ECB does need political backing to take on the LLR role overtly. The German and French leaders must make the case that this is the only way to preserve the monetary union. And the ECB also should receive explicit indemnities (guarantees) from finance ministers of the 17 member countries against capital losses the bank might incur on its sovereign bond purchases. Both the U.S. Federal Reserve and the Bank of England have received such indemnities in respect of their quantitative easing programs.

Then the ECB should make an expectations-changing announcement of the new policy, just as the Swiss National Bank did when it moved to cap the value of the Swiss franc. As that example shows, it is highly likely that if the commitment were made, the markets would recognize that betting against the bonds (a speculative attack) could not succeed, because the ECB has unlimited capacity to resist. Hence, it would not have to buy much, if at all.

Ideally, this short-run stabilizing policy should be complemented by long-run plans for fiscal stability and integration, as well as Eurobonds (issued at the Eurozone level with "joint and several liability"). That would establish the kind of "convergence play" that drove the markets smoothly into EMU at the end of the 1990s. There are several Eurobond proposals now on the table, but the leaders of the major countries have so far rejected them.

Meanwhile, although the ECB policy proposed above could buy time for economic reforms to work, long-run debt sustainability requires economic growth. But fiscal contraction is contractionary.[5] The only counterexample

[5]See Guajardo *et al.* (2011).

is that of Ireland in the 1980s, a very special case: a rather backward country catching up to the technological frontier; exporting into a boom in its major trading partners (especially the UK); creating an exceptionally favorable environment for foreign direct investment; and exploiting a well-educated diaspora willing to return.

The austerity policies championed by Germany and other apostles of fiscal rectitude, implemented enthusiastically by the European Commission, are not the solution, but rather a major part of the problem. They are driving the Eurozone into a new recession.[6] The debt of several Eurozone countries is not sustainable if they contract.

Moreover, fiscal contraction together with private sector deleveraging is not feasible without a current account surplus. We teach this in first-year macroeconomics:

$$CA = (S_p - I_p) + (T - G).$$

The current account must equal the sum of private sector net saving and government net saving. In the Eurozone, the surplus countries are those with the most "fiscal space." There will be no exit from the current debt traps and stagnation unless the surplus countries are willing to accept that they must allow the others to run surpluses, so that either they relax fiscal policy or they adopt policies to reduce private net savings. And the overall position would improve if the euro were to depreciate significantly — another reason for monetary easing (some will be coming soon, no doubt). But that is true for the United States and Japan as well.[7]

Germany and France have benefited greatly from the single currency over its first decade. Their business communities see this. One must still hope that the core Eurozone countries will eventually act in their own best interests. The global financial crisis need not lead to the demise of the single currency through a Eurozone crisis that could be resolved successfully if policymakers were to change course.

References

Guajardo, J., D. Leigh, and A. Pescatori, 2011, "Expansionary austerity: New international evidence," IMF, working paper, No. 11/158.

---

[6]See http://eurocoin.cepr.org/, where the Eurocoin coincident indicator has been firmly in negative territory over the past two months.

[7]This is not to say that "competitive quantitative easing" at the zero lower bound for interest rates will be ineffective or "beggar-thy-neighbor" policies — see Portes (2012).

Jacobides, M., R. Portes, and D. Vayanos, 2011, "Greece: The way forward," white paper, October 27, summarized at www.voxeu.org, November 30.

Palladini, G. and R. Portes, 2011, "Sovereign CDS and bond pricing dynamics in the euro area," CEPR discussion paper No. 8651, NBER working paper No. 17586, November.

Portes, R., 2010, "Ban naked CDS," available at www.eurointelligence.com, March 18.

Portes, R., 2011, "Restructure Ireland's debt," available at www.voxeu.org, April 26.

Portes, R., 2012, "Monetary policies and exchange rates at the zero lower bound," *Journal of Money, Credit and Banking*, Vol. 44, pp. 157–163.

Reinhart, C. and V. Reinhart, 2008, "Capital flow bonanzas," CEPR, discussion paper, No. 6996, October.

The Way Forward — Central Banks with Financial Stability Mandates: The Case of the Eurosystem

Anne Sibert*
Birkbeck, University of London and CEPR;
External member of the Central Bank of Iceland

1. Introduction

The liquidity, banking, and sovereign debt crises that have arisen sequentially since August 2007 have reminded us that central banks have a dual role. They should both maintain price stability and ensure the orderly functioning of financial markets.

Since the beginning of the financial crises, the Eurosystem has engaged in a range of actions that previously would have been hard to imagine. National Central Banks (NCBs) have conducted lender-of-last-resort actions for their governments' accounts. The ECB has massively expanded the range of securities it accepts as collateral in the repos and other collateralized loan transactions done by the NCBs. It has participated in currency swaps with other governments and provided repo facilities to non-Euro Area countries such as Hungary. On May 9, 2010, it announced that it would purchase Euro Area government bonds outright in secondary markets as part of the financial support scheme for heavily indebted Euro Area countries.

Not only has the Eurosystem taken significant risks with taxpayers' money; in some cases, it has gone beyond ensuring that markets and solvent financial institutions remained liquid and has used what is ultimately the taxpayers' money to subsidize or bail out institutions that were clearly insolvent or threatened with insolvency. The Governing Council initiated

* Anne Sibert is professor of economics at Birkbeck, University of London. She is also an external member of the Monetary Policy Committee of the Central Bank of Iceland, and a member of the panel of economic and monetary experts for the Committee for Economic and Monetary Affairs of the European Parliament.

the Securities Market Programme with the stated intent of ensuring "depth and liquidity in those markets which are dysfunctional." However, it later used this program to buy Greek debt at prices far above fair market value.

The financial stability activities that have been undertaken by the Eurosystem are likely perceived as far more political activities than the selection of a policy interest rate. They also require a different set of skills than those that are required for making monetary policy. In this paper I consider how the Eurosystem, and other central banks as well, need to be redesigned and staffed to maintain their legitimacy and to ensure their efficiency when they are required to maintain financial stability as well as make monetary policy.

2. The Central Bank's Legitimacy When It Has a Financial Stability Role

In this section I describe how a central bank's financial stability role is a political one. I specify how an unelected institution can be viewed as the legitimate provider of financial stability and discuss how the behavior of the Eurosystem so far has affected its legitimacy.

2.1 *The political nature of the central bank's financial stability role*

For a central bank to maintain financial stability, it must be willing to act both as the market-maker of last resort and as the lender of last resort. In a liquidity crisis, the markets for a range of financial assets become dysfunctional. Trading volume declines sharply and transactions only occur at prices that are far lower than would prevail in more orderly times. To restore market functioning, it may be necessary for the central bank to act as the market-maker of last resort by purchasing or accepting as collateral the financial assets that either cannot be sold in the market or can only be sold at fire-sale prices below but close to those that would prevail in normal times.

This action need not be inflationary. The central bank can sterilize this intervention by selling some of its other assets to avoid affecting the money supply. However, it then holds the illiquid assets on its balance sheet instead of the assets that it sells. Suppose that the assets that are sold are government bonds whose market value remains little changed. If the central bank is successful at reviving the dysfunctional market or markets and if it paid below-market prices for the financial assets it purchased, then the change in the composition of the central bank's balance sheet is profitable and the central bank's net worth increases. However, if the assets turn out to be worth less than expected, then it makes a loss relative to what it would have made if it had instead held the government bonds. The central bank's net worth declines.

Fear-driven markets may believe that a financial institution (or class of financial institutions or even a sovereign) is insolvent. Then this financial institution cannot borrow or can only borrow at far above market interest rates. As a result, the market participants' expectations are self-fulfilling and the financial institution is indeed insolvent, even though it would have been solvent otherwise. In scenarios where more than one outcome is possible, the central bank can act as the lender of last resort to ensure that the socially preferable outcome is realized. If there is the potential for a fear-driven run on potentially solvent financial institutions and the central bank is credible that it stands willing to act as lender of last resort and to lend as much as it takes to avert the run, the run may never happen. If the run does occur and the bank makes a loan to the threatened financial institution, the fear may pass and the financial institution can return to the market as normal.

As was the case when the central bank acts as market-maker of last resort, it need not be inflationary when the central bank acts as a lender of last resort, but it can increase the riskiness of its balance sheet. When the central bank makes a loan, it can sterilize it by selling some of its other assets. Again, suppose that these other assets are government bonds and their market value is stable. If the loan was made at a penalty rate and the illiquidity was temporary, a solvent borrower repays, the sterilization can be reversed, and the central bank makes a profit. If the illiquid borrower turns out to be insolvent as well, the loan is not repaid and the central bank's net worth declines.

To the degree that dysfunctional markets or illiquid financial institutions have systemic importance, the fates of other financial markets and institutions are affected by the central bank's intervention. In deciding whether to purchase an illiquid asset outright or accept it as collateral or whether or not to rescue an illiquid but possibly solvent financial institution, the central bank is making a decision that can affect the prices of all of the assets on its balance sheet as well as those assets held by the private sector. If the market or institution under consideration for rescue is sufficiently systemically important, the decision to intervene may even *reduce* the riskiness of the central bank's own balance sheet and that of the nation or area over whose markets it presides.

If when acting as market-maker or lender of last resort the central bank chooses its prices and penalty interest rates correctly, the expected increase in national or area wealth should more than compensate most of its citizenry for any additional risk. However, the central bank's actions redistribute expected wealth and may do so in a way that is perceived by many as unfair. Moreover, in choosing its counterparties and the terms of its contracts, there is the possibility that the central bank might be motivated by more than purely economic considerations. Even if the central bank policymakers always behave honorably, there is the possibility of an erroneous perception that they did not. Both the possibility of redistributing wealth in an unpopular way and of being thought of as corrupt introduce significant political elements into a central bank's role as provider of financial stability.

2.2 *The perceived legitimacy of the Eurosystem as provider of financial stability*

The Eurosystem is unique in its operational independence. Its decision-making bodies are specifically forbidden from taking direction from any European Community institution or body or any national government or body of a member state. All European Community institutions and bodies and member state governments are specifically prohibited from seeking to influence the decision-making bodies of the Eurosystem.[1] To impinge on this extraordinary degree of independence would require a change in the treaty and the statute, and this could happen only with the unanimous consent of all of the member states.

The Eurosystem also enjoys functional independence. It has been given most of the tools that it needs to make monetary policy and it gets to say how and when it uses them. The only exception is the exchange rate arrangement, which is the joint competency of the Council of Ministers and the ECB.

For independent and unelected central banks to be acceptable to society, they must be seen as legitimate. Given its remarkable operational and functional independence and its multinational nature, legitimacy is of particular importance to the Eurosystem.

Unelected central banks that have a financial stability role will only be viewed as legitimate if the citizenry believes that they have both the right

[1] See the treaty establishing the European Community, consolidated version, Article 111.

to do the financial stability tasks that they take on and that they are the most appropriate institution to perform them. There are two related sources of such legitimacy: output legitimacy and input legitimacy. Output legitimacy can occur if the central bank does its assigned tasks in a satisfactory manner and does not undertake tasks that it has not been assigned, even if it can do these tasks well. Input legitimacy can arise if the citizenry approve of the way that tasks were delegated to the central banks and if the central bank is accountable.

2.3 *The Eurosystem's output legitimacy*

The Eurosystem has not existed long enough to draw a firm conclusion about its competency in providing financial stability. Nevertheless, most economists would probably view the Eurosystem's performance in its financial stability role as being at least as good as that of the world's other major central banks. Thus, the Eurosystem has some output legitimacy because it is viewed as doing its job well. Indeed, it probably has more output legitimacy than the Fed in this regard as the Fed has been widely criticized for not foreseeing the current crises, which arose first in the United States, and — perhaps unfairly — for its part in contributing to the U.S. housing bubble or at least for not containing it. However, while the Eurosystem is perceived as relatively competent at the moment, bad luck alone might cause it or any other central bank to lose this source of output legitimacy in the future.

Central banks can also achieve output legitimacy by not taking on tasks that have not been assigned to them. Providing direct subsidies to counterparties by buying their assets or accepting their assets as collateral at a higher than fair value is equivalent to making a fiscal transfer, and this is not generally seen as an appropriate action for a central bank. The Eurosystem's purchases of Greek government debt since May 2010 are widely viewed as something that the Eurosystem was not only not assigned to do, but were something it was specifically *not* supposed to do. It is, however, generally understood that the ECB president Jean-Claude Trichet was uncomfortable with this task and did it only because there was no other entity able and willing to come up with the necessary funding at short notice and the systemic risk of a premature and disorderly Greek default was unacceptably high.

Federal Reserve chairman Ben Bernanke was put in a similar situation when he had to take on the distasteful task of bailing out the AIG without authorization from Congress. While the actions of Mr. Trichet and

Mr. Bernanke may be justified and even applauded, they did not enhance the legitimacy of their central banks. If governments want their central bank to have output legitimacy, they should ensure that they have the institutions in place so that they are not forced to become the fiscal policymakers of necessity.

While the Eurosystem's foray into the Greek sovereign debt market was done under duress, the Eurosystem has sometimes strayed into the role of fiscal subsidization quite voluntarily. While it is difficult to know exactly how often as the Eurosystem does not divulge the details of its transactions, a couple of examples come to mind. One is the national central bank of Luxembourg's long-standing policy of allowing Icelandic banks to borrow from it using each other's debt — known as *love letters* — as collateral.[2] Another was the unlimited one-year fixed rate liquidity provision of June 2009, which may have been a transfer of about €1 billion from taxpayers to happy banks.[3] It will be difficult for the Eurosystem to maintain output legitimacy if it is seen as playing reverse Robin Hood: subsidizing banks — Icelandic and otherwise — with taxpayer funds.

2.4 *Input legitimacy through the manner of the ECB's creation*

Acting as the lender of last resort or the market-maker of last resort is generally perceived as a legitimate role for the Federal Reserve. Indeed, the Federal Reserve Act came into being largely as a response to a series of financial crises. Unfortunately, there is much less of a perception that it is a legitimate role for the Eurosystem. The European Monetary Union came into being after unfortunate European experiences with bad monetary policy in the 1970s and 1980s. Thus, the treaty, which might have reinforced the input legitimacy of the Eurosystem in its financial stability role, focuses almost entirely on monetary policy. It has little to say about a financial stability role for the central bank, and what it does say is vague and ambiguous. In addition, it explicitly prohibits the Eurosystem from buying government debt directly in the primary issuer market. This limits the ability of the Eurosystem to act as an effective lender of last resort to the member state sovereigns by buying their new issuance of public debt, and it causes the Eurosystem's less effective purchases of government debt in secondary markets to be widely seen as a flouting of the spirit of the treaty.

[2]See Sibert (2010).

[3]See Buiter (2009).

As its output legitimacy could be threatened by chance, as it has taken on tasks that were not in its remit, and as it has little input legitimacy through the treaty, it is vital that the Eurosystem attain input legitimacy by being perceived as accountable.

2.5 *Accountability and the Eurosystem*

A typical view of what constitutes accountability of an institution to the citizenry is that the institution is accountable if it is obliged to inform the citizenry about its past and current actions and decisions, to justify them, and to suffer punishment in the case of misconduct or incompetency.[4] From this definition, it is seen that accountability has three components for a central bank: First, the public should be able to observe or be provided with the relevant information about the central bank's actions and decision-making processes; second, the central bank should explain and justify its actions; and third, it should be possible to punish central bank policymakers who engage in bad or incompetent behavior. The first two components are often referred to as *formal accountability*; the third component is often referred to as *substantive accountability*.[5]

The ECB's unusual degree of independence precludes the possibility of substantive accountability. Members of the Executive Board serve eight-year, non-renewable terms; NCB governors serve at least five-year terms. Their compensation is internally decided. Governors of NCBs and members of the Executive Board can be fired only in the event of incapacity or serious misconduct; gross incompetency does not count. No one, not the European Parliament, nor the Council of Ministers, nor the European Commission, can impose sanctions on the ECB. The ECB is also financially independent: Its arrangements are separate from those of the rest of the European Community. It has its own budget and its capital is subscribed to and held solely by the NCBs. It is telling that while the Federal Reserve Board chairman *testifies* before the U.S. Congress, the president of the ECB has a quarterly *dialogue* with a very polite and deferential European Parliament.

With virtually no substantive accountability, the ECB must be formally accountable to have input legitimacy. Unfortunately, the ECB — notoriously opaque in its conduct of monetary policy — is demonstrating even less transparency in its financial stability role.

[4]See Schedler (1999).

[5]See Buiter (2006, 2008).

The ECB uses market prices to value marketable securities as collateral. However, if there has been no recent trading of these securities, it computes theoretical prices. Unfortunately, the ECB refuses to say what these prices are, even after a lag to protect market-sensitive information. Moreover, it will not say what method it uses to compute these prices. This makes it impossible to tell whether the ECB is doing a good job at computing the prices, and it opens the door to the perception of corruption. If we do not know anything about the price that was paid, how do we know that only economic considerations played a role?

After deciding the value of a security, the ECB imposes a "haircut." Haircuts are not typically thought of as a penalty for default risk as this is supposed to be reflected in the security's value. Instead, they might be viewed as a compensation for a loss of liquidity or, perhaps, they might also be viewed as compensation for taking on the correlated default risks of the ECB's counterparty and of the issuer of the security offered as collateral by the counterparty. But just as with the theoretical prices, the ECB refuses to say how it computes its haircuts or even what it believes a haircut is supposed to be a penalty for.

When the European Parliament (Quarterly Dialogue, Dec. 2009) asked Jean-Claude Trichet how collateral is valued, his response was, "This is done by the system in ways which I considered appropriate but that we can improve at any time if we judge that they should be improved. . . ." Unfortunately, the oddity of the haircuts, coupled with a refusal to say how they came about, raises questions about the ECB's competency. Why, for example, do haircuts increase rapidly with an asset's maturity when there are secondary markets and potential illiquidity does not necessarily do so? This perverse policy may have contributed to the current situation where Euro Area banks simultaneously have huge short-term debt refinancing requirements and are scrambling for massive amounts of additional capital.

The Eurosystem also refuses to say who its counterparties are or how they were chosen. It is widely believed that the average discount to face value paid for the Greek sovereign debt acquired (prior to August, at least) under the Securities Market Programme was no more than 20 percent. Moreover, it appears that the NCBs sought out the fortunate counterparties. The possibilities for corruption under a system where a central bank is allowed to sell a security at any price to any eligible counterparty and where it never has to say who the counterparty was or how much they paid, are huge. One does not have to have much of an imagination to conjecture that the delighted counterparties were German and French banks.

The extraordinary opacity of the Eurosystem can be contrasted with what is now required of the Federal Reserve System. Section 1109(c) of the Dodd–Frank Act requires the Fed to publicly reveal the details of its emergency lending between December 2007 and July 2010. In December 2010, the Fed provided detailed information about this lending on its website, including the identity of the counterparty, the size of the transaction, and the terms. The Dodd–Frank Act exempted borrowing from the discount window during the crisis but mandated disclosure of loans made after July 21, 2010, with a two-year lag. In March 2011, the Supreme Court forced the Fed to disclose data on emergency discount window borrowing.

The Eurosystem's obsessive secrecy threatens its accountability, undermining its legitimacy and hence its credibility and its reputation as an institution. This will hamper its future ability to both make monetary policy and provide financial stability. As the ECB is one of the key governance institutions of the European Union, a loss of its legitimacy would threaten the legitimacy of all other European Union governance institutions, including the European Commission, the European Court of Justice, and the European Parliament.

Perhaps the Eurosystem may become more transparent under its new leadership. It is better for an institution's reputation for transparency if it is open of its own accord, rather than being forced to reveal information by a change in the law or a court order. However, if this does not occur, it is to be hoped that the sequence of financial crises might make it possible to revise the treaty so that the Eurosystem is forced to become more accountable.

3. Staffing the Central Bank When It Has a Financial Stability Role

As seen in the previous section, ensuring the orderly functioning of financial markets is a difficult technical task. A central bank must assess the likelihood of being able to restore a dysfunctional market and the probability that a financial institution or group of financial institutions, or even a sovereign, is merely illiquid rather than insolvent. It must decide the price of assets when markets are dysfunctional and the haircuts on assets it accepts as collateral and the terms of the loans that it offers.

Central banks that have been primarily focused on monetary policy tend to be staffed primarily with macroeconomists, and macroeconomists are not necessarily the people best suited to ensuring market stability. I provide two examples of this.

3.1 *Why macroeconomists are not enough*

The first example is the response to the liquidity crisis that arose in the summer of 2007. In early August 2007, the market for asset-backed securities became dysfunctional. On August 9, BNP Paribas froze three of its investment funds after what it called "the complete evaporation of liquidity in U.S. credit markets." Overnight, interest rates rose sharply and, led by a brigade of macroeconomists, the world's major central banks swung into action. The ECB, the Fed, and the Bank of Japan promptly injected well over $200 billion worth of liquidity into the markets to stop the relevant private benchmarks from rising above their policy rate targets, and on August 17, the Fed reduced its policy rate by 50 basis points.

This was the wrong response. The problem was not that market participants could not borrow at a reasonable interest rate against high-grade collateral. The market failure was that financial institutions were holding a vast amount of assets that were suddenly illiquid and could not be sold at any sensible price. Indeed, BNP Paribas' argument for freezing its funds was that it no longer had any way to value the funds' assets. When the Fed lowered the discount rate, the only effect was to provide a 50-basis-point subsidy to institutions that were able and willing to borrow at the discount window. What central banks should have done is what they later came to do: purchased illiquid securities outright in their open-market operations; accepted illiquid securities as collateral for repos and at the discount window; and widened the set of counterparties for liquidity-providing operations and at the discount window.

Unfortunately, the macroeconomists who staffed the central banks are not the natural people to respond to credit market failures. If central banks had been staffed by microeconomists who were interested in credit markets, the correct central bank response might have been timelier.

The second example is the failure of central banks to realize the amount of systemic risk in the financial system prior to autumn 2008. Macroeconomists at central banks were worried about house prices and global imbalances, but few appeared to realize that financial firms were so leveraged or to understand the nature of the real estate-backed assets that they held. Indeed, one wonders what fraction of the ECB's Governing Council or the Federal Reserve's FOMC could explain what a collateralized debt obligation was in early 2007.

Not only do macroeconomists tend to lack the necessary expertise to respond to liquidity crises or to evaluate systemic risk, they are macroeconomists because they are interested in macroeconomic issues such as monetary policy. As they are less interested in financial stability matters, they are apt to neglect thinking about how financial markets and the financial sector work until after a crisis arises. Jean-Claude Trichet appears to be an example of this. In his press conferences and Quarterly Dialogues with the European Parliament, Mr. Trichet has always spoken about monetary policy with enthusiasm. However, until autumn 2008, he had little to say about financial stability. It is a design error of central banks that the same people are in charge of both monetary policy and financial stability.

3.2 *Expertise for a financial stability role*

If a central bank is to provide financial stability, it needs to change its expertise. Such a central bank should have theories about why asset markets freeze up and about how contagion arises. It should have theories about what should determine the haircuts on the assets it accepts as collateral. It should know how to design an auction to sell illiquid assets. These tasks require a background in microeconomics and game theory; they are not tasks that macroeconomists are apt to be good at. A central bank with a financial stability role should have staff and senior policymakers who are serious microeconomists.

A larger fraction of the staff and senior policymakers at central banks should have understood and been able to debate the costs and benefits of fair-value accounting prior to the financial crises. In early 2008, one wonders what percentage of senior central bankers knew exactly what implanting FAS 157 required and had a view on whether it might force big banks to understate the value of their assets in a crisis. Macroeconomists sometimes tend to regard accounting as not particularly interesting, but accounting rules have played an important role in the financial crisis and central banks should hire more research accountants.

The existence of credit default swaps, collateralized debt obligations, and equity tranches of mortgage-backed securities should not have come as a surprise to most of the research staff at a central bank in 2007. But how would the staff have known of the existence and importance of such financial assets unless they spoke with practitioners? The staff at central banks should spend more time talking to traders. Traders may not like to volunteer their time, but since the central bank is a regulator they will do so. Some may even be eager to explain lurking problems that central banks may not be aware of.

In assessing a possible Greek debt restructuring, it is necessary to know what is legally possible and what the legal consequences of various options are. Central banks with a financial stability role need lawyers and legal scholars. On October 31, 2011, Greek prime minister George Papandreou announced that he intended to hold a referendum for the acceptance of the terms for a Euro Area bailout deal. Central banks with a financial stability role should have been able to immediately assess the likely outcome of the surprising move. Any major central bank with a serious financial stability role also needs political scientists.

Maintaining financial stability requires many types of expertise and a mastery of macroeconomics is just one of them. Central banks need senior policymakers and staff with an expertise in microeconomics, accounting, political science, and law. Of course, some central banks already have some of this expertise, but there is a tendency for them to be relatively overstaffed with macroeconomists.

4. Combining the Financial Stability and Monetary Policy Roles of a Central Bank

As argued in the previous section, providing financial stability and making monetary policy require different types of expertise. The more political nature of the financial stability role requires serious accountability and constraints on independence. The incentive of even benevolent governments to use monetary policy opportunistically means that monetary policymakers should be shielded from political influence. This suggests that separate groups should provide financial stability and make monetary policy.

Financial stability policy should be made by a Financial Stability Committee (FSC) within the central bank chaired by the head of the central bank. This committee must have a mandate to make risky decisions that might redistribute wealth if the stability of the financial system requires it, and it must be held accountable. It must be required to specify its collateral policies and how it decides them and to say how it chooses its counterparties. With an appropriate lag, it must provide the details of its transactions. Members must regularly testify before parliament or the analogous legislative body. It should be possible to fire members who are incompetent.

The Monetary Policy Committee (MPC) should be affiliated with but distinct from the central bank and charged *solely* with choosing policy interest rates or conducting monetary easing if necessary. The intersection of the FSC and the MPC should be small but not empty; the MPC need not be chaired by the head of the central bank and it need not and probably should not be populated primarily by employees of the central bank. This committee should have a point inflation target that is consistent with price stability and be given operational independence. Its members should serve fixed terms and dismissal should only be on grounds of gross misconduct. Accountability is satisfied if it publishes individual votes and its unattributed minutes. Monetary policy is primarily a technical job. As with other technical jobs, such as brain surgery or flying passenger planes, it is usually better to hire the best people rather than the best people of a specific nationality.

References

Buiter, Willem H., 2006, "How robust is the new conventional wisdom in monetary policy? The surprising fragility of the theoretical foundations of inflation targeting and central bank independence," European Institute, London School of Economics and Political Science, mimeo.

Buiter, Willem H., 2008, "Monetary economics and the political economy of central banking: Inflation targeting and central bank independence revisited," in *Monetary Policy under Uncertainty: Proceedings of the 2007 Money and Banking Seminar*, Jorge Carrera (ed.), Buenos Aires, Argentina: Banco Central de la República Argentina, pp. 218–243.

Buiter, Willem, 2009, "Recapitalising the banks through enhanced credit support: Quasi-fiscal shenanigans in Frankfurt," Maverecon, *Financial Times*, June 28.

Schedler, Andreas, 1999, "Conceptualizing accountability," in *The Self-Restraining State: Power and Accountability in New Democracies*, Andreas Schedler, Larry Diamond, Marc F. Plattner (eds.), London, UK: Lynne Rienner Publishers, pp. 13–28.

Sibert, Anne, 2010, "Accountability and the ECB," in *Central Banking after the Crisis: Proceedings of the 2010 Economics Conference*, Vienna: Central Bank of Austria, available at www.annesibert.co.uk/PolicyPapersandSpeeches.htm.

Conference Agenda

Thursday, November 10

9:00 AM Registration and Continental Breakfast

9:40 AM Welcoming Remarks
Charles L. Evans, President and Chief Executive Officer, Federal Reserve Bank of Chicago
Peter Praet, Member of the Executive Board, European Central Bank

10:00 AM Session I: The Role of Central Banks in Financial Stability: Historical Review and Critique
Moderator: Douglas D. Evanoff, Federal Reserve Bank of Chicago
Nellie Liang, Board of Governors of the Federal Reserve System
Martin Hellwig, Max Planck Institute for Research on Collective Goods, University of Bonn
Takeo Hoshi, University of California, San Diego
Carlos A. Vegh, University of Maryland

12:00 PM Luncheon and Keynote Address
Introduction: Charles L. Evans, President and Chief Executive Officer, Federal Reserve Bank of Chicago
Peter Praet, Member of the Executive Board, European Central Bank

2:00 PM Session II: Macroprudential Policies and Regulation: How to Address Systemic Risk
Moderator: Manfred Kremer, European Central Bank
Tobias Adrian, Federal Reserve Bank of New York
Mathias Drehmann, Bank for International Settlements
Jeremy C. Stein, Harvard University
Commentator: Richard Berner, U.S. Department of the Treasury

3:45 PM Break

4:00 PM SESSION III: CENTRAL BANKS AND ASSET PRICE BUBBLES
Moderator: Cornelia Holthausen, European Central Bank
Kenneth N. Kuttner, Williams College
Annette Vissing-Jørgensen, Northwestern University
Takatoshi Ito, University of Tokyo
Commentator: Andrew Filardo, Bank for International Settlements' Representative Office, Hong Kong

5:45 PM RECEPTION

6:45 PM DINNER AND KEYNOTE ADDRESS
Introduction: Daniel G. Sullivan, Executive Vice President and Director of Research, Federal Reserve Bank of Chicago
Willem Buiter, Chief Economist, Citigroup Inc.

Friday, November 11

7:30 AM REGISTRATION AND CONTINENTAL BREAKFAST

8:15 AM SESSION IV: CURRENT, PAST, AND POTENTIAL FUTURE THREATS TO FINANCIAL STABILITY
Moderator: Michael Pomerleano, World Bank
Asli Demirgüç-Kunt, World Bank
Giancarlo Corsetti, Cambridge University
Ronald I. McKinnon, Stanford University
Commentator: Liliana Rojas-Suarez, Center for Global Development, Washington, DC

10:00 AM BREAK

10:15 AM SESSION V: THE SOCIAL PRODUCTIVITY OF THE FINANCIAL SECTOR
Moderator: David Marshall, Federal Reserve Bank of Chicago
Ross Levine, Brown University
Josh Lerner, Harvard Business School
Alexander A. Popov, European Central Bank
Commentator: Gerard Caprio, Jr., Williams College

12:15 PM LUNCHEON AND KEYNOTE ADDRESS
Introduction: Charles L. Evans, President and Chief Executive Officer, Federal Reserve Bank of Chicago
Janet L. Yellen, Vice Chair, Board of Governors of the Federal Reserve System

2:15 PM SESSION VI: OPEN ISSUES IN THE REGULATORY DEBATE: FAILURE RESOLUTIONS, BAILOUTS, MORAL HAZARD, AND MARKET DISCIPLINE
Moderator: John H. Boyd, University of Minnesota
Edward J. Kane, Boston College
Joseph P. Hughes, Rutgers University
Reint Gropp, European Business School
David A. Skeel, University of Pennsylvania Law School

4:00 PM BREAK

4:15 PM SESSION VII: POLICY PANEL: WHERE TO FROM HERE?
George G. Kaufman, Loyola University Chicago
Benjamin M. Friedman, Harvard University
Richard C. Koo, Nomura Research Institute
Frederic Mishkin, Columbia University
Athanasios Orphanides, Central Bank of Cyprus
Richard Portes, London Business School
Anne Sibert, Birkbeck College, University of London

6:00 PM RECEPTION